LIONEL TRAINS
POCKET PRICE GUIDE

KALMBACH
BOOKS

Twenty-eighth Edition
Printed in Canada.

For more information, visit our Web site at www.kalmbachbooks.com.

Cover photo: Model no. 2349 Northern Pacific GP-9 diesel cataloged in 1959-60, provided by Kent Johnson

We constantly strive to improve Greenberg's Pocket Price Guides. If you find missing items or detect misinformation, please contact us. Send your comments, new information, or corrections via e-mail to books@kalmbach.com or by mail to

Lionel Pocket Price Guide Editor
Books Division
Kalmbach Publishing Co.
21027 Crossroads Circle
Waukesha, WI 53186

CONTENTS

The Latest and Greatest Guide

Welcome to the latest edition of what hobbyists regard as the most authoritative and trusted price guide for toy trains and accessories manufactured by the company now known as Lionel LLC. Whether you are a longtime Lionel enthusiast or a newcomer to the toy train hobby, you'll find the information needed to identify and evaluate thousands of items made by Lionel between 1901 and 2008. Most of all, you will have at your fingertips the most up-to-date prices for locomotives, freight and passenger cars, stations, tunnels, signals, track sections, transformers, catalogs, and more.

The *Lionel Pocket Price Guide 1901-2008* contains information on just about every toy train product marketed by Lionel since it brought out its first trains in 1901. Lionel has, with the exception of two years during World War II when federal restrictions prevented it from manufacturing toy trains (1943 and 1944), continued to bring out innovative and entertaining models ever since.

What's Listed and What isn't

Almost every Lionel model produced over the years is listed in the pages that follow. Even the toys Lionel developed in the 1930s that don't qualify as railroad related (windup boats and an electric range) have their own entries. The only notable items not included are the boxed train sets (what Lionel referred to as *outfits*) offered during just prior to and after World War II. These outfits are omitted because, to be considered complete, they must have all the items, including ancillary ones, that Lionel packed with them. Furthermore, they should be in their original boxes. This level of completeness puts outfits beyond the scope of this pocket guide.

Also left out of this pocket guide are some rare items that have surfaced. These unique pieces include mock-ups of products that were assembled by members of Lionel's Engineering Department. They include models created for company executives to evaluate different paint and lettering schemes. These items, some of which are truly one of a kind, are considered so scarce that values cannot be assigned to them.

This edition of the *Lionel Pocket Price Guide* contains information about new additions to the product line as described in Lionel catalogs, press releases, and other sources. Any additions that Lionel makes to its line after this book is printed will be reported in the 2009 edition.

In addition, the *Lionel Pocket Price Guide* provides information about items associated with Lionel yet not mentioned in its catalogs. These uncataloged or promotional items include unique train sets and specially decorated locomotives and cars that Lionel produces for national and regional toy train collecting and operating groups, museums, local railroad clubs, and other customers.

Models not Listed in the Guide

As hard as the contributors and editors try to make this guide complete, they occasionally miss something. If you discover a Lionel model that is not listed here, there are a few steps to take.

First, determine whether or not Lionel made it. Somewhere on almost every locomotive, car, and accessory, Lionel placed a mark to identify itself as the manufacturer.

Then, verify that your item was either a part of the cataloged line or a promotional piece offered by a toy train organization, museum, or other group. This process involves finding a reference to it in a Lionel catalog or in paperwork available from the sponsor.

Check that your item is legitimate by asking the opinion of other toy train enthusiasts, including dealers and hobby shop owners. Contact hobbyists with experience and knowledge of Lionel trains.

Once you are sure that you have a legitimate and original item, send a description and a color photograph of it to Kalmbach Publishing Co.

When to Consult this Guide

Many readers of the *Lionel Pocket Price Guide* use it after the fact. They already have some trains and accessories and now want to identify and evaluate those items. Maybe someone lucked upon a bridge at a garage sale and wants to know whether it's a 300 Hell Gate or a 314 deck girder type. Somebody else with a massive collection needs to provide his or her insurance agent with a complete list of O gauge locomotives that includes their conditions and current values. This guide contains the information any hobbyist needs to identify that bridge and ascertain present values for that engine roster.

In addition, the *Lionel Pocket Price Guide* can help you think about what to acquire in the future. That's really when the fun begins! You just have to spend some time considering how you want to approach the hobby. Collect, operate, or both? Prewar, postwar, or modern? Particular type of locomotive or car? Favorite railroad or two? Promotional items? Catalogs?

Once you have a general idea of how to enjoy this hobby, you can make informed decisions about which trains you want. The list can grow pretty rapidly, so try to keep it under control before you have to take out a second mortgage or get a third job!

Number	Description	Condition —— Good	Exc	Cond/$
6436-500	LV Girls' Hopper, lilac, "643657", *57–58**	95	270	___
X6454	NYC Boxcar, *48*			
	(A) Brown body	20	55	___
	(B) Orange body	45	140	___
	(C) Tan body	15	35	___
6475	Libby's Crushed Pineapple Vat Car, *63 u*	25	75	___

Identifying a Catalog Number

A Lionel catalog number is usually stamped, printed, engraved, or painted on an item. However, some products do not contain a catalog number. In these cases, you can match the product with its catalog number through a comprehensive reference book, such as one of Greenberg's Guide To books, or various Web sites including Lionel.com, where you can find past and current catalogs.

Two-, three-, and four-digit numbers predominated during the prewar and postwar periods. Four- and five-digit numbers have been most common during the modern era.

On the models, often catalog numbers double as road numbers, which were added to locomotives and cars to enhance an item's realism. Sometimes separate road numbers were added. Lionel also placed other numbers on its rolling stock to make it look more realistic. Numbers having a prefix of HT or WT refer to the height and weight of the full-sized prototype on which a car was modeled. And a Built or a New date may not indicate the actual year Lionel made or cataloged a car.

Locating an Item

Each section is arranged in numerical order by catalog numbers. Items with one or more zeroes as placeholders are listed before numbers without placeholders. For example, a 042 pair of switches is found in front of a 42 electric locomotive.

In the prewar and postwar sections, some items such as transformers and track pieces, are identified by a letter. These products follow the numbered items, and products without numbers are also found at the end of the section.

Reading an Entry

Every entry begins with the product's catalog number (or other number) assigned by Lionel.

A basic description of the model follows. It gives the type of product, lists the name of any railroad identified with it, and includes identifying characteristics, such as color or lettering. If the item has a road number that differs from its catalog number, that number is shown in quotation marks. Abbreviations used in the descriptions are listed at the back of the price guide.

Next, you'll find the year or years during which that item was part of Lionel's cataloged product line. The years are shown in italics. If a date is followed by *u*, then this item is considered to be uncataloged. It was not part of the cataloged line but was a promotional item that Lionel made or sponsored for an outside business or group.

Some entries show an asterisk (*) after the date, which means that one or more reissues of the item have been made. Lionel reissues of prewar Standard and O gauge trains and accessories appear in section 4.

Many entries feature variations, each indicated by a separate letter (A, B, and so forth). Variations amount to slight yet noteworthy differences in appearance that distinguish models that otherwise seem identical. These differences can relate to color, lettering, and details that were added or deleted. The letters *mv* indicate that there were many variations of an item.

An entry concludes with an indication of the value of the item for several common conditions.

Condition

Prewar and postwar trains are evaluated in Good and Excellent condition. Modern-era trains, including tinplate, are assessed in Excellent and New condition. Postwar and modern catalogs are also evaluated in Excellent and New condition. Regardless of the classifications used in this pocket price guide, Lionel enthusiasts should be familiar with these standards established by the Train Collectors Association for evaluating the condition of toy trains and accessories:

Fair: well-scratched, chipped, dented, rusted, or warped.

Good: scratched, small dents, and dirty.

Very Good: few scratches, no dents, rust, or warpage, very clean.

Excellent: minute scratches or nicks, exceptionally clean.

Like New: free of nicks or scratches, completely original (including box), vibrant colors, faint signs of handling or use.

New (Mint): brand new, absolutely unmarred, completely original (including box and all paperwork added by manufacturer), never used.

Besides the characteristics associated with the levels of condition, readers of the *Lionel Pocket Price Guide* should be aware of three other designations that are used.

CP (Current Production) refers to an item that's currently being manufactured, advertised, or sold by retail stores. Consequently, its value in New condition is equivalent to the current catalog or retail price.

NM (Never Manufactured) refers to an item that may have been mentioned or pictured in a Lionel catalog but was never mass-produced.

NRS (No Reported Sales) refers to an item for which adequate pricing data is not available. Typically, these items are so scarce that only a handful have been reported.

Determining a Model's Condition

Look over a model carefully to see whether it has suffered serious damage, including warping and breaking. Then note whether any parts are missing. Feel for dents in metal and cracks in plastic. Check for areas marred by rust, mildew, or chipped paint.

The condition standards will assist you in evaluating your model, such as deciding whether a prewar or postwar model falls below Good or above Excellent, the two grades with values specified for those models.

The assessment of a toy train's value is based on the expectations that it has not been modified and that all parts are present and original to it. Repainting or relettering a model seriously undermines a train's value, regardless of how beat-up and scratched it may have been before undergoing modification. Any model that has been altered should be labeled as a restoration; potential buyers deserve to be informed about how it has been modified, so they do not mistake it for an original.

A model that is missing some parts should be sold as-is or have those parts replaced by identical originals. A tank car cataloged in 1935 that needs a brake wheel must have a part from that year put on it to be considered a true original. Adding a brake wheel from 1936 undermines the car's legitimacy as much as a part from 2007 does.

The same rule applies to the ancillary items that came with various models. The value of a flatcar may depend largely on the miniature airplane or rocket packed with it; therefore, having a load that is a genuine original is essential to maintaining the value of that flatcar. Similarly, freight loaders must have whatever cargo came with them (coal, logs, trailers, and so forth); reproductions should be identified as such.

The *Lionel Pocket Price Guide* has been divided into six major sections according to the categories used by toy train enthusiasts. These categories are based primarily on time (the period associated with a particular item's manufacture) and size. Purpose largely defines other categories: whether a particular item was a reissue of an older one or whether Lionel authorized or produced an item to benefit an organization or business but did not publicize that item in its own catalogs. Finally, consumer catalogs, like other toy train "paper," belong in a separate group.

Spend any amount of time among knowledgeable Lionel hobbyists and you're sure to hear them toss around the terms *prewar*, *postwar*, and *modern*. These general terms refer to the period when a train or other item was described or pictured in a Lionel catalog.

The first two terms use World War II as a dividing point. Prewar fits anything cataloged by Lionel from its initial line in 1901 to 1942, when federal restrictions curtailed toy train production. Postwar fits anything cataloged from 1945 to 1969. In that year, the Lionel Corp. leased the rights to manufacture and market its trains to General Mills, an act that effectively concluded the postwar period of Lionel's history. What hobbyists refer to as the modern era now covers 38 years.

In all sections, the value of a steam locomotive includes a tender, even if the tender is not listed in detail. The value of steam locomotives, particularly prewar items, may be affected significantly by the type of tender included.

Lionel also marketed smaller HO scale trains between 1957 and 1966 and 1974 to 1977. None of these locomotives and cars are included in this price guide, nor are Lionel's large scale models.

Section 1: Prewar 1901-1942

Section 1 of the *Lionel Pocket Price Guide* is devoted to the prewar period. The entries cover just about every train, accessory, and transformer associated with Lionel's line during its first 42 years. The only outfits listed are those of articulated streamlined trains that consist of a powered unit and attached unpowered cars. Catalogs from the prewar era are not included in this section or in section 6.

Each entry contains a basic description of the item that specifies its gauge (the distance between the inside of the outermost rails). During this time, Lionel catalogued models in four sizes. It is noted in parentheses whether an item is 2⅞-inch, Standard (2¼ inches), O (1¼ inches), or OO (¾ inches). O gauge models intended to run on tighter 27-inch-diameter track belong to Lionel's O27 gauge line and are identified as such. Transformers, rheostats, and many accessories were not limited to a single gauge, so their descriptions do not specify a gauge.

Section 2: Postwar 1945-1969

Section 2 concentrates on the postwar period. Nearly every train and accessory (except outfits) that Lionel cataloged between 1945 and 1969 has its own listing. By this time, Lionel no longer made trains in 2⅞-inch, Standard, or OO gauge. Instead, it offered trains that ran on track that had a diameter of either 31 inches (O gauge) or 27 inches (O27 gauge). However, the entries in this section do not distinguish between O and O27 since only a handful of locomotives and cars could operate solely on the wider curves. Lionel consumer catalogs of the postwar era are listed in section 6.

Section 3: Modern Era 1970-2008

Section 3 shows the trains (including outfits), accessories, transformers, and other items that Lionel has cataloged since 1970. The modern era encompasses the products of three companies: Model Products Corp. (MPC, a division of General Mills), 1970-85; Lionel Trains Inc. (LTI), 1986-95; and Lionel LLC (LLC), 1996-2008.

These incarnations of Lionel are responsible for an enormous inventory of trains, accessories, transformers, and more. Cataloged and uncataloged O gauge items (ranging from the near-scale Standard O to the toy-like O27) can be found within the pages of this section, while reissues of prewar Standard and O gauge items appear in section 4.

All items in section 3 are arranged according to their Lionel catalog number (omitting the number 6 used as a prefix). The descriptions of products made during the modern era may include information that relates to where in the product line a particular item belongs. Models derived from MPC designs have been described as *traditional*. Rolling stock whose dimensions and features approach scale realism may be designated as Standard O (abbreviated as Std. O). Locomotives equipped with TrainMaster Command Control are identified as such, often with the abbreviation CC.

Section 4: Modern Tinplate

Section 4 covers a category of modern-era trains that is referred to as Modern Tinplate. Here you'll find reissues of Standard and O gauge trains and accessories dating from the prewar period that LTI and LLC have brought out for the purpose of satisfying a growing market. Also included in this section are a few Standard gauge trains that Lionel LLC has created, based on new designs.

Section 5: Club Cars and Special Production

Section 5 gathers the various items, principally locomotives and rolling stock, that Lionel has made or sponsored for different hobby organizations, museums, businesses, and so forth since the 1970s. These uncataloged club cars and special production items are arranged according to the groups that offered them for sale. Those groups are listed alphabetically; regional divisions of national organizations follow the parent organization's listing. Within each subordinate section, items are listed in a numerical (not chronological) order, with a basic description similar to that used for cataloged entries.

Section 6: Catalogs

Section 6 concludes this price guide with a chronological listing of the catalogs put out by Lionel during the postwar and modern eras. The dimensions of each consumer catalog are specified, as is the number of pages.

Every user of the *Lionel Pocket Price Guide* wants to know how the values are ascertained. There's nothing mysterious or arbitrary about the process. Over the years, we at Kalmbach Publishing Co. have gained the cooperation of many dealers and hobbyists, some of whom serve on our national review panel. These knowledgeable individuals share information about the trains and accessories they have bought and sold. They report on transactions conducted at meets across the United States and in retail outlets, auctions, and online. The editors of this guide study the information and supplement it with data from the publications of hobby groups that relates to buying and selling Lionel trains.

The values presented here are an averaged reflection of prices for items bought and sold across the country over the year prior to the publication of this edition. These values are offered as guidelines and should be viewed as starting points that buyers and sellers can use to begin informed and reasonable negotiations.

Values for individual items may differ from what is listed in this price guide due to a few key factors. Where collectible trains are scarce and demand outruns supply, actual values may exceed what is shown. Values may also rise where certain items are especially popular, often because of their road names. And as with all collectibles, national and local economic conditions will impact values, which tend to drop when times are tough and demand falls.

Another factor influencing what a toy train is worth relates to the venue in which it is being sold. Antiques dealers generally ask more for an item than do folks putting it out at a garage sale. Mail-order and retail outlets tend to charge more for trains than do individuals at shows because they need to be compensated for the additional costs generated by operating a store, compiling and distributing price lists, and packing and shipping trains. Of course, the cost of any item can balloon far beyond its listed value when two or more people compete for it at a live or online auction.

Original Boxes

Over the past 20 years, original boxes and other forms of packaging have assumed significance for some collectors. These hobbyists insist that the trains they buy come in the boxes and have the paperwork and ancillary pieces (inserts, instruction sheets, and envelopes) that the manufacturer packed with them before offering them for sale.

Cardboard boxes, inserts, and assorted sheets of paper are more fragile than die-cast metal or plastic trains. They were also deemed to be less important to the children playing with toy trains long ago and so were not treated with the same care. Instruction sheets were lost, and boxes were discarded. As a result, fewer boxes and instruction sheets have survived than have the trains and accessories that went with them.

When the first editions of this guide were published, less interest in boxes existed. That has since changed, although the consensus of opinion holds that only items in Like New or better condition require their original packaging to maintain their high level of value. For that reason and because demand for boxes and related paperwork affects only the top echelons of collecting, the values given for items in Good and Excellent condition are not based on the expectation that a box and other associated items are present.

Items that do have their original packaging, especially if it is complete and undamaged, command a premium among collectors of prewar and postwar trains. No hard-and-fast rules can be stated as to how much higher their value is over the same items in Excellent condition. In some cases the box that a particular locomotive, car, or even outfit came in is valued above the item itself. Generally speaking, though, boxed items in Like New condition are valued about 50 percent above the same item without a box.

Using the Values

The values listed should be considered to be what a consumer would pay – more or less – to get a particular item in a specific condition. One collector selling that item to another would probably ask the stated value and expect to get something close to it.

However, someone selling that same item to a person or business that intends to resell it (a train dealer) is unlikely to receive the stated value. Experience shows that sellers get about half the amount. Dealers offer less than the stated value so that they can then raise their asking price in hopes of earning a profit when reselling an item.

Regardless of whether you are buying or selling a toy train, you should proceed with care and acquire as much knowledge as you can. Start by consulting this pocket price guide and then, if possible, learn more about the item that interests you. You can read more about it in one of the comprehensive reference guides on toy trains and ask more experienced hobbyists for their opinion about the item's condition and value.

When buying, selling, or trading items, less-experienced collectors should seek the assistance and advice of friends or associates with more experience in the toy train hobby. With that in mind, use this price guide wisely and have fun in what many of us consider to be the world's greatest hobby.

The chances are pretty good that, if you've made it this far in the price guide, you already have a strong interest in toy trains. Perhaps you discovered your grandfather's Lionel accessories in the family attic and are attempting to determine their value. Maybe you received a Lionel outfit as a child and are trying to piece together what you remember playing with. Or you could be looking for a new hobby.

You've come to the right place! Enjoying toy trains is something that you can do by yourself or with family members and friends.

Finding a Specialty

Reasons to collect and operate Lionel trains and accessories abound. Some hobbyists are motivated by nostalgia. Other enthusiasts have fun restoring beat-up models. Buying and selling trains for a profit drives some others. Once you decide why you like Lionel trains, you can make some decisions about which items you want to collect or operate.

Many hobbyists choose to specialize and profess to having a favorite era of Lionel history. The post-World War II decades, when Lionel trains were the finest and most sophisticated toy a child could receive, boast the largest following among Lionel enthusiasts. Other people, including many who were born long after World War II, vote for prewar trains. Some opt for the beauty and heft of Standard gauge, and others vote for the colorful, toy-like models that characterized Lionel's O and O27 gauge lines.

The modern era of Lionel production is gaining more supporters, thanks to the tremendous variety of trains manufactured over the past 38 years. You can specialize in modern tinplate (and venture into the prewar period for original versions of these contemporary reissues). You can focus on a particular railroad and fill your train room with Illinois Central, New Haven, or Southern Pacific locomotives and rolling stock. You can acquire only steam locomotives, only boxcars, only freight loaders, only catalogs, or any other "only" that pleases you.

Finding and Buying Items

After compiling a list of what you're looking for – or at least have in mind a train or two that you'd love to own – you're ready to join the hunt. The information in this price guide will assist you when attending train meets and visiting hobby shops.

Some hobbyists report making great finds by combing through boxes at estate and garage sales or by placing ads for old trains in newspapers and magazines. By and large, however, you're less likely to discover an outfit in a private home or the bargain bin of a charitable group. Those sources, once so rich for collectors, are rapidly drying up.

What has jumped in importance for individuals buying and selling toy trains in recent years is the Internet. Rather than spread out their inventory on tables at a meet, people are depending on online auction sites to sell their trains. Buyers benefit because they no longer have to travel to search for the trains they want. Investigations can be conducted from your living room at any hour of the day.

The starting point when you're buying any toy train is to proceed with care and knowledge. If the train is not accessible, gather as much information as you can from pictures and descriptions of what's being offered.

And pose questions about the item. Don't hesitate to ask the seller about a car's condition and a locomotive's performance. (At some train meets, the sponsor has a test track on which locomotives can be tested.) Find out whether an outfit that's said to be complete has all its components, including paperwork. Discover whether an item purported to be original has been restored, right down to its couplers, trucks, and load.

Longtime hobbyists prefer to deal with individuals they know and have done business with previously. Newcomers should look to their more experienced friends and associates for guidance here, although most regular dealers conduct business fairly and honestly and so encourage customers to return. When buying from someone online, check the feedback that the seller has been given, so you know whether previous customers believe they have been treated in a fair and professional way.

Let's suppose that you have ample information about an item that you want. All your questions have been answered. You're satisfied with its condition and performance. And you understand that it is being sold as-is. What you do next depends on where you are.

If you're attending a train meet or yard sale, you can either pay the ticketed price or, as is the practice, make an offer 10 to 20 percent below it. Some sellers stick firmly to their asking price. Others enjoy the negotiating and recognize that they'll have to make a slight concession to close the deal.

If you're buying a train at a hobby shop, dickering over prices is less common, especially when the item purchased is brand new or in current production.

If you're participating in an live or online auction, be sure you have a firm sense of how much you can reasonably bid. Keep in mind that a buyer's premium will be added to the final price (the auctioneer may also tack on shipping and insurance charges).

Caring for your Trains

What you do with your Lionel trains and accessories once you acquire them is up to you. Arranging them on open shelving for the world to admire is one choice; putting them on a layout is another. Either way, however, your new prizes will gradually gather dust and maybe a bit of moisture. The lighting you install may affect their finish.

Should you be worried about your trains fading, corroding, or disintegrating? Not really. The metals that Lionel used (sheet as well as die-cast) and the types of plastic have, by and large, stood the test of time. So have the paints sprayed over the frames and chassis and the lettering added. Lionel trains and accessories are rugged and durable, so the chances of them being damaged by normal conditions in your home are small.

Still, your peace of mind will be made greater if you take some simple precautions when displaying and storing your trains, regardless of their age, materials, and value.

Temperature: Maintain your train room at an even and moderate temperature. Install a thermometer to ensure the room stays between 55 and 72 degrees Fahrenheit.

Humidity: Have one dehumidifier running at all times in your train room. Use two dehumidifiers if you store your models in a basement, where water vapor can cause metal parts to rust. Buy a hygrometer (available from hardware stores and home improvement centers) to measure the humidity, which should be kept at 50 to 60 percent.

Cleaning: Items kept out on shelves or a layout should be cleaned on a regular basis. Use a soft brush or a can of compressed air to remove dust. If a more thorough cleaning is necessary, use warm water and a mild soap (liquid dishwashing detergent works well). Avoid dampening lettering and decals that may be marred by the water. Finish by drying everything carefully with a warm cloth towel or a hairdryer.

Wrapping: Items not on display or in operation should be stored with care. Start by drying anything you plan to store with a warm cloth towel. When all the moisture has been removed, wrap sheet-metal and plastic items in two or three sheets of acid-free (alkaline) tissue paper. Do not wrap them in newspapers, plastic bubble wrap, or old clothes. Make sure to wrap flatcar loads separately, after removing elastic bands and tie-tapes.

Labeling: Once you have finished wrapping an item, add a note to identify it. Write down the catalog or product number, type of model, and other pertinent data.

Storing: Place wrapped and labeled items inside either the boxes they came in or storage boxes. Cover any staples or metal stabilizers in the boxes that can scratch your trains. Then place one or two packets of silica gel inside each box to reduce moisture, protecting the boxes from mold and mildew and the trains from rust. Store the trains in a cupboard, drawer, or other dark, dry area. Always keep them out of direct sunlight and fluorescent lighting.

Insuring your Trains

The protection you give individual models by cleaning and storing them properly in a climate-controlled environment should be matched by protection you give your entire collection. Valuable toy trains should be insured against damage or theft.

Information: Contact your insurance agent or company and ask whether it offers collectible insurance riders or policies. Discuss the coverage and rates available. Before signing an agreement, get information that applies specifically to toy train collections from agencies that advertise such policies in toy train and antiques magazines and publications put out by toy train collecting groups.

Inventory: Regardless of the size and value of your collection, it's smart to keep an up-to-date written inventory, which is required for most insurance policies. In addition, keep track of what you acquire to avoid purchasing duplicates.

Each entry should start with a description of the item, including its manufacturer, type of model, catalog number, year (if known), railroad name, color, original packaging (if relevant), and other important characteristics. Next, evaluate the item's condition. Finally, using this price guide, note the value of the item.

Pictures: In addition to your written inventory, you may wish to photograph your entire collection or layout. At the very least, take pictures of the most significant and expensive items that you own to supplement the written descriptions. A digital camera works well for creating a visual record of what you have. A video camera can also be used for this task, but be sure to take your time and get sharp, complete pictures of each model.

Policies: Blanket policies can be obtained to provide general coverage, but they may limit the amount of protection.

Exclusions characterize just about every collectibles insurance plan. They can include gradual depreciation and deterioration; damage caused by cold, dampness, heat, or insects; dishonesty; and negligence.

Limitations also characterize just about every collectibles insurance plan. They can include newly acquired items, models in transit, and paper-related memorabilia.

Deductibles come with these policies, and the designated amount varies.

Costs of policies can differ, depending on the insurance company or the location where the collection is kept. In general, a fair annual rate for collectibles insurance would be approximately $7 for every $1,000 worth of coverage.

Prewar Trains and Accessories

Nearly all the Lionel enthusiasts that specialize in prewar trains and accessories consider themselves collectors. Most of them acquire items that they display on shelves or in enclosed showcases. They search for items that share style or design traits or were part of a series of cataloged freight cars. The array of colors that Lionel used to paint its passenger cars fascinates some hobbyists, and they specialize in them.

To be sure, some prewar fans do build layouts, especially around the holidays. Everyone gets a kick out of seeing an antique electric train rumbling around a circle of track. Prewar accessories enhance even the smallest model railroad, and with flashing lights and remote-controlled animation, they delight kids of all ages.

Regardless of the approach you take, here are a few observations about the current market for prewar Lionel trains that the values in this guide corroborate.

First, the supply of prewar trains in all conditions on the market is increasing because the number of hobbyists who grew up with these trains is decreasing. Collections are hitting the market, and younger enthusiasts are finding great satisfaction in chasing after the colorful, toy-like models that Lionel cataloged 66 or more years ago.

Second, the demand for virtually any prewar Lionel item in Like New or better condition, especially if it has its original packaging, remains high. Perhaps the strongest segment of the current market consists of the scale and near-scale locomotives and rolling stock that Lionel introduced to its O gauge line in the late 1930s and early 1940s. Both prewar and postwar enthusiasts hunt for outstanding examples of these classics.

Also very hot right now are Standard gauge pieces, notably those that were cataloged during the classic era that lasted from the mid-1920s into the early 1930s. Accessories, principally the stations, bridges, tunnels, and railroad structures painted in bright colors, have never lost their appeal, especially for anyone planning a layout.

So how can you make inroads into the prewar market? If you want trains in Good or Excellent condition, you will find supplies – and bargains – to be plentiful. What the most critical collectors ignore may still look great in your train room or, even better, on a layout designed to capture the feel of a department store display from the Depression era.

Another smart move, besides relaxing your standards about condition, is to stray from the main line. Consider buying items other than those attracting so much attention. Small Standard gauge locomotives and passenger cars, lithographed O27 freight cars, and O gauge trains from the 1920s always seem to get short shrift when enthusiasts describe what they dream of owning. Learn more about these items and see how nice they look.

However, if you are determined to own examples of some of the finest prewar trains but have a fairly limited budget for hobby expenses, you need not go home empty-handed. The Modern Tinplate line that LTI and LLC developed features reissues of outstanding Standard and O gauge trains and accessories. The gorgeous colors, shiny details, and superb motors on these updated versions make them perfect additions, especially if you want to operate prewar trains and accessories.

The Modern Tinplate line has enabled hobbyists, younger ones in particular, to experience the joy of seeing prewar trains at their best. Some of these newcomers then have been motivated to look for actual prewar pieces to complement their reissues. They combine older models that are still affordable with reissues of outfits and pieces whose values remain out of sight. Best of all, the selection of reissues continues to broaden.

Whether with originals or reissues, hobbyists who confess to a preference for prewar Lionel trains, especially Standard gauge, should find this a good time to specialize in these antiques. The supply appears to be increasing, and demand remains strong. Secondary fields offer bargains for those enthusiasts who enjoy collecting or even restoring old trains. Operators, meanwhile, benefit from reasonable prices on assorted original trains, particularly in O and O27 gauges, and the Modern Tinplate offerings.

Postwar Trains and Accessories

This is a curious time to be concentrating on postwar Lionel. On the one hand, serious collectors are paying record prices for Like New and Mint items, boxes are escalating in value, and demand for original and complete outfits, top-of-the-line locomotives, and scarce variations continues to rise.

On the other hand, the need that operators once felt to acquire postwar pieces to run on their O gauge layouts has all but vanished. Lionel catalogs continue to display a mind-boggling selection of steam and diesel locomotives and near-scale rolling stock that just gets greater every year.

As a result, folks who want to run trains can choose from models that promise superior performance and outstanding detail. Few enthusiasts can say that the postwar line surpassed what is available today, which is why operators are devouring new catalogs and paying less attention to what was offered 50 years ago.

Anyone who wants Good and even Excellent trains to display or operate will find that all but the most deluxe and exotic models are available in abundant supply and at affordable prices. Collectors with deep pockets and high standards may turn up their noses at common pieces as well as notable trains because those items are graded below Like New or do not come with all their original packaging.

So collectors willing to forgo a box and accept a scratch or paint chip may find items available that they once thought were beyond their aspirations. They may also benefit from the shift of operators away from postwar trains to contemporary ones. Operating cars, especially those models and road names that are considered fairly common, deserve more attention. In contrast, passenger cars continue to dazzle serious collectors, and so their prices have stayed at the same level or even climbed.

Demand for certain items in the higher grades seems stronger, which means that those same trains and accessories in Good or possibly Excellent condition may be overlooked. For example, many of the items that Lionel cataloged in the late 1940s, particularly those at the upper end, continue to gain strength on the collector market. The same can be said of the less mundane motorized units, in particular, intact examples (most of the top motorized units show up with key parts broken or missing). Original and complete flatcar loads also draw attention, probably because reproductions (marked and unmarked) have inundated the market. Alco diesels and switchers command more interest as collectors search for models they had overlooked.

Now may be a great time to collect or operate postwar trains, provided you're willing to make a few compromises in the appearance, performance, and packaging of the locomotives, cars, and accessories you buy. Most F3 and Train Master diesels are available, and so are Berkshire and small Hudson steam locomotives (be sure to get the correct tender). Nearly all the boxcars in the esteemed 6464 series can be found in good quantities through train shows, mail-order dealers, and Internet sites. Accessories also appear plentiful, so you can easily acquire the freight loaders, signals, bridges, and stations needed for a layout or a tabletop display at the holidays.

Consumer catalogs from the entire postwar period are available at low prices. As bound volumes of catalog reproductions go out of print, demand for originals should rise, which logically means that Lionel wish books in Excellent and better condition will go up in value. If you love the postwar era and don't have a complete set of catalogs, this is the time to buy the missing ones.

Original and complete boxed outfits are not included in this pocket price guide. Anyone familiar with the current hobby knows that the prices for genuine outfits keep skyrocketing. Luckily for most enthusiasts, the

Postwar Celebration Series created by LLC has done for postwar trains what the Modern Tinplate line has for prewar. It offers reissues of neat items in dazzling colors with the latest motors at reasonable prices. The Postwar Celebration Series also includes reissues of some motorized units and other items that as originals cost too much for most hobbyists.

Finally, for the postwar fanatic who craves everything Lionel, there are the boxcars and other models that Lionel LLC is cataloging as part of its Archives Series. Product developers have searched the company archives to find models and paint schemes that were considered but rejected in the 1950s and 1960s. Some of these unique and innovative prototypes are being mass-produced, so collectors and operators can own replicas of models that at one time only members of Lionel's inner circle could examine.

Modern Trains and Accessories

Anyone who wants to assess the history of Lionel and the current state of the toy train hobby need only observe the pages in this guide. The assorted trains and accessories that Lionel cataloged in the 42 years of the prewar period are covered in approximately 35 pages, as are the trains of the 25-year postwar period. But the modern era, covering the past 38 years, requires 200 pages to describe and present values for all the O and O27 items Lionel has produced. There is no doubt that, based on the huge variety of items available, today's toy train lovers are living in a golden age.

Flip through section 3 and you'll come across models of every major type of steam or diesel locomotive and any kind of freight or passenger car imaginable. Railroads, large and small, prominent and forgotten, are represented.

Increasing numbers of Lionel enthusiasts are jumping on the contemporary bandwagon and buying trains of recent vintage to operate on their layouts. This trend doesn't mean that nobody is collecting modern-era trains. The boxcars and refrigerator cars put out by MPC to advertise brands of cigarettes, beer, and spirits are rising steadily in value. Demand is also growing for similar rolling stock decorated with the names of national fast food chains, candy, and local short lines that burst forth, only to disappear from the scene almost overnight.

While you're paging through the section on modern era trains, don't miss all the models that Lionel has decorated with beloved cartoon characters on them. Every Disney favorite has ridden over Lionel's three-rail track. So have such Warner Bros. heroes as Bugs Bunny, Wile E. Coyote, and Porky Pig. The latest animated stars to hitch a ride come from *The Simpsons*. These models, along with the recent Polar Express outfit, also capture the attention of collectors of miniature trains, toys, and movie memorabilia.

Returning to the realm of more traditional railroad models, collectors have expanded their rosters of prized diesel locomotives by mixing postwar classics, such as F3s and Train Masters, with the new road names added to those models in the 1980s and 1990s. Cabooses have definitely been hot, too, with new styles and paint schemes coming out in the past few decades to augment what was cataloged in the postwar decades.

Nonetheless, it is the operators who have found real enjoyment. They have dozens of new locomotives to run and hundreds of cars to couple behind them. Better yet, the performance of those diesels and steamers took on an added dimension of sophistication and excitement when Lionel introduced its TrainMaster system of command control (and RailSounds sound effects) in the 1990s. Operators have adopted these great systems and seen how fun it can be to run trains without having to plant themselves at the handles of an ancient ZW transformer and a network of glowing remote-control switch machines.

What is remarkable about the modern era, too, are the brand-new accessories that the engineering staff at Lionel has developed. Many layouts feature the different freight loaders, cranes, and animated railroad facilities that hit the market over the past 16 years. Lionel's growing roster of structure kits and tractor-trailers has also made an impact on the O gauge model railroads that are being constructed. These items have retained their value, and demand for them continues to stay strong.

Additional evidence of the popularity of Lionel trains can be found in section 5, which focuses on uncataloged club cars and special production. Every year, more locomotives and cars are used by groups to promote themselves. Because the size of the production run of these unique items is small, collectors and operators snap them up. If you're looking for bargains or something to spice up your roster, the promotional pieces listed in section 5 will give you lots of possibilities.

Section 1
PREWAR 1901-1942

		Good	Exc	Cond/$
001	Steam 4-6-4 (OO), *38–42*	195	395	___
1	Bild-A-Motor, *28–31*	60	140	___
1	Trolley (Std.), *06–14*			
	(A) Cream body, orange band/roof	1900	4750	___
	(B) White body, blue band/roof	1750	4750	___
	(C) Cream body, blue band/roof	1300	3150	___
	(D) Cream body, blue band/roof, Curtis Bay	2150	5550	___
	(E) Blue, cream band, blue roof	1450	3150	___
1/111	Trolley Trailer (Std.), *06–14*	1000	2700	___
002	Steam 4-6-4 (OO), *39–42*	160	315	___
2	Bild-A-Motor, *28–31*	100	180	___
2	Countershafting, *04–11*		NRS	___
2	Trolley (Std.), *06–16**			
	(A) Yellow, red band	1200	2250	___
	(B) Red, yellow band	1200	2250	___
2/200	Trolley Trailer (Std.), *06–16*	1000	1800	___
003	Steam 4-6-4 (OO), *39–42*			
	(A) With 003W whistling Tender	190	395	___
	(B) With 003T non-whistling Tender	175	355	___
3	Trolley (Std.), *06–13*			
	(A) Cream, orange band	1400	3100	___
	(B) Cream, dark olive green band	1400	3100	___
	(C) Orange, dark olive green band	1400	3100	___
	(D) Dark green, cream windows	1400	3100	___
	(E) Green, cream window, "BAY SHORE	1650	3700	___
3/300	Trolley Trailer (Std.), *06–13*	1500	3500	___
004	Steam 4-6-4 (OO), *39–42*			
	(A) With 004W whistling Tender	210	350	___
	(B) With 004T non-whistling Tender	190	310	___
4	Electric 0-4-0 (O), *28–32**			
	(A) Orange, black frame	550	900	___
	(B) Gray, apple green stripe	580	1050	___
4	Trolley (Std.), *06–12*			
	(A) Cream, dark olive green band	3000	4950	___
	(B) Green or olive green, cream roof	3000	4950	___
4U	#4 Kit Form (O), *28–29*	1150	1600	___
5	Steam 0-4-0, no Tender, Early (Std.), *06–07*			
	(A) "N.Y.C. & H.R.R."	1000	1450	___
	(B) "PENNSYLVANIA"	1400	2300	___
	(C) "N.Y.C. & H.R.R.R." (3 Rs)	1250	2050	___
	(D) "B. & O. R.R."	1500	2400	___
5	Steam 0-4-0, w/ Tender, Early Special	980	1300	___

		Good	Exc	Cond/$
	(Std.), *06–09*			
5	Steam 0-4-0, no Tender, Later (Std.), *10–11*	750	1150	___
5	Steam 0-4-0, w/ Tender, Later Special (Std.), *10–11*	920	1200	___
5/51	Steam 0-4-0, w/ Tender, Latest (Std.), *12–23*	800	1100	___
6	Steam 4-4-0 (Std.), *06–23*	860	1250	___
6	Steam 0-4-0 Special (Std.), *08–09*	2050	2950	___
7	Steam 4-4-0 (Std.), *10–23**	1850	2300	___
8	Electric 0-4-0 (Std.), *25–32*			
	(A) Maroon, brass windows/trim	235	250	___
	(B) Olive green or mojave w/brass	155	205	___
	(C) Red, brass or cream window	195	250	___
	(D) Peacock, orange windows	520	750	___
8	Trolley (Std.), *08–14**			
	(A) Cream, orange band and roof	3000	5400	___
	(B) Dark green, cream windows	3000	5400	___
8E	Electric 0-4-0 (Std.), *26–32*			
	(A) Mojave, brass windows/trim	175	240	___
	(B) Red, brass or cream window	150	225	___
	(C) Peacock, orange windows	370	590	___
	(D) Pea green, cream stripe	465	670	___
9	Electric 0-4-0 (Std.), 29*	1200	2150	___
9	Motor Car (Std.), *09–12*		NRS	___
9	Trolley (Std.), *09*	3000	5400	___
9E	Electric 0-4-0 (Std.), *28–35**			
	(A) 0-4-0, orange	700	1250	___
	(B) 2-4-2, two-tone green	880	1600	___
	(C) 2-4-2, gun-metal gray	860	1100	___
9U	Electric 0-4-0 Kit (Std.), *28–29*	1050	1750	___
10	Electric 0-4-0 (Std.), *25–29**			
	(A) Mojave, brass trim	150	215	___
	(B) Gray, brass trim	125	205	___
	(C) Peacock, brass inserts	145	205	___
	(D) Red, cream stripe	580	880	___
10	Interurban (Std.), *10–16*			
	(A) Maroon	3000	5750	___
	(B) Dark olive green	1200	2150	___
10E	Electric 0-4-0 (Std.), *26–30*			
	(A) Olive green, black frame		NRS	___
	(B) Peacock, dark green or black frame	295	400	___
	(C) State brown, dark green frame	435	630	___
	(D) Gray, black frame	165	220	___
	(E) Red, cream stripe	620	890	___
011	Switches, pair (O), *33–37*	17	35	___
11	Flatcar, Early (Std.), *06–08*	150	360	___
11	Flatcar, Later (Std.), *09–15*	50	90	___

		Good	Exc	Cond/$
11	Flatcar, Latest (Std.), *16–18*	50	90	___
11	Flatcar, Lionel Corp. (Std.), *18–26*	50	80	___
012	Switches, pair (O), *27–33*	21	42	___
12	Gondola, Early (Std.), *06–08*	150	360	___
12	Gondola, Later (Std.), *09–15*	50	100	___
12	Gondola, Latest (Std.), *16–18*	45	70	___
12	Gondola, Lionel Corp. (Std.), *18–26*	50	70	___
013	012 Switches w/ 439 Panel Board, *27–33*	120	190	___
13	Cattle Car, Early (Std.), *06–08*	300	450	___
13	Cattle Car, Later (Std.), *09–15*	150	225	___
13	Cattle Car, Latest (Std.), *16–18*	65	115	___
13	Cattle Car, Lionel Corp. (Std.), *18–26*	65	115	___
0014	Boxcar (OO), *38–42*			
	(A) Yellow, "Lionel Lines"	80	155	___
	(B) Tuscan body, "PENNSYLVANIA	50	75	___
14	Boxcar, Early (Std.), *06–08*	195	435	___
14	Boxcar, Later (Std.), *09–15*	80	105	___
14	Boxcar, Latest (Std.), *16–18*	80	105	___
14	Boxcar, Lionel Corp. (Std.), *18–26*	80	105	___
0015	Tank Car (OO), *38–42*			
	(A) Silver, "SUN OIL"	40	90	___
	(B) Black, "SHELL"	40	75	___
15	Oil Car, Early (Std.), *06–08*	200	360	___
15	Oil Car, Later (Std.), *09–15*	75	115	___
15	Oil Car, Latest (Std.), *16–18*	75	115	___
15	Oil Car, Lionel Corp. (Std.), *18–26*	75	115	___
0016	Hopper Car (OO), *38–42*			
	(A) Gray	75	145	___
	(B) Black	75	115	___
16	Ballast (Dump) Car, Early (Std.), *06–11*	400	700	___
16	Ballast (Dump) Car, Later (Std.), *09–15*	95	175	___
16	Ballast (Dump) Car, Latest (Std.), *16–18*	95	175	___
16	Ballast (Dump) Car, Lionel Corp. (Std.), *18–26*	95	175	___
0017	Caboose (OO), *38–42*	50	90	___
17	Caboose, Early (Std.), *06–08*	220	440	___
17	Caboose, Later (Std.), *09–15*	70	135	___
17	Caboose, Latest (Std.), *16–18*	75	135	___
17	Caboose, Lionel Corp. (Std.), *18–26*	50	90	___
18	Pullman (Std.), 08			
	(A) Dark olive green, unremovable roof	700	2150	___
	(B) Dark olive green, removable roof	105	215	___
	(C) Yellow-orange, removable roof	315	870	___
	(D) Orange, removable roof	90	205	___
	(E) Mojave, removable roof	305	890	___
18	Pullman (Std.), *11–13*	600	900	___
18	Pullman (Std.), *13–15*	150	270	___

		Good	Exc	Cond/$
18	Pullman (Std.), *15–18*	150	270	___
18	Pullman (Std.), *18–22*	90	155	___
18	Pullman (Std.), *23–26*	270	530	___
19	Combine (Std.), *08*			
	(A) Dark olive green, unremovable roof	1100	2600	___
	(B) Dark olive green, removable roof	90	145	___
	(C) Yellow-orange, removable roof	260	430	___
	(D) Orange, removable roof	115	205	___
	(E) Mojave, removable roof	305	890	___
19	Combine (Std.), *11–13*	600	900	___
19	Combine (Std.), *13–15*	200	270	___
19	Combine (Std.), *15–18*	200	270	___
19	Combine (Std.), *18–22*	90	155	___
19	Combine (Std.), *23–26*	265	520	___
020	90° Crossover (O), *15–42*	2	5	___
020X	45° Crossover (O), *17–42*	2.50	9	___
20	90° Crossover (Std.), *09–32*	4	10	___
20	Direct Current Reducer, *06*		195	___
20X	45° Crossover (Std.), *28–32*	5	10	___
021	Switches, pair (O), *15–37*	20	48	___
21	Switches, pair (Std.), *15–25*	40	70	___
21	90° Crossover (Std.), *06*	10	18	___
022	Switches, pair, Remote (O), *38–42*	38	70	___
22	Switches, pair (Std.), *06–25*	47	75	___
023	Bumper (O), *15–33*	15	37	___
23	Bumper (Std.), *06–23*	17	39	___
0024	PRR Boxcar (OO), *39–42*	45	75	___
24	Railway Station (Std.), *06*		NRS	___
025	Bumper (O), *28–42*	22	33	___
0025	Tank Car (OO), *39–42*			
	(A) Black, "SHELL"	40	90	___
	(B) Silver, "SUNOCO"	40	80	___
25	Open Station (Std.), *06*		NRS	___
25	Bumper (Std.), *27–42*	30	47	___
26	Passenger Bridge (Std.), *06*		40	___
0027	Caboose (OO), *39–42*	40	70	___
27	Lighting Set, *11–23*	15	41	___
27	Station (Std.), *09–12*		NRS	___
28	Double Station w/ dome, *09–12*		NRS	___
29	Day Coach (Std.), *07–22*			
	(A) Dark olive green, 9-window	1500	3000	___
	(B) Maroon, 10-window body	1200	1500	___
	(C) Dark green, 10-window body	3000	4500	___
	(D) Dark olive green, 10-window	680	1000	___
	(E) Dark green, 10-window body	500	900	___
31	Combine (Std.), *21–25*			

		Good	Exc	Cond/$
	(A) Maroon	70	90	___
	(B) Orange	125	195	___
	(C) Dark olive green	70	90	___
	(D) Brown	75	95	___
32	Mail Car (Std.), *21–25*			
	(A) Maroon	85	125	___
	(B) Orange	120	185	___
	(C) Dark olive green	65	85	___
	(D) Brown	70	90	___
32	Miniature Figures, *09–18*	85	155	___
33	Electric 0-6-0, Early (Std.), 13			
	(A) Dark olive green, NYC in oval	90	175	___
	(B) Black, NYC LINES in oval	440	950	___
	(C) Dark olive green, NYC	440	950	___
	(D) "PENNSYLVANIA RAILROAD"	580	1250	___
33	Electric 0-4-0, Later (Std.), *13–24*			
	(A) Dark olive green or black, NYC	105	170	___
	(B) Black, lettered "C & O"	395	720	___
	(C) Maroon, red, or peacock	340	620	___
34	Electric 0-6-0, Early (Std.), *12*	520	860	___
34	Electric 0-4-0 (Std.), *13*	200	385	___
35	Blvd. Lamp, 6⅛" high, *40–42*	25	50	___
35	Pullman (Std.), *12–13*			
	(A) Dark blue	470	900	___
	(B) Dark olive green	170	235	___
35	Pullman (Std.), *14–16*			
	(A) Dark olive green, maroon windows	50	70	___
	(B) Maroon, green windows	85	105	___
	(C) Orange, maroon windows	135	195	___
35	Pullman (Std.), *15–18*	50	70	___
35	Pullman (Std.), *18–23*			
	(A) Dark olive green, maroon windows	36	50	___
	(B) Maroon, green windows	30	45	___
	(C) Orange, maroon windows	120	210	___
	(D) Brown, green windows	36	50	___
35	Pullman (Std.), *24*	40	55	___
35	Pullman (Std.), *25–26*	40	55	___
36	Observation (Std.), *12–13*			
	(A) Dark blue	315	810	___
	(B) Dark olive green	145	205	___
36	Observation (Std.), *14–16*			
	(A) Dark olive green, maroon windows	70	95	___
	(B) Maroon, green windows	50	70	___
	(C) Orange, maroon windows	180	290	___
	(D) Brown, green windows	60	75	___
36	Observation (Std.), *15–18*	60	80	___

		Good	Exc	Cond/$
36	Observation (Std.), *18–23*			
	(A) Dark olive green, maroon windows	40	55	___
	(B) Maroon, green windows	40	55	___
	(C) Orange, maroon windows	130	215	___
	(D) Brown, green windows	40	55	___
36	Observation (Std.), *24*	40	55	___
36	Observation (Std.), *25–26*	40	55	___
38	Electric 0-4-0 (Std.), *13–24*			
	(A) Black	100	135	___
	(B) Red	475	680	___
	(C) Mojave or pea green	405	540	___
	(D) Dark green	270	360	___
	(E) Brown	270	315	___
	(F) Red, cream trim	405	540	___
	(G) Maroon	170	270	___
	(H) Gray	110	125	___
41	Accessory Contactor, *37–42*	1	3	___
042	Switches, pair (O), *38–42*	17	39	___
42	Electric 0-4-4-0, square hood, Early (Std.), *12**	760	1650	___
42	Electric 0-4-4-0, round hood, Later (Std.), *13–23*			
	(A) Black or gray	300	510	___
	(B) Maroon	1250	2050	___
	(C) Dark gray	375	600	___
	(D) Dark green or mojave	500	800	___
	(E) Peacock	1100	1800	___
	(F) Olive or dark olive green	750	1200	___
043/43	Bild-A-Motor Gear Set, *29*		85	___
43	Boat, Runabout, *33–36, 39–41*	480	700	___
0044	Boxcar (OO), *39–42*	41	80	___
0044K	Boxcar Kit (OO), *39–42*	75	120	___
44	Boat, Speedster, *35–36*	510	780	___
0045	Tank Car (OO), *39–42*			
	(A) Black, "SHELL"	40	95	___
	(B) Silver, "SUNOCO"	40	80	___
0045K	Tank Car Kit (OO), *39–42*	75	120	___
45/045/45N	Automatic Gateman, *35–42*	40	70	___
0046	Hopper Car (OO), *39–42*	50	90	___
0046K	Hopper Car Kit (OO), *39–42*			
	(A) "SOUTHERN PACIFIC"	75	135	___
	(B) "READING"		NRS	___
46	Crossing Gate, *39–42*	75	120	___
0047	Caboose (OO), *39–42*	31	60	___
0047K	Caboose Kit (OO), *39–42*	75	135	___
47	Crossing Gate, *39–42*	70	140	___
48W	Whistle Station, *37–42*	22	65	___

		Good	Exc	Cond/$
49	Lionel Airport, *37–39*	160	410	___
50	Airplane, *36–39*	135	320	___
50	Electric 0-4-0 (Std.), 24			
	(A) Dark green or dark gray	145	250	___
	(B) Maroon	315	600	___
	(C) Mojave	175	345	___
50	Cardboard Train, Cars, Accessory (O), *43**	200	360	___
51	Steam 0-4-0, Late 8-wheel (Std.), *12–23*	800	1150	___
51	Lionel Airport, 36, *38*	155	395	___
52	Lamp Post, *33–41*	44	95	___
53	Electric 0-4-4-0, Early (Std.), *12–14*	1200	2450	___
53	Electric 0-4-0, Later (Std.), *15–19*			
	(A) Maroon	550	950	___
	(B) Mojave	670	1350	___
	(C) Dark olive green	560	1150	___
53	Electric 0-4-0, Latest (Std.), *20–21*	200	450	___
53	Lamp Post, *31–42*	33	49	___
53	Electric 0-6-6-0, Early (Std.), *11*		NRS	___
54	Electric 0-4-4-0, Early (Std.), *12**	2500	4050	___
54	Electric 0-4-4-0, Late (Std.), *13–23*	1800	2700	___
54	Lamp Post, *29–35*	45	80	___
55	Airplane w/ stand, *37–39*	190	520	___
56	Lamp Post, removable lens and cap, *24–42*	35	70	___
57	Lamp Post w/ street names, *22–42*	36	85	___
58	Lamp Post, 7⅜" high, *22–42*	33	50	___
59	Lamp Post, 8¾" high, *20–36*	40	85	___
60/060	Telegraph Post (Std./O), *29–42*	11	23	___
60	Electric 0-4-0, FAO Schwartz (Std.), *15 u*		NRS	___
61	Electric 0-4-4-0, FAO Schwartz (Std.), *15 u*		NRS	___
61	Lamp Post, one globe, *14–36*	40	65	___
62	Electric 0-4-0, FAO Schwartz (Std.), *24–32 u*		NRS	___
62	Semaphore, *20–32*	25	50	___
63	Lamp Post, two globes, *33–42*	135	265	___
63	Semaphore, *15–21*	25	50	___
64	Lamp Post, *40–42*	33	70	___
64	Semaphore, 6¾" high, *15–21*	30	60	___
65	Semaphore, one-arm, *15–26*	30	60	___
65	Whistle Controller, *35*	5	7	___
66	Semaphore, two-arm, *15–26*	35	70	___
66	Whistle Controller, *36–39*	9	10	___
67	Lamp Post, *15–32*	85	145	___
67	Whistle Controller, *36–39*	4	8	___
68/068	Crossing Sign, *25–42*	11	19	___
69/069/69N	Electric Warning Signal, *21–42*	33	75	___
70	Outfit: 62 (2), 59 (1), 68 (1), *21–32*	60	130	___
071	060 Telegraph Poles, 6, (Std.), *24–42*	70	160	___

		Good	Exc	Cond/$
71	60 Telegraph Poles, 6, (Std.), *29–42*	70	160	___
0072	Switches, pair (OO), *38–42*	225	355	___
0074	Boxcar (OO), *39–42*	36	70	___
0075	Tank Car (OO), *39–42*	48	90	___
076/76	Block Signal, *23–28*	25	65	___
76	Warning Bell and Shack, *39–42*	65	245	___
0077	Caboose (OO), *39–42*	34	60	___
77/077/77N	Automatic Crossing Gate, *23–39*	28	55	___
78/078	Train Signal (Std.), *24–32*	40	100	___
79	Flashing Signal, *28–40*	115	145	___
80	Automobile, *12–16*	340	660	___
80/080/80N	Semaphore (Std.), *26–42*	50	120	___
81	Automobile, *12–16*	720	1450	___
81	Controlling Rheostat, *27–33*	2	6	___
82/082/82N	Semaphore, *27–42*	50	120	___
83	Flashing Traffic Signal, *27–42*	65	195	___
084	Semaphore, *28–32*	60	100	___
84	Semaphore, *27–32*	55	85	___
84	Automobiles (2), *12–16*	1400	2900	___
85	Telegraph Pole (Std.), *29–42*	15	27	___
85	Automobiles (2), *12–16*	1400	2900	___
86	Telegraph Poles (6), *29–42*	60	120	___
87	Flashing Crossing Signal, *27–42*	85	205	___
88	Battery Rheostat, *15–27*	3	9	___
88	Rheostat Controller, *33–42*	3	5	___
89	Flag Pole, *23–34*	44	75	___
90	Flag Pole, *27–42*	39	95	___
91	Circuit Breaker, *30–42*	34	55	___
092	Signal Tower, *23–27*	90	190	___
92	Floodlight Tower, *31–42**	150	290	___
93	Water Tower, *31–42*	60	125	___
94	High Tension Tower, *32–42**	150	290	___
95	Controlling Rheostat, *34–42*	2.50	6	___
96	Coal Elevator, manual, *38–40*	165	220	___
097	Telegraph Set (O)	50	75	___
97	Coal Elevator, *38–42*	125	250	___
98	Coal Bunker, *38–40*	160	375	___
99/099/99N	Train Control, *32–42*	44	155	___
100	Electric Locomotive (2⅞"), *03–05**	2900	5200	___
100	Trolley (Std.), *10–16*			
	(A) Blue, white windows	1300	2700	___
	(B) Blue, cream windows	1850	3600	___
	(C) Red, cream windows	1300	2700	___
100	Bridge Approaches (2), (Std.), *20–31*	20	36	___
100	Wooden Gondola (2⅞"), *01*		NRS	___
101	Bridge Span, Approaches (2), (Std.), *20–31*	65	120	___

		Good	Exc	Cond/$
101	Summer Trolley (Std.), *10–13*	1300	2700	___
102	Bridge Spans (2), Approaches (2) (Std.), *20–31*	70	175	___
103	Bridge (Std.), *13–16*	50	70	___
103	Bridge Spans (3), Approaches (2) (Std.), *20–31*	60	145	___
104	Bridge Span (Std.), *20–31*	20	45	___
104	Tunnel (Std.), *09–14*	50	135	___
105	Bridge (Std.), *11–14*	40	70	___
105	Bridge Approaches (2), (O), *20–31*	50	70	___
106	Bridge Span, Approaches (2), (O), *20–31*	30	65	___
107	DC Reducer, 110V, *23–32*		NRS	___
108	Bridge Spans (2), Approaches (2), (O), *20–31*	50	90	___
109	Bridge Spans, (3) Approaches (2), (O), *20–32*	50	115	___
109	Tunnel (Std.), *13–14*	30	70	___
110	Bridge Span (O), *20–31*	12	23	___
111	Box of 50 Bulbs, *20–31*	55	105	___
112	Gondola, Early (Std.), *10–12*	225	400	___
112	Gondola, Later (Std.), *12–16*	40	65	___
112	Gondola, Latest (Std.), *16–18*	40	65	___
112	Gondola, Lionel Corp. (Std.), *18–26*	40	65	___
112	Station, *31–35*	145	270	___
113	Cattle Car, Later (Std.), *12–16*	50	70	___
113	Cattle Car, Latest (Std.), *16–18*	50	70	___
113	Cattle Car, Lionel Corp. (Std.), *18–26*	40	55	___
113	Station, *31–34*	150	295	___
114	Boxcar, Later (Std.), *12–16*	50	90	___
114	Boxcar, Latest (Std.), *16–18*	40	70	___
114	Boxcar, Lionel Corp. (Std.), *18–26*	40	70	___
114	Station, *31–34*	530	1200	___
115	Station, *35–42**	235	440	___
116	Station, *35–42**	640	1450	___
116	Ballast Car, Early and Later (Std.), *10–16*	85	115	___
116	Ballast Car, Latest (Std.), *16–18*	65	105	___
116	Ballast Car, Lionel Corp. (Std.), *18–26*	55	95	___
117	Caboose, Early (Std.), *12*	60	70	___
117	Caboose, Later (Std.), *12–16*	50	70	___
117	Caboose, Latest (Std.), *16–18*	50	70	___
117	Caboose, Lionel Corp. (Std.), *18–26*	38	60	___
117	Station, *36–42*	90	235	___
118	Tunnel, 8" long, (O), *22–32*	20	55	___
118L	Tunnel, 8" long, *27*	20	55	___
119	Tunnel, 12" long, *20–42*	22	60	___
119L	Tunnel, 12" long, *27–33*	20	55	___
120	Tunnel, 17" long, *22–27*	27	75	___
120L	Tunnel, *27–42*	75	160	___

		Good	Exc	Cond/$
121	Station (Std.), *09–16*			___
	(A) 14" x 10" x 9"		NRS	___
	(B) 13" x 9" x 13"	150	300	___
121	Station (Std.), *20–26*	75	165	___
121X	Station (Std.), *17–19*	110	255	___
122	Station (Std.), *20–30*	80	190	___
123	Station (Std.), *20–23*	75	205	___
123	Tunnel, 18½" long (O), *33–42*	105	235	___
124	Station, "Lionel City", *20–36**			___
	(A) Tan or gray base, pea green	90	200	___
	(B) Pea green base, red roof	200	360	___
125	Station, "Lionelville", *23–25*	80	185	___
125	Track Template, *38*	1	5	___
126	Station, "Lionelville", *23–36*	95	205	___
127	Station, "Lionel Town", *23–36*	90	160	___
128	124 Station & Terrace, *31–34**	900	1900	___
128	115 Station & Terrace, *35–42**	900	1900	___
129	Terrace, *28–42**	600	1100	___
130	Tunnel, 26" long, *20–36*	100	450	___
130L	Tunnel, 26" long, *27–33*	150	450	___
131	Corner Display, *24–28*	125	295	___
132	Corner Grass Plot, *24–28*	125	295	___
133	Heart-shaped Plot, *24–28*	125	295	___
134	Oval-shaped Plot, *24–28*	125	300	___
134	Station, "Lionel City", w/ stop, *37–42*	230	390	___
135	Circular Plot, *24–28*	125	295	___
136	Large Elevation, *24–28*		NRS	___
136	Station, "Lionelville", w/ stop, *37–42*	85	180	___
137	Station, w/ stop, *37–42*	85	135	___
140L	Tunnel, 37" long, *27–32*	460	1050	___
150	Electric 0-4-0, Early (O), *17*	90	160	___
150	Electric 0-4-0, Late (O), *18–25*			___
	(A) Brown, brown or olive windows	95	150	___
	(B) Maroon, dark olive windows	90	135	___
152	Electric 0-4-0 (O), *17–27*			___
	(A) Dark green	90	135	___
	(B) Gray	115	160	___
	(C) Mojave	340	680	___
	(D) Peacock	340	680	___
152	Crossing Gate, *40–42*	18	38	___
153	Block Signal, *40–42*	23	45	___
153	Electric 0-4-0 (O), *24–25*			___
	(A) Dark green	100	160	___
	(B) Gray	100	160	___
	(C) Mojave	100	160	___
154	Electric 0-4-0 (O), *17–23*	100	180	___

		Good	Exc	Cond/$
154	Highway Signal, *40–42*	21	47	___
	(A) Black base	21	49	___
	(B) Orange base	40	120	___
155	Freight Shed, *30–42**			
	(A) Cream base, terra cotta floor	180	320	___
	(B) Ivory base, red floor	240	400	___
156	Electric 4-4-4 (O), *17–23*			
	(A) Dark green	475	810	___
	(B) Maroon	540	890	___
	(C) Olive green	600	1050	___
	(D) Gray	670	1200	___
156	Electric 0-4-0 (O), *17–23*	400	720	___
156	Station Platform, *39–42*	85	140	___
156X	Electric 0-4-0 (O), *23–24*			
	(A) Maroon	380	495	___
	(B) Olive green	440	550	___
	(C) Gray	530	710	___
	(D) Brown	470	600	___
157	Hand Truck, *30–32*	25	41	___
158	Electric 0-4-0 (O), *19–23*			
	(A) Gray or red windows	75	205	___
	(B) Black	95	250	___
158	156 (2) and 136 (1), *40–42*	120	280	___
159	Block Actuator, *40*	10	27	___
161	Baggage Truck, *30–32**	42	80	___
162	Dump Truck, *30–32**	42	80	___
163	157 (2), 162 (1), 161 (1), boxed, *30–42**	220	360	___
164	Log Loader, *40–42*	160	225	___
165	Magnetic Crane, *40–42*	175	290	___
166	Whistle Controller, *40–42*	3	7	___
167	Whistle Controller, *40–42*	6	14	___
167X	Whistle Controller (OO), *40–42*	5	14	___
169	Controller, *40–42*	3	8	___
170	DC Reducer, 220V, *14–38*	3	8	___
171	DC to AC Inverter, 110V, *36–42*	3	15	___
172	DC to AC Inverter, 229V, *39–42*	3	7	___
180	Pullman (Std.), *11–13*			
	(A) Maroon body and roof	145	205	___
	(B) Brown body and roof	145	255	___
180	Pullman (Std.), *13–15*	80	160	___
180	Pullman (Std.), *15–18*	80	160	___
180	Pullman (Std.), *18–22*	80	135	___
181	Combine (Std.), *11–13*			
	(A) Maroon, dark olive doors	145	205	___
	(B) Brown, dark olive doors	145	205	___
	(C) Yellow-orange, orange door	350	495	___

		Good	Exc	Cond/$
181	Combine (Std.), *13–15*	80	160	___
181	Combine (Std.), *15–18*	80	160	___
181	Combine (Std.), *18–22*	80	135	___
182	Observation (Std.), *11–13*			
	(A) Maroon, dark olive doors	145	205	___
	(B) Brown, dark olive doors	145	205	___
	(C) Yellow-orange, orange door	350	495	___
182	Observation (Std.), *13–15*	80	160	___
182	Observation (Std.), *15–18*	80	160	___
182	Observation (Std.), *18–22*	80	135	___
183	Pullman (Std.)		NM	___
184	Bungalow, illuminated, *23–32**	65	110	___
184	Combine (Std.), *11*		NM	___
185	Bungalow, *23–24*	50	115	___
185	Observation (Std.), *11*		NM	___
186	184 Bungalows (5), *23–32*	195	610	___
186	Log Loader Outfit, *40–41*	130	340	___
187	185 Bungalows (5), *23–24*	170	590	___
188	Elevator and Car Set, *38–41*	115	370	___
189	Villa, illuminated, *23–32**	165	225	___
190	Observation (Std.), 08			
	(A) Dark olive green, unremovable roof	1150	2600	___
	(B) Dark olive green, removable roof	115	205	___
	(C) Yellow-orange, removable roof	320	620	___
	(D) Orange, removable roof	115	205	___
	(E) Mojave, removable roof	345	870	___
190	Observation (Std.), *11–13*	600	900	___
190	Observation (Std.), *13–15*	200	295	___
190	Observation (Std.), *15–18*	200	295	___
190	Observation (Std.), *18–22*	80	135	___
190	Observation (Std.), *23–26*	230	475	___
191	Villa, illuminated, *23–32**	180	325	___
192	Villa Set, illuminated: 189, 191, 184 (2) *27–32*		800	___
193	Accessory Set, boxed, *27–29*	150	325	___
194	Accessory Set, boxed, *27–29*	100	325	___
195	Terrace, *27–30*	350	740	___
196	Accessory Set, *27*	200	335	___
200	Electric Express (2⅞"), *03*	4150	5600	___
200	Turntable, *28–33**	85	190	___
200	Wooden Gondola (2⅞"), *01–02*		NRS	___
200	Trailer, matches #2 Trolley (Std.), *11–16*		2400	___
200	Electric Express (2⅞"), *03–05**	4000	6300	___
201	Steam 0-6-0 (O), *40–42*			
	(A) With 2201B Tender w/ bell	375	760	___
	(B) With 2201T Tender w/o bell	345	690	___

		Good	Exc	Cond/$
202	Summer Trolley (Std.), *10–13*			
	(A) "ELECTRIC RAPID TRANSIT"	1300	2700	___
	(B) "PRESTON ST."	3250	4500	___
203	Armored 0-4-0 (O), *17–21*	1100	1800	___
203	Steam 0-6-0 (O), *40–42*			
	(A) With 2203B Tender w/ bell	400	590	___
	(B) With 2203T Tender w/o bell	365	550	___
204	Steam 2-4-2 (O), *40–42* u			
	(A) Black locomotive	55	105	___
	(B) Gun-metal gray locomotive	80	165	___
205	LCL Merchandise Containers (3), *30–38**	130	290	___
206	Sack of Coal, *38–42*	5	18	___
208	Tool Set, boxed, *34–42**	65	150	___
0209	Barrels, *34–42*	5	21	___
209	Wooden Barrels, *34–42*	8	19	___
210	Switches, pair (Std.), 26, *34–42*	42	75	___
211	Flatcar (Std.), *26–40**	125	225	___
212	Gondola (Std.), *26–40**			
	(A) Gray or light green	100	205	___
	(B) Maroon	75	135	___
213	Cattle Car (Std.), *26–40**			
	(A) Mojave, maroon roof	160	365	___
	(B) Terra-cotta, pea green roof	130	285	___
	(C) Cream, maroon roof	300	650	___
214	Boxcar (Std.), *26–40**			
	(A) Terra-cotta, green roof	195	295	___
	(B) Cream body, orange roof	150	270	___
	(C) Yellow, brown roof	300	495	___
214R	Refrigerator Car (Std.), *29–40**			
	(A) Ivory or white, peacock roof	325	495	___
	(B) White, light blue nickel roof	435	790	___
215	Tank Car (Std.), *26–40**			
	(A) Pea green	150	215	___
	(B) Ivory	220	360	___
	(C) Aluminum	315	720	___
216	Hopper Car (Std.), *26–38**			
	(A) Dark green, brass plates	195	335	___
	(B) Dark green, nickel plates	445	1100	___
217	Caboose (Std.), *26–40**			
	(A) Orange, maroon roof	250	510	___
	(B) Red, peacock roof	120	245	___
	(C) Red body/roof, ivory doors	150	320	___
217	Lighting Set, *14–23*		NRS	___
218	Dump Car (Std.), *26–38**	220	365	___
219	Crane (Std.), *26–40**			
	(A) Peacock, red boom	135	250	___

		Good	Exc	Cond/$
	(B) Yellow, light green or red boom	270	440	___
	(C) Ivory, light green boom	270	480	___
220	Floodlight Car (Std.), *31–40**			
	(A) Terra-cotta base	225	385	___
	(B) Green base	340	485	___
220	Switches, pair (Std.), *26**	25	90	___
222	Switches, pair (Std.), *26–32*	40	100	___
223	Switches, pair (Std.), *32–42*	33	120	___
224/224E	Steam 2-6-2 (O), *38–42*			
	(A) Black, die-cast 2224 Tender	155	290	___
	(B) Black, plastic 2224 Tender	110	195	___
	(C) Gun-metal, die-cast 2224 Tender	385	950	___
	(D) Gun-metal, 2689 Tender	120	210	___
225	222 Switches, 439 Panel, *29–32*	115	260	___
225/225E	Steam 2-6-2 (O), *38–42*			
	(A) Black, 2235 or 2245 Tender	210	370	___
	(B) Black, 2235 plastic Tender	185	320	___
	(C) Gun-metal, 2225 or 2265 Tender	210	360	___
	(D) Gun-metal, 2235 die-cast Tender	285	730	___
226/226E	Steam 2-6-4 (O), *38–41*	345	670	___
227	Steam 0-6-0 (O), *39–42*			
	(A) With 2227B Tender w/ bell	600	1250	___
	(B) With 2227T Tender w/o bell	600	1150	___
228	Steam 0-6-0 (O), *39–42*			
	(A) With 2228B Tender w/ bell	600	1250	___
	(B) With 2228T Tender w/o bell	600	1150	___
229	Steam 2-4-2 (O), *39–42*			
	(A) Black or gun-metal w/ 2689W	155	280	___
	(B) Black or gun-metal w/ 2689T	120	200	___
	(C) Black w/ 2666W whistle Tender	155	280	___
	(D) Black w/ 2666T non-whistle Tender	120	200	___
230	Steam 0-6-0 (O), *39–42*	1100	2050	___
231	Steam 0-6-0 (O), *39*	1000	1800	___
232	Steam 0-6-0 (O), *40–42*	1000	1800	___
233	Steam 0-6-0 (O), *40–42*	1000	1800	___
238	Steam 4-4-2 (O), *39–40 u*	430	710	___
238E	Steam 4-4-2 (O), *36–38*			
	(A) W/265W or 2225W whistle Tender	280	365	___
	(B) W/265 or 2225T non-whistling Tender	275	360	___
248	Electric 0-4-0 (O), *27–32*	150	240	___
249/249E	Steam 2-4-2 (O), *36–39*			
	(A) Gun-metal, 265T or 265W Tender	100	200	___
	(B) Black, 265W Tender	110	210	___
250	Electric 0-4-0, Early (O), *26*	125	220	___
250	Electric 0-4-0, Late (O), *34*			
	(A) Yellow-orange, terra-cotta frame	145	245	___

		Good	Exc	Cond/$
	(B) Terra-cotta body, maroon frame	160	275	___
250E	Steam 4-4-2 Hiawatha (O), *35–42**	400	1100	___
251	Electric 0-4-0 (O), *25–32*			
	(A) Gray body, red windows	190	340	___
	(B) Red body, ivory stripe	215	410	___
	(C) Red body, w/o ivory stripe	200	380	___
251E	Electric 0-4-0 (O), *27–32*			
	(A) Red body, ivory stripe	225	425	___
	(B) Red body, w/o ivory stripe	215	395	___
	(C) Gray, red trim	195	350	___
252	Electric 0-4-0 (O), *26–32*			
	(A) Peacock or olive green	95	170	___
	(B) Terra-cotta or yellow-orange	125	255	___
252E	Electric 0-4-0 (O), *33–35*			
	(A) Terra-cotta	145	250	___
	(B) Yellow-orange	125	205	___
253	Electric 0-4-0 (O), *24–32*			
	(A) Maroon	180	430	___
	(B) Dark green	105	195	___
	(C) Mojave	105	235	___
	(D) Terra-cotta	180	430	___
	(E) Peacock	95	195	___
	(F) Red	210	475	___
253E	Electric 0-4-0 (O), *31–36*			
	(A) Green	150	205	___
	(B) Terra-cotta	190	305	___
254	Electric 0-4-0 (O), *24–32*	240	340	___
254E	Electric 0-4-0 (O), *27–34*	190	285	___
255E	Steam 2-4-2 (O), *35–36*	485	1000	___
256	Electric 0-4-4-0 (O), *24–30**			
	(A) Rubber-stamped lettering	470	1250	___
	(B) w/o outline and "LIONEL"	425	770	___
	(C) "LIONEL" and "256" on brass	450	1050	___
257	Steam 2-4-0 (O), *30–35* u			
	(A) Black Tender	145	305	___
	(B) Black crackle-finish Tender	240	435	___
258	Steam 2-4-0, Early (O), *30–35* u			
	(A) With 4-wheel 257 Tender	85	170	___
	(B) With 8-wheel 258 Tender	100	195	___
258	Steam 2-4-2, Late (O), *41 u*			
	(A) Black	60	90	___
	(B) Gun-metal	85	135	___
259	Steam 2-4-2 (O), *32*	70	135	___
259E	Steam 2-4-2 (O), *33–42*	80	155	___
260E	Steam 2-4-2 (O), *30–35**			
	(A) Black, green or black frame	385	520	___

		Good	Exc	Cond/$
	(B) Dark gun-metal body and frame	440	640	___
261	Steam 2-4-2 (O), *31*	125	210	___
261E	Steam 2-4-2 (O), *35*	190	285	___
262	Steam 2-4-2 (O), *31–32*	215	375	___
262E	Steam 2-4-2 (O), *33–36*			
	(A) Gloss black, copper/brass trim	100	210	___
	(B) Satin black, nickel trim	125	265	___
263E	Steam 2-4-2 (O), *36–39**			
	(A) Gun-metal gray	315	610	___
	(B) 2-tone blue, from Blue Comet	415	950	___
264E	Steam 2-4-2 (O), *35–36*			
	(A) Red, "RED COMET"	150	295	___
	(B) Black	220	380	___
265E	Steam 2-4-2 (O), *35–40*			
	(A) Black or gun-metal	170	330	___
	(B) Light blue, "BLUE STREAK"	460	800	___
267E/267W	Sets: 616, 617 (2), 618, *35–41*		560	___
270	Bridge, 10" long (O), *31–42*	18	50	___
270	Lighting Set, *15–23*		NRS	___
271	270 Spans (2), (O), *31–33, 35–40*	65	150	___
271	Lighting Set, *15–23*		NRS	___
272	270 Spans (3), (O), *31–33, 35–40*	60	165	___
280	Bridge, 14" long (Std.), *31–42*	50	115	___
281	Bridge Spans (2), (Std.), *31–33, 35–40*	90	205	___
282	Bridge Spans (3), (Std.), *31–33, 35–40*	105	265	___
289E	Steam 2-4-2 (O), *37 u*	120	305	___
300	Electric Trolley Car (2⅞"), *01–05*	2000	3600	___
300	Hell Gate Bridge (Std.), *28–42**			
	(A) Cream towers, green truss	800	1350	___
	(B) Ivory towers, aluminum truss	700	1600	___
301	Batteries, set of 4 (2⅞"), *03–05*		NRS	___
302	Plunge Battery (2⅞"), *01–02*		NRS	___
303	Summer Trolley, *10–13*	1500	3150	___
303	Carbon Cylinders (2⅞"), *02*		NRS	___
304	Composite Zincs (2⅞"), *02*		NRS	___
306	Glass Jars (2⅞"), *02*		NRS	___
308	Signs (5), (O), *40–42*	26	70	___
309	Electric Trolley Trailer (2⅞"), *01–05*	2500	4050	___
309	Pullman (Std.), *26–39*			
	(A) Maroon body/roof, mojave window	100	160	___
	(B) Mojave body/roof, maroon window	100	160	___
	(C) Light brown body, dark brown roof	120	185	___
	(D) Medium blue body, dark blue roof	170	280	___
	(E) Apple green body, dark green roof	170	280	___
	(F) Pale blue body, silver roof	100	185	___
	(G) Maroon body, terra-cotta roof	130	195	___

		Good	Exc	Cond/$
310	Baggage (Std.), *26–39*			
	(A) Maroon body/roof, mojave window	100	160	___
	(B) Mojave body/roof, maroon window	100	160	___
	(C) Light brown body, dark brown roof	115	185	___
	(D) Medium blue body, dark blue roof	170	280	___
	(E) Apple green body, dark green roof	170	280	___
	(F) Pale blue body, silver roof	100	175	___
310	Rails and Ties, complete section (2⅞"), *01–02*	5	14	___
312	Observation (Std.), *24–39*			
	(A) Maroon body/roof, mojave window	100	160	___
	(B) Mojave body/roof, maroon window	100	160	___
	(C) Light brown body, dark brown roof	120	185	___
	(D) Medium blue body, dark blue roof	170	280	___
	(E) Apple green body, dark green roof	170	280	___
	(F) Pale blue body, silver roof	100	175	___
	(G) Maroon body, terra-cotta roof	130	195	___
313	Bascule Bridge (O), *40–42*			
	(A) Silver bridge	235	500	___
	(B) Gray bridge	250	590	___
314	Girder Bridge (O), *40–42*	17	40	___
315	Trestle Bridge (O), *40–42*	28	80	___
316	Trestle Bridge (O), *40–42*	21	48	___
318	Electric 0-4-0 (Std.), *24–32*			
	(A) Gray, dark gray, or mojave	150	250	___
	(B) Pea green	150	250	___
	(C) State brown	250	395	___
318E	Electric 0-4-0, *26–35*			
	(A) Gray, mojave, or pea green	150	250	___
	(B) State brown	275	440	___
	(C) Black	550	1050	___
319	Pullman (Std.), *24–27*	105	175	___
320	Baggage (Std.), *25–27*	100	175	___
320	Switch and Signal (2⅞"), *02–05*		NRS	___
322	Observation (Std.), *24–27, 29–30 u*	100	175	___
330	Crossing, 90° (2⅞"), *02–05*		NRS	___
332	Baggage (Std.), *26–33*			
	(A) Red body and roof, cream doors	80	120	___
	(B) Peacock body/roof, orange doors	75	115	___
	(C) Gray body/roof, maroon doors	75	115	___
	(D) Olive green body/roof, red doors	90	145	___
	(E) State brown body, dark brown roof	190	430	___
337	Pullman (Std.), *25–32*			
	(A) Red body/roof, cream doors	95	190	___
	(B) Mojave body/roof, maroon doors	95	190	___
	(C) Olive green body/roof, red doors	105	225	___
	(D) Olive green body/roof, maroon doors	95	190	___

		Good	Exc	Cond/$
	(E) Pea green body/roof, cream doors	210	500	___
338	Observation (Std.), *25–32*			
	(A) Red body/roof, cream doors	95	190	___
	(B) Mojave body/roof, maroon doors	95	190	___
	(C) Olive green body/roof, red doors	105	225	___
	(D) Olive green body/roof, maroon doors	95	190	___
339	Pullman (Std.), *25–33*			
	(A) Peacock body/roof, orange doors	55	100	___
	(B) Gray body/roof, maroon doors	55	100	___
	(C) State brown body, dark brown roof	135	380	___
	(D) Peacock body, dark green roof	75	130	___
	(E) Mojave body, maroon roof/doors	145	230	___
340	Suspension Bridge (2⅞"), *02–05**		NRS	___
341	Observation (Std.), *25–33*			
	(A) Peacock body/roof, orange doors	50	70	___
	(B) Gray body/roof, maroon doors	50	70	___
	(C) State brown body, dark brown roof	125	275	___
	(D) Peacock body, dark green roof	65	95	___
	(E) Mojave body, maroon roof/doors	135	165	___
350	Track Bumper (2⅞"), *02–05*		550	___
370	Jars and Plates (2⅞"), *02–03*		NRS	___
380	Electric 0-4-0 (Std.), *23–27*	310	440	___
380	Elevated Pillars (2⅞"), *04–05**	30	70	___
380E	Electric 0-4-0 (Std.), *26–29*			
	(A) Mojave	445	630	___
	(B) Maroon	295	400	___
	(C) Dark green	370	460	___
381	Electric 4-4-4 (Std.), *28–29**	1600	2100	___
381E	Electric 4-4-4 (Std.), *28–36**			
	(A) State green, apple green sub-frame	1500	2500	___
	(B) State green, red sub-frame	1900	3250	___
381U	Electric 4-4-4 Kit (Std.), *28–29*	1600	4100	___
384	Steam 2-4-0 (Std.), *30–32**	415	730	___
384E	Steam 2-4-0 (Std.), *30–32**	425	650	___
385E	Steam 2-4-2 (Std.), *33–39**	370	670	___
390	Steam 2-4-2 (Std.), *29**	460	820	___
390E	Steam 2-4-2 (Std.), *29–31**			
	(A) Black, w/ or w/o orange stripe	460	690	___
	(B) 2-tone blue, cream-orange stripe	650	1050	___
	(C) 2-tone green, orange or green stripe	990	2050	___
392E	Steam 4-4-2 (Std.), *32–39**			
	(A) Black, 384 Tender	750	1250	___
	(B) Black, large 12-wheel Tender	1050	1150	___
	(C) Gun-metal gray	1000	1800	___
400	Express Trail Car (2⅞"), *03–05**	3500	5850	___
400E	Steam 4-4-4 (Std.), *31–39**			

		Good	Exc	Cond/$
	(A) Black	1400	2150	___
	(B) Medium blue boiler	1550	2400	___
	(C) Crackle black finish	1550	2400	___
402	Electric 0-4-4-0 (Std.), *23–27*	365	570	___
402E	Electric 0-4-4-0 (Std.), *26–29*	345	550	___
404	Summer Trolley (Std.), *10*		NRS	___
408E	Electric 0-4-4-0 (Std.), *27–36**			
	(A) Apple green or mojave, red pilots	770	980	___
	(B) 2-tone brown, brown pilots	2100	2650	___
	(C) Dark green, red pilots	1850	3400	___
412	Pullman, "California" (Std.), *29–35**			
	(A) Light green body, dark green roof	590	1750	___
	(B) Light brown body, dark brown roof	620	2100	___
413	Pullman, "Colorado" (Std.), *29–35**			
	(A) Light green body, dark green roof	590	1750	___
	(B) Light brown body, dark brown roof	620	2100	___
414	Pullman, "Illinois" (Std.), *29–35**			
	(A) Light green body, dark green roof	590	2050	___
	(B) Light brown body, dark brown roof	620	2050	___
416	Observation, "New York" (Std.), *29–35**			
	(A) Light green body, dark green roof	590	1750	___
	(B) Light brown body, dark brown roof	620	2100	___
418	Pullman (Std.), *23–32**	225	320	___
419	Combination (Std.), *23–32**	205	280	___
420	Pullman, "Faye" (Std.), *30–40**			
	(A) Brass trim	485	900	___
	(B) Nickel trim	500	1200	___
421	Pullman, "Westphal" (Std.), *30–40**			
	(A) Brass trim	500	900	___
	(B) Nickel trim	500	1200	___
422	Observation, "Tempel" (Std.), *30–40**			
	(A) Brass trim	485	900	___
	(B) Nickel trim	500	1200	___
424	Pullman, "Liberty Belle" (Std.), *31–40**			
	(A) Brass trim	350	530	___
	(B) Nickel trim	385	650	___
425	Pullman, "Stephen Girard" (Std.), *31–40**			
	(A) Brass trim	350	530	___
	(B) Nickel trim	385	650	___
426	Observation, "Coral Isle" (Std.), *31–40**			
	(A) Brass trim	350	530	___
	(B) Nickel trim	385	650	___
427	Diner (Std.), *30*		NM	___
428	Pullman (Std.), *26–30**			
	(A) Dark green body and roof	250	385	___
	(B) Orange body/roof, apple green window	390	890	___

		Good	Exc	Cond/$
429	Combine (Std.), *26–30**			
	(A) Dark green body and roof	250	385	___
	(B) Orange body/roof, apple green window	390	890	___
430	Observation (Std.), *26–30**			
	(A) Dark green body and roof	250	385	___
	(B) Orange body/roof, apple green window	390	890	___
431	Diner (Std.), *27–32**			
	(A) Mojave body, screw-mounted roof	350	540	___
	(B) Mojave body, hinged roof	465	720	___
	(C) Dark green body, orange windows	410	720	___
	(D) Orange body, apple green window	410	720	___
	(E) Apple green body, red window	410	720	___
435	Power Station, *26–38**	215	400	___
436	Power Station, *26–37**			
	(A) "POWER STATION" plate	135	265	___
	(B) "EDISON SERVICE" plate	270	610	___
437	Switch/Signal Tower, *26–37**	190	430	___
438	Signal Tower, *27–39**			
	(A) Mojave base, orange house	215	410	___
	(C) Black base, ivory house	325	640	___
439	Panel Board, *28–42**	80	145	___
440/0440/440N Signal Bridge, *32–42**		180	445	___
440C	Panel Board, *32–42*	90	145	___
441	Weighing Station (Std.), *32–36*	495	1400	___
442	Landscape Diner, *38–42*	250	350	___
444	Roundhouse (Std.), *32–35**	1350	2850	___
444-18	Roundhouse Clip, *33*		NRS	___
450	Electric 0-4-0, Macy's (O), *30 u*			
	(A) Red, black frame	295	700	___
	(B) Apple green, dark green frame	415	880	___
450	Set: 450, matching 605, 606 (2), *30 u*	750	1800	___
455	Electric Range, 30, *32–33*	355	1000	___
490	Observation (Std.), *23–32**	190	255	___
500	Dealer Display, *27–28*		NRS	___
500	Electric Derrick Car (2⅞"), *03–04**	5000	6750	___
501	Dealer Display, *27–28*		NRS	___
502	Dealer Display, *27–28*		NRS	___
503	Dealer Display, *27–28*		NRS	___
504	Dealer Display, *24–28*		NRS	___
505	Dealer Display, *24–28*		NRS	___
506	Dealer Display, *24–28*		NRS	___
507	Dealer Display, *24–28*		NRS	___
508	Dealer Display, *24–28*		NRS	___
509	Dealer Display, *24–28*		NRS	___
510	Dealer Display, *27–28*		NRS	___
511	Flatcar (Std.), *27–40*	65	115	___

		Good	Exc	Cond/$
	(A) Dark green	65	115	___
	(B) Medium green	75	165	___
512	Gondola (Std.), *27–39*			
	(A) Peacock	38	70	___
	(B) Light green	50	95	___
513	Cattle Car (Std.), *27–38*			
	(A) Olive green, orange roof	70	165	___
	(B) Orange, pea green roof	60	110	___
	(C) Cream, maroon roof	90	175	___
514	Boxcar (Std.), *29–40*			
	(A) Cream, orange roof	90	155	___
	(B) Yellow, brown roof	115	285	___
514	Refrigerator Car (Std.), *27–28*			
	(A) Ivory or white, peacock roof	240	400	___
	(B) Cream, peacock roof	215	340	___
	(C) Ivory, peacock roof	285	800	___
514R	Refrigerator Car (Std.), *29–40*			
	(A) Ivory, peacock roof, brass plates	140	190	___
	(B) Ivory, light blue roof, nickel plate	420	580	___
	(C) White, light blue roof, brass plates	140	180	___
515	Tank Car (Std.), *27–40*			
	(A) Terra-cotta	90	160	___
	(B) Light tan	105	185	___
	(C) Silver	90	175	___
	(D) Orange, red "SHELL" decal	340	690	___
516	Hopper Car (Std.), *28–40*		395	
	(A) Red	170	240	___
	(B) Red with rubber-stamped data	200	300	___
	(C) Light red, nickel trim	200	325	___
517	Caboose (Std.), *27–40*			
	(A) Pea green, red roof	50	100	___
	(B) Red body and roof	105	155	___
	(C) Red, black roof, orange windows	355	640	___
520	Floodlight Car (Std.), *31–40*			
	(A) Terra-cotta base	110	210	___
	(B) Green base	110	240	___
529	Pullman (O), *26–32*			
	(A) Olive green body and roof	25	45	___
	(B) Terra-cotta body and roof	25	60	___
530	Observation (O), *26–32*			
	(A) Olive green body and roof	25	45	___
	(B) Terra-cotta body and roof	25	60	___
550	Miniature Figures, boxed (Std.), *32–36**	175	350	___
551	Engineer (Std.), *32*	25	45	___
552	Conductor (Std.), *32*	21	42	___
553	Porter (Std.) with stool, *32*	25	50	___

		Good	Exc	Cond/$
554	Male Passenger (Std.), *32*	25	45	___
555	Female Passenger (Std.), *32*	25	45	___
556	Red Cap Figure (Std.) with suitcase, *32*	25	65	___
600	Derrick Trailer (2⅞"), *03–04**	5000	8550	___
600	Pullman, Early (O), *15–23*			
	(A) Dark green	65	170	___
	(B) Maroon or brown	48	85	___
600	Pullman, Late (O), *33–42*			
	(A) Light red or gray, red roof	50	90	___
	(B) Light blue, aluminum roof	70	120	___
601	Observation, Late (O), *33–42*			
	(A) Light red body and roof	50	90	___
	(B) Light gray, red roof	50	90	___
	(C) Light blue body, aluminum roof	70	120	___
601	Pullman, Early (O), *15–23*	50	70	___
602	Baggage, Lionel Lines, Late (O), *33–42*			
	(A) Light red or gray; red roof	60	110	___
	(B) Light blue body, aluminum roof	90	150	___
602	Baggage, NYC (O), *15–23*	30	45	___
602	Observation (O), *22 u*	30	36	___
603	Pullman, Early (O), *22 u*	40	70	___
603	Pullman, Later (O), *20–25*	20	45	___
603	Pullman, Latest (O), *31–36*			
	(A) Light red body and roof	45	85	___
	(B) Red body, black roof	35	60	___
	(C) Stephen Girard green, dark green roof	35	60	___
	(D) Maroon body/roof, "MACY SPCL"	60	125	___
604	Observation, Later (O), *20–25*	35	60	___
604	Observation, Latest (O), *31–36*			
	(A) Light red body and roof	44	85	___
	(B) Red body, black roof	35	60	___
	(C) Yellow-orange body, terra-cotta roof	35	60	___
	(D) Stephen Girard green, dark green roof	35	60	___
	(E) Maroon body and roof	70	150	___
605	Pullman (O), *25–32*			
	(A) Gray, "LIONEL LINES"	85	170	___
	(B) Gray, "ILLINOIS CENTRAL"	85	170	___
	(C) Red, "LIONEL LINES"	170	255	___
	(D) Red, "ILLINOIS CENTRAL"	255	340	___
	(E) Orange, "LIONEL LINES"	170	255	___
	(F) Orange, "ILLINOIS CENTRAL"	300	430	___
	(G) Olive green, "LIONEL LINES"	255	340	___
606	Observation (O), *25–32*			
	(A) Gray, "LIONEL LINES"	130	215	___
	(B) Gray, "ILLINOIS CENTRAL"	90	170	___
	(C) Red, "LIONEL LINES"	170	255	___

		Good	Exc	Cond/$
	(D) Red, "ILLINOIS CENTRAL"	255	340	___
	(E) Orange, "LIONEL LINES"	170	255	___
	(F) Orange, "ILLINOIS CENTRAL"	170	255	___
	(G) Olive green, "LIONEL LINES"	255	340	___
607	Pullman (O), *26–27*			
	(A) Peacock, "LIONEL LINES"	50	70	___
	(B) Peacock, "ILLINOIS CENTRAL	75	115	___
	(C) 2-tone green, "LIONEL LINES"	50	75	___
	(D) Red, "LIONEL LINES"	75	110	___
608	Observation (O), *26–37*			
	(A) Peacock, "LIONEL LINES"	50	70	___
	(B) Peacock, "ILLINOIS CENTRAL	75	115	___
	(C) 2-tone green, "LIONEL LINES"	50	75	___
	(D) Red, "LIONEL LINES"	75	110	___
609	Pullman (O), *37*	60	85	___
610	Pullman, Early (O), *15–25*			
	(A) Dark green body and roof	50	65	___
	(B) Maroon body and roof	60	95	___
	(C) Mojave body and roof	60	95	___
610	Pullman, Late (O), *26–30*			
	(A) Olive green body and roof	65	80	___
	(B) Mojave body and roof	55	80	___
	(C) Terra-cotta body, maroon roof	100	155	___
	(D) Pea green body and roof	70	115	___
	(E) Light blue body, aluminum roof	130	260	___
	(F) Light red, aluminum finish roof	100	155	___
611	Observation (O), *37*	55	90	___
612	Observation, Early (O), *15–25*			
	(A) Dark green body and roof	50	60	___
	(B) Maroon body and roof	70	90	___
	(C) Mojave body and roof	70	90	___
612	Observation, Late (O), *26–30*			
	(A) Olive green body and roof	55	80	___
	(B) Mojave body and roof	55	80	___
	(C) Terra-cotta body, maroon roof	100	155	___
	(D) Pea green body and roof	70	115	___
	(E) Light blue body, aluminum roof	130	260	___
	(F) Light red, aluminum finish roof	100	155	___
613	Pullman (O), *31–40**			
	(A) Terra-cotta, maroon/terra-cotta roof	85	195	___
	(B) Light red, light red/aluminum roof	175	350	___
	(C) Blue, two-tone blue roof	115	225	___
614	Observation (O), *31–40**			
	(A) Terra-cotta, maroon/terra-cotta roof	100	190	___
	(B) Light red, light red/aluminum roof	175	350	___
	(C) Blue, two-tone blue roof	115	225	___

		Good	Exc	Cond/$
615	Baggage (O), *33–40**	150	260	___
616E/616W	Diesel only (O), *35–41*	90	215	___
616E/616W	Set: 616, 617 (2), 618	310	570	___
617	Coach (O), *35–41*			
	(A) Blue and white	55	85	___
	(B) Chrome, gun-metal skirts	55	85	___
	(C) Chrome, chrome skirts	55	85	___
	(D) Silver finish	55	85	___
618	Observation (O), *35–41*			
	(A) Blue and white	55	85	___
	(B) Chrome, gun-metal skirts	55	85	___
	(C) Chrome, chrome skirts	55	85	___
	(D) Silver finish	55	85	___
619	Combine (O), *36–38*			
	(A) Blue, white window band	100	205	___
	(B) Chrome, chrome skirts	100	205	___
620	Floodlight Car (O), *37–42*	50	85	___
629	Pullman (O), *24–32*			
	(A) Dark green body and roof	30	40	___
	(B) Orange body and roof	30	40	___
	(C) Red body and roof	20	32	___
	(D) Light red body and roof	40	55	___
630	Observation, *24–32*			
	(A) Dark green body and roof	30	40	___
	(B) Orange body and roof	30	40	___
	(C) Red body and roof	20	32	___
	(D) Light red body and roof	40	55	___
636W	Diesel only (O), *36–39*	90	175	___
636W	Set: 636W, 637 (2), 638, *36–39*	375	640	___
637	Coach (O), *36–39*	70	105	___
638	Observation (O), *36–39*	70	105	___
651	Flatcar (O), *35–40*	28	55	___
652	Gondola (O), *35–40*	28	55	___
653	Hopper Car (O), *34–40*	35	65	___
654	Tank Car (O), *34–42*			
	(A) Orange or aluminum finish	38	60	___
	(B) Gray	42	75	___
655	Boxcar (O), *34–42*			
	(A) Cream, maroon roof	35	60	___
	(B) Cream, tuscan roof	47	75	___
656	Cattle Car (O), *35–40*			
	(A) Light gray, vermilion roof	40	75	___
	(B) Burnt orange, tuscan roof	70	125	___
657	Caboose (O), *34–42*			
	(A) Red body and roof	20	34	___
	(B) Red, tuscan roof	25	42	___

		Good	Exc	Cond/$
659	Dump Car (O), *35–42*	40	75	___
700	Electric 0-4-0 (O), *15–16*	360	690	___
700	Window Display (2⅞"), *03–05*		NRS	___
700E	Steam 4-6-4, Scale Hudson, 5344 (O) *37–42**	1400	2950	___
700K	Steam 4-6-4, unbuilt (O), *38–42*	4400	5950	___
701	Electric 0-4-0 (O), *15–16*	390	660	___
701	Steam 0-6-0 (see 708)		2350	___
702	Baggage (O), *17–21*	115	305	___
703	Electric 4-4-4 (O), *15–16*	1400	2350	___
706	Electric 0-4-0 (O), *15–16*	375	630	___
708	Steam 0-6-0, "8976" on boiler front (O) *39–42**	1450	2850	___
710	Pullman (O), *24–34*			
	(A) Red, "LIONEL LINES"	200	300	___
	(B) Orange, "LIONEL LINES"	150	225	___
	(C) Orange, "NEW YORK CENTRAL"	200	225	___
	(D) Orange, "ILLINOIS CENTRAL"	300	450	___
	(E) 2-tone blue, "LIONEL LINES	300	415	___
	(F) Orange, "NEW YORK CENTRAL"	200	260	___
711	R.C. Switches, pair (O72), *35–42*	80	150	___
712	Observation (O), *24–34*			
	(A) Red, "LIONEL LINES"	185	355	___
	(B) Orange, "LIONEL LINES"	140	265	___
	(C) Orange, "NEW YORK CENTRAL"	185	310	___
	(D) Orange, "ILLINOIS CENTRAL"	280	530	___
	(E) 2-tone blue, "LIONEL LINES	280	485	___
	(F) Orange, "NEW YORK CENTRAL"	185	310	___
714	Boxcar (O), *40–42**	350	610	___
714K	Boxcar, unbuilt (O), *40–42*		480	___
715	Tank Car (O), *40–42**			
	(A) "S.E.P.S. 8124" decal	340	610	___
	(B) "S.U.N.X. 715" decal	435	880	___
715K	Tank Car, unbuilt (O), *40–42*		530	___
716	Hopper Car (O), *40–42**	310	415	___
716K	Hopper, unbuilt (O), *40–42*		730	___
717	Caboose (O), *40–42**	340	510	___
717K	Caboose, unbuilt (O), *40–42*		590	___
720	90° Crossing (O72), *35–42*	21	40	___
721	Manual Switches, pair (O72), *35–42*	50	105	___
730	90° Crossing (O72), *35–42*	20	36	___
731	R.C. Switches, pair, T-rail (O72), *35–42*	80	135	___
751E/751W	Set: 752, 753 (2), 754 (O), *34–41**	640	1050	___
752E	Diesel only (O), *34–41*			
	(A) Yellow and brown	190	355	___
	(B) Aluminum finish	180	340	___

		Good	Exc	Cond/$
753	Coach (O), *36–41*			
	(A) Yellow and brown	100	185	___
	(B) Aluminum finish	95	180	___
754	Observation (O), *36–41*			
	(A) Yellow and brown	100	185	___
	(B) Aluminum finish	95	180	___
760	Curved Track, 16 pieces, (O72), *35–42*	37	70	___
761	Curved Track (O72), *34–42*	1	2.50	___
762	Straight Track (O72), *34–42*	1	2.50	___
762	Inside Straight Track (O72), *34–42*	2	5	___
763E	Steam 4-6-4 (O), *37–42*			
	(A) Gun-metal, 263 or 2263W Tender	1200	2650	___
	(B) Gun-metal, 2226X or 2226WX	1350	2950	___
	(C) Black, 2226WX Tender	1200	2650	___
771	Curved Track, T-rail (O72), *35–42*	3	10	___
772	Straight Track, T-rail (O72), *35–42*	4	12	___
773	Fishplate Outfit (O72), *36–42*	25	32	___
782	Hiawatha Combine (O), *35–41**	230	380	___
783	Hiawatha Coach (O), *35–41**	140	290	___
784	Hiawatha Observation (O), *35–41**	205	445	___
792	Rail Chief Combine (O), *37–41**	215	580	___
793	Rail Chief Coach (O), *37–41**	290	800	___
794	Rail Chief Observation (O), *37–41**	250	800	___
800	Boxcar (O), *15–26*			
	(A) Light orange, brown-maroon roof	45	70	___
	(B) Orange body/roof, "PENN RR"	30	43	___
800	Boxcar (2⅞"), *04–05**	2500	4050	___
801	Caboose (O), *15–26*	36	46	___
802	Stock Car (O), *15–26*	43	60	___
803	Hopper Car, Early (O), *23–28*	28	55	___
803	Hopper Car, Late (O), *29–34*	39	55	___
804	Tank Car (O), *23–28*	28	49	___
805	Boxcar (O), *27–34*			
	(A) Pea green, terra-cotta roof	35	60	___
	(B) Pea green, maroon roof	44	115	___
	(C) Orange, maroon roof	44	95	___
806	Stock Car (O), *27–34*			
	(A) Pea green, terra-cotta roof	42	75	___
	(B) Orange, various color roof	35	60	___
807	Caboose (O), *27–40*			
	(A) Peacock, dark green roof	20	35	___
	(B) Red, peacock roof	20	35	___
	(C) Light red body and roof	23	40	___
809	Dump Car (O), *31–41*			
	(A) Orange bin	40	75	___
	(B) Green bin	40	85	___

No.	Description	Good	Exc	Cond/$
810	Crane (O), *30–42*			
	(A) Terra-cotta cab, maroon roof	170	215	___
	(B) Cream cab, vermilion roof	130	205	___
811	Flatcar (O), *26–40*			
	(A) Maroon	40	70	___
	(B) Aluminum finish	47	100	___
812	Gondola (O), *26–42*	44	90	___
812T	Tool Set, *30–41*	40	95	___
813	Stock Car (O), *26–42*			
	(A) Orange, pea green roof	65	145	___
	(B) Orange, maroon roof	55	135	___
	(C) Cream, maroon roof	100	225	___
	(D) Tuscan body and roof		1600	___
814	Boxcar (O), *26–42*			
	(A) Cream, orange roof	46	105	___
	(B) Cream, maroon roof	115	140	___
	(C) Yellow, brown roof	110	120	___
814R	Refrigerator Car (O), *29–42*			
	(A) Ivory, peacock roof	100	190	___
	(B) White, light blue roof	120	265	___
	(C) Flat white, brown roof	600	900	___
815	Tank Car (O), *26–42*			
	(A) Pea green, maroon frame	250	510	___
	(B) Pea green, black frame	70	155	___
	(C) Aluminum, black frame	50	115	___
	(D) Orange-yellow, black frame	150	255	___
816	Hopper Car (O), *27–42*			
	(A) Olive green	85	155	___
	(B) Red body	65	135	___
	(C) Black body	370	680	___
817	Caboose (O), *26–42*			
	(A) Peacock, dark green roof	45	80	___
	(B) Red, peacock roof	45	80	___
	(C) Light red body and roof	45	80	___
820	Boxcar (O), *15–26*			
	(A) Orange, "ILLINOIS CENTRAL"	45	80	___
	(B) Orange, "UNION PACIFIC"	65	105	___
820	Floodlight Car (O), *31–42*			
	(A) Terra-cotta	100	175	___
	(B) Green	100	175	___
	(C) Light green	105	180	___
821	Stock Car (O), *15–16, 25–26*	45	85	___
822	Caboose (O), *15–26*	35	65	___
831	Flatcar (O), *27–34*	24	48	___
840	Industrial Power Station, *28–40**	1200	3050	___
900	Ammunition Car (O), *17–21*	120	340	___

		Good	Exc	Cond/$
900	Box Trail Car (2⅞"), *04–05**	2000	3600	___
901	Gondola (O), *19–27*	25	49	___
902	Gondola (O), *27–34*	29	50	___
910	Grove of Trees, *32–42*	70	155	___
911	Country Estate, *32–42*	195	410	___
912	Suburban Home	300	620	___
913	Landscaped Bungalow, *40–42*	140	285	___
914	Park Landscape, *32–35*	90	205	___
915	Tunnel, 32, *34–35*	160	435	___
916	Tunnel, 29¼" long, *35*	95	180	___
917	Scenic Hillside, *32–36*	90	205	___
918	Scenic Hillside, *32–36*	90	205	___
919	Park Grass, bag, *32–42*	8	17	___
920	Village, *32–33*	600	1600	___
921	Scenic Park, 3 pieces, *32–33*	980	2600	___
921C	Park Center, *32–33*	400	1050	___
922	Terrace, *32–36*	90	175	___
923	Tunnel, 40¼" long, *33–42*	90	225	___
924	Tunnel, 30" long (O72), *35–42*	50	135	___
925	Lubricant, *35–42*	1	2.50	___
927	Flag Plot, *37–42*	70	135	___
1000	Passenger Car (2⅞"), 05*	4500	6750	___
1000	Trolley Trailer (Std.), *10–16*	1400	2250	___
1010	Electric 0-4-0, Winner (O), *31–32*	90	160	___
1010	Interurban Trailer (Std.), *10–16*	1000	1800	___
1011	Pullman, Winner (O), *31–32*	55	75	___
1011	Interurban (Std.), *10*		NM	___
1012	Station, *32*	50	70	___
1015	Steam 0-4-0 (O), *31–32*	100	205	___
1017	Winner Station, *33*	25	70	___
1019	Observation (O), *31–32*	50	70	___
1020	Baggage (O), *31–32*	65	110	___
1021	90° Crossover (O27), *32–42*	1	4	___
1022	Tunnel, 18¾" long (O), *35–42*	15	32	___
1023	Tunnel, 19" long, *34–42*	20	41	___
1024	Switches, pair (O27), *37–42*	4	15	___
1025	Bumper (O27), *40–42*	14	25	___
1027	Transformer, Tin Station, *34*	50	115	___
1028	Transformer, 40 watts, *39*	3	11	___
1030	Electric 0-4-0 (O), *32*	75	135	___
1035	Steam 0-4-0 (O), *32*	75	115	___
1045	Watchman, *38–42*	15	50	___
1050	Passenger Car Trailer (2⅞"), 05*	5000	7200	___
1100	Handcar, Mickey Mouse, *35–37**			
	(A) Red base	405	640	___
	(B) Apple green base, orange shoes	500	880	___

		Good	Exc	Cond/$
	(C) Orange base	600	1200	___
1100	Summer Trolley Trailer (Std.), *10–13*		NRS	___
1103	Handcar, Peter Rabbit (O), *35–37**	330	820	___
1105	Handcar, Santa Claus (O), *35–35**			
	(A) Red base	660	1050	___
	(B) Green base	720	1200	___
1107	Transformer, Tin Station, *33*	25	70	___
1107	Handcar, Donald Duck (O), *36–37**			
	(A) White dog house w/ red roof	475	1200	___
	(B) White dog house w/ green roof	450	1100	___
	(C) Orange dog house w/ green roof	640	1850	___
1121	Switches, pair (O27), *37–42*	15	34	___
1506L	Steam 0-4-0 (O), *33–34*	95	125	___
1506M	Steam 0-4-0 (O), *35*	250	430	___
1508	Steam 0-4-0, Commodore Vanderbilt w/ Mickey in 1509 Stoker Tender, *35*	420	690	___
1511	Steam 0-4-0 (O), *36–37*	110	160	___
1512	Gondola (O), *31–33, 36–37*	29	47	___
1514	Boxcar (O), *31–37*	23	41	___
1515	Tank Car (O), *33–37*	25	41	___
1517	Caboose (O), *31–37*	25	41	___
1518	Mickey Mouse Diner (O), *35*	120	260	___
1519	Mickey Mouse Band (O), *35*	120	260	___
1520	Mickey Mouse Animal (O), *35*	120	260	___
1536	Circus: 1508, 1509, 1518, 1519, 1520 *15–20*	770	1350	___
1550	Switches, pair, windup, *33–37*	2	5	___
1555	90° Crossover, windup, *33–37*	1	2.50	___
1560	Station, *33–37*	15	34	___
1569	Accessory Set, 8 pieces, *33–37*	35	70	___
1588	Steam 0-4-0 (O), *36–37*	150	250	___
1630	Pullman (O), *38–42*			
	(A) Aluminum windows	35	70	___
	(B) Light gray windows	47	80	___
1631	Observation (O), *38–42*			
	(A) Aluminum windows	35	70	___
	(B) Light gray windows	47	80	___
1651E	Electric 0-4-0 (O), *33*	130	240	___
1661E	Steam 2-4-0 (O), *33*	75	160	___
1662	Steam 0-4-0 (O27), *40–42*	275	445	___
1663	Steam 0-4-0 (O27), *40–42*	200	385	___
1664/1664E	Steam 2-4-2 (O27), *38–42*			
	(A) Gun-metal	60	100	___
	(B) Black	60	95	___
1666/1666E	Steam 2-6-2 (O27), *38–42*			
	(A) Gun-metal	115	170	___

		Good	Exc	Cond/$
	(B) Black	95	145	___
1668/1668E	Steam 2-6-2 (O27), *37–41*			
	(A) Gun-metal	75	115	___
	(B) Black	75	130	___
1673	Coach (O), *36–37*			
	(A) Aluminum windows	35	75	___
	(B) Light gray windows	47	90	___
1674	Pullman (O), *36–37*	35	75	___
1675	Observation (O), *36–37*	30	70	___
1677	Gondola (O), *33–35, 39–42*			
	(A) "IVES/R.R. LINES", light blue	40	60	___
	(B) "LIONEL", blue or red	21	37	___
1679	Boxcar (O), *33–42*			
	(A) Cream, "IVES" on side	23	38	___
	(B) Cream, "LIONEL" on side	23	38	___
	(C) Cream or yellow, "BABY RUTH"	23	38	___
1680	Tank Car (O), *33–42*	65	170	___
	(A) Aluminum, "IVES TANK LINES"	80	95	___
	(B) Aluminum, no "IVES" lettering	19	34	___
	(C) Orange, "Shell Oil"	15	29	___
1681	Steam 2-4-0 (O), *34–35*			
	(A) Black, red frame	55	120	___
	(B) Red, red frame	110	145	___
1681E	Steam 2-4-0 (O), *34–35*			
	(A) Black, red frame	65	130	___
	(B) Red, red frame	130	165	___
1682	Caboose (O), *33–42*			
	(A) Vermilion, "IVES" on side	34	70	___
	(B) Red or tuscan, "LIONEL"	17	40	___
1684	Steam 2-4-2 (O27), *41–42*			
	(A) Black	45	70	___
	(B) Gun-metal	45	70	___
1685	Coach (O), *33–37 u*			
	(A) Gray, maroon roof	240	495	___
	(B) Red, maroon roof	170	335	___
	(C) Blue, silver roof	170	315	___
1686	Baggage (O), *33–37 u*			
	(A) Gray, maroon roof	240	495	___
	(B) Red, maroon roof	170	335	___
	(C) Blue, silver roof	170	315	___
1687	Observation (O), *33–37 u*			
	(A) Gray, maroon roof	170	315	___
	(B) Red, maroon roof	180	315	___
	(C) Blue, silver roof	170	315	___
1688/1688E	Steam 2-4-2 (O27), *36–46*	50	85	___
1689E	Steam 2-4-2 (O27), *36–37*			

		Good	Exc	Cond/$
	(A) Gun-metal	75	115	___
	(B) Black	60	100	___
1690	Pullman (O), *33–40*	35	60	___
1691	Observation (O), *33–40*	35	60	___
1692	Pullman (O27), *39 u*	45	70	___
1693	Observation (O27), *39 u*	45	70	___
1700E	Diesel, power unit only (O27), *35–37*	45	70	___
1700E	Set: 1700, 1701 (2), 1702 (O27), *35–37 u*			
	(A) Aluminum and light red	140	250	___
	(B) Chrome and light red	140	250	___
	(C) Orange and gray	155	285	___
1701	Coach (O27), *35–37*			
	(A) Chrome sides and roof	20	46	___
	(B) Silver sides and roof	30	55	___
	(C) Orange and gray	75	150	___
1702	Observation (O27), *35–37*			
	(A) Chrome sides and roof	20	46	___
	(B) Silver sides and roof	30	55	___
	(C) Orange and gray	75	150	___
1703	Observation w/ hooked coupler, *35–37 u*	49	110	___
1717	Gondola (O), *33–40 u*	30	48	___
1717X	Gondola (O), *40 u*	27	48	___
1719	Boxcar (O), *33–40 u*	30	50	___
1719X	Boxcar (O), *41–42 u*	30	50	___
1722	Caboose (O), *33–42 u*	25	50	___
1722X	Caboose (O), *39–40 u*	26	41	___
1766	Pullman (Std.), *34–40**			
	(A) Terra-cotta, maroon roof, brass trim	300	650	___
	(B) Red, maroon roof, nickel trim	300	540	___
1767	Baggage Car (Std.), *34–40**			
	(A) Terra-cotta, maroon roof, brass trim	295	850	___
	(B) Red, maroon roof, nickel trim	295	700	___
1768	Observation (Std.), *34–40**			
	(A) Terra-cotta, maroon roof, brass trim	300	650	___
	(B) Red, maroon roof, nickel trim	300	540	___
1811	Pullman (O), *33–37*	32	70	___
1812	Observation (O), *33–37*	30	65	___
1813	Baggage Car (O), *33–37*	60	135	___
1816/1816W	Diesel (O), *35–37*	100	240	___
1817	Coach (O), *35–37*	22	50	___
1818	Observation (O), *35–37*	22	50	___
1835E	Steam 2-4-2 (Std.), *34–39*	470	730	___
1910	Electric 0-6-0, Early (Std.), *10–11*	920	1550	___
1910	Electric 0-6-0, Late (Std.), *12*	550	1350	___
1910	Pullman (Std.), *09–10 u*	860	1800	___
1911	Electric 0-4-0, Early (Std.), *10–12*	860	1700	___

		Good	Exc	Cond/$
1911	Electric 0-4-0, Late (Std.), *13*	700	1100	___
1911	Electric 0-4-4-0, Special (Std.), *11–12*	860	2500	___
1912	Electric 0-4-4-0 (Std.), *10–12**			
	(A) NY, New Haven & Hartford	1550	3200	___
	(B) "NEW YORK CENTRAL LINES"	1300	2700	___
1912	Electric 0-4-4-0 Special (Std.), *11**	2500	4500	___
2200	Summer Trolley Trailer (Std.), *10–13*	1100	2250	___
2600	Pullman (O), *38–42*	80	155	___
2601	Observation (O), *38–42*	60	115	___
2602	Baggage Car (O), *38–42*	90	185	___
2613	Pullman (O), *38–42**			
	(A) Blue, 2-tone blue roof	100	270	___
	(B) State green, 2-tone green roof	200	440	___
2614	Observation (O), *38–42**			
	(A) Blue, 2-tone blue roof	100	270	___
	(B) State green, 2-tone green roof	200	440	___
2615	Baggage Car (O), *38–42**			
	(A) Blue, 2-tone blue roof	115	270	___
	(B) State green, 2-tone green roof	200	420	___
2620	Floodlight Car (O), *38–42*	65	100	___
2623	Pullman (O), *41–42*			
	(A) "IRVINGTON"	175	335	___
	(B) "MANHATTAN"	165	310	___
2624	Pullman (O), *41–42*	750	1700	___
2630	Pullman (O), *38–42*	30	70	___
2631	Observation (O), *38–42*	30	70	___
2640	Pullman, illuminated (O), *38–42*			
	(A) Light blue, aluminum roof	30	70	___
	(B) State green, dark green roof	28	70	___
2641	Observation, illuminated (O), *38–42*			
	(A) Light blue, aluminum roof	30	70	___
	(B) State green, dark green roof	28	70	___
2642	Pullman (O), *41–42*	32	70	___
2643	Observation (O), *41–42*	30	65	___
2651	Flatcar (O), *38–42*	30	50	___
2652	Gondola (O), *38–41*	26	55	___
2653	Hopper Car (O), *38–42*			
	(A) Stephen Girard green	38	70	___
	(B) Black	60	100	___
2654	Tank Car (O), *38–42*			
	(A) Aluminum finish, "SUNOCO"	35	60	___
	(B) Orange, "SHELL"	35	60	___
	(C) Light gray, "SUNOCO"	41	70	___
2655	Boxcar (O), *38–42*			
	(A) Cream, maroon roof	35	65	___
	(B) Cream, tuscan roof	38	75	___

		Good	Exc	Cond/$
2656	Stock Car (O), *38–41*			
	(A) Light gray, red roof	45	75	___
	(B) Burnt orange, tuscan roof	75	115	___
2657	Caboose (O), *40–41*	26	45	___
2657X	Caboose (O), *40–41*	25	41	___
2659	Dump Car (O), *38–41*	40	70	___
2660	Crane (O), *38–42*	85	95	___
2672	Caboose (O27), *41–42*	22	35	___
2677	Gondola (O27), *39–41*	26	37	___
2679	Boxcar (O27), *38–42*	26	34	___
2680	Tank Car (O27), *38–42*			
	(A) Aluminum finish, "SUNOCO"	15	41	___
	(B) Orange, "SHELL"	15	41	___
2682	Caboose (O27), *38–42*	18	32	___
2682X	Caboose (O27), *38–42*	22	35	___
2717	Gondola (O), *38–42 u*	21	41	___
2719	Boxcar (O), *38–42 u*	29	50	___
2722	Caboose (O), *38–42 u*	25	50	___
2755	Tank Car (O), *41–42*	65	130	___
2757	Caboose (O), *41–42*	26	38	___
2757X	Caboose (O), *41–42*	25	36	___
2758	Automobile Boxcar (O), *41–42*	38	55	___
2810	Crane (O), *38–42*	145	205	___
2811	Flatcar (O), *38–42*	65	115	___
2812	Gondola (O), *38–42*			
	(A) Green	42	90	___
	(B) Dark orange	44	95	___
2813	Stock Car (O), *38–42*	120	250	___
2814	Boxcar (O), *38–42*			
	(A) Cream, maroon roof	85	210	___
	(B) Orange, brown roof	85	205	___
2814R	Refrigerator Car (O), *38–42*			
	(A) White, light blue roof, nickel plates	150	250	___
	(B) White, brown roof, no plates	375	660	___
2815	Tank Car (O), *38–42*			
	(A) Aluminum finish	85	165	___
	(B) Orange	135	250	___
2816	Hopper Car (O), *35–42*			
	(A) Red	100	190	___
	(B) Black	110	205	___
2817	Caboose (O), *36–42*			
	(A) Light red body and roof	90	145	___
	(B) Flat red, tuscan roof	140	225	___
2820	Floodlight Car (O), *38–42*			
	(A) Stamped nickel searchlight	110	235	___
	(B) Gray die-cast searchlights	120	260	___

		Good	Exc	Cond/$
2954	Boxcar (O), *40–42**	145	360	___
2955	Sunoco Tank Car (O), *40–42**			
	(A) "SHELL" decal	225	560	___
	(B) "SUNOCO" decal	340	780	___
2956	Hopper Car (O), *40–42**	160	400	___
2957	Caboose (O), *40–42**	145	375	___
3300	Summer Trolley Trailer (Std.), *10–13*	1400	2250	___
3651	Operating Lumber Car (O), *39–42*	24	55	___
3652	Operating Gondola (O), *39–42*	36	85	___
3659	Operating Dump Car (O), *39–42*	26	44	___
3811	Operating Lumber Car (O), *39–42*	33	65	___
3814	Operating Merchandise Car (O), *39–42*	125	245	___
3859	Operating Dump Car (O), *38–42*	44	105	___
A	Miniature Motor, *04*	50	95	___
A	Transformer, 40, 60 watts, *27–37*	8	25	___
B	New Departure Motor, *06–16*	75	135	___
B	Transformer, 50, 75 watts, *16–38*	6	24	___
C	New Departure Motor, *06–16*	100	180	___
D	New Departure Motor, *06–14*	100	180	___
E	New Departure Motor, *06–14*	100	180	___
F	New Departure Motor, *06–14*	100	180	___
G	Battery Fan Motor, *06–14*	100	180	___
K	Power Motor, *05*	100	180	___
K	Transformer, 150, 200 watts, *13–38*	19	95	___
L	Power Motor, *05*	50	100	___
L	Transformer, 50, 75 watts, *13–38*	8	24	___
M	Battery Motor, *15–20*	30	80	___
N	Transformer, 50 watts, *41–42*	7	23	___
Q	Transformer, 50, 75 watts, *14–15*	13	32	___
R	Battery Motor, *15–20*	30	75	___
R	Transformer, 100 watts, *38–42*	27	60	___
S	Transformer, 50, 80 watts, *14–17*	18	37	___
T	Transformer, 75, 100,150 watts, *19–28*	10	30	___
U	Transformer, Aladdin, *32–33*	6	16	___
V	Transformer, 150 watts, *39–42*	55	90	___
W	Transformer, 75 watts, *32–33*	8	25	___
Y	Battery Motor, *15–20*	40	80	___
Z	Transformer, 250 watts, *39–42*	110	170	___

Other Transformers and Rheostats Made by Lionel

106	Rheostat, *11–14*	3	9	___
1029	25 watts, *36*	6	18	___
1030	40 watts, *35–38*	6	23	___
1031	Rheostat, circa 1938, *38*	2	4	___

		Good	Exc	Cond/$
1036	Rheostat, circa 1941, *40*	2	5	___
1037	Transformer, 40 watts, *40–42*	7	23	___
1038	Rheostat, circa 1940, *40*	2	4	___
1039	Transformer, 35 watts, *37–40*	7	18	___
1040	Transformer, 60 watts, *37–39*	12	27	___
1041	Transformer, 60 watts, *39–42*	13	30	___

Track, Lockons, and Contactors

	Good	Exc	Cond/$
O Straight	0.25	0.70	___
O Curve	0.25	0.70	___
O72 Straight	1	2	___
O72 Curve	1	2	___
O27 Straight	0.10	0.50	___
O27 Curve	0.10	0.45	___
Standard Straight	0.70	3	___
Standard Curve	0.60	2	___
O Gauge Lockon	0.10	0.55	___
Standard Gauge Lockon	0.35	1	___
UTC Lockon	0.35	0.95	___
145C Contactor	0.85	3	___
153C Contactor	0.75	3	___

Section 2
POSTWAR 1945-1969

		Good	Exc	Cond/$
011-11	Fiber Pins (O), *46–50*	0.10	0.15	___
011-43	Insulating Pins, dz. (O), *61*	1	1.50	___
020	90° Crossover (O), *45–61*	8	11	___
020X	45° Crossover (O), *46–59*	7	10	___
022	RC Switches, pair (O), *45–69*	34	43	___
022-500	Adapter Set (O), *57–61*	1	3	___
022A	RC Switches, pair (O), *47*	32	155	___
025	Bumper (O), *46–47*	8	22	___
026	Bumper, gray, *48*	20	68	___
026	Bumper, gray, *48*	20	68	___
027C-1	Track Clips, dz. (O27), *47, 49*	0.55	0.90	___
30	Water Tower, *47–50*	75	105	___
31	Curved Track (Super O), *57–66*	1	1.50	___
31-7	Power Blade Connection (Super O), *57–61*		0.35	___
31-15	Ground Rail Pin (Super O), *57–66*		0.60	___
31-45	Power Blade Connection (Super O), *61–66*		0.60	___
32	Straight Track (Super O), *57–66*	1	3	___
32-10	Insulating Pin (Super O), *57–60*		0.35	___
32-20	Power Blade Insulator (Super O), *57–60*		0.15	___
32-25	Insulating Pin (Super O), *57–61*		0.15	___
32-30	Ground Pin (Super O), *57–61*		0.15	___
32-31	Power Pin (Super O), *57–61*		0.15	___
32-32	Insulating Pin (Super O), *57–61*		0.15	___
32-33	Ground Pin (Super O), *57–61*		0.15	___
32-34	Power Pin (Super O), *57–61*		0.15	___
32-45	Power Blade Insulators, dz. (Super O), *61–66*	0.85	1.50	___
32-55	Insulating Pins, dz. (Super O), *61–66*	1	2	___
33	Half Curved Track (Super O), *57–66*	1	3	___
34	Half Straight Track (Super O), *57–66*	1	3	___
35	Boulevard Lamp, *45–49*	15	40	___
36	Remote Control Set (Super O), *57–66*	11	16	___
37	Uncoupling Track Set (Super O), *57–66*	7	13	___
38	Water Tower, *46–47*	160	400	___
38	Accessory Adapter Track (Super O), *51–61*	6	13	___
39	Operating Set (Super O), *57*	4	8	___
39-5	Operating Set (Super O), *57–58*	4	8	___
39-10	Operating Set (Super O), *58*	4	8	___
39-15	Operating Set, w/ blade (Super O), *57–58*	4	8	___
39-20	Operating Set (Super O), *57–58*	4	8	___
39-25	Operating Set (Super O), *61–66*	4	9	___

		Good	Exc	Cond/$
39-35	Operating Set (Super O), *59*	4	9	___
40	Hookup Wire, *50–51, 53–63*	4	37	___
40-25	Conductor Wire, *56–59*	6	21	___
40-50	Cable Reel, *60–61*	4	14	___
41	Contactor (Super O)	0.50	1.50	___
41	U.S. Army Switcher, *55–57*	65	95	___
42	Picatinny Arsenal Switcher, *57*	155	365	___
042/42	Manual Switches, pair (O), *46–59*	16	39	___
43	Power Track (Super O), *59–66*	4	7	___
44	U.S. Army Mobile Launcher, *59–62*	105	200	___
44-80	Missiles, *59–60*	11	21	___
45	U.S. Marines Mobile Launcher, *60–62*	155	300	___
45	Automatic Gateman, *46–49*	28	48	___
45N	Automatic Gateman, *45*	32	55	___
48	Insulated Straight Track (Super O), *57–66*	4	10	___
49	Insulated Curved Track (Super O), *57–66*	4	10	___
50	Lionel Gang Car (mv), *54–64*			
	(A) Gray bumpers w/ rotating blue man and fixed olive men, *54*	275	650	
51	Navy Yard Switcher, *56–57*	75	145	
52	Fire Car, *58–61*	95	165	
53	Rio Grande Snowplow, *57–60*			
	(A) Backwards "a" in Rio Grande	165	300	___
	(B) Correctly printed "a"	360	675	___
54	Ballast Tamper, *58–61, 66, 68–69*	105	175	___
55	Tie-jector, *57–61*	100	185	___
55-150	Ties, *57–60*	5	19	___
56	Lamp Post, *46–49*	23	55	___
56	M&StL Mine Transport, *58*	265	470	___
57	AEC Switcher, *59–60*	395	690	___
58	Lamp Post, *46–50*	20	65	___
58	GN Snowplow, *59–61*	235	425	___
59	Minuteman Switcher, *62–63*	255	510	___
60	Lionelville Rapid Transit Trolley, *55–58*	85	135	___
61	Ground Lockon (Super O), *57–66*	0.25	0.50	___
62	Power Lockon (Super O), *57–66*	0.25	0.50	___
64	Street Lamp, *45–49*	29	60	___
65	Lionel Lines Handcar, *62–66*	145	270	___
68	Executive Inspection Car, *58–61*	145	230	___
69	Lionel Maintenance Car, *60–62*	125	200	___
69	Lionel Maintenance Car, *60–62*	125	200	___
70	Yard Light, *49–50*	25	55	___
71	Lamp Post, *49–59*	15	18	___
75	Goose Neck Lamp, set of 2, *61–63*	12	21	___
76	Blvd. Street Lamp, set of 3, *59–66, 68–69*	16	35	___

		Good	Exc	Cond/$
80	Controller	11	20	___
88	Controller, *46–60*	4	8	___
89	Flagpole, *56–58*	17	47	___
90	Controller	3	8	___
91	Circuit Breaker, *57–60*	13	25	___
92	Circuit Breaker, *59–66, 68–69*	8	19	___
93	Water Tower, *46–49*	25	55	___
96C	Controller	3	9	___
97	Coal Elevator, *46–50*	95	170	___
100	Multivolt-DC/AC Transformer, *58–66*		70	___
108	Trestle Set	25	36	___
109	Partial Trestle Set, *61*		30	___
110	Graduated Trestle Set, *55–69*	14	23	___
111	Elevated Trestle Set, *56–69*	10	17	___
111-100	Two Elevated Trestle Piers, *60–63*	10	24	___
112	RC Switches, pair (Super O), *57–66*	75	115	___
114	Newsstand w/ horn, *57–59*	44	100	___
115	Passenger Station, *46–49*	165	315	___
118	Newsstand w/ whistle, *57–58*	46	105	___
119	Landscaped Tunnel, *57–58*		NRS	___
120	90° Crossing (Super O), *57–66*	7	11	___
121	Landscaped Tunnel, *59–66*		NRS	___
122	Lamp Assortment, *48–52*		165	___
123	Lamp Assortment, *55–59*	85	185	___
123-60	Lamp Assortment, *60–63*		150	___
125	Whistle Shack, *50–55*	26	44	___
128	Animated Newsstand, *57–60*	70	150	___
130	60° Crossing (Super O), *57–61*	7	13	___
131	Curved Tunnel, *59–66*		NRS	___
132	Passenger Station, *49–55*	37	85	___
133	Passenger Station, *57, 61–62, 66*	28	75	___
137	Passenger Station, *46*	87	180	___
138	Water Tower, *53–57*	65	100	___
140	Automatic Banjo Signal, *54–66*	22	40	___
142	Manual Switches, pair (Super O), *57–66*	32	65	___
145	Automatic Gateman, *50–66*	27	48	___
145C	Contactor, *50–60*	1	13	___
147	Whistle Controller, *61–66*	1	4	___
148	Dwarf Trackside Signal, *57–60*	23	45	___
150	Telegraph Pole Set, *47–50*	38	75	___
151	Automatic Semaphore, *47–69*			
	(A) Black base, *47*	26	45	___
	(C) With red blade, *47*	160	400	___
	(B) Green base, *47*	30	75	___
152	Automatic Crossing Gate, *45–49*	12	29	___

		Good	Exc	Cond/$
153	Automatic Block Control, Signal, *45–59*	20	35	___
153C	Contactor	1	8	___
154	Automatic Highway Signal, *45–69*	16	43	___
155	Blinking Light Signal w/ bell, *55–57*	32	60	___
156	Station Platform, *46–49*	45	100	___
157	Station Platform, *52–59*	29	60	___
160	Unloading Bin, *52–57*			
	(A) Plastic	1	3	___
	(B) Metal	13	65	___
161	Mail Pickup Set, *61–63*	34	85	___
163	Single Target Block Signal, *61–69*	17	30	___
164	Log Loader, *46–50*	100	180	___
167	Whistle Controller, *45–46*	5	9	___
175	Rocket Launcher, *58–60*	85	185	___
175-50	Extra Rocket, *59–60*	5	18	___
182	Magnetic Crane, *46–49*	155	265	___
192	Operating Control Tower, *59–60*	110	255	___
	(A) Red, *53–55*	90	95	___
	(B) Black, *53*	100	160	___
195	Floodlight Tower, *57–69*	27	60	___
195-75	Eight-Bulb Extension, *58–60*	25	65	___
196	Smoke Pellets, *46–47*	50	60	___
197	Rotating Radar Antenna, *57–59*	50	105	___
199	Microwave Relay Tower, *58–59*	28	65	___
202	UP Alco A Unit, *57*	49	85	___
204	Santa Fe Alco AA Units, *57*	125	240	___
205	Missouri Pacific Alco AA Units, *57–58*	50	115	___
206	Artificial Coal, large bag, *46–68*	5	13	___
207	Artificial Coal, small bag, *46–48*	3	10	___
208	Santa Fe Alco AA Units, *58–59*	105	245	___
209	New Haven Alco AA Units, *58*	295	760	___
209	Wooden Barrels, set of 4, *46–50*	9	21	___
210	Texas Special Alco AA Units, *58*	85	140	___
211	Texas Special Alco AA Units, *62–66*	95	160	___
212	USMC Alco A Unit, *58–59*	85	155	___
212	Santa Fe Alco AA Units, *64–66*	80	160	___
212T	USMC Dummy A Units, *58–59* u	300	610	___
213	Railroad Lift Bridge, *50*		NM	___
213	M&StL Alco AA Units, *64*	90	200	___
214	Plate Girder Bridge, *53–69*	9	25	___
215	Santa Fe Alco Units, *65 u*			
	(A) AB Units	85	165	___
	(B) Double A Units (usually w/ 212T)	80	160	___
216	Burlington Alco A Unit, *58*	105	350	___
216	M&StL Alco AA Units, (usually w/ 213T), *64 u*	90	200	___

		Good	Exc	Cond/$
217	B&M Alco AB Units, *59*	95	210	___
218	Santa Fe Alco Units, *59–63*			
	(A) Double A Units	70	165	___
	(B) AB Units	70	165	___
	(C) Double A Unit with solid nose decal	75	265	___
219	Missouri Pacific Alco AA Units, *59 u*	80	145	___
220	Santa Fe Alco Units, *60–61*			
	(A) A Unit only	75	115	___
	(B) AA Units	100	205	___
221	2-6-4, 221T/221W Tender, *46–47*			
	(A) Gray die-cast body	80	165	___
	(B) Black die-cast body	80	160	___
	(C) w/ aluminum colored wheels and 221W Tender, *46*	100	250	___
221	Rio Grande Alco A Unit, *63–64*	65	105	___
221	USMC Alco A Unit, *63–64 u*	145	450	___
221	Santa Fe Alco A Unit, *63–64 u*	165	485	___
222	Rio Grande Alco A Unit, *62*	34	60	___
223	218C Santa Fe Alco AB Units, *63*	110	220	___
224	Steam 2-6-2, 2466T/2466W Tender, *45–46*	95	150	___
224	U.S. Navy Alco AB Units, *60*	160	330	___
225	C&O Alco A Unit, *60*	65	105	___
226	B&M Alco AB Units, *60 u*	85	185	___
227	CN Alco A Unit, *60 u*	85	155	___
228	CN Alco A Unit, *61 u*	80	145	___
229	M&StL Alco Units, *61–62*			
	(A) A Unit only, *61*	65	110	___
	(B) AB Units, *62*	95	205	___
230	C&O Alco A Unit, *61*	75	135	___
231	Rock Island Alco A Unit, *61–63*	100	170	___
232	New Haven Alco A Unit, *62*	60	115	___
233	Steam 2-4-2, 233W Tender, *61–62*	43	80	___
235	Steam 2-4-2, 1130T/1060T Tender, *60 u*	60	140	___
236	Steam 2-4-2, 1130T/1050T Tender, *61–62*			
	(A) 1050T slope-back Tender	18	41	___
	(B) 1130T Tender	18	41	___
237	Steam 2-4-2, *63–66*			
	(A) w/ 1060T Tender	25	55	___
	(B) w/ 234W Tender	45	90	___
238	Steam 2-4-2, 234W Tender, *63–64*	55	115	___
239	Steam 2-4-2, 234W Tender, *65–66*	55	90	___
240	Steam 2-4-2, 242T, *64 u*	140	235	___
241	Steam 2-4-2 w/ 234W Tender, *65 u*	70	135	___
242	Steam 2-4-2 w/ 1060T Tender or 1062T Tender, *62–66*	23	48	___

		Good	Exc	Cond/$
243	Steam 2-4-2, 243W Tender, *60*	55	115	___
244	Steam 2-4-2, 244T/1130T Tender, *60–61*	25	41	___
245	Steam 2-4-2, 1130T Tender, *59 u*		95	___
246	Steam 2-4-2, 244T/1130T Tender, *59–61*	22	41	___
247	Steam 2-4-2, 247T Tender, *59*	27	47	___
248	Steam 2-4-2, 1130T Tender, *58*	34	100	___
249	Steam 2-4-2, 250T Tender, *58*	22	50	___
250	Steam 2-4-2, 250T Tender, *57*	22	49	___
251	Steam 2-4-2, 1062T Tender, *66 u*			
	(A) Slope-back Tender	160	305	___
	(B) 250T-type Tender	155	300	___
252	Crossing Gate, *50–62*	23	33	___
253	Block Control Signal, *56–59*	17	26	___
256	Illuminated Freight Station, *50–53*			
	(A) Standard	25	40	___
	(B) Light green roof	50	150	___
257	Freight Station w/ diesel horn, *56–57*	37	100	___
260	Bumper, *51–69*			
	(A) Die-cast	9	19	___
	(B) Black plastic	22	45	___
262	Highway Crossing Gate, *62–69*	22	65	___
264	Operating Forklift Platform w/ 6264, *57–60*	155	310	___
270	Metal Bridge (O), *46*	19	50	___
282	Gantry Crane, *54–57*	100	150	___
282R	Gantry Crane, *56–57*	110	185	___
299	Code Transmitter Beacon Set, *61–63*	85	185	___
308	Railroad Sign Set, die-cast, *45–49*	28	50	___
309	Yard Sign Set, plastic, *50–59*	14	27	___
310	Billboard Set, *50–68*	15	26	___
313	Bascule Bridge, *46–49*	220	490	___
313-82	Fiber Pins, *46–60*		0.05	___
313-121	Fiber Pins, dozen, *61*		1.50	___
314	Scale Model Girder Bridge, *45–50*	13	32	___
315	Trestle Bridge, *46–48*	60	120	___
316	Trestle Bridge, *49*	17	39	___
317	Trestle Bridge, *50–56*	19	39	___
321	Trestle Bridge, *58–64*	13	37	___
332	Arch-Under Bridge, *59–66*	17	37	___
334	Operating Dispatching Board, *57–60*	150	275	___
342	Culvert Loader, *56–58*	125	355	___
345	Culvert Unloader, *57–59*	185	350	___
346	Manual Culvert Unloader, *65*	60	130	___
347	Cannon Firing Range Set, *64 u*	170	520	___
348	Manual Culvert Unloader, *66–69*	80	190	___
350	Engine Transfer Table, *57–60*	215	370	___

		Good	Exc	Cond/$
350-50	Transfer Table Extension, *57–60*	105	250	___
352	Ice Depot, includes 6352, *55–57*	100	170	___
353	Trackside Control Signal, *60–61*	17	40	___
356	Operating Freight Station, *52–57*			
	(A) With dark green roof, *52–57*	60	95	___
	(B) With light green roof, *57*	75	180	___
362	Barrel Loader, *52–57*	70	90	___
362-78	Wooden Barrels, *52–57*	7	23	___
364	Conveyor Lumber Loader, *48–57*	65	85	___
364C	On/Off Switch, *48–64*	3	10	___
365	Dispatching Station, *58–59*	75	125	___
375	Turntable, *62–64*	160	300	___
390C	Switch, double-pole, double-throw, *60–64*	8	13	___
394	Rotary Beacon, *49–53*	27	65	___
395	Floodlight Tower, *49–56*	32	55	___
397	Diesel Operating Coal Loader w/ yellow generator, *48*	125	350	___
397	Diesel Operating Coal Loader w/ blue generator, *49–57*	90	120	___
400	B&O RDC Passenger, *56–58*	160	210	___
404	B&O RDC Baggage-Mail, *57–58*	175	330	___
410	Billboard Blinker, *56–58*	33	55	___
413	Countdown Control Panel, *62*	44	80	___
415	Diesel Fueling Station, *55–57*	80	120	___
419	Heliport Control Tower, *62*	175	410	___
443	Missile Launch Platform w/ 943 Ammo Dump, *60–62*	17	41	___
445	Switch Tower, lighted, *52–57*	36	65	___
448	Missile Firing Range Set, w/ 6448, *61–63*	80	155	___
450	Signal Bridge, two-track, *52–58*	28	47	___
450L	Signal Light Head, *52–58*	17	46	___
452	Signal Bridge, single-track, *61–63*	75	145	___
455	Operating Oil Derrick, *50–54*	105	150	___
456	Coal Ramp w/ 3456 Hopper, *50–55*	135	175	___
460	Piggyback Transportation w/ 3460, *55–57*	60	125	___
460P	Piggyback Platform, *55–57*	29	80	___
461	Platform w/ Truck and Trailer, *66*	65	160	___
462	Derrick Platform Set, *61–62*	200	325	___
464	Lumber Mill, *56–60*	85	170	___
465	Sound Dispatching Station, *56–57*	60	115	___
470	Missile Launching Platform w/ 6470, *59–62*	75	110	___
479-1	Truck for 6362 Truck Car, *55–56*	14	85	___
480-25	Conversion Coupler, *50–60*	1	3	___
480-32	Conversion Magnetic Coupler, *61–69*	1	3	___
494	Rotary Beacon, *54–66*	24	39	___

		Good	Exc	Cond/$
497	Coaling Station, *53–58*	80	190	___
520	Lionel Lines Box Cab Electric, *56–57*	55	80	___
600	MKT NW-2 Switcher, *55*			
	(A) Black frame and end rails	80	140	___
	(B) Gray frame and yellow or black end rails	220	360	___
601	Seaboard NW-2 Switcher, *56*	105	205	___
602	Seaboard NW-2 Switcher, *57–58*	115	190	___
610	Erie NW-2 Switcher, *55*			
	(A) Black frame	85	145	___
	(B) Yellow frame	285	620	___
611	Jersey Central NW-2 Switcher, *57–58*	90	140	___
613	UP NW-2 Switcher, *58*	115	340	___
614	Alaska NW-2 Switcher, *59–60*			
	(A) Plastic bell, no brake	115	175	___
	(B) No bell, yellow brake/air	135	205	___
	(C) w/ "BUILT BY LIONEL"	225	390	___
616	Santa Fe NW-2 Switcher, *61–62*			
617	Santa Fe NW-2 Switcher, *63*	135	255	___
621	Jersey Central NW-2 Switcher, *56–57*	75	180	___
622	Santa Fe NW-2 Switcher, *49–50*			
	(A) Large "GM" decal on cab	190	320	___
	(B) Small "GM" decal on cab	145	290	___
623	Santa Fe NW-2 Switcher, *52–54*	135	210	___
624	C&O NW-2 Switcher, *52–54*	120	200	___
625	LV GE 44-ton Switcher, *57–58*	80	135	___
626	B&O GE 44-ton Switcher, *56–57, 59*	110	300	___
627	LV GE 44-ton Switcher, *56–57*	70	110	___
628	NP GE 44-ton Switcher, *56–57*	105	140	___
629	Burlington GE 44-ton Switcher, *56*	195	340	___
633	Santa Fe NW-2 Switcher, *62*	110	175	___
634	Santa Fe NW-2 Switcher, *63, 65–66*			
	(A) w/ safety stripes	85	165	___
	(B) w/o safety stripes	50	110	___
635	UP NW-2 Switcher, *65 u*	70	130	___
637	Steam 2-6-4, 2046W/736W Tender, *59–63*			
	(A) 2046W "LIONEL LINES" Tender	55	140	___
	(B) 736W "PENNSYLVANIA" Tender	65	160	___
638-2361	Van Camp's Pork & Beans Boxcar, *62 u*	21	38	___
645	Union Pacific NW-2 Switcher, *69*	60	115	___
646	Steam 4-6-4, 2046W Tender, *54–58*	125	250	___
665	Steam 4-6-4, 2046W/6026W/736W Tender *54–59, 66*	110	245	___
670	Pennsylvania Turbine, 6-8-6, *52*		NM	___

		Good	Exc	Cond/$
671	Steam 6-8-6, *46–49*			
	(A) 671W Tender	100	215	___
	(B) 2671W Tender	150	300	___
671R	Steam 6-8-6, 4424W/4671 Tender, *46–49*	130	280	___
671RR	Steam 6-8-6, 2046W-50 Tender, *52*	125	230	___
671S	Smoke Conversion Kit		40	___
674	Steam 2-6-4, *52*		NM	___
675	Steam 2-6-2, 2466W/2466WX/6466WX Tender *47–49*; 2–6–4, *52*			
	(A) 2-6-2, disc drivers	90	170	___
	(B) 2-6-4, spoked drivers	85	165	___
681	Steam Turbine, 6-8-6, 2046W-50/2671W Tender, *50–51, 53*	135	185	
682	Steam 6-8-6, 2046W-50 Tender, *54–55*	230	315	___
685	Steam 4-6-4, 6026W Tender, *53*	90	225	___
703	Steam 4-6-4, Hudson, *46*		NM	___
703-10	Special Smoke Bulb, *46*		23	___
725	Steam 2-8-4, Berkshire, *52*		NM	___
726	Steam 2-8-4 Berkshire, *47–49*			
	(A) 2426W Tender, *46*	250	490	___
	(B) 2426W Tender, *47–49*	270	395	___
726RR	Steam 2-8-4 Berkshire, 2046W Tender, *52*	210	345	___
726S	Smoke Conversion Kit	40	435	___
736	Steam 2-8-4, 2671WX/2046W/736W Tender, *50–66*	225	320	___
746	N&W Steam 4-8-4, *57–60*			
	(A) Long stripe Tender	560	990	___
	(B) Short stripe Tender	480	890	___
760	Curved Track, 16 sections (O72), *54–57*	19	37	___
773	Steam 4-6-4 Hudson, 2426W Tender, *50*	870	1350	___
773	Steam 4-6-4 Hudson, *64–66*			
	(A) w/ 773W Tender	540	1000	___
	(B) w/ 736W Tender	465	730	___
902	Elevated Trestle Set, *60*		NRS	___
909	Smoke Fluid, *57–66, 68–69*		9	___
919	Artificial Grass, *46–64*		15	___
920	Scenic Display Set, *57–58*	55	95	___
920-2	Tunnel Portals, pair, *58–59*	29	50	___
920-3	Green Grass, *57*		11	___
920-4	Yellow Grass, *57*		11	___
920-5	Artificial Rock, *57–58*	3	7	___
920-8	Dyed Lichen, *57–58*	1	11	___
925	Lionel Lubricant, large tube, *46–69*	1	6	___
926	Lionel Lubricant, small tube, *55*	1	2	___
926-5	Instruction Booklet, *46–48*	1	5	___

		Good	Exc	Cond/$
927	Lubricating Kit, *50–59*	12	25	___
928	Maintenance and Lubricating Kit, *60–63*	28	70	___
943	Ammo Dump, *59–61*	28	50	___
950	U.S. Railroad Map, *58–66*	22	50	___
951	Farm Set w/ box, *58*	23	65	___
952	Figure Set w/ box, *58*	25	55	___
953	Figure Set w/ box, *59–62*	29	70	___
954	Swimming Pool/Playground Set w/ box, *59*	27	65	___
955	Highway Set w/ box, *58*	24	60	___
956	Stockyard Set w/ box, *59*	22	48	___
957	Farm Building and Animal Set w/ box, *58*	33	75	___
958	Vehicle Set w/ box, *58*	17	55	___
959	Barn Set w/ box, *58*	21	50	___
960	Barnyard Set w/ box, *59–61*	16	45	___
961	School Set w/ box, *59*	17	55	___
962	Turnpike Set w/ box, *58*	33	85	___
963	Frontier Set w/ box, *59–60*	32	90	___
963-100	Frontier Set for Halloween General Set w/ box, *60*	115	215	___
964	Factory Site Set w/ box, *59*	21	55	___
965	Farm Set, *59*	23	55	___
966	Firehouse Set w/ box, *58*	21	55	___
967	Post Office Set w/ box, *58*	21	55	___
968	TV Transmitter Set w/ box, *58*	16	46	___
969	Construction Set w/ box, *60*	19	55	___
970	Ticket Booth, *58–60*	50	145	___
971	Lichen Package w/ box, *60–64*	11	19	___
972	Landscape Tree Assortment w/ box, *61–64*	10	17	___
973	Complete Landscaping Set w/ box, *60–64*	14	34	___
974	Scenery Set w/ box, *58*	7	18	___
980	Ranch Set w/ box, *60*	22	75	___
981	Freight Yard Set w/ box, *60*	16	55	___
982	Suburban Split Level Set w/ box, *60*	16	47	___
983	Farm Set w/ box, *60–61*	16	55	___
984	Railroad Set w/ box, *61–62*	16	55	___
985	Freight Area Set w/ box, *61*	18	55	___
986	Farm Set w/ box, *62*	28	50	___
987	Town Set w/ box, *62*	28	50	___
988	Railroad Structure Set w/ box, *62*	28	50	___
1001	Steam 2-4-2, 1001T Tender, *48*			
	(A) Plastic	22	41	___
	(B) Die-cast	275	540	___

		Good	Exc	Cond/$
1002	Lionel Gondola, *48–52*			
	(A) Black w/ white lettering	5	10	___
	(B) Blue w/ white lettering	6	11	___
	(C) Silver w/ black lettering	110	380	___
	(D) Yellow w/ black lettering	115	350	___
	(E) Red w/ white lettering	110	425	___
	(F) Light blue w/ black lettering		NRS	___
X1004	PRR Baby Ruth Boxcar, *48–52*	6	14	___
1005	Sunoco 1-D Tank Car, *48–50*	8	13	___
1007	LL SP-type Caboose, *48–52*	5	13	___
1008	Camtrol Uncoupling Unit (O27), *57–62*	0.55	1	___
1008-50	Camtrol w/ track (O27), *48*	0.25	0.90	___
1010	Transformer, 35 watts, *61–66*	8	21	___
1011	Transformer, 25 watts, *48–49*	8	18	___
1012	Transformer, 35 watts, *50–54*	7	15	___
1013	Curved Track (O27), *45–69*	0.10	0.35	___
1013-17	Steel Pins (O27), *46–60*		0.05	___
1013-42	Steel Pins (O27), *61–68*		0.50	___
1014	Transformer, 40 watts, *55*	13	22	___
1015	Transformer, 45 watts, *56–60*	8	31	___
1016	Transformer, 35 watts, *59–60*	7	24	___
1018	Straight Track (O27), *45–69*	0.15	0.40	___
1018	Half Straight Track (O27), *55–69*	0.15	0.40	___
1019	RC Track Set (O27), *46–48*	2	9	___
1020	90° Crossing (O27), *55–69*	3	6	___
1021	90° Crossing (O27), *45–54*	2	5	___
1022	Manual Switches, pair (O27), *53–69*	12	19	___
1023	45° Crossing (O27), *56–69*	2	5	___
1024	Manual Switches, pair (O27), *46–52*	8	14	___
1025	Illuminated Bumper (O27), *46–47*	13	15	___
1025	Transformer, 45 watts, *61–69*	13	27	___
1026	Transformer, 25 watts, *61–64*	5	14	___
1032	Transformer, 75 watts, *48*	26	47	___
1033	Transformer, 90 watts, *48–56*	22	42	___
1034	Transformer, 75 watts, *48–54*	19	28	___
1035	Transformer, 60 watts, *47*	22	41	___
1037	Transformer, 40 watts, *46–47*	10	25	___
1041	Transformer, 60 watts, *45–46*	15	25	___
1042	Transformer, 75 watts, *47–48*	22	44	___
1043	Transformer, *53–58*			
	(A) 50 watts, black, *53–57*	13	27	___
	(B) 60 watts, ivory, *57–58*	55	105	___
1044	Transformer, 90 watts, *57–69*	34	60	___
1045	Operating Watchman, *46–50*	16	47	___
1047	Operating Switchman, *59–61*	49	165	___

		Good	Exc	Cond/$
1050	Steam 0-4-0, 1050 Tender, 59 u	85	285	___
1053	Transformer, 60 watts, 56–60	19	45	___
1055	Texas Special Alco A Unit, 59–60	49	95	___
1060	Steam 2-4-2, 1050T/1060T Tender, 60–62	10	33	___
1061	Steam 0-4-0, 1061T Tender, 64; 2–4–2, 69			
	(A) Slope-back "LIONEL LINES"	14	33	___
	(B) 1130T "SOUTHERN PACIFIC"	17	41	___
	(C) With paper number labels	50	250	___
	(D) No number stamped on cab	39	135	___
1062	Steam 2-4-2, 1062T Tender, 63–64			
	(A) 0-4-0 wheel arrangement	12	27	___
	(B) 2-4-2 wheel arrangement	12	27	___
1063	Transformer, 75 watts, 60–64	16	45	___
1065	Union Pacific Alco A Unit, 61	31	65	___
1066	Union Pacific Alco A Unit, 64 u	50	90	___
1073	Transformer, 60 watts, 61–66	19	50	___
1101	Steam 2-4-2, 1001T Tender, 48	20	38	___
1101	Transformer, 25 watts, 48	8	14	___
1110	Steam 2-4-2, 1001T Tender, 49, 51–52	17	24	___
1120	Steam 2-4-2, 1001T Tender, 50	19	35	___
1121	RC Switches, pair (O27), 46–51	14	26	___
1122	RC Switches, pair (O27), 52–53	10	26	___
1122E	RC Switches, pair (O27), 53–69	13	28	___
1122-34	RC Switches, pair, 52–53	14	34	___
1122-500	Gauge Adapter (O27), 57–66	0.30	1	___
1130	Steam 2-4-2, 6066T/1130T Tender, 53–54			
	(A) Plastic body	20	36	___
	(B) Die-cast body	48	110	___
1615	Steam 0-4-0, 1615T Tender, 55–57			
	(A) No grab-irons	95	165	___
	(B) Grab-irons on chest/Tender	165	355	___
1625	Steam 0-4-0, 1625T Tender, 58	130	350	___
1640-100	Presidential Kit, 60	75	250	___
1654	Steam 2-4-2, 1654W Tender, 46–47	33	65	___
1655	Steam 2-4-2, 6654W Tender, 48–49	35	70	___
1656	Steam 0-4-0, 6403B Tender, 48–49	130	300	___
1665	Steam 0-4-0, 2403B Tender, 46	190	370	___
1666	Steam 2-6-2, 2466W/2466WX Tender, 46–47	37	150	___
1862	General 4-4-0, 1862T Tender, 59–62			
	(A) Gray smoke stack	85	205	___
	(B) Black smoke stack	95	205	___
1865	Western & Atlantic Coach, 59–62	28	50	___
1866	Western & Atlantic Mail-Baggage, 59–62	33	60	___
1872	General 4-4-0, 1872T Tender, 59–62	95	350	___
1875	Western & Atlantic Coach, 59–62	165	290	___

		Good	Exc	Cond/$
1875W	W&A Coach w/ whistle, *59–62*	80	195	___
1876	Western & Atlantic Baggage, *59–62*	28	70	___
1877	Flatcar w/ fence and horses, *59–62*	39	75	___
1882	General 4-4-0, 1882T Tender, *60 u*	250	500	___
1885	Western & Atlantic Coach, *60 u*	100	305	___
1887	Flatcar w/ fences and horses, *60 u*	75	150	___
2001	Track Make-up Kit (027), *63*		NRS	___
2002	Track Make-up Kit (027), *63*		NRS	___
2003	Track Make-up Kit (027), *63*		NRS	___
2016	Steam 2-6-4, 6026W Tender, *55–56*	49	120	___
2018	Steam 2-6-4, *56–59, 61*			
	(A) 6026T Tender	40	70	___
	(B) 6026W Tender	60	115	___
	(C) 1130T Tender	43	75	___
2020W	Steam 6-8-6, Tender, *46*	170	205	___
2020	Steam 6-8-6, 2020W/6020W Tender, *46–49*	105	165	___
2023	Union Pacific Alco AA Units, *50–51*			
	(A) Yellow body	130	245	___
	(B) Gray nose and side frames		NRS	___
	(C) Silver body	145	250	___
2024	C&O Alco A, *69*	34	75	___
2025	Steam 2-6-2 w/ 2466WX or 6466WX Tender;	80	155	___
	2-6-4 w/ 6466W Tender, *47–49, 52*			
2026	Steam 2-6-2, 2-6-4, *48–49, 51–53*			
	(A) 6466W or 6466WX	50	115	___
	(B) 6466T or 6066T	40	80	___
2028	Pennsylvania GP-7, *55*			
	(A) Gold lettering	165	250	___
	(B) Yellow lettering	140	260	___
	(C) Tan frame	275	540	___
2029	Steam 2-6-4, 234W Tender, *64–69*			
	(A) 243W "LIONEL LINES" Tender	70	115	___
	(B) 243W "PENNSYLVANIA" Tender	255	325	___
	(C) (A) w/ "Hagerstown, Maryland"	90	135	___
2031	Rock Island Alco AA Units, *52–54*	155	250	___
2032	Erie Alco AA Units, *52–54*	140	225	___
2033	Union Pacific Alco AA Units, *52–54*	150	295	___
2034	Steam 2-4-2, 6066T Tender, *52*	34	65	___
2035	Steam 2-6-4, 6466W Tender, *50–51*	65	150	___
2036	Steam 2-6-4, 6466W Tender, *50*	65	120	___
2037	Steam 2-6-4, black engine, *54–55, 57–63*			
	(A) w/ 6026T, 1130T	45	80	___
	(B) w/ 6026W, 233W, 234W	70	160	___
2037-500	Steam 2-6-4, pink engine	400	820	___
	w/ 1130T-500 Tender, *57–58*			

		Good	Exc	Cond/$
2041	Rock Island Alco AA Units, *69*	70	135	___
2046	Steam 4-6-4, 2046W Tender, *50–51, 53*	150	185	___
2055	Steam 4-6-4, 2046W/6026W Tender, *53–55*	105	190	___
2056	Steam 4-6-4, 2046W Tender, *52*	105	205	___
2065	Steam 4-6-4, 2046W/6026W Tender, *54–56*	105	200	___
2240	Wabash F-3 AB Units, *56*	380	700	___
2242	New Haven F-3 AB Units, *58–59*	425	770	___
2243	Santa Fe F-3 AB Units, *55–57*	235	325	___
2243C	Santa Fe F-3 B Unit, *55–57*	100	235	___
2245	Texas Special F-3 AB Units, *54–55*			
	(A) B Unit w/ portholes, *54*	250	500	___
	(B) B Unit w/o portholes, *55*	400	720	___
2257	Lionel SP-type caboose, *47*	8	13	___
	(A) Red, no stack	7	13	___
	(B) Tuscan, w/ stack	55	265	___
	(C) Red, w/ stack	75	485	___
2321	Lackawanna Train Master, *54–56*			
	(A) Gray roof	270	465	___
	(B) Maroon roof	390	700	___
2322	Virginian Train Master, *65–66*			
	(A) Unpainted blue stripe	340	610	___
	(B) Painted blue stripe	400	770	___
2328	Burlington GP-7, *55–56*	225	285	___
2329	Virginian Rectifier, *58–59*	275	530	___
2330	Pennsylvania GG-1, green, *50*	480	840	___
2331	Virginian Train Master, *55–58*			
	(A) Black stripe/gold lettering, *55*	550	990	___
	(B) Blue stripe/yellow lettering, *56–58*	310	670	___
	(C) Blue and yellow, gray mold	680	1250	___
2332	Pennsylvania GG-1, *47–49*			
	(A) Black	880	1750	___
	(B) Green	300	540	___
2333	Santa Fe F-3 AA Units, *48–49*	210	365	___
2333	NYC F-3 AA Units, *48–49*			
	(A) Rubber-stamped lettering	410	800	___
	(B) Heat-stamped lettering	285	610	___
2337	Wabash GP-7, *58*	140	310	___
2338	Milwaukee Road GP-7, *55–56*			
	(A) Orange band around shell	900	1450	___
	(B) Interrupted orange band	145	250	___
2339	Wabash GP-7, *57*	150	360	___
2340	Pennsylvania GG-1, *55*			
	(A) Tuscan	630	1100	___
	(B) Dark green	560	940	___

		Good	Exc	Cond/S
2341	Jersey Central Train Master, *56*			
	(A) High gloss orange	1050	1750	___
	(B) Dull orange	950	1700	___
2343	Santa Fe F-3 AA Units, *50–52*	170	310	___
2343C	Santa Fe F-3 B Unit, *50–55*			
	(A) Screen roof vents	100	220	___
	(B) Louver roof vents	115	245	___
2344	NYC F-3 AA Units, *50–52*	220	600	___
2344C	NYC F-3 B Unit, *50–55*	130	305	___
2345	Western Pacific F-3 AA Units, *52*	630	770	___
2346	B&M GP-9, *65–66*	175	345	___
2347	C&O GP-7, 6*5 u*	1400	2600	___
2348	M&StL GP-9, *58–59*	160	405	___
2349	Northern Pacific GP-9, *59–60*	190	495	___
2350	New Haven EP-5, *56–58*			
	(A) White "N" painted nose	370	680	___
	(B) White "N" decal nose	210	380	___
	(C) Orange "N" painted nose	900	1550	___
	(D) Orange "N" decal nose	510	910	___
	(E) White "N" orange paint through doors	395	750	___
2351	Milwaukee Road EP-5, *57–58*	185	435	___
2352	Pennsylvania EP-5, *58–59*			
	(A) Tuscan body	225	650	___
	(B) Chocolate brown body	220	480	___
2353	Santa Fe F-3 AA Units, *53–55*	365	550	___
2354	NYC F-3 AA Units, *53–55*	290	660	___
2355	Western Pacific F-3 AA Units, *53*	695	1200	___
2356	Southern F-3 AA Units, *54–56*	460	750	___
2356C	Southern F-3 B Unit, *54–56*	175	330	___
2357	Lionel SP-type Caboose, *47–48*			
	(A) Red w/ red stack	160	470	___
	(B) Tuscan w/ tuscan stack	15	31	___
	(C) Tile red, no stack, "6357" stamped on bottom, *46–47*	17	34	___
2358	Great Northern EP-5, *59–60*	400	860	___
2359	Boston & Maine GP-9, *61–62*	170	365	___
2360	Penn GG-1, *56–58, 61–63*			
	(A) Tuscan, 5 gold stripes	600	1250	___
	(B) Dark green, 5 gold stripes	475	1100	___
	(C) Tuscan, gold stripe, heat-stamped letters	490	880	___
	(D) Tuscan, gold stripe, decaled lettering	455	760	___
2363	Illinois Central F-3 AB Units, *55–56*			
	(A) Black lettering	435	960	___
	(B) Brown lettering	450	980	___
2365	C&O GP-7, *62–63*	115	220	___

		Good	Exc	Cond/$
2367	Wabash F-3 AB Units, *55*	350	620	___
2368	B&O F-3 AB Units, *56*	550	1300	___
2373	CP F-3 AA Units, *57*	1350	2200	___
2378	Milwaukee Road F-3 AB Units, *56*			
	(A) w/ yellow roof line stripes	1050	1600	___
	(B) w/o roof line stripes	870	1300	___
2379	Rio Grande F-3 AB Units, *57–58*	415	620	___
2383	Santa Fe F-3 AA Units, *58–66*	260	455	___
2400	Maplewood Pullman, green, *48–49*	80	220	___
2401	Hillside Observation, green, *48–49*	75	145	___
2402	Chatham Pullman, green, *48–49*	65	155	___
2404	Santa Fe Vista Dome, *64–65*	29	75	___
2405	Santa Fe Pullman, *64–65*	29	65	___
2406	Santa Fe Observation, *64–65*	28	60	___
2408	Santa Fe Vista Dome, *66*	41	85	___
2409	Santa Fe Pullman, *66*	38	75	___
2410	Santa Fe Observation, *66*	34	70	___
2411	Lionel Lines Flatcar, *46–48*			
	(A) w/ pipes, *46*	50	90	___
	(B) w/ logs, *47–48*	16	28	___
2412	Santa Fe Vista Dome, *59–63*	33	95	___
2414	Santa Fe Pullman, *59–63*	30	115	___
2416	Santa Fe Observation, *59–63*	27	65	___
2419	DL&W Work Caboose, *46–47*	25	60	___
2420	DL&W Work Caboose, w/ light, *46–48*	60	100	___
	(A) Light or dark gray, heat-stamped serif lettering	70	175	___
	(B) Light or dark gray, rubber-stamped sans-serif lettering	100	375	___
2421	"Maplewood" Pullman, *50–53*			
	(A) Gray roof	40	80	___
	(B) Silver roof	43	70	___
2422	"Chatham" Pullman, *50–53*			
	(A) Gray roof	39	80	___
	(B) Silver roof	38	70	___
2423	"Hillside" Observation, *50–53*			
	(A) Gray roof	40	75	___
	(B) Silver roof	38	65	___
2429	"Livingston" Pullman, *52–53*			
	(A) Gray roof	44	120	___
	(B) Aluminum roof, no stripe	55	110	___
2430	Blue Pullman, *46–47*	31	75	___
2431	Blue Observation, *46–47*	31	70	___
2432	"Clifton" Vista Dome, *54–58*	42	105	___
2434	"Newark" Pullman, *54–58*	34	75	___

		Good	Exc	Cond/$
2435	"Elizabeth" Pullman, *54–58*	39	85	___
2436	"Mooseheart" Observation, *57–58*	28	75	___
2436	Summit Observation, *54–56*	25	65	___
2440	Green Pullman, *46–47*	32	80	___
2441	Green Observation, *46–47*	25	60	___
2442	"Clifton" Vista Dome, red stripe, *56*	60	135	___
2442	Brown Pullman, *46–48*			
	(A) Silver lettering	26	80	___
	(B) White lettering	25	65	___
2443	Brown Observation, *46–48*			
	(A) Silver lettering	23	75	___
	(B) White lettering	25	65	___
2444	"Newark" Pullman, *56*	50	115	___
2445	"Elizabeth" Pullman, *56*	90	315	___
2446	"Summit" Observation, *56*	55	165	___
2452	Pennsylvania Gondola, *45–47*	9	23	___
2452X	Pennsylvania Gondola, *46–47*	7	25	___
X2454	Pennsylvania Boxcar, *46*			
	(A) Brown door	85	185	___
	(B) Orange door	120	255	___
X2454	Baby Ruth Boxcar, PRR logo, *46–47*	12	28	___
2456	Lehigh Valley Hopper, *48*	9	29	___
2457	PRR Caboose, metal, N5, *45–47*			
	(A) Red, white lettering	17	38	___
	(B) Brown, white lettering	27	55	___
X2458	Pennsylvania Boxcar, *46–48*	18	55	___
2458	Automobile Boxcar (O), postwar trucks "2758", *41–42*	34	65	
2460	Bucyrus Erie Crane, *12*-wheel, *46–50*			
	(A) Gray cab	85	205	___
	(B) Black cab	35	75	___
2461	Transformer Car, die-cast, *47–48*			
	(A) Red transformer	42	105	___
	(B) Black transformer	30	75	___
2465	Sunoco 2-D Tank Car, *46–48*			
	(A) "GAS/SUNOCO/OILS" in diamond	38	85	___
	(B) "SUNOCO" in diamond	10	20	___
	(C) "SUNOCO" goes past diamond	10	18	___
2472	PRR Caboose, metal, N5, *46–47*	12	27	___
2481	"Plainfield" Pullman, yellow, *50*	125	305	___
2482	"Westfield" Pullman, yellow, *50*	120	295	___
2483	"Livingston" Observation, yellow, *50*	105	260	___
2521	"President McKinley" Observation, *62–66*	85	170	___
2522	"President Harrison" Vista Dome, *62–66*	80	135	___
2523	"President Garfield" Pullman, *62–66*	70	145	___

		Good	Exc	Cond/$
2530	REA Baggage, *54–60*			
	(A) Large doors	280	525	___
	(B) Small doors	90	200	___
2531	"Silver Dawn" Observation, *52–60*	80	160	___
2532	"Silver Range" Vista Dome, *52–60*	75	140	___
2533	"Silver Cloud" Pullman, *52–59*	60	110	___
2534	"Silver Bluff" Pullman, *52–59*	70	140	___
2541	"Alexander Hamilton" Observation, *55–56**	85	260	___
2542	"Betsy Ross" Vista Dome, *55–56**	85	190	___
2543	"William Penn" Pullman, *55–56**	70	140	___
2544	"Molly Pitcher" Pullman, *55–56**	85	200	___
2550	B&O RDC Baggage/Mail, *57–58*	245	610	___
2551	"Banff Park" Observation, *57**	135	270	___
2552	"Skyline 500" Vista Dome, *57**	110	215	___
2553	"Blair Manor" Pullman, *57**	245	455	___
2554	"Craig Manor" Pullman, *57**	215	450	___
2555	Sunoco 1-D Tank Car, *46–48*	21	60	___
2559	B&O RDC Passenger, *57–58*	155	350	___
2560	Lionel Lines Crane, 8-wheel, *46–47*			
	(A) Black boom	25	65	___
	(B) Brown boom	22	55	___
	(C) Green boom	25	70	___
	(D) Black boom from 2460 crane, *47*	22	55	___
2561	"Vista Valley" Observation, *59–61**	130	300	___
2562	"Regal Pass" Vista Dome, *59–61**	145	340	___
2563	"Indian Falls" Pullman, *59–61**	145	340	___
2625	"Madison" Pullman, *46–47**	115	230	___
2625	"Manhattan" Pullman, *46–47**	100	210	___
2625	"Irvington" Pullman, *46–50**			
	(A) w/o silhouettes	85	185	___
	(B) w/ silhouettes	115	250	___
2627	"Madison" Pullman, *48–50**			
	(A) w/o silhouettes	90	195	___
	(B) w/ silhouettes	90	230	___
2628	"Manhattan" Pullman, *48–50**			
	(A) w/o silhouettes	100	190	___
	(B) w/ silhouettes	115	235	___
2671	TCA Tender, *68*		95	___
2855	SUNX 1-D Tank Car, *46–47*			
	(A) Black	65	215	___
	(B) Black, "GAS/OILS" omitted	55	220	___
	(C) Gray	43	185	___
2856	B&O Scale Hopper Car, *46–47*		NM	___
2857	NYC Scale Caboose, *46*		NM	___

		Good	Exc	Cond/$
3309	Turbo Missile Launch Car, *63–64*			
	(A) Red body	23	50	___
	(B) Olive body	100	440	___
3330	Flatcar w/ submarine kit, *60–62*	36	140	___
3330-100	Operating Submarine Kit, *60–61*	55	120	___
3349	Turbo Missile Launch Car, *62–65*			
	(A) Red body	26	47	___
	(B) Olive drab body	100	445	___
3356	Operating Horse Car only, *56–60, 64–66*	50	95	___
3356	Operating Horse Car and Corral Set *56–60, 64–66*	65	120	___
3356-100	Black Horses (9), *56–59*	8	34	___
3356-150	Horse Car Corral, *57–60*	30	75	___
3357	Hydraulic Maintenance Car, *62–64*	34	80	___
3359	Lionel Lines Two-bin Dump, *55–58*	20	46	___
3360	Operating Burro Crane, *56–57*	150	270	___
3361	Operating Log Dump Car, *55–58*	21	40	___
3362	Flatcar w/ helium tanks or logs, *61–63*	14	42	___
3362/3364	Log Dump Car, *65–69*	15	32	___
3366	Circus Car Corral Set, *59–62*	80	165	___
3366	Circus Car only, *59–62*	90	170	___
3366-100	White Horses (9), *59–60*	31	75	___
3370	W&A Outlaw Car, *61–64*	30	75	___
3376	Bronx Zoo Car, *60–66, 69*			
	(A) Blue w/ white lettering	20	55	___
	(B) Green w/ yellow lettering	35	100	___
	(C) Blue w/ yellow lettering	115	290	___
3386	Bronx Zoo Car, *60*	29	65	___
3409	Helicopter Car, *61*	46	100	___
3410	Helicopter Car, *61–63*	40	85	___
3413	Mercury Capsule Car, *62–64*	75	150	___
3419	Helicopter Car, *59–65*	55	75	___
3424	Wabash Operating Boxcar, *56–58*	33	70	___
3424-100	Low Bridge Signal Set, *56–58*	15	75	___
3428	U.S. Mail Operating Boxcar, *59–60*	49	115	___
3429	USMC Helicopter Car, *60*	195	405	___
3434	Poultry Dispatch Car, *59–60, 64–66*	60	110	___
3435	Traveling Aquarium Car, *59–62*			
	(A) Gold circle	430	970	___
	(B) Tank 1, tank 2	280	770	___
	(C) Gold lettering	155	320	___
	(D) Yellow rubber stamp	100	230	___
3444	Erie Operating Gondola, *57–59*	50	70	___
3451	Operating Log Dump Car, *46–48*	17	44	___

		Good	Exc	Cond/$
3454	PRR Operating Merchandise Car, *46–47*			
	(A) Red lettering		NRS	___
	(B) Blue lettering	55	115	___
3456	N&W Operating Hopper Car, *50–55*	17	75	___
3459	LL Operating Dump Car, *46–48*			
	(A) Aluminum bin	100	310	___
	(B) Black bin	21	48	___
	(C) Green bin	27	85	___
3460	Flatcar w/ trailers, *55–57*	29	70	___
3461	Lionel Operating Log Car, *49–55*			
	(A) Black car	17	39	___
	(B) Green car	28	75	___
3462	Automatic Milk Car, *47–48*	24	65	___
	(A) Plain	21	55	___
	(B) Glossy eggshell white		450	___
3462P	Milk Car Platform, *47–48*	8	15	___
X3464	ATSF Operating Boxcar, *49–52*	11	26	___
X3464	NYC Operating Boxcar, *49–52*	11	30	___
3469	LL Operating Dump Car, *49–55*	17	55	___
3470	Target Launcher, *62–64*			
	(A) Dark blue car	30	70	___
	(B) Light blue car	60	140	___
3472	Automatic Milk Car, *49–53*	24	75	___
3474	Western Pacific Boxcar, *52–53*	31	85	___
3482	Automatic Milk Car, *54–55*			
	(A) "RT34672"	45	130	___
	(B) "RT3482"	35	75	___
3484	Pennsylvania Operating Boxcar, *53*			
	(A) White lettering	15	45	___
	(B) Gold lettering	15	45	___
3484-25	ATSF Operating Boxcar, *54*			
	(A) White lettering	33	90	___
	(B) Black lettering	42	120	___
3494-1	NYC Pacemaker Boxcar, *55*	55	130	___
3494-150	MP Operating Boxcar, *56*	65	140	___
3494-275	State of Maine Operating Boxcar, *56–58*	60	135	___
3494-550	Monon Operating Boxcar, *57–58*	120	390	___
3494-625	Soo Operating Boxcar, *57–58*	150	490	___
3509	Satellite Car, *61*	27	55	___
3510	Satellite Car, *62*	40	145	___
3512	Fireman and Ladder Car, *59–61*			
	(A) Black rooftop ladder	60	125	___
	(B) Silver rooftop ladder	85	230	___
3519	Satellite Car, *61–64*	22	50	___
3520	Searchlight Car, *52–53*	24	55	___

		Good	Exc	Cond/$
3530	GM Generator Car, *56–58*			
	(A) Blue fuel tank	60	125	___
	(B) Black fuel tank	65	135	___
3530-50	Searchlight w/ pole and base, *56–56*	29	90	
3535	A E C Security Car, *60–61*	37	120	
3540	Operating Radar Car, *59–60*	42	145	
3545	Lionel TV Car, *61–62*	55	180	
3559	Operating Coal Dump Car, *46–48*	17	41	
3562-1	ATSF Operating Barrel Car, black, *54*			
	(A) Black trough	75	185	___
	(B) Yellow trough	75	185	___
3562-25	ATSF Operating Barrel Car, gray, *54*			
	(A) Red lettering	165	475	___
	(B) Blue lettering	22	55	___
3562-50	ATSF Operating Barrel Car, yellow, *55–56*			
	(A) Painted	45	105	___
	(B) Unpainted	20	55	___
3562-75	ATSF Operating Barrel Car, orange, *57–58*	40	85	___
3619	Helicopter Boxcar, *62–64*			
	(A) Light yellow	33	90	___
	(B) Dark yellow	40	145	___
3620	Searchlight Car, *54–56*			
	(A) Gray searchlight	27	50	___
	(B) Orange generator/light	55	160	___
3650	Extension Searchlight Car, *56–59*			
	(A) Light gray	38	70	___
	(B) Dark gray	70	145	___
3656	Armour Operating Cattle Car, *49–55*			
	(A) Black letters, Armour sticker	75	225	___
	(B) White letters, Armour sticker	34	75	___
	(C) No Armour sticker, black lettering	42	120	___
	(D) White lettering	31	75	___
	(E) White letters, no decal, open coil below frame	38	95	___
3656	Stockyard w/ cattle	33	85	___
3662	Automatic Milk Car, *55–60, 64–66*	36	70	___
3665	Minuteman Operating Car, *61–64*			
	(A) Medium blue roof	75	155	___
	(B) Dark blue roof	55	115	___
3666	Minuteman Boxcar w/ missile, *64 u*	165	460	
3672	Bosco Operating Boxcar, *59–60*			
	(A) Unpainted	85	220	___
	(B) Painted	115	315	___
3820	Flatcar w/ submarine, *60–62*	75	215	___
3830	Flatcar w/ submarine, *60–63*	40	96	___

		Good	Exc	Cond/$
3854	Operating Merchandise Car, *46–47*	185	395	___
3927	Lionel Lines Track Cleaner, *56–60*	55	75	___
3927-50	Track Cleaning Fluid, *57–69*	2.50	11	___
3927-75	Track Cleaning Pads, *57–69*	6	25	___
4357	PRR SP-type Caboose, electric, *48–49*			___
4452	PRR Gondola, electronic, *46–49*	43	80	___
4454	Baby Ruth PRR Boxcar, electronic, *46–49*	60	160	___
4457	PRR N5 Caboose, electronic, *46–47*	45	150	___
4681	Steam 6-8-6, electronic, *50*		NM	___
5159	Maintenance Kit, *63–65*	28	80	___
5159-50	Maintenance and Lube Kit, *66–69*	28	80	___
5160	Viewing Stand, *63*	50	130	___
5459	LL Dump Car, electronic, *46–49*	49	150	___
6002	NYC Gondola, *50*	5	13	___
X6004	Baby Ruth PRR Boxcar, *50*	4	7	___
6007	Lionel Lines SP-type Caboose, *50*	3	8	___
6009	RC Uncoupling Track, *53–54*	1	6	___
6012	Lionel Gondola, *51–56*	2	7	___
6014	Airex Boxcar, 6*0 u*	26	55	___
6014	Bosco PRR Boxcar, *58*			
	(A) White body	35	50	___
	(B) Red body	4	7	___
	(C) Orange body	4	7	___
6014	Chun King Boxcar, 5*7 u*	65	125	___
6014	Frisco Boxcar, *57, 63–69*			
	(A) White body	4	9	___
	(B) Red body	4	7	___
	(C) White w/ coin slot	25	45	___
	(D) Orange body	22	39	___
	(E) Orange, Type I body	20	80	___
X6014	Baby Ruth PRR Boxcar, *51–56*			
	(A) White	5	9	___
	(B) Red	10	26	___
6014-150	Wix Boxcar, 5*9 u*	95	170	___
6015	Sunoco 1-D Tank Car, *54–55*			
	(A) Painted tank	45	155	___
	(B) Unpainted tank	4	10	___
6017	Lionel Lines SP-type Caboose, *51–62*	3	11	___
6017	Lionel SP-type Caboose, *56*	14	34	___
6017-50	USMC SP-type Caboose, *58*	29	75	___
6017-85	LL SP-type Caboose, gray, *58*	21	55	___
6017-100	B&M SP-type Caboose, *59, 62, 65–66*			
	(A) Purplish blue	255	475	___
	(B) Medium or light blue	11	41	___
6017-185	ATSF SP-type Caboose, *59–60*	13	46	___

		Good	Exc	Cond/$
6017-200	U.S. Navy SP-type Caboose, *60*	49	110	___
6017-225	ATSF SP-type Caboose, c. 6*3 u, 61–62*	15	55	___
6017-235	ATSF SP-type Caboose, *62*	18	70	___
6019	RCS Track Set (O27), *48–66*	2.50	12	___
6024	Nabisco Shredded Wheat Boxcar, *57*	13	30	___
6024	RCA Whirlpool Boxcar, 5*7 u*	28	60	___
6025	Gulf 1-D Tank Car, *56–58*			
	(A) Gray, blue lettering	5	16	___
	(B) Orange, blue lettering	5	14	___
	(C) Black, red "GULF" emblem	5	14	___
6027	Alaska SP-type Caboose, *59*	28	80	___
6029	Remote Control Uncoupling Track, *55–63*	1	6	___
6032	Lionel Gondola, black (O27), *52–54*	2.50	7	___
X6034	Baby Ruth PRR Boxcar, *53–54*			
	(A) Orange, blue lettering	5	11	___
	(B) Red, white lettering	5	11	___
	(C) Orange, black lettering	5	11	___
6035	Sunoco 1-D Tank Car, *52–53*	3	9	___
6037	Lionel Lines SP-type Caboose, *52–54*	3	8	___
6042	Lionel Gondola, *59–61, 62–64* u	2	8	___
6044	Airex Boxcar, orange lettering, *59–60* u			
	(A) Medium blue	6	21	___
	(B) Teal blue	40	80	___
	(C) Dark blue/purple	90	315	___
6044-1X	Nestles/McCall's Boxcar w/o letters, *62–63 u*	450	810	___
6045	Lionel Lines 2-D Tank Car, *59–64*			
	(A) Gray	15	21	___
	(B) Orange	15	37	___
6045	Cities Service 2-D Tank, 6*0 u*	13	40	___
6047	Lionel Lines SP-type Caboose, *62*			
	(A) Unpainted, medium red	2.50	6	___
	(B) Brown-painted	100	300	___
6050	Lionel Savings Bank Boxcar, *61*	12	26	___
	(A) w/ "BLT", *61*	13	32	___
	(B) w/ "BUILT"	100	225	___
6050	Swift Refrigerator Car, *62–63*			
	(A) Red body	11	23	___
	(B) w/ 2 open holes in roof walk	35	150	___
6050	Libby's Boxcar, 6*3 u*			
	(A) Green stems on tomatoes	18	41	___
	(B) Green stems missing	21	49	___
6057	LL SP-type Caboose, *59–62*			
	(A) Unpainted	3	9	___
	(B) Painted	38	190	___
6057-50	LL SP-type Caboose, orange, *62*	12	32	___

		Good	Exc	Cond/$
6058	C&O SP-type Caboose, *61*			
	(A) Blue lettering	18	45	___
	(B) Black lettering	18	50	___
6059	M&StL SP-type Caboose, *61–69*			
	(A) Painted, red	13	25	___
	(B) Unpainted, red	4	8	___
	(C) Unpainted, maroon	7	12	___
6062	NYC Gondola, w/ cable reels, *59–62*			
	(A) Without metal undercarriage	12	29	___
	(B) With metal undercarriage	40	100	___
6062-50	NYC Gondola, w/ 2 canisters, *69*	6	21	___
6067	Caboose (no lettering), SP-type, *62*	3	6	___
6076	ATSF Hopper, *63 u*	11	22	___
6076	LV Hopper, red, black or gray body, *63*			
	(A) Gray body	7	14	___
	(B) Black body	7	13	___
	(C) Red body	7	13	___
	(D) Yellow body	7	13	___
6076	Hopper, no lettering, *63*			
	(A) Yellow body	50	90	___
	(B) Gray body	10	18	___
6110	Steam 2-4-2, 6001T Tender, *50–51*	14	32	___
6111	Flatcar w/ logs, *55–57*	9	19	___
6112	Lionel Gondola, *56–58*			
	(A) Black body	3	7	___
	(B) Blue body	4	10	___
	(C) White body	11	25	___
6119	DL&W Work Caboose, red, *55–56*	13	31	___
6119-25	DL&W Work Caboose, orange, *56–59*	9	33	___
6119-50	DL&W Caboose, brown, *56*	19	65	___
6119-75	DL&W Work Caboose, *57*			
	(A) Gray frame w/ heat-stamped letters	14	39	___
	(B) With closely spaced letters on frame	75	225	___
6119-100	DL&W Work Caboose, red/gray, *57–66, 69*			
	(A) Red/gray	12	34	___
	(B) Heat-stamped "Built By Lionel", *66*	125	227	___
6119-125	Rescue Unit Work Caboose, no number olive drab, *63–64* u	65	175	___
6120	Work Caboose, no lettering, yellow, *61–62*	7	23	___
6121	Flatcar w/ pipes, *56–57*			
	(A) various colors	5	15	___
	(B) Wine red	29	95	___
6130	ATSF Work Caboose, *61, 65–69*	12	38	___
6139	RC Uncoupling Track (O27), *63*	1	4	___
6142	Lionel Gondola, *63–66, 69*			

		Good	Exc	Cond/$
	(A) Green, blue or black	3	8	___
	(B) Olive drab	32	125	___
6149	RC Uncoupling Track (O27), *64–69*	1	5	___
6151	Flatcar (various colors) w/ patrol truck, *58*			
	(A) Yellow	40	110	___
	(B) Orange	40	110	___
	(C) Cream	40	110	___
6162	NYC Gondola, *59–68*			
	(A) Blue body	5	11	___
	(B) Red body	70	415	___
6162-60	Alaska Gondola, *59*	38	95	___
6167	LL SP-type Caboose, red, *63*			
	(A) Unpainted	3	9	___
	(B) Painted	100	240	___
6167	Unstamped SP-type Caboose w/o end rails			
	(A) Red body	3	9	___
	(B) Yellow body	11	26	___
	(C) Brown body	15	36	___
	(D) Olive body		425	___
6167-85	UP SP-type Caboose, *69*	10	34	___
6175	Flatcar w/ rocket, *58–61*			
	(A) Black car	25	65	___
	(B) Red car	25	70	___
6176	LV Hopper, *64–66, 69*			
	(A) Yellow	3	9	___
	(B) Gray	3	8	___
	(C) Black	3	8	___
6176	Hopper (no lettering), *64*			
	(A) Yellow	6	18	___
	(B) Gray	5	14	___
	(C) Olive	32	95	___
6219	C&O Work Caboose, *60*	27	65	___
6220	Santa Fe NW-2 Switcher, *49–50*			
	(A) Large "GM" decal on cab	125	280	___
	(B) Small "GM" decal on cab	125	265	___
6250	Seaboard NW-2 Switcher, *54–55*			
	(A) Decals	125	280	___
	(B) Rubber-stamped	110	230	___
6257	Lionel SP-type Caboose, *48–56, 63–64*	3	14	___
6257-25	Lionel SP-type Caboose	3	7	___
6257-50	Lionel SP-type Caboose	3	7	___
6257-100	Lionel Lines SP-type Caboose	7	17	___
6257X	Lionel SP-type Caboose, *48*	15	55	___

		Good	Exc	Cond/$
6262	Flatcar w/ wheels, *56–57*			
	(A) Black, *56–57*	30	65	___
	(B) Red, *56*	170	490	___
6264	Flatcar w/ lumber for Fork Lift Set, *57–60*			
	(A) No box	20	75	___
	(B) Separate-sale box	100	390	___
6311	Flatcar w/ 3 pipes, *55*	19	49	___
6315	Gulf 1-D Chemical Tank Car, *56–59, 68–69*			
	(A) Early, painted	38	65	___
	(B) Late, unpainted	30	65	___
	(C) Late, unpainted w/ built date	43	85	___
6315	Lionel Lines 1-D Tank Car, *63–66*			
	(A) Unpainted orange body	15	30	___
	(B) Painted orange body	100	250	___
6342	NYC Gondola, *56–58, 64–66*	17	48	___
6343	Barrel Ramp Car, *61–62*	15	39	___
6346	Alcoa Quad Hopper, *56*	31	75	___
6352	PFE Reefer from 352 Ice Depot, *55–57*			
	(A) No box	65	195	___
	(B) Separate-sale box	650	1700	___
6356	NYC Stock Car, 2-level, *54–55*			
	(A) Heat-stamped letterng	15	37	___
	(B) Rubber-stamped lettering	40	100	___
6357	Lionel SP-type Caboose, *48–61*	9	25	___
6357-25	Lionel SP Type Caboose, maroon body and stack, *53–56*	100	215	___
6357-50	ATSF SP-type Caboose, *60*	325	1000	___
6361	Flatcar w/ timber, *60–61, 64–69*	31	80	___
6362	Truck Car w/ 3 trucks, *55–56*			
	(A) Shiny orange	24	55	___
	(B) Dull orange	80	130	___
6376	LL Circus Stock Car, *56–57*	40	85	___
6401	Flatcar, no load, gray, *60*	2	7	___
6402	Flatcar w/ reels or boat, *62, 64–66, 69*			
	(A) w/ reels	6	18	___
	(B) w/ boat	25	60	___
6404	Black Flatcar w/ auto, *60*			
	(A) w/ red auto	20	115	___
	(B) w/ yellow auto		300	___
	(C) w/ brown auto		495	___
	(D) w/ green auto		495	___
6405	Maroon Flatcar w/ trailer, *61*	15	45	___

		Good	Exc	Cond/$
6406	Flatcar w/ auto, *61*			
	(A) Maroon w/ red auto	23	65	___
	(B) Maroon w/ yellow auto	45	190	___
	(C) Gray w/ dark brown auto	95	355	___
	(D) Gray w/ green auto	95	350	___
	(E) Gray w/ yellow auto	35	75	___
6407	Flatcar w/ rocket, *63*	105	320	___
6408	Flatcar w/ pipes, *63*	14	36	___
6409	Flatcar w/ pipes, *63*	14	36	___
6411	Flatcar w/ logs, *48–50*	15	31	___
6413	Mercury Project Car, *62–63*			
	(A) Powder blue car	75	130	___
	(B) Aquamarine car	95	150	___
6414	Evans Auto Loader w/ 4 cars, *55–66*			
	(A) Cars w/ windows, chrome bumpers and rubber tires; red, yellow, blue, and white	49	130	___
	(B) 4 cars, w/o trim, 2 red, 2 yellow	275	520	___
	(C) 4 red cars w/ gray bumpers	50	165	___
	(D) 4 yellow cars w/ gray bumpers	150	375	___
	(E) Dark yellow, gray bumpers		NRS	___
	(F) Dark brown, chrome bumpers		NRS	___
	(G) 4 brown cars w/ gray bumpers	350	850	___
	(H) Medium green, chrome bumpers		NRS	___
	(I) 4 green cars w/ gray bumpers	360	950	___
6415	Sunoco 3-D Tank Car, *53–55, 64–66, 69*	13	36	___
6416	Boat Loader Car, *61–63*	95	245	___
6417	PRR Porthole Caboose, *53–57*			
	(A) w/ "NEW YORK ZONE"	11	45	___
	(B) w/o "NEW YORK ZONE"	105	270	___
6417-25	Lionel Lines N5C Caboose, *54*	15	40	___
6417-50	LV porthole Caboose, *54*			
	(A) Tuscan	375	1050	___
	(B) Gray	50	145	___
6418	Flatcar w/ steel girders, *55–57*	48	105	___
6419	DL&W Work Caboose, early frame *48–50, 52–57*	17	50	___
6419-25	DL&W Work Caboose, *54–55*	16	41	___
6419-50	DL&W Work Caboose, late frame, *56–57*	17	50	___
6419-75	DL&W Work Caboose, late frame, *56–57*	17	50	___
6419-100	N&W Work Caboose, *57–58*	39	120	___
6420	DL&W Work Caboose, w/ light, *48–50*	28	80	___
6424	Autoloader w/ 6805 slots in floor and rail stops, *58–59*	85	235	___
6424	Flatcar w/ 2 autos, *56–59*	25	44	___
6425	Gulf 3-D Tank Car, *56–58*	17	45	___

		Good	Exc	Cond/$
6427	Lionel Lines Porthole Caboose, *54–60*	12	31	___
6427-60	Virginian Porthole Caboose, *58*	155	420	___
6427-500	PRR Porthole Caboose, Girls', *57–58**	145	310	___
6428	U.S. Mail Boxcar, *60–61, 65–66*	20	39	___
6429	DL&W Work Caboose w/ AAR trucks, *63*	140	320	___
6430	Flatcar w/ Cooper-Jarrett vans, *56–58*			
	(A) Gray vans	22	60	___
	(B) White vans	20	55	___
6431	Flatcar w/ vans, *66*	90	225	___
6434	Poultry Dispatch, *58–59*	42	70	___
6436-1	LV Quad Hopper, black, *55*	15	36	___
6436-25	LV Quad Hopper, maroon, *55–57*	16	33	___
6436-110	LV Quad Hopper, red, *63–68*			
	(A) w/o cover, no built date	20	43	___
	(B) w/ cover and "NEW 3-55"	100	275	___
	(C) w/o cover and "NEW 3-55"	40	80	___
6436-500	LV Girls' Hopper, lilac, "643657", *57–58**	95	270	___
6437	PRR Porthole Caboose, *61–68*	16	41	___
6440	Flatcar with vans, *61–63*	26	85	___
6440	Green Pullman, *48–49*	28	65	___
6441	Green Observation, *48–49*	29	65	___
6442	Brown Pullman, *49*	31	75	___
6443	Brown Observation, *49*	35	60	___
6445	Fort Knox Gold Reserve, *61–63*	60	135	___
6446	N&W Quad Hopper "546446", black or gray, *54–55*	19	49	___
6446-25	N&W Quad Hopper "644625", black or gray, *55–57*			
	(A) Black, white lettering	19	65	___
	(B) Gray, black lettering	19	75	___
6447	PRR Porthole Caboose, *63*	155	450	___
6448	Target Car, *61–64*			
	(A) Red, white lettering	17	38	___
	(B) White, red lettering	17	38	___
6452	Pennsylvania Gondola, black, *48–49*	6	23	___
X6454	Baby Ruth PRR Boxcar, *48*	75	245	___
X6454	NYC Boxcar, *48*			
	(A) Brown body	20	55	___
	(B) Orange body	45	140	___
	(C) Tan body	15	35	___
X6454	Santa Fe Boxcar, *48*	17	47	___
X6454	SP Boxcar, *49–52*	15	46	___
X6454	Erie Boxcar, *49–52*	21	55	___
X6454	PRR Boxcar, *49–52*	25	60	___

		Good	Exc	Cond/$
6456	Lehigh Valley Short Hopper, *48–55*			
	(A) Black	9	16	___
	(B) Maroon	6	17	___
	(C) Gray	16	36	___
	(D) Enamel red, yellow lettering	60	165	___
	(E) Enamel red, white lettering	240	700	___
	(F) Enamel gray, maroon letter		NRS	___
6457	Lionel SP-type Caboose, *49–52*	19	34	___
6460	Bucyrus Erie Crane, 8-wheel, *52–54*			
	(A) Black cab	18	55	___
	(B) Red cab	29	80	___
6460-25	Bucyrus Erie Crane, red cab, 8-wheel w/ box, *54*	48	140	___
6461	Transformer Car, *49–50*	25	70	___
6462	Pennsylvania Gondola, black, *49*	10	25	___
6462	NYC Gondola, *49–57*			
	(A) Black	9	15	___
	(B) Green	8	28	___
	(C) Red	5	18	___
6462-500	NYC Girls' Gondola, pink, *57–58**	65	165	___
6463	Rocket Fuel 2-D Tank, *62–63*	13	42	___
6464-1	WP Boxcar, *53–54*			
	(A) Blue lettering	31	65	___
	(B) Red lettering	450	1150	___
	(C) Orange, silver lettering		NRS	___
6464-25	GN Boxcar, *53–54*	34	80	___
6464-50	M&StL Boxcar, *53–56*	37	65	___
6464-75	RI Boxcar, *53–54, 69*	36	75	___
6464-100	WP Boxcar, *54–55*			
	(A) Silver body, yellow feather	60	145	___
	(B) Orange body, blue feather	380	810	___
	(C) Orange, blue feather, "1954"		NRS	___
	(D) w/ "6464-100"		NRS	___
6464-125	NYC Boxcar, *54–56*	42	125	___
6464-150	MP Boxcar, *54–55, 57*	30	100	___
6464-175	Rock Island Boxcar, *54–55*			
	(A) Blue lettering	50	90	___
	(B) Black lettering	450	950	___
6464-200	Pennsylvania Boxcar, *54–55, 69*	75	130	___
6464-225	SP Boxcar, *54–56*	65	135	___
6464-250	WP Boxcar, *66*	115	225	___
6464-275	State of Maine Boxcar, *55, 57–59*			
	(A) Striped doors	48	80	___
	(B) Solid doors	55	135	___

		Good	Exc	Cond/$
6464-300	Rutland Boxcar, *55–56*			
	(A) Rubber-stamped	40	75	___
	(B) Split door	310	650	___
	(C) Solid shield	850	2250	___
	(D) Heat-stamped	50	135	___
6464-325	B&O Sentinel Boxcar, *56*	280	560	___
6464-350	MKT Katy Boxcar, *56*	145	265	___
6464-375	Central of Georgia Boxcar, *56–57, 66*			
	(A) Unpainted, maroon body	55	100	___
	(B) Painted, red body	800	1550	___
6464-400	B&O Time-saver Boxcar, *56–57, 69*			
	(A) w/ "BLT 5-54"	44	110	___
	(B) w/ "BLT 2-56"	95	265	___
6464-425	New Haven Boxcar, *56–58*	23	55	___
6464-450	Great Northern Boxcar, *56–57, 66*	65	135	___
6464-475	B&M Boxcar, *57–60, 65–66, 68*	42	135	___
6464-500	Timken Boxcar, yellow and white charcoal lettering, *57–59, 69*	75	150	___
6464-510	NYC Pacemaker Boxcar, *57–58*	345	725	___
6464-515	MKT Boxcar, *57–58*	315	640	___
6464-525	M&StL Boxcar, *57–58, 64–66*			
	(A) Red, white lettering	30	60	___
	(B) Maroon, white lettering		530	___
6464-650	D&RGW Boxcar, *57–58, 66*			
	(A) Unpainted yellow body	50	115	___
	(B) w/o black stripe	150	195	___
	(C) Painted yellow body and roof	500	900	___
6464-700	Santa Fe Boxcar, *61, 66*	49	105	___
6464-725	New Haven Boxcar, *62–66, 68*			
	(A) Orange body	30	55	___
	(B) Black body	70	250	___
6464-825	Alaska Boxcar, *59–60*	160	390	___
6464-900	NYC Boxcar, *60–66*	70	150	___
6465	Sunoco 2-D Tank Car, *48–56*			
	(A) "6465" stamped	6	18	___
	(B) "6455" stamped	7	26	___
	(C) No number	7	21	___
6465	Cities Service 2-D Tank, *60–62*	17	45	___
6465	Gulf 2-D Tank Car, *58*			
	(A) Black tank	25	60	___
	(B) Gray tank	10	23	___
6465	LL 2-D Tank Car, *59, 63–64*			
	(A) Black tank	10	26	___
	(B) Orange tank	5	16	___
6467	Bulkhead Flatcar, *56*	20	49	___

		Good	Exc	Cond/$
6468	B&O Auto Boxcar, *53–55*			
	(A) Tuscan	150	350	___
	(B) Blue, glossy or flat	20	58	___
6468-25	NH Auto Boxcar, *56–58*			
	(A) Black "N" over white "H"	41	135	___
	(B) White "N" over black "H"	215	470	___
6469	Lionel Liquefied Gases Car, *63*	50	125	___
6470	Explosives Boxcar, *59–60*	13	32	___
6472	Refrigerator Car, *50–53*	17	39	___
6473	Horse Transport Car, *62–69*	9	27	___
6475	Heinz 57 Vat Car, *65–66*	55	105	___
6475	Libby's Crushed Pineapple Vat Car, *63 u*	25	75	___
6475	Pickles Vat Car, *60–62*	26	55	___
6476	LV Hopper, red, black, or gray body, *57–69*			
	(A) Red body	4	10	___
	(B) Gray body	4	9	___
	(C) Black body	4	10	___
6476-135	LV Hopper, yellow, *64–66, 68*	6	11	___
6476-160	LV Hopper, black, *69*	7	16	___
6476-185	LV Hopper, yellow, *69*	6	14	___
6477	Bulkhead Car w/ pipes, *57–58*	22	60	___
6480	Explosives Boxcar, red, *61*	28	49	___
6482	Refrigerator Car, *57*	30	65	___
6500	Flatcar w/ Bonanza plane, *62, 65*			
	(A) Plane w/ red top and wings	350	660	___
	(B) Plane w/ white top and wings	350	650	___
6501	Flatcar w/ jet boat, *62–63*	70	130	___
6502	Flatcar w/ bridge girder, *62*	17	38	___
6511	Flatcar w/ pipes, *53–56*	19	42	___
6512	Cherry Picker Car, *62–63*	33	95	___
6517	LL Bay Window Caboose, *55–59*			
	(A) Underscored	30	70	___
	(B) Not underscored	22	70	___
6517-75	Erie B/W Caboose, *66*	185	445	___
6518	Transformer Car, *56–58*	43	110	___
6519	Allis-Chalmers Flatcar, *58–61*			
	(A) Dark/medium orange base	35	70	___
	(B) Dull light orange base	40	100	___
6520	Searchlight Car, *49–51*			
	(A) Tan diesel generator	200	450	___
	(B) Green diesel generator	175	395	___
	(C) Maroon or orange diesel generator	25	70	___
	(D) Orange generator, gray light	24	65	___

		Good	Exc	Cond/$
6530	Firefighting Car, red, *60–61*			
	(A) Red, white lettering	34	70	___
	(B) Black, white lettering		415	___
6536	M&StL Quad Hopper, *58–59, 63*	23	55	___
6544	Missile Firing Car, *60–64*			
	(A) White-lettered console	45	115	___
	(B) Black-lettered console	180	390	___
6555	Sunoco 1-D Tank Car, *49–50*	16	38	___
6556	MKT Stock Car, *58*	95	365	___
6557	Lionel SP-type Caboose, smoke, *58–59*	95	230	___
6560	Bucyrus Erie Crane w/ stack, 8-wheel, *55–58, 68–69*			
	(A) Reddish-orange or black cab, early	65	170	___
	(B) Gray cab	40	85	___
	(C) Red cab	24	48	___
	(D) Dark blue w/ "Hagerstown"	40	85	___
6560-25	Bucyrus Erie Crane, 8-wheel, *56*	35	75	___
6561	Reel Car, *53–56*			
	(A) Orange reels	22	60	___
	(B) Gray reels	25	65	___
6562	NYC Gondola w/ canisters, *56–58*			
	(A) Gray body, *56*	16	47	___
	(B) Red body, *56, 58*	15	38	___
	(C) Black body, *57*	16	44	___
6572	REA Refrigerator Car, *58–59, 63*	60	120	___
6630	IRBM Rocket Launcher, *61*	27	95	___
6636	Alaska Quad Hopper, *59–60*	19	55	___
6640	USMC Rocket Launcher, *60*	85	200	___
6646	Lionel Lines Stock Car, *57*	18	55	___
6650	IRBM Rocket Launcher, *59–63*	23	49	___
6650-80	Missile, *60*	3	9	___
6651	USMC Cannon Car, *64 u*	75	190	___
6656	Lionel Lines Stock Car, *49–55*			
	(A) w/ brown "ARMOUR" decal	47	90	___
	(B) w/o decal	10	25	___
6657	Rio Grande SP-type Caboose, *57–58*	75	195	___
6660	Flatcar w/ crane, *58*	31	75	___
6670	Flatcar w/ crane, *59–60*	18	60	___
6672	Santa Fe Refrigerator Car, *54–56*			
	(A) Blue lettering, 2 lines	25	65	___
	(B) Black lettering, 2 lines	22	65	___
	(C) Blue lettering, 3 lines	85	265	___
6736	Detroit & Mackinac Quad Hopper, *60–62*	13	34	___
6800	Flatcar w/ airplane, *57–60*			
	(A) Yellow plane w/ black top	80	175	___
	(B) Black plane w/ yellow top	75	160	___

		Good	Exc	Cond/$
6801	Flatcar w/ boat, *57–60*			
	(A) Boat with blue hull	45	100	___
	(B) Brownish-yellow boat hull	45	100	___
	(C) Boat with white hull	38	85	___
6802	Flatcar w/ bridge, *58–59*	17	31	___
6803	Flatcar w/ tank and truck, *58–59*	60	135	___
6804	Flatcar w/ USMC trucks, *58–59*	70	165	___
6805	Atomic Disposal Flatcar, *58–59*	55	165	___
6806	Flatcar w/ USMC trucks, *58–59*	70	160	___
6807	Lionel Flatcar w/ boat, *58–59*	60	135	___
6808	Flatcar w/ USMC trucks, *58–59*	100	215	___
6809	Flatcar w/ USMC trucks, *58–59*	70	165	___
6810	Flatcar w/ trailer, *58*	25	50	___
6812	Track Maintenance Car, *59*			
	(A) Dark yellow-gold superstructure	18	80	___
	(B) Black base and gray top	18	80	___
	(C) Gray base, black top	18	80	___
	(D) Cream base and top	19	95	___
	(E) Light yellow base and top	18	80	___
6814	Lionel Rescue Caboose, *59–61*	33	115	___
6816	Flatcar w/ Allis-Chalmers tractor dozer, *59–60*			
	(A) Red car	240	425	___
	(B) Black car	325	730	___
6816-100	Allis-Chalmers tractor dozer, *59–60*			
	(A) No box	75	250	___
	(B) Separate-sale box	250	1000	___
6817	Flatcar w/ Allis-Chalmers motor scraper, *59–60*			
	(A) Red car	230	430	___
	(B) Black car	425	940	___
6817-100	Allis-Chalmers motor scraper, *59–60*			
	(A) No box	105	250	___
	(B) Separate-sale box		NRS	___
6818	Transformer Car, *58*	18	39	___
6819	Flatcar w/ helicopter, *59–60*	19	65	___
6820	Flatcar w/ missile transport helicopter, *60–61*			
	(A) Light blue-painted flatcar	80	205	___
	(B) Darker blue flatcar	50	135	___
6821	Flatcar w/ crates, *59–60*	22	38	___
6822	Searchlight Car, *61–69*			
	(A) Black base, gray light	20	44	___
	(B) Gray base, black light	21	48	___
6823	Flatcar w/ IRBM missiles, *59–60*	33	80	___
6824	USMC Work Caboose, *60*	65	200	___
6825	Flatcar w/ bridge, *59–62*	19	37	___
6826	Flatcar w/ trees, *59–60*	38	80	___

		Good	Exc	Cond/$
6827	Flatcar w/ steam shovel, *60–63*	55	135	___
6827-100	Harnischfeger tractor shovel, *60*			
	(A) No box	55	110	___
	(B) Separate-sale box	105	185	___
6828	Flatcar w/ crane, *60–63, 66*	85	175	___
6828-100	Harnischfeger construction crane, *60*			
	(A) No box	55	135	___
	(B) Separate-sale box	115	225	___
6830	Flatcar w/ submarine, *60–61*	50	110	___
6844	Flatcar w/ missiles, *59–60*			
	(A) Black plastic flatcar	23	90	___
	(B) Red plastic flatcar	300	590	___
A	Transformer, 90 watts, *47–48*	25	70	___
CTC	Lockon (O and O27), *47–69*		0.75	___
ECU-1	Electronic Control Unit, *46*	22	65	___
KW	Transformer, 190 watts, *50–65*	90	120	___
LTC	Lockon (O and O27), *50–69*	2	3	___
LW	Transformer, 125 watts, *55–56*	70	95	___
OC	Curved Track (O), *45–61*		1.50	___
OC1/2	Half Section Curve Track (O), *45–66*		1.50	___
OCS	Curved Insulated Track (O), *46–50*	40	75	___
OS	Straight Track (O), *45–61*		1.50	___
OSS	Straight Insulated Track, *46–50*		75	___
OTC	Lockon Track (O and O27)		3	___
Q	Transformer, 75 watts, *46*	20	60	___
R	Transformer, 110 watts, *46–47*	55	55	___
RW	Transformer, 110 watts, *48–54*	37	55	___
RCS	Remote Control Track (O), *45–48*	5	9	___
S	Transformer, 80 watts, *48*	27	43	___
SP	Smoke Pellets, bottle, *48–69*	8	30	___
SW	Transformer, 130 watts, *61–66*	49	90	___
TW	Transformer, 175 watts, *53–60*	55	95	___
TOC	Curved Track (O), *62–66, 68–69*		1.50	___
TOC1/2	Half Section Straight Track (O), *62–66*		1.50	___
TOS	Straight Track (O), *62–69*		1.50	___
UCS	Remote Control Track (O), *45–69*	8	16	___
UTC	Lockon (O, O27, Standard), *45*		1.50	___
V	Transformer, 150 watts, *46–47*	85	150	___
VW	Transformer, 150 watts, *48–49*	65	110	___
Z	Transformer, 250 watts, *45–47*	65	125	___
ZW	Transformer, 250 watts, *48–49*	105	210	___
ZW	Transformer, 275 watts, *50–66*	140	170	___

Unnumbered Items

Flatcar (see 6401, 6402, 6406)
Gondola (see 6142)
Hopper (see 6176)
Rolling Stock (see 3413, 3510, 6111, 6121, 6151, 6407, 6408, 6409, 6469, 6500, 6501, 6502, 6512)
SP-type Caboose, (see 6067, 6167)
Turbo Missile Car (see 3309, 3349)
Work Caboose, (see 6119-125, 6120)

Section 3
MODERN ERA 1970-2008

		Exc	New	Cond/$
79C95204C	Sears Santa Fe Diesel Set, *71 u*	150	165	___
79C9715C	Sears 4-unit Set, *75 u*	50	65	___
79C9717C	Sears 7-unit Set, *75 u*	150	165	___
79N95223C	Sears 6-unit Set, *74 u*	150	165	___
79N9552C	Sears 6-unit Set, *72 u*	150	165	___
79N9553C	Sears 6-unit Diesel Set, *72 u*	150	165	___
79N96178C	Sears 4-unit Set, *74 u*	50	65	___
79N97082C	Sears Set, *70 u*		NRS	___
79N97101C	Sears 5-unit Set, *75 u*	150	165	___
79N98765C	Sears Logging Empire Set, *78 u*	100	115	___
0512	Toy Fair Reefer, *81 u*	60	70	___
550C	Curved Track 31" (O), *70*	0.85	1.50	___
550S	Straight Track (O), *70*	0.85	1.50	___
634	Santa Fe NW-2, *70 u*	55	110	___
665E	Johnny Cash "Blue Train" 4-6-4, *71 u*		NRS	___
1050	New Englander Set, *80–81*	155	205	___
1051	T&P Diesel Set, *80*		NM	___
1052	Chesapeake Flyer Set, *80*	140	150	___
1053	The James Gang Set, *80–82*	155	195	___
1070	The Royal Limited Set, *80*	285	350	___
1071	Mid Atlantic Limited Set, *80*	225	230	___
1072	Cross Country Express Set, *80–81*	240	385	___
1076	Lionel Clock, *76–77 u*	590	680	___
1081	Wabash Cannonball Set, *70–72*	105	120	___
1082	Yard Boss Set, *70*	120	165	___
1083	Pacemaker Set, *70*	105	120	___
1084	Grand Trunk & Western Set, *70*	120	140	___
1085	Santa Fe Express Diesel Freight Set, *70*	175	190	___
1086	The Mountaineer Set, *70*		NM	___
1087	Midnight Express Set, *70*		NM	___
1091	Sears Special Set, *70 u*	150	165	___
1092	79N97081C Sears Set, *70 u*	150	165	___
1092	79C97105C Sears 6-unit Set, *71 u*	150	165	___
1100	Happy Huff n' Puff, *74–75 u*	55	70	___
1150	L.A.S.E.R. Train Set, *81–82*	155	195	___
1151	Union Pacific Thunder Freight Set, *81–82*	150	175	___

		Exc	New	Cond/$
1153	JCPenney Thunderball Freight Set, *81 u*	165	180	___
1154	Reading Yard King Set, *81–82*	170	190	___
1155	Cannonball Freight Set, *82*	75	85	___
1157	Lionel Leisure Wabash Cannonball Set, *81 u*		250	___
1158	Maple Leaf Limited Set, *81*	405	435	___
1159	Toys "R" Us Midnight Flyer Set, *81 u*	130	140	___
1160	Great Lakes Limited Set, *81*	280	330	___
T-1171	CN Steam Locomotive Set, *71 u*	240	275	___
T-1172	Yardmaster Set, *71 u*		200	___
T-1173	Grand Trunk & Western Set, *71–73 u*	175	195	___
T-1174	Canadian National Set, *71–73 u*	265	300	___
1182	The Yardmaster Set, *71–72*	85	105	___
1183	The Silver Star Set, *71–72*	65	80	___
1184	The Allegheny Set, *71*	120	150	___
1186	Cross Country Express Set, *71–72*	210	260	___
1187	Illinois Central Set (SSS), *71*	400	485	___
1190	Sears Special #1 Set, *71 u*	85	100	___
1195	JCPenney Special Set, *71 u*	150	165	___
1198	Unnamed Set, *71 u*		175	___
1199	Ford-Autolite Allegheny Set, *71 u*	175	195	___
1200	Gravel Gus, *75 u*	75	100	___
1250	New York Central Set (SSS), *72*	315	380	___
1252	Heavy Iron Set, *82–83*	90	130	___
1253	Quicksilver Express Set, *82–83*	265	340	___
1254	Black Cave Flyer Set, *82*	75	105	___
1260	Continental Limited Set, *82*	290	385	___
1261	49N95211 Sears Black Cave Flyer Set, *82 u*	165	195	___
1262	Toys "R" Us Heavy Iron Set, *82 u*	150	165	___
1263	XU671-0701A JCPenney Overland Freight Set, *82 u*	150	165	___
1264	Nibco Express Set, *82 u*	190	195	___
1265	Tappan Special Set, *82 u*	130	155	___
T-1272	Yardmaster Set, *72–73 u*	150	165	___
T-1273	Silver Star Set, *72–73 u*	90	115	___
1280	Kickapoo Valley & Northern Set, *72*	60	75	___
1284	Allegheny Set, *72*	140	165	___
1285	Santa Fe Twin Diesel Set, *72*	95	140	___
1287	Pioneer Dockside Switcher Set, *72*	95	100	___
1290	Sears Set, *72 u*	150	165	___
1291	Sears Set, *72 u*	150	165	___
1300	Gravel Gus Junior, *75 u*	70	90	___

		Exc	New	Cond/$
1350	Canadian Pacific Set (SSS), *73*	460	620	___
1351	Baltimore & Ohio Set, *83–84*	205	280	___
1352	Rocky Mountain Freight Set, *83–84*	75	95	___
1353	Southern Streak Set, *83–85*	75	95	___
1354	Northern Freight Flyer Set, *83–85*	230	280	___
1355	Commando Assault Train Set, *83–84*	175	280	___
1359	Train Display Case for Set 1355, *83 u*	75	95	___
1361	Gold Coast Limited Set, *83*	390	400	___
1362	Lionel Leisure BN Express Set, *83 u*	200	300	___
1380	U.S. Steel Industrial Switcher Set, *73–75*	60	75	___
1381	Cannonball, *73–75*	70	75	___
1382	Yardmaster Set, *73–74*	110	135	___
1383	Santa Fe Freight Set, *73–75*	100	125	___
1384	Southern Express Set, *73–76*	75	120	___
1385	Blue Streak Freight Set, *73–74*	100	120	___
1386	Rock Island Express Set, *73–74*	120	140	___
1387	Milwaukee Road Special Set, *73*	185	285	___
1388	Golden State Arrow Set, *73–75*	215	240	___
1390	Sears 7-unit Set, *73 u*	170	190	___
1392	79C95224C Sears 8-unit Set, *73 u*	150	165	___
1393	79C95223C Sears 6-unit Set, *73 u*	150	165	___
1395	JCPenney Set, *73 u*	150	165	___
1400	Happy Huff n' Puff Junior, *75 u*	130	140	___
1402	Chessie System Set, *84–85*	125	150	___
1403	Redwood Valley Express Set, *84–85*	170	205	___
1450	D&RGW Set (SSS), *74*	335	415	___
1451	Erie-Lackawanna Limited Set, *84*	415	465	___
1460	Grand National Set, *74*	300	330	___
1461	Black Diamond Set, *74 u, 75*	100	120	___
1463	Coca-Cola Special Set, *74 u, 75*	175	220	___
1487	Broadway Limited Set, *74–75*	160	255	___
1489	Santa Fe Double Diesel Set, *74–76*	140	165	___
1492	79N96185C Sears 7-unit Set, *74 u*	150	165	___
1493	79N96185C Sears 7-unit Set, *74 u*	150	165	___
1499	JCPenney Great Express Set, *74 u*	150	165	___
1501	Midland Freight Set, *85–86*	75	95	___
1502	Yard Chief Set, *85–86*	205	230	___
1506	Sears Chessie System Set, *85 u*	165	195	___
1512	JCPenney Midland Freight Set, *85 u*	90	115	___
1549	Toys "R" Us Heavy Iron Set, *85–89 u*	180	215	___

		Exc	New	Cond/$
1552	Burlington Northern Limited Set, *85*	500	570	___
1560	North American Express Set, *75*	275	365	___
1562	Fast Freight Flyer Set, *85 u*	120	140	___
1577	Liberty Special Set, *75 u*	205	205	___
1579	Milwaukee Road Set (SSS), *75*	325	410	___
1581	Thunderball Freight Set, *75–76*	90	100	___
1582	Yard Chief Set, *75–76*	115	155	___
1584	N&W "Spirit of America" Set, *75*	160	180	___
1585	75th Anniversary Special Set, *75–77*	190	205	___
1586	Chesapeake Flyer Set, *75–77*	160	190	___
1587	Capitol Limited Set, *75*	270	300	___
1593	Sears Set, *75 u*		100	___
1595	79C9716C Sears 6-unit Set, *75 u*	150	165	___
1602	Nickel Plate Special Set, *86–91*	120	125	___
1606	Sears Nickel Plate Special Set, *86 u*	165	195	___
1608	American Express General Set, *86 u*	205	320	___
1615	Cannonball Express Set, *86–90*	65	75	___
1632	Santa Fe Work Train Set (SSS), *86*	220	255	___
1652	B&O Freight Set, *86*	140	185	___
1658	Town House TV and Appliances Set, *86 u*	80	95	___
1660	Yard Boss Set, *76*	100	115	___
1661	Rock Island Line Set, *76–77*	80	100	___
1662	Black River Freight Set, *76–78*	75	95	___
1663	Amtrak Lake Shore Limited Set, *76–77*	215	265	___
1664	Illinois Central Freight Set, *76–77*	265	355	___
1665	NYC Empire State Express Set, *76*	310	435	___
1672	Northern Pacific Set (SSS), *76*	215	280	___
1685	True Value Freight Flyer Set, *86–87 u*	60	75	___
1686	Kay Bee Toys Freight Flyer Set, *86 u*	150	165	___
1687	Freight Flyer Set, *87–90*	39	47	___
1693	Toys "R" Us Rock Island Line Set, *76 u*	110	130	___
1694	Toys "R" Us Black River Freight Set, *76 u*	110	130	___
1696	Sears Set, *76 u*	110	130	___
1698	True Value Rock Island Line Set, *76 u*	125	145	___
1760	Trains n' Truckin' Steel Hauler Set, *77–78*	105	110	___
1761	Trains n' Truckin' Cargo King Set, *77–78*	95	165	___
1762	Wabash Cannonball Set, *77*	135	190	___
1764	Heartland Express Set, *77*	185	240	___
1765	Rocky Mountain Special Set, *77*	210	315	___
1766	B&O Budd Car Set (SSS), *77*	335	390	___

		Exc	New	Cond/$
1776	Seaboard U36B, *74–76*	175	260	___
1790	Lionel Leisure Steel Hauler Set, *77 u*	150	200	___
1791	Toys "R" Us Steel Hauler Set, *77 u*	130	175	___
1792	True Value Rock IslandLine Set, *77 u*	100	135	___
1793	Toys "R" Us Black River Freight Set, *77 u*	120	155	___
1796	JCPenney Cargo Master Set, *77 u*		200	___
1860	Workin' on the Railroad Timberline Set, *78*	65	85	___
1862	Workin' on the Railroad Logging Empire Set, *78*	85	110	___
1864	Santa Fe Double Diesel Set, *78–79*	155	190	___
1865	Chesapeake Flyer Set, *78–79*	155	180	___
1866	Great Plains Express Set, *78–79*	195	285	___
1867	Milwaukee Road Limited Set, *78*	230	275	___
1868	M&StL Set (SSS), *78*	215	255	___
1892	JCPenney Logging Empire Set, *78 u*	95	125	___
1893	Toys "R" Us Logging Empire Set, *78 u*	175	225	___
1960	Midnight Flyer Set, *79–81*	55	75	___
1962	Wabash Cannonball Set, *79*	90	105	___
1963	Black River Freight Set, *79–81*	75	85	___
1964	Radio Control Express Set, *79 u*		NM	___
1965	Smokey Mountain Line Set, *79*	65	85	___
1970	Southern Pacific Limited Set, *79 u*	340	365	___
1971	Quaker City Limited Set, *79*	315	335	___
1990	Mystery Glow Midnight Flyer Set, *79 u*	75	90	___
1991	JCPenney Wabash Cannonball Deluxe Express Set, *79 u*	150	165	___
1993	Toys "R" Us Midnight Flyer Set, *79 u*	110	130	___
2110	Graduated Trestle Set (22), *70–88*	9	13	___
2111	Elevated Trestle Set (10), *70–88*	8	11	___
2113	Tunnel Portals (2), *84–87*	11	17	___
2115	Dwarf Signal, *84–87*	12	13	___
2117	Block Target Signal, *84–87*	23	29	___
2122	Extension Bridge w/ rock piers, *76–87*	24	34	___
2125	Whistling Freight Shed, *71*	36	43	___
2126	Whistling Freight Shed, *76–87*	25	26	___
2127	Diesel Horn Shed, *76–87*	25	30	___
2128	Operating Switchman, *83–86*	26	29	___
2129	Illuminated Freight Station, *83–86*	30	33	___
2133	Lighted Freight Station, *72–78*, *80–84*	34	38	___
2140	Automatic Banjo Signal, *70–84*	17	21	___
2145	Automatic Gateman, *72–84*	31	47	___
2151	Operating Semaphore, *78–82*	15	19	___

		Exc	New	Cond/$
2152	Automatic Crossing Gate, *70–84*	21	25	___
2154	Automatic Highway Flasher, *70–87*	19	24	___
2156	Illuminated Station Platform, *70–71*	26	34	___
2162	Automatic Crossing Gate and Signal "262", *70–87, 94, 96–98, 05*	16	27	___
2163	Block Target Signal, *70–78*	14	19	___
2170	Street Lamps (3), *70–87*	13	19	___
2171	Gooseneck Street Lamps (2), *80–81, 83–84*	15	18	___
2175	Sandy Andy Gravel Loader Kit, *76–79*	34	55	___
2180	Road Signs (16) "307", *77–98*		6	___
2181	Telephone Pole Set "150", *77–98*		5	___
2195	Floodlight Tower, *70–71*	38	50	___
2199	Microwave Tower, *72–75*	30	39	___
2214	Girder Bridge, *70–71, 72 u, 73–87*	5	9	___
2256	Station Platform, *73–81*	17	18	___
2260	Illuminated Bumper, *70–71, 72 u, 73*	23	35	___
2280	Non-Illuminated Bumpers (3), *73–84*	2.50	4	___
2282	Die-Cast Bumpers (2), *83 u*	17	18	___
2283	Die-Cast Illuminated Bumpers "260", *84–99*	15	16	___
2290	Illuminated Bumpers (2), *75 u, 76–86*	10	11	___
2292	Station Platform, *85–87*	5	9	___
2300	Operating Oil Drum Loader, *83–87*	80	90	___
2301	Operating Sawmill, *80–84*	60	65	___
2302	Union Pacific Manual Gantry Crane, *80–82*	24	31	___
2303	Santa Fe Manual Gantry Crane, *80–81, 83 u*	17	21	___
2305	Getty Operating Oil Derrick, *81–84*	105	115	___
2306	Operating Ice Station w/ 6700 PFE Ice Car, *82–83*	90	105	___
2307	Lighted Billboard, *82–86*	12	13	___
2308	Animated Newsstand, *82–83*	105	120	___
2309	Mechanical Crossing Gate, *82–92*	4	7	___
2310	Mechanical Crossing Gate, *73–77*	2.50	4	___
2311	Mechanical Semaphore, *82–92*	4	7	___
2312	Mechanical Semaphore, *73–77*	2.50	4	___
2313	Floodlight Tower, *75–86*	22	27	___
2314	Searchlight Tower, *75–84*	22	27	___
2315	Operating Coaling Station, *83–84*	80	105	___
2316	N&W Operating Gantry Crane, *83–84*	90	125	___
2317	Operating Drawbridge, *75 u, 76–81*	100	130	___
2318	Operating Control Tower, *83–86*	60	65	___
2319	Illuminated Watchtower, *75–78, 80*	22	26	___

		Exc	New	Cond/$
2320	Flagpole Kit, *83–87*	10	14	___
2321	Operating Sawmill, *84, 86–87*	115	145	___
2323	Operating Freight Station, *84–87*	43	47	___
2324	Operating Switch Tower, *84–87*	60	65	___
2390	Lionel Mirror, *82 u*	60	100	___
2494	Rotary Beacon, *72–74*	37	44	___
2709	Rico Station Kit, *81–98*		42	___
2710	Billboards (5), *70–84*	4	10	___
2714	Tunnel, *75 u, 76–77*	36	43	___
2716	Short Extension Bridge, *88–98*	3	8	___
2717	Short Extension Bridge, *77–87*	2.50	4	___
2718	Barrel Platform Kit, *77–84*	3	5	___
2719	Watchman's Shanty Kit, *77–87*	3	5	___
2720	Lumber Shed Kit, *77–84, 87*	3	5	___
2721	Operating Log Mill Kit, *78*	2.50	4	___
2722	Barrel Loader Kit, *78*	2.50	4	___
2729	Water Tower Kit, *85*		NM	___
2783	Freight Station Kit, *84*	6	10	___
2784	Freight Platform Kit, *81–90*	5	8	___
2785	Engine House Kit, *73–77*	31	39	___
2786	Freight Platform Kit, *73–77*	4	6	___
2787	Freight Station Kit, *73–77, 83*	7	10	___
2788	Coal Station Kit, *75 u, 76–77*	18	30	___
2789	Water Tower Kit, *75–77, 80*	19	24	___
2791	Cross Country Set, *70–71*	22	30	___
2792	Whistle Stop Set, *70–71*	24	34	___
2792	Layout Starter Pack, *80–84*	9	21	___
2793	Alamo Junction Set, *70–71*	22	30	___
2796	Grain Elevator Kit, *76 u, 77*	43	47	___
2797	Rico Station Kit, *76–77*	23	37	___
2900	Lockon, *70–98*		1.50	___
2901	Track Clips (12) (O27), *71–98*		6	___
2905	Lockon and Wire, *74–00*		3	___
2909	Smoke Fluid, *70–98*		4	___
2910	OTC Contactor, *84–86, 88*	4	7	___
2911	Smoke Pellets, *70–73*	10	12	___
2925	Lubricant, *70–71, 72 u, 73–75*		1.50	___
2927	Maintenance Kit, *70, 78–98*		11	___
2928	Oil, *71*		1.50	___
2951	Track Layout Book, *70–86*	0.85	1.50	___

		Exc	New	Cond/$
2952	Train and Accessory Manual, *70–74*	0.85	1.50	___
2953	Train and Accessory Manual, *75–86*	0.85	1.50	___
2960	Lionel 75th Anniversary Book, *75 u, 76*	10	22	___
2980	Magnetic Conversion Coupler, *70–71*	0.85	1.50	___
2985	The Lionel Train Book, *86–98*		11	___
3100	Great Northern 4-8-4 (FARR #3), *81*	335	415	___
4044	Transformer, 45-watt, *70–71*	2.50	4	___
4045	Safety Transformer, *70–71*	2.50	3	___
4050	Safety Transformer, *72–79*	2.50	3	___
4060	Power Master Transformer, *80–93*		13	___
4065	DC Hobby Transformer, *81–83*	2.50	3	___
4090	Power Master Transformer, *70–84*	47	65	___
4125	Transformer, 25-watt, *72*	2.50	3	___
4150	Trainmaster Transformer, *72–73, 75–77*	6	15	___
4250	Trainmaster Transformer, *74*	5	10	___
4651	Trainmaster Transformer, *78–79*	1.50	2.50	___
4690	MW Transformer, *86–89*	60	80	___
4851	DC Transformer, *85–91, 94–96*	5	10	___
4870	DC Hobby Transformer and Throttle Controller, *77–78*	2.50	3	___
5012	Curved Track 27", card of 4 (O27), *70–96*		17	___
5013	Curved Track 27" (O27), *70–78*		0.45	___
5014	Half-Curved Track 27" (O27), *70–98*		0.70	___
5016	36" Straight Track (O27), *87–88*	1.50	2.50	___
5017	Straight Track, card of 4 (O27), *70–96*		4	___
5018	Straight Track (O27), *70–78*	0.45	0.65	___
5019	Half-Straight Track (O27), *70–98*		0.70	___
5020	90° Crossover (O27), *70–98*		7	___
5021	Left Manual Switch 27" (O27), *70–98*	15	15	___
5022	Right Manual Switch 27" (O27), *70–98*		15	___
5023	45° Crossover (O27), *70–98*		6	___
5024	35" Straight Track (O27), *88–98, 05*		CP	___
5025	Manumatic Uncoupler, *71–72*	0.85	1.50	___
5027	Pair Manual Switches 27" (O27), *74–84*	13	21	___
5030	Track Expander Set (O27), *71–84*	18	26	___
5031	Ford-Autolite Layout Expander Set, *71 u*	50	65	___
5033	Curved Track 27" (O27), *79–98*		0.85	___
5038	Straight Track (O27), *79–98*		0.85	___
5041	Insulator Pins (12) (O27), *70–98*		1.50	___
5042	Steel Pins (12) (O27), *70–98*		1.50	___
5044	Curved Track Ballast 42" (O27), *88*		NM	___

		Exc	New	Cond/$
5045	Curved Track Ballast 54" (O27), *87–88*	0.85	1.50	___
5046	Curved Track Ballast 27" (O27), *87–88*	0.85	1.50	___
5047	Straight Track Ballast (O27), *87–88*	0.85	1.50	___
5049	Curved Track 42" (O27), *88–98*	0.85	1.50	___
5090	Manual Switches 27", 3 pair, (O27), *78–84*	55	70	___
5113	Curved Track 54" (O27), *79–98*	0.85	1.50	___
5121	Left Remote Switch 27" (O27), *70–98*	18	22	___
5122	Right Remote Switch 27" (O27), *70–98*	20	22	___
5125	Pair Remote Switches 27" (O27), *71–83*	20	30	___
5132	Right Remote Switch 31" (O), *80–94*	29	30	___
5133	Left Remote Switch 31" (O), *80–94*	22	30	___
5149	Remote Uncoupling Section (O27), *70–98*		7	___
5165	Right Remote Switch 72" (O), *87–98*	23	65	___
5166	Left Remote Switch 72" (O), *87–98*	23	75	___
5167	Right Remote Switch 42" (O27), *88–98*	25	37	___
5168	Left Remote Switch 42" (O27), *88–98*	25	37	___
5193	Remote Switches 27", 3 pair, (O27), *78–83*	80	95	___
5500	Straight Track 10" (O), *71–98*		1.50	___
5501	Curved Track 31" (O), *71–98*		1.50	___
5502	Remote Uncoupling Section (O), *71–72*	7	9	___
5504	Half Curved Track 31" (O), *83–98*		0.85	___
5505	Half Straight Track (O), *83–98*		0.85	___
5520	90° Crossover (O), *71–72*	6	9	___
5522	36" Straight, *87–88*		3	___
5523	40" Straight Track (O), *88–98*		4	___
5530	Remote Uncoupling Section (O), *81–98*	10	19	___
5540	90° Crossover (O), *81–98*		10	___
5543	Insulator Pins (12) (O), *70–98*		1.50	___
5545	45° Crossover (O), *83–98*		11	___
5551	Steel Pins (12) (O), *70–98*		1.50	___
5554	Curved Track 54" (O), *90–98*		2.50	___
5560	Curved Track Ballast 72" (O), *87–88*	0.85	1.50	___
5561	Curved Track Ballast 31" (O), *87–88*	0.85	1.50	___
5562	Straight Track Ballast (O), *87–88*	0.85	1.50	___
5572	Curved Track 72" (O), *79–98*	2	3	___
5600	Curved Track (TT), *73–74*	0.85	1.50	___
5601	Curved Track, card of 4 (TT), *73–74*	6	10	___
5602	Curved Track Ballast, card of 4 (TT), *73–74*	5	9	___
5605	Straight Track (TT), *73–74*	0.85	1.50	___
5606	Straight Track, card of 4 (TT), *73–74*	5	9	___

		Exc	New	Cond/$
5607	Straight Track Ballast, card of 4 (TT), *73–74*	5	9	___
5620	Left Manual Switch (TT), *73–74*	4	13	___
5625	Left Remote Switch (TT), *73–74*	9	17	___
5630	Right Manual Switch (TT), *73–74*	4	13	___
5635	Right Remote Switch (TT), *73–74*	9	17	___
5640	Left Switch Ballast, card of 2 (TT), *73–74*	5	9	___
5650	Right Switch Ballast, card of 2 (TT), *73–74*	5	9	___
5655	Lockon (TT), *73–74*	0.85	1.50	___
5660	Terminal Track w/ lockon (TT), *74*	1.50	3	___
5700	Oppenheimer Reefer, *81*	30	38	___
5701	Dairymen's League Reefer, *81*	21	23	___
5702	National Dairy Despatch Reefer, *81*	16	21	___
5703	North American Despatch Reefer, *81*	22	26	___
5704	Budweiser Reefer, *81–82*	60	65	___
5705	Ball Glass Jars Reefer, *81–82*	30	35	___
5706	Lindsay Brothers Reefer, *81–82*	26	27	___
5707	American Refrigerator Reefer, *81–82*	20	20	___
5708	Armour Reefer, *82–83*	16	21	___
5709	REA Reefer, *82–83*	22	26	___
5710	Canadian Pacific Reefer, *82–83*	22	25	___
5711	Commercial Express Reefer, *82–83*	13	15	___
5712	Lionel Lines Reefer, *82 u*	165	195	___
5713	Cotton Belt Reefer, *83–84*	19	22	___
5714	Michigan Central Reefer, *83–84*	17	24	___
5715	Santa Fe Reefer, *83–84*	19	26	___
5716	Central Vermont Reefer, *83–84*	20	23	___
5717	Santa Fe Bunk Car, *83*	22	30	___
5719	Canadian National Reefer, *84*	15	16	___
5720	Great Northern Reefer, *84*	75	90	___
5721	Soo Line Reefer, *84*	21	23	___
5722	NKP Reefer, *84*	16	18	___
5724	PRR Bunk Car, *84*	20	22	___
5726	Southern Bunk Car, *84 u*	22	27	___
5727	USMC Bunk Car, *84–85*	25	30	___
5728	Canadian Pacific Bunk Car, *86*	18	23	___
5730	Strasburg RR Reefer, *85–86*	20	27	___
5731	L&N Reefer, *85–86*	19	24	___
5732	Jersey Central Reefer, *85–86*		24	___
5733	Lionel Lines Bunk Car, *86 u*	18	24	___
5735	NYC Bunk Car, *85–86*	33	35	___

		Exc	New	Cond/$
5739	B&O Tool Car, *86*	32	37	___
5745	Santa Fe Bunk Car (SSS), *86*	39	45	___
5760	Santa Fe Tool Car (SSS), *86*	30	35	___
5900	AC/DC Converter, *79–83*	3	5	___
6076	LV Hopper (O27), *70 u*	17	21	___
6100	ON Covered Quad Hopper, *81–82*	30	34	___
6101	BN Covered Quad Hopper, *81–82*	17	31	___
6102	GN Covered Quad Hopper (FARR #3), *81*	26	28	___
6103	Canadian National Covered Quad Hopper, *81*	35	38	___
6104	Southern Quad Hopper w/ coal load (FARR #4), *83*	50	60	___
6105	Reading Operating Hopper, *82*	34	39	___
6106	N&W Covered Quad Hopper, *82*	30	40	___
6107	Shell Covered Quad Hopper, *82*	22	26	___
6109	C&O Operating Hopper, *83*	29	41	___
6110	MP Covered Quad Hopper, *83–84*	17	27	___
6111	L&N Covered Quad Hopper, *83–84*	13	20	___
6113	Illinois Central Hopper (O27), *83–85*	15	25	___
6114	C&NW Covered Quad Hopper, *83*	75	85	___
6115	Southern Hopper (O27), *83–86*	15	19	___
6116	Soo Line Ore Car, *84*	21	29	___
6117	Erie Operating Hopper, *84*	29	39	___
6118	Erie Covered Quad Hopper, *84*	31	45	___
6122	Penn Central Ore Car, *84*	20	25	___
6123	PRR Covered Quad Hopper (FARR #5), *84–85*	55	105	___
6124	D&H Covered Quad Hopper, *84*	19	32	___
6126	Canadian National Ore Car, *86*	18	24	___
6127	Northern Pacific Ore Car, *86*	20	24	___
6131	Illinois Terminal Covered Quad Hopper, *85–86*	15	21	___
6134	Burlington Northern 2-Bay ACF Hopper (Std. O), *86 u*	95	115	___
6135	C&NW 2-Bay ACF Hopper (Std. O), *86 u*	65	80	___
6137	NKP Hopper (O27), *86–91*	13	17	___
6138	B&O Quad Hopper w/ coal load, *86*	21	28	___
6142	Lionel Gondola, black, 1970	15	25	___
6150	Santa Fe Hopper (O27), *85–86, 92 u*	10	15	___
6177	Reading Hopper (O27), *86–90*	14	19	___
6200	FEC Gondola w/ canisters, *81–82*	13	24	___
6201	Union Pacific Animated Gondola, *82–83*	19	25	___
6202	WM Gondola w/ coal load, *82*	34	36	___
6203	Black Cave Gondola (O27), *82*	2.50	4	___

		Exc	New	Cond/$
6205	CP Gondola w/ canisters, *83*	18	26	___
6206	C&IM Gondola w/ canisters, *83–85*	18	26	___
6207	Southern Gondola w/ canisters (O27), *83–85*	6	8	___
6208	Chessie System Gondola w/ canisters, *83 u*	21	24	___
6209	NYC Gondola w/ coal load (Std. O), *84–85*	42	46	___
6210	Erie-Lackawanna Gondola w/ canisters, *84*	21	30	___
6211	C&O Gondola w/ canisters, *84–85*		10	___
6214	Lionel Lines Gondola w/ canisters, *84 u*	38	45	___
6230	Erie-Lackawanna Reefer (Std. O), *86 u*	95	120	___
6231	Railgon Gondola w/ coal load (Std. O), *86 u*	80	90	___
6232	Illinois Central Boxcar (Std. O), *86 u*	65	80	___
6233	CP Flatcar w/ stakes (Std. O), *86 u*	47	50	___
6234	Burlington Northern Boxcar (Std. O), *85*	55	75	___
6235	Burlington Northern Boxcar (Std. O), *85*	33	43	___
6236	Burlington Northern Boxcar (Std. O), *85*	33	43	___
6237	Burlington Northern Boxcar (Std. O), *85*	32	47	___
6238	Burlington Northern Boxcar (Std. O), *85*	33	43	___
6239	Burlington Northern Boxcar (Std. O), *86 u*	37	55	___
6251	NYC Coal Dump Car, *85*	25	42	___
6254	NKP Gondola w/ canisters, *86–91*	10	11	___
6258	Santa Fe Gondola w/ canisters (O27), *85–86, 92 u*		3	___
X6260	NYC Gondola w/ canisters, *85–86*	13	15	___
6272	Santa Fe Gondola w/ cable reels (SSS), *86*	20	25	___
6300	Corn Products 3-D Tank Car, *81–82*	19	25	___
6301	Gulf 1-D Tank Car, *81*	20	26	___
6302	Quaker State 3-D Tank Car, *81*	38	42	___
6304	GN 1-D Tank Car (FARR #3), *81*	44	55	___
6305	British Columbia 1-D Tank Car, *81*	55	85	___
6306	Southern 1-D Tank Car (FARR #4), *83*	45	50	___
6307	PRR 1-D Tank Car (FARR #5), *84–85*	70	75	___
6308	Alaska 1-D Tank Car (O27), *82–83*	27	35	___
6310	Shell 2-D Tank Car (O27), *83–84*	19	24	___
6312	C&O 2-D Tank Car (O27), *84–85*	18	26	___
6313	Lionel Lines 1-D Tank Car, *84 u*	43	50	___
6314	B&O 3-D Tank Car, *86*	31	38	___
6317	Gulf 2-D Tank Car (O27), *84–85*	18	22	___
6357	Frisco 1-D Tank Car, *83*	42	50	___
6401	Virginian B/W Caboose, *81*	37	47	___
6403	Amtrak Vista Dome Car (O27), *76–77*	30	31	___
6404	Amtrak Passenger Car (O27), *76–77*	24	31	___

		Exc	New	Cond/$
6405	Amtrak Passenger Car (O27), *76–77*	24	31	___
6406	Amtrak Observation Car (O27), *76–77*	22	29	___
6410	Amtrak Passenger Car (O27), *77*	28	48	___
6411	Amtrak Passenger Car (O27), *77*	24	35	___
6412	Amtrak Vista Dome Car (O27), *77*	22	33	___
6420	Reading Transfer Caboose, *81–82*	20	28	___
6421	Joshua L. Cowen B/W Caboose, *82*	34	40	___
6422	DM&IR B/W Caboose, *81*	32	38	___
6425	Erie-Lackawanna B/W Caboose, *83–84*	35	43	___
6426	Reading Transfer Caboose, *82–83*	14	24	___
6427	BN Transfer Caboose, *83–84*	12	21	___
6428	C&NW Transfer Caboose, *83–85*	22	25	___
6430	Santa Fe SP-type Caboose, *83–89*	4	7	___
6431	Southern B/W Caboose (FARR #4), *83*	42	55	___
6432	Union Pacific SP-type Caboose, *81–82*	9	10	___
6433	Canadian Pacific B/W Caboose, *81*	60	70	___
6435	U.S. Transfer Caboose, *83–84*	9	17	___
6438	GN B/W Caboose (FARR #3), *81*	48	65	___
6439	Reading B/W Caboose, *84–85*	22	30	___
6441	Alaska B/W Caboose, *82–83*	45	50	___
6446-25	N&W Covered Quad Hopper, *70 u*	130	230	___
6449	Wendy's N5C Caboose, *81–82*	50	60	___
6464-500	Timken Boxcar, yellow, *70 u*	225	350	___
6464-2003	Maddox Retirement Boxcar, *02*		100	___
6476-135	LV Hopper "25000" (O27), *70–71 u*	6	11	___
6478	Black Cave SP-type Caboose, *82*	5	9	___
6482	Nibco Express SP-type Caboose, *82 u*	26	34	___
6485	Chessie System SP-type Caboose, *84–85*	6	10	___
6486	Southern SP-type Caboose, *83–85*	5	7	___
6490	NKP N5C Caboose, *84 u*		NRS	___
6491	Erie-Lackawanna Transfer Caboose, *85–86*	9	17	___
6493	L&C B/W Caboose, *86–87*	21	34	___
6494	Santa Fe Bobber Caboose, *85–86*	7	9	___
6496	Santa Fe Work Caboose (SSS), *86*	21	29	___
6504	L.A.S.E.R. Flatcar w/ helicopter (O27), *81–82*	18	26	___
6505	L.A.S.E.R. Radar Car, *81–82*	17	25	___
6506	L.A.S.E.R. Security Car, *81–82*	18	26	___
6507	L.A.S.E.R. Flatcar w/ cruise missile, *81–82*	21	30	___
6508	Canadian Pacific Crane Car, *81*	50	70	___
6509	Depressed Flatcar w/ girders, *81*	60	85	___

		Exc	New	Cond/$
6510	Union Pacific Crane Car, *82*	55	60	___
6515	Union Pacific Flatcar (O27), *83–84, 86*	5	9	___
6521	NYC Flatcar w/ stakes (Std. O), *84–85*	29	35	___
6522	C&NW Searchlight Car, *83–85*	27	30	___
6524	Erie Crane Car, *84*	55	60	___
6526	Searchlight Car, *84–85*	23	25	___
6529	NYC Searchlight Car, *85–86*	21	27	___
6531	Express Mail Flatcar w/ trailers, *85–86*	23	32	___
6560	Bucyrus Erie Crane Car, *71*	100	130	___
6561	Flatcar w/ cruise missile (O27), *83–84*	13	26	___
6562	Flatcar w/ fences (O27), *83–84*	13	21	___
6564	Flatcar w/ 2 USMC tanks (O27), *83–84*	13	21	___
6573	Redwood Valley Express Flatcar w/ dump bin (O27), *84–85*	8	13	___
6574	Redwood Valley Express Flatcar w/ crane (O27), *84–85*	7	13	___
6575	Redwood Valley Express Flatcar w/ fences (O27), *84–85*	7	13	___
6576	Santa Fe Flatcar w/ crane (O27), *85–86, 92 u*	7	10	___
6579	NYC Crane Car, *85–86*	36	44	___
6585	PRR Flatcar w/ fences (O27), *86–90*	5	9	___
6587	W&ARR Flatcar w/ horses, *86 u*	18	26	___
6593	Santa Fe Crane Car (SSS), *86*	41	48	___
6700	PFE Ice Car, *82–83*		70	___
6900	N&W E/V Caboose, *82*	60	65	___
6901	Ontario Northland E/V Caboose, *82 u*	44	55	___
6903	Santa Fe E/V Caboose, *83*	80	95	___
6904	Union Pacific E/V Caboose, *83*	115	135	___
6905	NKP E/V Caboose, *83 u*	50	65	___
6906	Erie-Lackawanna E/V Caboose, *84*	75	90	___
6907	NYC Wood-sided Caboose (Std. O), *86 u*	90	100	___
6908	PRR N5C Caboose (FARR #5), *84–85*	43	47	___
6910	NYC E/V Caboose, *84 u*	55	60	___
6912	Redwood Valley Express SP-type Caboose *84–85*	9	16	___
6913	Burlington Northern E/V Caboose, *85*	70	90	___
6916	NYC Work Caboose, *85–86*	16	22	___
6917	Jersey Central E/V Caboose, *86*	42	50	___
6918	B&O SP-type Caboose, *86*	10	15	___
6919	Nickel Plate Road SP-type Caboose, *86–91*	5	9	___
6920	B&A Wood-sided Caboose (Std. O), *86 u*	65	80	___

		Exc	New	Cond/$
6921	PRR SP-type Caboose, *86–90*	5	9	___
7200	Quicksilver Passenger Car (O27), *82–83*	26	34	___
7201	Quicksilver Passenger Car (O27), *82–83*	26	34	___
7202	Quicksilver Observation Car (O27), *82–83*	26	34	___
7203	N&W Dining Car "491", *82 u*	130	180	___
7204	Southern Pacific Dining Car, *82 u*	190	235	___
7207	NYC Dining Car, *83 u*	70	140	___
7208	PRR Dining Car, *83 u*	80	105	___
7210	Union Pacific Dining Car, *84*	85	110	___
7211	Southern Pacific Vista Dome Car, *83 u*	145	185	___
7215	B&O Passenger Car, *83–84*	43	50	___
7216	B&O Passenger Car, *83–84*	43	50	___
7217	B&O Baggage Car, *83–84*	43	50	___
7220	Illinois Central Baggage Car, *85*, *87*	105	135	___
7221	Illinois Central Combination Car, *85*, *87*	85	105	___
7222	Illinois Central Passenger Car, *85*, *87*	85	105	___
7223	Illinois Central Passenger Car, *85*, *87*	85	105	___
7224	Illinois Central Dining Car, *85*, *87*	75	90	___
7225	Illinois Central Observation Car, *85*, *87*	95	115	___
7227	Wabash Dining Car (FF #1), *86–87*	115	130	___
7228	Wabash Baggage Car (FF #1), *86–87*	90	100	___
7229	Wabash Combination Car (FF #1), *86–87*	90	100	___
7230	Wabash Passenger Car (FF #1), *86–87*	90	100	___
7231	Wabash Passenger Car (FF #1), *86–87*	90	100	___
7232	Wabash Observation Car (FF #1), *86–87*	85	95	___
7241	W&ARR Passenger Car, *86 u*	43	50	___
7242	W&ARR Baggage Car, *86 u*	43	50	___
7301	Norfolk & Western Stock Car, *82*	44	45	___
7302	Texas & Pacific Stock Car (O27), *83–84*	11	14	___
7303	Erie Stock Car, *84*	41	50	___
7304	Southern Stock Car (FARR #4), *83 u*	41	45	___
7309	Southern Stock Car (O27), *85–86*	12	16	___
7312	W&ARR Stock Car (O27), *86 u*	25	30	___
7401	Chessie System Stock Car (O27), *84–85*	13	17	___
7404	Jersey Central Boxcar, *86*	31	40	___
7500	Lionel 75th Anniversary U36B, *75–77*	115	135	___
7501	Lionel 75th Anniversary Boxcar, *75–77*	21	28	___
7502	Lionel 75th Anniversary Reefer, *75–77*	24	33	___
7503	Lionel 75th Anniversary Reefer, *75–77*	26	37	___
7504	Lionel 75th Anniversary Covered Quad Hopper, *75–77*	25	37	___

		Exc	New	Cond/$
7505	Lionel 75th Anniversary Boxcar, *75–77*	26	37	___
7506	Lionel 75th Anniversary Boxcar, *75–77*	15	20	___
7507	Lionel 75th Anniversary Reefer, *75–77*	26	37	___
7508	Lionel 75th Anniversary N5C Caboose, *75–77*	22	27	___
7509	Kentucky Fried Chicken Reefer, *81–82*	43	50	___
7510	Red Lobster Reefer, *81–82*	42	45	___
7511	Pizza Hut Reefer, *81–82*	43	45	___
7512	Arthur Treacher's Reefer, *82*	38	41	___
7513	Bonanza Reefer, *82*	34	41	___
7514	Taco Bell Reefer, *82*	49	75	___
7515	Denver Mint Car, *81*	65	70	___
7517	Philadelphia Mint Car, *82*	38	40	___
7518	Carson City Mint Car, *83*	34	41	___
7519	Toy Fair Reefer, *82 u*	35	42	___
7520	Nibco Express Boxcar, *82 u*	265	440	___
7521	Toy Fair Reefer, *83 u*	50	65	___
7522	New Orleans Mint Car, *84 u*	33	38	___
7523	Toy Fair Reefer, *84 u*	44	49	___
7524	Toy Fair Reefer, *85 u*	55	60	___
7525	Toy Fair Boxcar, *86 u*	65	80	___
7530	Dahlonega Mint Car, *86 u*	37	48	___
7600	Frisco "Spirit of '76" N5C Caboose, *74–76*	33	39	___
7601	Delaware Boxcar, *74–76*	16	19	___
7602	Pennsylvania Boxcar, *74–76*	23	27	___
7603	New Jersey Boxcar, *74–76*	23	24	___
7604	Georgia Boxcar, *74 u, 75–76*	22	26	___
7605	Connecticut Boxcar, *74 u, 75–76*	22	32	___
7606	Massachusetts Boxcar, *74 u, 75–76*	25	29	___
7607	Maryland Boxcar, *74 u, 75–76*	22	34	___
7608	South Carolina Boxcar, *75 u, 76*	38	50	___
7609	New Hampshire Boxcar, *75 u, 76*	38	46	___
7610	Virginia Boxcar, *75 u, 76*	155	200	___
7611	New York Boxcar, *75 u, 76*	50	65	___
7612	North Carolina Boxcar, *75 u, 76*	35	60	___
7613	Rhode Island Boxcar, *75 u, 76*	36	50	___
7700	Uncle Sam Boxcar, *75 u*	35	39	___
7701	Camel Boxcar, *76–77*	42	50	___
7702	Prince Albert Boxcar, *76–77*	44	65	___
7703	Beechnut Boxcar, *76–77*	25	38	___
7704	Toy Fair Boxcar, *76 u*	110	120	___

		Exc	New	Cond/$
7705	Canadian Toy Fair Boxcar, *76 u*	130	145	___
7706	Sir Walter Raleigh Boxcar, *77–78*	43	50	___
7707	White Owl Boxcar, *77–78*	43	55	___
7708	Winston Boxcar, *77–78*	45	60	___
7709	Salem Boxcar, *78*	39	50	___
7710	Mail Pouch Boxcar, *78*	48	60	___
7711	El Producto Boxcar, *78*	46	60	___
7712	Santa Fe Boxcar (FARR #1), *79*	25	29	___
7800	Pepsi Boxcar, *76 u, 77*	60	70	___
7801	A&W Boxcar, *76 u, 77*	38	50	___
7802	Canada Dry Boxcar, *76 u, 77*	43	55	___
7803	Trains n' Truckin' Boxcar, *77 u*	20	26	___
7806	Season's Greetings Boxcar, *76 u*	70	95	___
7807	Toy Fair Boxcar, *77 u*	70	95	___
7808	Northern Pacific Stock Car, *77*	37	44	___
7809	Vernors Boxcar, *77 u, 78*	50	65	___
7810	Orange Crush Boxcar, *77 u, 78*	40	55	___
7811	Dr Pepper Boxcar, *77 u, 78*	44	60	___
7813	Season's Greetings Boxcar, *77 u*	65	90	___
7814	Season's Greetings Boxcar, *78 u*	70	95	___
7815	Toy Fair Boxcar, *78 u*	65	85	___
7816	Toy Fair Boxcar, *79 u*	65	85	___
7817	Toy Fair Boxcar, *80 u*	95	105	___
7900	D&RGW Operating Cowboy Car (O27), *82–83*	22	26	___
7901	LL Cop and Hobo Car (O27), *82–83*	24	27	___
7902	Santa Fe Boxcar (O27), *82–85*	5	9	___
7903	Rock Island Boxcar (O27), *83*	8	13	___
7904	San Diego Zoo Giraffe Car (O27), *83–84*	44	55	___
7905	Black Cave Boxcar (O27), *82*	6	9	___
7908	Tappan Boxcar (O27), *82 u*	39	55	___
7909	L&N Boxcar (O27), *83–84*	40	49	___
7910	Chessie System Boxcar (O27), *84–85*	18	23	___
7912	Toys "R" Us Giraffe Car (O27), *82–84 u*	70	80	___
7913	Turtleback Zoo Giraffe Car (O27), *85–86*	50	60	___
7914	Toys "R" Us Giraffe Car (O27), *85–89 u*	70	90	___
7920	Sears Centennial Boxcar (O27), *85–86 u*	39	44	___
7925	Erie-Lackawanna Boxcar (O27), *86–90*	10	18	___
7926	NKP Boxcar (O27), *86–91*	8	10	___
7930	True Value Boxcar (O27), *86–87 u*	34	50	___
7931	Town House TV and Appliances Boxcar (O27), *86 u*	31	39	___

		Exc	New	Cond/S
7932	Kay Bee Toys Boxcar (O27), *86–87 u*	40	49	___
8001	NKP 2-6-4, *80 u*	55	65	___
8002	Union Pacific 2-8-4 (FARR #2), *80*	345	310	___
8003	Chessie System 2-8-4, *80*	360	540	___
8004	Rock Island 4-4-0, *80–82*	220	220	___
8005	Santa Fe 4-4-0, *80–82*	65	75	___
8006	ACL 4-6-4, *80 u*	245	340	___
8007	NYNH&H 2-6-4, *80–81*	65	75	___
8008	Chessie System 4-4-2, *80*	65	75	___
8010	Santa Fe NW-2, *70, 71 u*	25	65	___
8020	Santa Fe Alco A Unit, *70–72, 74–76*	65	85	___
8020	Santa Fe Alco A Unit Dummy, *70*	45	60	___
8021	Santa Fe Alco B Unit, *71–72, 74–76*	47	70	___
8022	Santa Fe Alco A Unit, *71 u*	80	105	___
8025	CN Alco A Unit, *71–73 u*	85	105	___
8025	CN Alco A Unit Dummy, *71–73 u*	45	65	___
8030	Illinois Central GP-9, *70–72*	125	145	___
8031	Canadian National GP-7, *71–73 u*	80	150	___
8031	Illinois Central GP-9 Dummy, *70*		NM	___
8040	NKP 2-4-2, *70–72*	26	34	___
8040	Canadian National 2-4-2, *71 u*	43	85	___
8041	NYC 2-4-2, *70*	55	65	___
8041	PRR 2-4-2, *71 u*	55	65	___
8042	GTW 2-4-2, *70, 71–73 u*	26	34	___
8043	NKP 2-4-2, *70 u*	45	65	___
8050	D&H U36C, *80*	105	220	___
8051	D&H U36C Dummy, *80*	95	115	___
8054/8055	Burlington F-3 AA Set, *80*	360	385	___
8056	C&NW FM Trainmaster, *80*	200	250	___
8057	Burlington NW-2, *80*	100	115	___
8059	Pennsylvania F-3 B Unit, *80 u*	190	290	___
8060	Pennsylvania F-3 B Unit, *80 u*	335	420	___
8061	Chessie System U36C, *80*	110	140	___
8062	Great Northern 4-6-4, *70*		NM	___
8062	Burlington F-3 B Unit, *80 u*	205	255	___
8063	Seaboard SD-9, *80*	80	100	___
8064	Florida East Coast GP-9, *80*	150	200	___
8065	Florida East Coast GP-9 Dummy, *80*	95	120	___
8066	TP&W GP-20, *80–81, 83 u*	65	80	___
8067	Texas & Pacific Alco A Unit, *80*		NM	___

		Exc	New	Cond/$
8071	Virginian SD-18, *80 u*	135	155	___
8072	Virginian SD-18 Dummy, *80 u*	75	110	___
8100	Norfolk & Western 4-8-4 "611", *81*	360	405	___
8101	Chicago & Alton 4-6-4 "659", *81*	275	445	___
8102	Union Pacific 4-4-2, *81–82*	49	65	___
8104	Union Pacific 4-4-0 "3", *81 u*	180	235	___
8111	DT&I NW-2, *71–74*	55	65	___
8140	Southern 2-4-0, *71 u*	22	30	___
8141	PRR 2-4-2, *71–72*	41	43	___
8142	C&O 4-4-2, *71–72*		55	___
8150	PRR GG-1 "4935", *81*	330	395	___
8151	Burlington SD-28, *81*	120	145	___
8152	Canadian Pacific SD-24, *81*	170	180	___
8153	Reading NW-2, *81–82*	100	155	___
8154	Alaska NW-2, *81–82*	120	160	___
8155	Monon U36B, *81–82*	110	135	___
8156	Monon U36B Dummy, *81–82*		65	___
8157	Santa Fe FM Trainmaster, *81*	280	325	___
8158	DM&IR GP-35, *81–82*	90	150	___
8159	DM&IR GP-35 Dummy, *81–82*	55	75	___
8160	Burger King GP-20, *81–82*	85	105	___
8161	L.A.S.E.R. Diesel Switcher, *81–82*	23	55	___
8162	Ontario Northland SD-18, *81 u*	150	210	___
8163	Ontario Northland SD-18 Dummy, *81 u*	95	140	___
8164	Pennsylvania F-3 B Unit, *81 u*	340	370	___
8182	Nibco Express NW-2, *82 u*	90	130	___
8190	Diesel Horn Kit, *81 u*		30	___
8200	"Kickapoo" Dockside 0-4-0T, *72*	30	39	___
8203	PRR 2-4-2, *72, 74 u, 75*	26	34	___
8204	C&O 4-4-2, *72*	55	60	___
8206	NYC 4-6-4, *72–75*	140	155	___
8209	"Pioneer" Dockside 0-4-0T w/ tender, *72*	45	65	___
8209	"Pioneer" Dockside 0-4-0T w/o tender, *73–76*	42	55	___
8210	Joshua L. Cowen 4-6-4, *82*	245	350	___
8212	Black Cave 0-4-0, *82*	30	49	___
8213	D&RGW 2-4-2, *82–83, 84–91 u*	65	70	___
8214	Pennsylvania 2-4-2, *82–83*	55	65	___
8215	Nickel Plate Road 2-8-4 "779", *82 u*	245	285	___
8250	Santa Fe GP-9, *72, 74–75*	120	145	___
8251-50	Horn/Whistle Controller, *72–74*	1.50	2.50	___

		Exc	New	Cond/$
8252	D&H Alco A Unit, *72*	85	125	___
8253	D&H Alco B Unit, *72*	50	70	___
8254	Illinois Central GP-9 Dummy, *72*	60	65	___
8255	Santa Fe GP-9 Dummy, *72*	60	65	___
8258	Canadian National GP-7 Dummy, *72–73 u*	65	85	___
8260/8262	Southern Pacific F-3 AA Set, *82*	490	520	___
8261	Southern Pacific F-3 B Unit, *82 u*	435	445	___
8263	Santa Fe GP-7, *82*	65	80	___
8264	CP Vulcan Switcher w/ snowplow, *82*	105	125	___
8265	Santa Fe SD-40, *82*	205	225	___
8266	Norfolk & Western SD-24, *82*	150	225	___
8268	Quicksilver Alco A Unit, *82–83*	85	105	___
8269	Quicksilver Alco A Unit Dummy, *82–83*	55	65	___
8272	Pennsylvania EP-5, *82 u*	205	265	___
8300	Santa Fe 2-4-0, *73–74*	22	25	___
8302	Southern 2-4-0, *73–76*	29	30	___
8303	Jersey Central 2-4-2, *73–74*	55	59	___
8304	Rock Island 4-4-2, *73–75*	85	105	___
8304	Pennsylvania 4-4-2, *74–75*	75	105	___
8304	B&O 4-4-2, *75*	75	105	___
8304	C&O 4-4-2, *75–77*	75	105	___
8305	Milwaukee Road 4-4-2, *73*	95	120	___
8307	Southern Pacific 4-8-4 "4449", *83*	490	560	___
8308	Jersey Central 2-4-2, *73–74 u*	36	43	___
8309	Southern 2-8-2 "4501" (FARR #4), *83*	385	495	___
8310	Nickel Plate Road 2-4-0, *73 u*	26	50	___
8310	Santa Fe 2-4-0, *74–75 u*	26	34	___
8310	Jersey Central 2-4-0, *74–75 u*	26	50	___
8311	Southern 0-4-0, *73 u*	26	34	___
8313	Santa Fe 0-4-0, *83–84*	13	17	___
8314	Southern 2-4-0, *83–85*	17	21	___
8315	B&O 4-4-0, *83–84*	85	120	___
8341	ACL SP-type Caboose, *86 u, 87–90*	6	8	___
8350	U.S. Steel Diesel Switcher, *73–75*	18	26	___
8351	Santa Fe Alco A Unit, *73–75*	60	65	___
8352	Santa Fe GP-20, *73–75*	65	105	___
8353	Grand Trunk GP-7, *73–75*	90	120	___
8354	Erie NW-2, *73, 75*	80	105	___
8355	Santa Fe GP-20 Dummy, *73–74*	65	90	___
8356	Grand Trunk GP-7 Dummy, *73–75*	65	75	___

		Exc	New	Cond/$
8357	PRR GP-9, *73–75*	100	120	___
8358	PRR GP-9 Dummy, *73–75*	55	100	___
8359	Chessie System GP-7 "GM50", *73*	95	120	___
8360	Long Island GP-20, *73–74*	70	105	___
8361	Western Pacific Alco A Unit, *73–75*	50	70	___
8362	Western Pacific Alco B Unit, *73–75*	45	65	___
8363	B&O F-3 A Unit, *73–75*	280	310	___
8364	B&O F-3 A Unit Dummy, *73–75*	120	160	___
8365/8366	CP F-3 AA Set (SSS), *73*	355	405	___
8367	Long Island GP-20 Dummy, *73–75*	80	100	___
8368	Alaska Vulcan Switcher, *83*	120	160	___
8369	Erie-Lackawanna GP-20, *83–85*	125	140	___
8370/8372	NYC F-3 AA Set, *83*	330	435	___
8371	NYC F-3 B Unit, *83*	105	150	___
8374	Burlington Northern NW-2, *83–85*	105	110	___
8375	C&NW GP-7, *83–85*	135	165	___
8376	Union Pacific SD-40, *83*	175	200	___
8377	U.S. Diesel Switcher, *83–84*	55	65	___
8378	Wabash FM Trainmaster "550", *83 u*	500	690	___
8379	PRR Fire Car, *83 u*	80	100	___
8380	Lionel Lines SD-28, *83 u*	235	315	___
8402	Reading 4-4-2, *84–85*	47	55	___
8403	Chessie System 4-4-2, *84–85*	55	65	___
8404	PRR 6-8-6 "6200" (FARR #5), *84–85*	360	460	___
8406	NYC 4-6-4 "783", *84*	445	600	___
8410	Redwood Valley Express 4-4-0, *84–85*	34	50	___
8452	Erie Alco A Unit, *74–75*	75	95	___
8453	Erie Alco B Unit, *74–75*	55	75	___
8454	D&RGW GP-7, *74–75*	80	110	___
8455	D&RGW GP-7 Dummy, *74–75*	50	85	___
8458	Erie-Lackawanna SD-40, *84*	190	190	___
8459	D&RGW Vulcan Rotary Snowplow, *84*	145	165	___
8460	MKT NW-2, *74–75*	45	65	___
8463	Chessie System GP-20, *74 u*	130	190	___
8464/8465	D&RGW F-3 AA Set (SSS), *74*	220	325	___
8466	Amtrak F-3 A Unit, *74–76*	225	250	___
8467	Amtrak F-3 A Unit Dummy, *74–76*	80	90	___
8468	B&O F-3 B Unit, *74–75*	95	100	___
8469	CP F-3 B Unit (SSS), *74*	85	110	___
8470	Chessie System U36B, *74*	80	110	___

		Exc	New	Cond/$
8471	Pennsylvania NW-2, *74–76*	170	195	___
8473	Coca-Cola NW-2, *74 u, 75*	95	120	___
8474	D&RGW F-3 B Unit (SSS), *74*	95	110	___
8475	Amtrak F-3 B Unit, *74*	85	105	___
8477	NYC GP-9, *84 u*	150	205	___
8480/8482	Union Pacific F-3 AA Set, *84*	280	365	___
8481	Union Pacific F-3 B Unit, *84*	150	155	___
8485	USMC NW-2, *84–85*	105	135	___
8500	Pennsylvania 2-4-0, *75–76*	17	21	___
8502	Santa Fe 2-4-0, *75*	17	21	___
8506	PRR 0-4-0, *75–77*	75	90	___
8507	Santa Fe 2-4-0, *75 u*	25	30	___
8512	Santa Fe 0-4-0T, *85–86*	22	30	___
8516	NYC 0-4-0, *85–86*	115	140	___
8550	Jersey Central GP-9, *75–76*	120	155	___
8551	Pennsylvania EP-5, *75–76*	115	120	___
8552/8553/8554	SP Alco ABA Set, *75–76*	200	245	___
8555/8557	Milwaukee Road F-3 AA Set (SSS), *75*	240	315	___
8556	Chessie System NW-2, *75–76*	160	200	___
8558	Milwaukee Road EP-5, *76–77*	160	195	___
8559	N&W GP-9 "1776", *75*	115	145	___
8560	Chessie System U36B Dummy, *75*	85	130	___
8561	Jersey Central GP-9 Dummy, *75–76*	70	95	___
8562	Missouri Pacific GP-20, *75–76*	145	130	___
8563	Rock Island Alco A Unit, *75–76 u*	65	90	___
8564	Union Pacific U36B, *75*	110	155	___
8565	Missouri Pacific GP-20 Dummy, *75–76*	55	70	___
8566	Southern F-3 A Unit, *75–77*	220	370	___
8567	Southern F-3 A Unit Dummy, *75–77*	105	135	___
8568	Preamble Express F-3 A Unit, *75 u*	90	115	___
8569	Soo Line NW-2, *75–77*	60	65	___
8570	Liberty Special Alco A Unit, *75 u*	75	90	___
8571	Frisco U36B, *75–76*	75	95	___
8572	Frisco U36B Dummy, *75–76*		55	___
8573	Union Pacific U36B Dummy, *75 u*	145	190	___
8575	Milwaukee Road F-3 B Unit (SSS), *75*	105	160	___
8576	Penn Central GP-7, *75 u, 76–77*	90	120	___
8578	NYC Ballast Tamper, *85, 87*	85	90	___
8580/8582	Illinois Central F-3 AA Set, *85, 87*	420	485	___
8581	Illinois Central F-3 B Unit, *85, 87*	130	155	___

		Exc	New	Cond/$
8585	Burlington Northern SD-40, *85*	355	385	___
8587	Wabash GP-9 "484", *85 u*	250	280	___
8600	NYC 4-6-4, *76*	175	195	___
8601	Rock Island 0-4-0, *76–77*	17	21	___
8602	D&RGW 2-4-0, *76–78*	22	26	___
8603	C&O 4-6-4, *76–77*	135	190	___
8604	Jersey Central 2-4-2, *76 u*	39	44	___
8606	B&A 4-6-4 "784", *86 u*	720	760	___
8610	Wabash 4-6-2 "672" (FF #1), *86–87*	435	610	___
8615	L&N 2-8-4 "1970", *86 u*	540	630	___
8616	Santa Fe 4-4-2, *86*	60	65	___
8617	Nickel Plate Road 4-4-2, *86–91*	60	65	___
8625	Pennsylvania 2-4-0, *86–90*	21	34	___
8630	W&ARR 4-4-0 "3", *86 u*	125	150	___
8635	Santa Fe 0-4-0 (SSS), *86*	80	100	___
8650	Burlington Northern U36B, *76–77*	120	170	___
8651	Burlington Northern U36B Dummy, *76–77*	70	90	___
8652	Santa Fe F-3 A Unit, *76–77*	260	510	___
8653	Santa Fe F-3 A Unit Dummy, *76–77*	135	160	___
8654	Boston & Maine GP-9, *76–77*	155	195	___
8655	Boston & Maine GP-9 Dummy, *76–77*	90	110	___
8656	Canadian National Alco A Unit, *76*	150	195	___
8657	Canadian National Alco B Unit, *76*	60	75	___
8658	Canadian National Alco A Unit Dummy, *76*	85	170	___
8659	Virginian Rectifier, *76–77*	125	150	___
8660	CP Rail NW-2, *76–77*	100	135	___
8661	Southern F-3 B Unit, *76*	165	170	___
8662	B&O GP-7, *86*	120	130	___
8664	Amtrak Alco A Unit, *76–77*	85	120	___
8665	BAR "Jeremiah O'Brien" GP-9 "1776", *76 u*	100	170	___
8666	Northern Pacific GP-9 (SSS), *76*	125	175	___
8667	Amtrak Alco B Unit, *76–77*	60	80	___
8668	Northern Pacific GP-9 Dummy (SSS), *76*	100	130	___
8669	Illinois Central Gulf U36B, *76–77*	125	165	___
8670	Chessie System Diesel Switcher, *76*	30	55	___
8679	Northern Pacific GP-20, *86*	90	105	___
8687	Jersey Central FM Trainmaster, *86*	270	325	___
8690	Lionel Lines Trolley, *86*	105	115	___
8701	W&ARR 4-4-0 "3", *77–79*	285	300	___
8702	Southern 4-6-4, *77–78*	280	470	___

		Exc	New	Cond/$
8703	Wabash 2-4-2, *77*	22	30	___
8750	Rock Island GP-7, *77–78*	110	125	___
8751	Rock Island GP-7 Dummy, *77–78*	50	70	___
8753	Pennsylvania GG-1, *77 u*	290	315	___
8754	New Haven Rectifier, *77–78*	100	120	___
8755	Santa Fe U36B, *77–78*	130	150	___
8756	Santa Fe U36B Dummy, *77–78*	75	95	___
8757	Conrail GP-9, *76 u*, *77–78*	110	140	___
8758	Southern GP-7 Dummy, *77 u*, *78*	75	95	___
8759	Erie-Lackawanna GP-9, *77–79*	115	175	___
8760	Erie-Lackawanna GP-9 Dummy, *77–79*	95	115	___
8761	GTW NW-2, *77–78*	95	130	___
8762	Great Northern EP-5, *77–78*	130	140	___
8763	Norfolk & Western GP-9, *76 u*, *77–78*	110	120	___
8764	B&O Budd RDC Passenger (SSS), *77*	110	135	___
8765	B&O Budd RDC Baggage Dummy (SSS), *77*	80	100	___
8766	B&O Budd RDC Baggage (SSS), *77*		310	___
8767	B&O Budd RDC Passenger Dummy (SSS), *77*	85	105	___
8768	B&O Budd RDC Passenger Dummy (SSS), *77*	85	105	___
8769	Republic Steel Diesel Switcher, *77–78*	22	39	___
8770	EMD NW-2, *77–78*		65	___
8771	Great Northern U36B, *77*	110	140	___
8772	GM&O GP-20, *77*	85	95	___
8773	Mickey Mouse U36B, *77–78*	440	610	___
8774	Southern GP-7, *77 u*, *78*	110	135	___
8775	Lehigh Valley GP-9, *77 u*, *78*	85	105	___
8776	C&NW GP-20, *77 u*, *78*	120	155	___
8777	Santa Fe F-3 B Unit (SSS), *77*	160	175	___
8778	Lehigh Valley GP-9 Dummy, *77 u*, *78*	90	110	___
8779	C&NW GP-20 Dummy, *77 u*, *78*	110	135	___
8800	Lionel Lines 4-4-2, *78–81*	75	105	___
8801	Blue Comet 4-6-4, *78–80*	380	500	___
8803	Santa Fe 0-4-0, *78*	14	24	___
8850	Penn Central GG-1, *78 u*, *79*	250	305	___
8851/8852	New Haven F-3 AA Set, *78 u*, *79*	320	430	___
8854	CP Rail GP-9, *78–79*	100	120	___
8855	Milwaukee Road SD-18, *78*		115	___
8857	Northern Pacific U36B, *78–80*	140	180	___
8858	Northern Pacific U36B Dummy, *78–80*	55	85	___
8859	Conrail Rectifier, *78–82*	105	150	___

		Exc	New	Cond/$
8860	Rock Island NW-2, *78–79*	85	100	___
8861	Santa Fe Alco A Unit, *78–79*	65	85	___
8862	Santa Fe Alco B Unit, *78–79*	36	43	___
8864	New Haven F-3 B Unit, *78*	85	105	___
8866	M&StL GP-9 (SSS), *78*	85	120	___
8867	M&StL GP-9 Dummy (SSS), *78*	65	95	___
8868	Amtrak Budd RDC Baggage, *78, 80*	195	235	___
8869	Amtrak Budd RDC Passenger Dummy, *78, 80*	75	95	___
8870	Amtrak Budd RDC Passenger Dummy, *78, 80*	85	115	___
8871	Amtrak Budd RDC Baggage Dummy, *78, 80*	85	105	___
8872	Santa Fe SD-18, *78 u, 79*	125	155	___
8873	Santa Fe SD-18 Dummy, *78 u, 79*	60	85	___
8900	Santa Fe 4-6-4 (FARR #1), *79*	355	310	___
8902	ACL 2-4-0, *79–82, 86 u, 87–90*	13	17	___
8903	D&RGW 2-4-2, *79–81*	17	21	___
8904	Wabash 2-4-2, *79, 81 u*	30	34	___
8905	"Smokey Mountain" Dockside 0-4-0T, *79*	9	17	___
8950	Virginian FM Trainmaster, *79*	230	285	___
8951	Southern Pacific FM Trainmaster, *79*	265	350	___
8952/8953	PRR F-3 AA Set, *79*	350	500	___
8955	Southern U36B, *79*	120	195	___
8956	Southern U36B Dummy, *79*	80	125	___
8957	Burlington Northern GP-20, *79*	120	150	___
8958	Burlington Northern GP-20 Dummy, *79*	85	90	___
8960	Southern Pacific U36C, *79 u*	130	180	___
8961	Southern Pacific U36C Dummy, *79 u*	70	80	___
8962	Reading U36B, *79*	115	130	___
8970/8971	PRR F-3 AA Set, *79 u, 80*	330	425	___
9001	Conrail Boxcar (O27), *86–87 u, 88–90*	5	10	___
9010	GN Hopper (O27), *70–71*	6	8	___
9011	GN Hopper (O27), *70 u, 75–76, 78–83*	8	10	___
9012	TA&G Hopper (O27), *71–72*	7	8	___
9013	Canadian National Hopper (O27), *72–76*	5	8	___
9014	Trailer Train Flatcar (O27), *78–79*		NM	___
9015	Reading Hopper (O27), *73–75*	17	21	___
9016	Chessie System Hopper (O27) *75–79, 87–88, 89 u*	4	6	___
9017	Wabash Gondola w/ canisters (O27), *78–82*	3	5	___
9018	DT&I Hopper (O27), *78–79, 81–82*	6	7	___
9019	Unlettered Flatcar (O27), *78*	2.50	3	___
9020	Union Pacific Flatcar (O27), *70–78*	3	5	___

		Exc	New	Cond/$
9021	Santa Fe Work Caboose, *70–71, 73–75*	9	13	___
9022	Santa Fe Bulkhead Flatcar (O27), *70–72, 75–79*	7	13	___
9023	MKT Bulkhead Flatcar (O27), *73–74*	7	10	___
9024	C&O Flatcar (O27), *73–75*	3	6	___
9025	DT&I Work Caboose, *71–74, 77–78*	8	10	___
9026	Republic Steel Flatcar (O27), *75–82*	5	7	___
9027	Soo Line Work Caboose, *75–76*	7	9	___
9030	"Kickapoo" Gondola (O27), *72, 79*	5	9	___
9031	NKP Gondola w/ canisters (O27) *73–75, 82–83, 84–91 u*	4	7	___
9032	SP Gondola w/ canisters (O27), *75–78*		3	___
9033	PC Gondola w/ canisters (O27) *76–78, 82, 86 u, 87–90, 92 u*		3	___
9034	Lionel Leisure Hopper (O27), *77 u*	30	34	___
9035	Conrail Boxcar (O27), *78–82*	5	9	___
9036	Mobilgas 1-D Tank Car (O27), *78–82*	7	13	___
9037	Conrail Boxcar (O27), *78 u, 80*	7	10	___
9038	Chessie System Hopper (O27), *78 u, 80*	15	19	___
9039	Mobilgas 1-D Tank Car (O27), *78 u, 80*	10	15	___
9040	General Mills Wheaties Boxcar (O27), *70–72*	9	13	___
9041	Hershey's Boxcar (O27), *70–71, 73–76*	16	25	___
9042	Ford-Autolite Boxcar (O27), *71 u, 72, 74–76*	13	21	___
9043	Erie-Lackawanna Boxcar (O27), *73–75*	13	20	___
9044	D&RGW Boxcar (O27), *75–76*	5	8	___
9045	Toys "R" Us Boxcar (O27), *75 u*	35	42	___
9046	True Value Boxcar (O27), *76 u*	26	34	___
9047	Toys "R" Us Boxcar (O27), *76 u*	40	43	___
9048	Toys "R" Us Boxcar (O27), *76 u*	33	41	___
9049	Toys "R" Us Boxcar (O27), *78 u*		NRS	___
9050	Sunoco 1-D Tank Car (O27), *70–71*	17	23	___
9051	Firestone 1-D Tank Car (O27), *74–75, 78*	15	19	___
9052	Toys "R" Us Boxcar (O27), *77 u*	26	34	___
9053	True Value Boxcar (O27), *77 u*	28	40	___
9054	JCPenney Boxcar (O27), *77 u*	14	19	___
9055	Republic Steel Gondola w/ canisters, *78 u*	9	10	___
9057	CP Rail SP-type Caboose, *78–79*	10	15	___
9058	Lionel Lines SP-type Caboose, *78–79, 83*	5	7	___
9059	Lionel Lines SP-type Caboose, *79 u, 81 u*	7	9	___
9060	Nickel Plate Road SP-type Caboose, *70–72*	5	7	___
9061	Santa Fe SP-type Caboose, *70–76*	5	8	___
9062	Penn Central SP-type Caboose, *70–72, 74–76*	5	9	___

		Exc	New	Cond/$
9063	GTW SP-type Caboose, *70, 71–73 u*	15	19	___
9064	C&O SP-type Caboose, *71–72, 75–77*	7	10	___
9065	Canadian National SP-type Caboose, *71–73 u*	19	24	___
9066	Southern SP-type Caboose, *73–76*	7	9	___
9067	Kickapoo Valley Bobber Caboose, *72*	6	9	___
9068	Reading Bobber Caboose, *73–76*	5	7	___
9069	Jersey Central SP-type Caboose *73–74, 75–76 u*	5	8	___
9070	Rock Island SP-type Caboose, *73–74*	13	17	___
9071	Santa Fe Bobber Caboose, *74 u, 77–78*	7	9	___
9073	Coca-Cola SP-type Caboose, *74 u, 75*	17	22	___
9075	Rock Island SP-type Caboose, *75–76 u*	13	17	___
9076	"We The People" SP-type Caboose, *75 u*	19	28	___
9077	D&RGW SP-type Caboose, *76–83, 84–91 u*	7	8	___
9078	Rock Island Bobber Caboose, *76–77*	5	7	___
9079	GTW Hopper (O27), *77*	31	30	___
9080	Wabash SP-type Caboose, *77*	9	10	___
9085	Santa Fe Work Caboose, *79–82*	4	5	___
9090	General Mills Mini-Max Car, *71*	24	28	___
9106	Miller Vat Car, *84–85*	31	46	___
9107	Dr Pepper Vat Car, *86–87*	24	33	___
9110	B&O Quad Hopper, *71*	25	30	___
9111	N&W Quad Hopper, *72–75*	15	20	___
9112	D&RGW Covered Quad Hopper, *73–75*	20	23	___
9113	Norfolk & Western Quad Hopper (SSS), *73*	27	32	___
9114	Morton Salt Covered Quad Hopper, *74–76*	18	27	___
9115	Planter's Covered Quad Hopper, *74–76*	21	30	___
9116	Domino Sugar Covered Quad Hopper, *74–76*	22	29	___
9117	Alaska Covered Quad Hopper (SSS), *74–76*	29	36	___
9120	Northern Pacific Flatcar w/ trailers, *70–71*	33	38	___
9121	L&N Flatcar w/ bulldozer and scraper, *71–79*	47	50	___
9122	Northern Pacific Flatcar w/ trailers, *72–75*	19	32	___
9123	C&O Auto Carrier, 3-tier, *72 u, 73–74*	18	27	___
9124	P&LE Flatcar w/ log load, *73–74*	18	25	___
9125	Norfolk & Western Auto Carrier 2-tier, *73–77*	23	28	___
9126	C&O Auto Carrier, 3-tier, *73–75*	23	34	___
9128	Heinz Vat Car, *74–76*	23	30	___
9129	N&W Auto Carrier, 3-tier, *75–76*	17	19	___
9130	B&O Quad Hopper, *70*	23	24	___
9131	D&RGW Gondola w/ canisters, *73–77*	5	8	___

		Exc	New	Cond/$
9132	Libby's Vat Car (SSS), *75–77*	16	23	___
9133	BN Flatcar w/ trailers, *76–77, 80*	20	28	___
9134	Virginian Covered Quad Hopper, *76–77*		32	___
9135	N&W Covered Quad Hopper, *70 u, 71, 75*	19	23	___
9136	Republic Steel Gondola w/ canisters, *72–76, 79*	8	11	___
9138	Sunoco 3-D Tank Car (SSS), *78*	33	38	___
9139	PC Auto Carrier, 3-tier, *76–77*	21	29	___
9140	Burlington Gondola w/ canisters *70, 73–82, 87–89*	7	9	___
9141	BN Gondola w/ canisters, *70–72*	8	10	___
9143	CN Gondola w/ canisters, *71–73 u*	30	34	___
9144	D&RGW Gondola w/ canisters (SSS), *74–76*	9	13	___
9145	ICG Auto Carrier, 3-tier, *77–80*	21	29	___
9146	Mogen David Vat Car, *77–81*	21	26	___
9147	Texaco 1-D Tank Car, *77–78*	39	55	___
9148	Du Pont 3-D Tank Car, *77–81*	25	31	___
9149	CP Rail Flatcar w/ trailers, *77–78*	22	35	___
9150	Gulf 1-D Tank Car, *70 u, 71*	22	28	___
9151	Shell 1-D Tank Car, *72*	27	31	___
9152	Shell 1-D Tank Car, *73–76*	25	34	___
9153	Chevron 1-D Tank Car, *74–76*	25	30	___
9154	Borden 1-D Tank Car, *75–76*	33	47	___
9156	Mobilgas 1-D Tank Car, *76–77*	30	40	___
9157	C&O Flatcar w/ crane, *76–78, 81–82*	35	44	___
9158	PC Flatcar w/ shovel, *76–77, 80*	40	55	___
9159	Sunoco 1-D Tank Car, *76*	35	50	___
9160	Illinois Central N5C Caboose, *70–72*	17	23	___
9161	CN N5C Caboose, *72–74*	14	25	___
9162	PRR N5C Caboose, *72–76*	25	30	___
9163	Santa Fe N5C Caboose, *73–76*	17	24	___
9165	Canadian Pacific N5C Caboose (SSS), *73*	21	30	___
9166	D&RGW SP-type Caboose (SSS), *74–75*	20	25	___
9167	Chessie System N5C Caboose, *74–76*	24	31	___
9168	Union Pacific N5C Caboose, *75–77*	17	19	___
9169	Milwaukee Road SP-type Caboose (SSS), *75*	16	19	___
9170	N&W N5C Caboose "1776", *75*	27	30	___
9171	MP SP-type Caboose, *75 u, 76–77*	19	20	___
9172	Penn Central SP-type Caboose, *75 u, 76–77*	23	31	___
9173	Jersey Central SP-type Caboose, *75 u, 76–77*	22	33	___
9174	NYC P&E B/W Caboose, *76*	65	70	___
9175	Virginian N5C Caboose, *76–77*	24	26	___

		Exc	New	Cond/$
9176	BAR N5C Caboose, *76 u*	18	30	___
9177	Northern Pacific B/W Caboose (SSS), *76*	25	35	___
9178	ICG SP-type Caboose, *76–77*	19	24	___
9179	Chessie System Bobber Caboose, *76*	7	11	___
9180	Rock Island N5C Caboose, *77–78*	12	23	___
9181	B&M N5C Caboose, *76 u, 77*	39	49	___
9182	N&W N5C Caboose, *76 u, 77–80*	20	26	___
9183	Mickey Mouse N5C Caboose, *77–78*	32	50	___
9184	Erie B/W Caboose, *77–78*	24	30	___
9185	GTW N5C Caboose, *77*	21	28	___
9186	Conrail N5C Caboose, *76 u, 77–78*	27	35	___
9188	GN Bay Window Caboose, *77*	22	27	___
9189	Gulf 1-D Tank Car, *77*	40	60	___
9193	Budweiser Vat Car, *83–84*	80	105	___
9200	Illinois Central Boxcar, *70–71*	19	25	___
9201	Penn Central Boxcar, *70*	17	25	___
9202	Santa Fe Boxcar, *70*	20	23	___
9203	Union Pacific Boxcar, *70*		21	___
9204	Northern Pacific Boxcar, *70*		21	___
9205	Norfolk & Western Boxcar, *70*	22	25	___
9206	Great Northern Boxcar, *70–71*		20	___
9207	Soo Line Boxcar, *71*	11	16	___
9208	CP Rail Boxcar, *71*	21	23	___
9209	Burlington Northern Boxcar, *71–72*	16	21	___
9210	B&O DD Boxcar, *71*	20	16	___
9211	Penn Central Boxcar, *71*	17	28	___
9213	M&StL Covered Quad Hopper (SSS), *78*	20	29	___
9214	Northern Pacific Boxcar, *71–72*	16	21	___
9215	Norfolk & Western Boxcar, *71*	19	24	___
9216	Great Northern Auto Carrier, 3-tier, *78*	25	39	___
9217	Soo Line Operating Boxcar, *82–84*	29	36	___
9218	Monon Operating Boxcar, *81*	25	30	___
9219	Missouri Pacific Operating Boxcar, *83*	27	33	___
9220	Borden Milk Car, *83–86*	95	125	___
9221	Poultry Dispatch Operating Chicken Car, *83–85*	45	50	___
9222	L&N Flatcar w/ trailers, *83–84*	38	60	___
9223	Reading Operating Boxcar, *84*	33	40	___
9224	Churchill Downs Operating Horse Car, *84–86*	85	110	___
9225	Conrail Operating Barrel Car, *84*	42	55	___
9226	Delaware & Hudson Flatcar w/ trailers, *84–85*	31	36	___

		Exc	New	Cond/$
9228	Canadian Pacific Operating Boxcar, *86*	24	37	___
9229	Express Mail Operating Boxcar, *85–86*	21	27	___
9230	Monon Boxcar (SSS), *71, 72 u*	17	24	___
9231	Reading B/W Caboose, *79*	24	32	___
9232	Allis-Chalmers Condenser Car, *80–81, 83 u*	42	50	___
9233	Depressed Flatcar w/ transformer, *80*	55	65	___
9234	Lionel Radioactive Waste Car, *80*	50	75	___
9235	Union Pacific Derrick Car, *83–84*	16	22	___
9236	C&NW Derrick Car, *83–85*	22	30	___
9237	UPS Operating Boxcar, *84*		NM	___
9238	Northern Pacific Log Dump Car, *84*	16	24	___
9239	Lionel Lines N5C Caboose, *83 u*	50	60	___
9240	NYC Operating Hopper, *86*	32	39	___
9240	NYC Hopper (O27), *87 u*	20	29	___
9241	PRR Log Dump Car, *85–86*	21	27	___
9245	Illinois Central Derrick Car, *85*		NM	___
9250	WaterPoxy 3-D Tank Car, *70–71*	23	26	___
9260	Reynolds Aluminum Covered Quad Hopper, *75–7*	19	22	___
9261	Sun-maid Raisins Covered Quad Hopper, *75 u, 76*	20	26	___
9262	Ralston Purina Covered Quad Hopper, *75 u, 76*	34	55	___
9263	PRR Covered Quad Hopper, *75 u, 76–77*	23	30	___
9264	Illinois Central Covered Quad Hopper, *75 u, 76–77*	28	39	___
9265	Chessie System Covered Quad Hopper, *75 u, 76–77*	21	27	___
9266	Southern "Big John" Covered Quad Hopper, *76*	46	65	___
9267	Alcoa Covered Quad Hopper (SSS), *76*	20	25	___
9268	Northern Pacific B/W Caboose, *77 u*	33	40	___
9269	Milwaukee Road B/W Caboose, *78*	34	47	___
9270	Northern Pacific N5C Caboose, *78*	14	27	___
9271	M&StL B/W Caboose (SSS), *78–79*	18	30	___
9272	New Haven B/W Caboose, *78–80*	20	34	___
9273	Southern B/W Caboose, *78 u*	36	45	___
9274	Santa Fe B/W Caboose, *78 u*	40	47	___
9276	Peabody Quad Hopper, *78*	19	28	___
9277	Cities Service 1-D Tank Car, *78*	41	45	___
9278	Life Savers 1-D Tank Car, *78–79*	105	145	___

		Exc	New	Cond/$
9279	Magnolia 3-D Tank Car, *78, 79 u*	13	19	___
9280	Santa Fe Operating Stock Car (O27), *77–81*	20	24	___
9281	Santa Fe Auto Carrier, 3-tier, *78–80*	21	27	___
9282	GN Flatcar w/ trailers, *78–79, 81–82*	22	33	___
9283	Union Pacific Gondola w/ canisters, *77*	15	21	___
9284	Santa Fe Gondola w/ canisters, *77*	16	27	___
9285	ICG Flatcar w/ trailers, *77*	47	55	___
9286	B&LE Covered Quad Hopper, *77*	14	26	___
9287	Southern N5C Caboose, *77 u, 78*	18	30	___
9288	Lehigh Valley N5C Caboose, *77 u, 78, 80*	25	31	___
9289	C&NW N5C Caboose, *77 u, 78, 80*	25	36	___
9290	Union Pacific Operating Barrel Car, *83*	65	75	___
9300	PC Log Dump Car, *70–75, 77*	18	24	___
9301	U.S. Mail Operating Boxcar, *73–84*	32	42	___
9302	L&N Searchlight Car, *72 u, 73–78*	21	24	___
9303	Union Pacific Log Dump Car, *74–78, 80*	17	22	___
9304	C&O Coal Dump Car, *74–78*	12	23	___
9305	Santa Fe Operating Cowboy Car (O27), *80–82*	16	23	___
9306	Santa Fe Flatcar w/ horses, *80–82*	18	26	___
9307	Erie Animated Gondola, *80–84*	55	70	___
9308	Aquarium Car, *81–84*	125	130	___
9309	TP&W B/W Caboose, *80–81, 83 u*	19	25	___
9310	Santa Fe Log Dump Car, *78 u, 79–83*	13	24	___
9311	Union Pacific Coal Dump Car, *78 u, 79–82*	13	24	___
9312	Conrail Searchlight Car, *78 u, 79–83*	18	27	___
9313	Gulf 3-D Tank Car, *79 u*	43	50	___
9315	Southern Pacific Gondola w/ canisters, *79 u*	16	23	___
9316	Southern Pacific B/W Caboose, *79 u*	47	50	___
9317	Santa Fe B/W Caboose, *79*	21	36	___
9320	Fort Knox Mint Car, *79 u*	110	135	___
9321	Santa Fe 1-D Tank Car (FARR #1), *79*	25	31	___
9322	Santa Fe Covered Quad Hopper (FARR #1), *79*	42	47	___
9323	Santa Fe B/W Caboose (FARR #1), *79*	39	49	___
9324	Tootsie Roll 1-D Tank Car, *79–81*	60	85	___
9325	Norfolk & Western Flatcar w/ fences, *79–81 u*	6	10	___
9326	Burlington Northern B/W Caboose, *79–80*	34	44	___
9327	Bakelite 3-D Tank Car, *80*	19	29	___
9328	Chessie System B/W Caboose, *80*	33	42	___
9329	Chessie System Crane Car, *80*	40	47	___
9330	"Kickapoo" Dump Car, *72, 79*	3	7	___

		Exc	New	Cond/$
9331	Union 76 1-D Tank Car, *79*	39	44	___
9332	Reading Crane Car, *79*	37	50	___
9333	Southern Pacific Flatcar w/ trailers, *79–80*	33	46	___
9334	Humble 1-D Tank Car, *79*	21	26	___
9335	B&O Log Dump Car, *86*	16	22	___
9336	CP Rail Gondola w/ canisters, *79*	20	29	___
9338	Penn Power Quad Hopper, *79*	60	75	___
9339	GN Boxcar (O27), *79–83, 85 u, 86*	7	10	___
9340	Illinois Central Gondola w/ canisters (O27), *79–81, 82 u, 83*	5	9	___
9341	ACL SP-type Caboose, *79–82, 86 u, 87–90*	6	8	___
9344	Citgo 3-D Tank Car, *80*	23	38	___
9345	Reading Searchlight Car, *84–85*	20	25	___
9346	Wabash SP-type Caboose, *79*	6	10	___
9348	Santa Fe Crane Car (FARR #1), *79 u*	60	70	___
9349	San Francisco Mint Car, *80*	55	70	___
9351	PRR Auto Carrier, 3-tier, *80*	23	40	___
9352	Trailer Train Flatcar w/ C&NW trailers, *80*	29	55	___
9353	Crystal Line 3-D Tank Car, *80*	18	26	___
9354	Pennzoil 1-D Tank Car, *80, 81 u*	60	85	___
9355	Delaware & Hudson B/W Caboose, *80*	37	45	___
9356	Life Savers Stik-O-Pep 1-D Tank Car, *80 u*		NM	___
9357	Smokey Mountain Bobber Caboose, *79*	8	10	___
9359	National Basketball Association Boxcar (O27), *79–80 u*	19	24	___
9360	National Hockey League Boxcar (O27), *79–80 u*	21	26	___
9361	C&NW B/W Caboose, *80*	47	55	___
9362	Major League Baseball Boxcar (O27), *79–80 u*	17	21	___
9363	N&W Flatcar w/ dump bin "9325" (O27), *79*	4	7	___
9364	N&W Flatcar w/ crane "9325" (O27), *79*	7	9	___
9365	Toys "R" Us Boxcar (O27), *79 u*	30	37	___
9366	UP Covered Quad Hopper (FARR #2), *80*	19	23	___
9367	Union Pacific 1-D Tank Car (FARR #2), *80*	21	30	___
9368	Union Pacific B/W Caboose (FARR #2), *80*	30	36	___
9369	Sinclair 1-D Tank Car, *80*	60	85	___
9370	Seaboard Gondola w/ canisters, *80*	19	21	___
9371	Atlantic Sugar Covered Quad Hopper, *80*	19	22	___
9372	Seaboard B/W Caboose, *80*	30	41	___
9373	Getty 1-D Tank Car, *80–81, 83 u*	31	42	___
9374	Reading Covered Quad Hopper, *80–81, 83 u*	39	40	___

		Exc	New	Cond/$
9375	Union Pacific Flatcar w/ fences (O27), *80*		NM	___
9376	Texas & Pacific SP-type Caboose, *80*		NM	___
9376	Soo Line Boxcar (O27), *81 u*	40	50	___
9377	Missouri Pacific Boxcar (O27), *80*		NM	___
9378	Lionel Derrick Car, *80–82*	18	22	___
9379	Santa Fe Gondola w/ canisters, *80–81, 83 u*	22	30	___
9380	NYNH&H SP-type Caboose, *80–81*	9	10	___
9381	Chessie System SP-type Caboose, *80*	7	9	___
9382	Florida East Coast B/W Caboose, *80*	34	48	___
9383	UP Flatcar w/ trailers (FARR #2), *80 u*	27	34	___
9384	Great Northern Operating Hopper, *81*	50	55	___
9385	Alaska Gondola w/ canisters, *81*	27	34	___
9386	Pure Oil 1-D Tank Car, *81*	38	50	___
9387	Burlington B/W Caboose, *81*	46	60	___
9388	Toys "R" Us Boxcar (O27), *81 u*	38	45	___
9389	Lionel Radioactive Waste Car, *81–82*	60	75	___
9398	PRR Coal Dump Car, *83–84*	28	35	___
9399	C&NW Coal Dump Car, *83–85*	17	22	___
9400	Conrail Boxcar, *78*	14	20	___
9401	Great Northern Boxcar, *78*	18	23	___
9402	Susquehanna Boxcar, *78*	30	33	___
9403	Seaboard Coast Line Boxcar, *78*	12	17	___
9404	NKP Boxcar, *78*	19	21	___
9405	Chattahoochee Boxcar, *78*	14	19	___
9406	D&RGW Boxcar, *78–79*	17	21	___
9407	Union Pacific Stock Car, *78*	24	25	___
9408	Lionel Lines Circus Stock Car (SSS), *78*	31	40	___
9411	Lackawanna Phoebe Snow Boxcar, *78*	35	44	___
9412	RF&P Boxcar, *79*	21	28	___
9413	Napierville Junction Boxcar, *79*	18	24	___
9414	Cotton Belt Boxcar, *79*	19	23	___
9415	Providence & Worcester Boxcar, *79*	17	25	___
9416	MD&W Boxcar, *79, 81*	13	19	___
9417	CP Rail Boxcar, *79*	45	50	___
9418	FARR Boxcar, *79 u*	50	60	___
9419	Union Pacific Boxcar (FARR #2), *80*	15	20	___
9420	B&O "Sentinel" Boxcar, *80*	25	28	___
9421	Maine Central Boxcar, *80*	10	17	___
9422	EJ&E Boxcar, *80*	12	20	___
9423	NYNH&H Boxcar, *80*	14	22	___

		Exc	New	Cond/$
9424	TP&W Boxcar, *80*	17	21	___
9425	British Columbia DD Boxcar, *80*	27	31	___
9426	Chesapeake & Ohio Boxcar, *80*	19	30	___
9427	Bay Line Boxcar, *80–81*	14	18	___
9428	TP&W Boxcar, *80–81, 83 u*		23	___
9429	"The Early Years" Boxcar, *80*	20	27	___
9430	"The Standard Gauge Years" Boxcar, *80*	22	25	___
9431	"The Prewar Years" Boxcar, *80*	20	25	___
9432	"The Postwar Years" Boxcar, *80*	50	55	___
9433	"The Golden Years" Boxcar, *80*	50	60	___
9434	Joshua Lionel Cowen "The Man" Boxcar, *80 u*	29	37	___
9436	Burlington Boxcar, *81*	25	30	___
9437	Northern Pacific Stock Car, *81*	22	36	___
9438	Ontario Northland Boxcar, *81*	25	31	___
9439	Ashley Drew & Northern Boxcar, *81*	11	19	___
9440	Reading Boxcar, *81*	50	65	___
9441	Pennsylvania Boxcar, *81*	32	42	___
9442	Canadian Pacific Boxcar, *81*	13	21	___
9443	Florida East Coast Boxcar, *81*	19	22	___
9444	Louisiana Midland Boxcar, *81*	14	18	___
9445	Vermont Northern Boxcar, *81*	14	17	___
9446	Sabine River & Northern Boxcar, *81*	15	21	___
9447	Pullman Standard Boxcar, *81*	16	21	___
9448	Santa Fe Stock Car, *81–82*	34	40	___
9449	Great Northern Boxcar (FARR #3), *81*	27	31	___
9450	Great Northern Stock Car (FARR #3), *81 u*	50	60	___
9451	Southern Boxcar (FARR #4), *83*	26	32	___
9452	Western Pacific Boxcar, *82–83*	12	16	___
9453	MPA Boxcar, *82–83*	14	19	___
9454	New Hope & Ivyland Boxcar, *82–83*	21	27	___
9455	Milwaukee Road Boxcar, *82–83*	15	19	___
9456	PRR DD Boxcar (FARR #5), *84–85*	24	30	___
9461	Norfolk & Southern Boxcar, *82*	25	43	___
9462	Southern Pacific Boxcar, *83–84*	18	23	___
9463	Texas & Pacific Boxcar, *83–84*	15	19	___
9464	NC&StL Boxcar, *83–84*	16	22	___
9465	Santa Fe Boxcar, *83–84*	12	19	___
9466	Wanamaker Boxcar, *82 u*	60	70	___
9467	Tennessee World's Fair Boxcar, *82 u*	26	31	___
9468	Union Pacific DD Boxcar, *83*	31	34	___

		Exc	New	Cond/$
9469	NYC "Pacemaker" Boxcar (Std. O), *84–85*	47	55	___
9470	Chicago Beltline Boxcar, *84*	15	20	___
9471	Atlantic Coast Line Boxcar, *84*	13	17	___
9472	Detroit & Mackinac Boxcar, *84*	22	26	___
9473	Lehigh Valley Boxcar, *84*	24	28	___
9474	Erie-Lackawanna Boxcar, *84*	31	35	___
9475	D&H "I Love NY" Boxcar, *84 u*	28	41	___
9476	PRR Boxcar (FARR #5), *84–85*	27	28	___
9480	MN&S Boxcar, *85–86*	15	18	___
9481	Seaboard System Boxcar, *85–86*	15	18	___
9482	Norfolk & Southern Boxcar, *85–86*	13	17	___
9483	Manufacturers Railway Boxcar, *85–86*	14	19	___
9484	Lionel 85th Anniversary Boxcar, *85*	22	26	___
9486	GTW "I Love Michigan" Boxcar, *86*	23	34	___
9490	Christmas Boxcar for Lionel Employees, *85 u*		1750	___
9491	Christmas Boxcar, *86 u*	26	37	___
9492	Lionel Lines Boxcar, *86*	23	28	___
9500	Milwaukee Road Passenger Car, *73*	40	75	___
9501	Milwaukee Road Passenger Car, *73 u, 74–76*	33	37	___
9502	Milwaukee Road Observation Car, *73*	30	48	___
9503	Milwaukee Road Passenger Car, *73*	33	48	___
9504	Milwaukee Road Passenger Car, *73 u, 74–76*	33	37	___
9505	Milwaukee Road Passenger Car, *73 u, 74–76*	35	38	___
9506	Milwaukee Road Combination Car *74 u, 75–76*	32	37	___
9507	PRR Passenger Car, *74–75*	34	55	___
9508	PRR Passenger Car, *74–75*	32	50	___
9509	PRR Observation Car, *74–75*	41	60	___
9510	PRR Combination Car, *74 u, 75–76*	30	47	___
9511	Milwaukee Road Passenger Car, *74 u*	33	48	___
9513	PRR Passenger Car, *75–76*	25	44	___
9514	PRR Passenger Car, *75–76*	23	36	___
9515	PRR Passenger Car, *75–76*	22	34	___
9516	B&O Passenger Car, *76*	27	42	___
9517	B&O Passenger Car, *75*	45	65	___
9518	B&O Observation Car, *75*	45	65	___
9519	B&O Combination Car, *75*	55	85	___
9521	PRR Baggage Car, *75 u, 76*	65	95	___
9522	Milwaukee Road Baggage Car, *75 u, 76*	65	80	___
9523	B&O Baggage Car, *75 u, 76*	60	70	___
9524	B&O Passenger Car, *76*	27	37	___

		Exc	New	Cond/$
9525	B&O Passenger Car, *76*	30	43	___
9527	Milwaukee Road Campaign Observation Car, *76 u*	50	75	___
9528	PRR Campaign Observation Car, *76 u*	65	95	___
9529	B&O Campaign Observation Car, *76 u*	44	70	___
9530	Southern Baggage Car, *77–78*	45	65	___
9531	Southern Combination Car, *77–78*	29	37	___
9532	Southern Passenger Car, *77–78*	33	47	___
9533	Southern Passenger Car, *77–78*	27	38	___
9534	Southern Observation Car, *77–78*	31	47	___
9536	Blue Comet Baggage Car, *78–80*	39	55	___
9537	Blue Comet Combination Car, *78–80*	35	50	___
9538	Blue Comet Passenger Car, *78–80*	35	47	___
9539	Blue Comet Passenger Car, *78–80*	35	48	___
9540	Blue Comet Observation Car, *78–80*	27	40	___
9541	Santa Fe Baggage Car, *80–82*	21	30	___
9545	Union Pacific Baggage Car, *84*	135	200	___
9546	Union Pacific Combination Car, *84*	85	105	___
9547	Union Pacific Observation Car, *84*	85	105	___
9548	UP "Placid Bay" Passenger Car, *84*	90	110	___
9549	UP "Ocean Sunset" Passenger Car, *84*	85	105	___
9551	W&ARR Baggage Car, *77 u, 78–80*	36	48	___
9552	W&ARR Passenger Car, *77 u, 78–80*	46	60	___
9553	W&ARR Flatcar w/ horses, *77 u, 78–80*	32	50	___
9554	Chicago & Alton Baggage Car, *81*	55	85	___
9555	Chicago & Alton Combination Car, *81*	50	75	___
9556	Chicago & Alton "Wilson" Passenger Car, *81*	50	75	___
9557	Chicago & Alton "Webster Groves" Passenger Car, *81*	45	65	___
9558	Chicago & Alton Observation Car, *81*	50	75	___
9559	Rock Island Baggage Car, *81–82*	42	65	___
9560	Rock Island Passenger Car, *81–82*	43	65	___
9561	Rock Island Passenger Car, *81–82*	42	65	___
9562	N&W Baggage Car "577", *81*	80	110	___
9563	N&W Combination Car "578", *81*	80	105	___
9564	N&W Passenger Car "579", *81*	90	100	___
9565	N&W Passenger Car "580", *81*	85	100	___
9566	N&W Observation Car "581", *81*	90	95	___
9567	N&W Vista Dome Car "582", *81 u*	160	255	___
9569	PRR Combination Car, *81 u*	115	160	___
9570	PRR Baggage Car, *79*	85	115	___

		Exc	New	Cond/$
9571	PRR Passenger Car, *79*	125	145	___
9572	PRR Passenger Car, *79*	110	125	___
9573	PRR Vista Dome Car, *79*	95	120	___
9574	PRR Observation Car, *79*	75	100	___
9575	PRR Passenger Car, *79–80 u*	100	135	___
9576	Burlington Baggage Car, *80*	145	175	___
9577	Burlington Passenger Car, *80*	95	105	___
9578	Burlington Passenger Car, *80*	105	110	___
9579	Burlington Vista Dome Car, *80*	95	110	___
9580	Burlington Observation Car, *80*	95	110	___
9581	Chessie System Baggage Car, *80*	55	65	___
9582	Chessie System Combination Car, *80*	47	55	___
9583	Chessie System Passenger Car, *80*	40	47	___
9584	Chessie System Passenger Car, *80*	31	37	___
9585	Chessie System Observation Car, *80*	55	65	___
9586	Chessie System Dining Car, *86 u*	85	90	___
9588	Burlington Vista Dome Car, *80 u*	110	120	___
9589	Southern Pacific Baggage Car, *82–83*	110	135	___
9590	Southern Pacific Combination Car, *82–83*	90	105	___
9591	SP "Pullman" Passenger Car, *82–83*	85	105	___
9592	SP "Chair" Passenger Car, *82–83*	85	105	___
9593	Southern Pacific Observation Car, *82–83*	100	130	___
9594	NYC Baggage Car, *83–84*	105	130	___
9595	NYC Combination Car, *83–84*	75	85	___
9596	NYC "Wayne County" Passenger Car, *83–84*	80	95	___
9597	NYC "Hudson River" Passenger Car, *83–84*	70	85	___
9598	NYC Observation Car, *83–84*	75	85	___
9599	Chicago & Alton Dining Car, *86 u*	80	90	___
9600	Chessie System Hi-Cube Boxcar, *75 u, 76–77*	19	25	___
9601	ICG Hi-Cube Boxcar, *75 u, 76–77*	20	21	___
9602	Santa Fe Hi-Cube Boxcar, *75 u, 76–77*	17	20	___
9603	Penn Central Hi-Cube Boxcar, *76–77*	17	18	___
9604	Norfolk & Western Hi-Cube Boxcar, *76–77*	23	26	___
9605	NH Hi-Cube Boxcar, *76–77*	17	21	___
9606	Union Pacific Hi-Cube Boxcar, *76 u, 77*	16	17	___
9607	Southern Pacific Hi-Cube Boxcar, *76 u, 77*	12	15	___
9608	Burlington Northern Hi-Cube Boxcar, *76 u, 77*	21	23	___
9610	Frisco Hi-Cube Boxcar, *77*	25	34	___
9620	NHL Wales Boxcar, *80*	27	35	___
9621	NHL Campbell Boxcar, *80*	27	34	___

MODERN ERA 1970-2008

		Exc	New	Cond/$
9622	NBA Western Boxcar, *80*	24	30	___
9623	NBA Eastern Boxcar, *80*	26	34	___
9624	National League Baseball Boxcar, *80*	27	34	___
9625	American League Baseball Boxcar, *80*	27	35	___
9626	Santa Fe Hi-Cube Boxcar, *82–84*	10	14	___
9627	Union Pacific Hi-Cube Boxcar, *82–83*	15	21	___
9628	Burlington Northern Hi-Cube Boxcar, *82–84*	14	19	___
9629	Chessie System Hi-Cube Boxcar, *83–84*	23	34	___
9660	Mickey Mouse Hi-Cube Boxcar, *77–78*	25	37	___
9661	Goofy Hi-Cube Boxcar, *77–78*	48	55	___
9662	Donald Duck Hi-Cube Boxcar, *77–78*	34	46	___
9663	Dumbo Hi-Cube Boxcar, *77 u, 78*	40	55	___
9664	Cinderella Hi-Cube Boxcar, *77 u, 78*	55	85	___
9665	Peter Pan Hi-Cube Boxcar, *77 u, 78*	48	75	___
9666	Pinocchio Hi-Cube Boxcar, *78*	105	155	___
9667	Snow White Hi-Cube Boxcar, *78*	325	440	___
9668	Pluto Hi-Cube Boxcar, *78*	145	185	___
9669	Bambi Hi-Cube Boxcar, *78 u*	65	100	___
9670	Alice In Wonderland Hi-Cube Boxcar, *78 u*	60	90	___
9671	Fantasia Hi-Cube Boxcar, *78 u*	55	90	___
9672	Mickey Mouse 50th Anniversary Hi-Cube Boxcar, *78 u*	350	415	___
9700	Southern Boxcar, *72–73*	24	31	___
9701	B&O DD Boxcar, *72*	14	19	___
9702	Soo Line Boxcar, *72–73*	15	21	___
9703	CP Rail Boxcar, *72*	34	44	___
9704	Norfolk & Western Boxcar, *72*	10	17	___
9705	D&RGW Boxcar, *72*	13	20	___
9706	C&O Boxcar, *72*	17	19	___
9707	MKT Stock Car, *72–75*	14	19	___
9708	U.S. Mail Boxcar, *72–75*	18	23	___
9708	U.S. Mail Toy Fair Boxcar, *73 u*	85	95	___
9709	BAR "State of Maine" Boxcar (SSS), *72–74*	29	32	___
9710	Rutland Boxcar (SSS), *72–74*	24	28	___
9711	Southern Boxcar, *74–75*	19	25	___
9712	B&O DD Boxcar, *73–74*	31	34	___
9713	CP Rail Boxcar, *73–74*	24	30	___
9713	CP Rail Season's Greetings Boxcar, *74 u*	95	120	___
9714	D&RGW Boxcar, *73–74*	16	20	___
9715	C&O Boxcar, *73–74*	17	22	___
9716	Penn Central Boxcar, *73–74*	15	20	___

		Exc	New	Cond/$
9717	Union Pacific Boxcar, *73–74*	21	25	___
9718	Canadian National Boxcar, *73–74*	23	31	___
9719	New Haven DD Boxcar, *73 u*	23	32	___
9723	Western Pacific Boxcar (SSS), *73–74*	27	29	___
9723	Western Pacific Toy Fair Boxcar, *74 u*	75	85	___
9724	Missouri Pacific Boxcar (SSS), *73–74*	21	24	___
9725	MKT Stock Car (SSS), *73–75*	15	18	___
9726	Erie-Lackawanna Boxcar (SSS), *78*	25	30	___
9729	CP Rail Boxcar, *78*		34	___
9730	CP Rail Boxcar, *74–75*	23	27	___
9731	Milwaukee Road Boxcar, *74–75*	16	21	___
9732	Southern Pacific Boxcar, *79 u*	24	31	___
9734	Bangor & Aroostook Boxcar, *79*	30	38	___
9735	Grand Trunk Boxcar, *74–75*	15	21	___
9737	Central Vermont Boxcar, *74–76*	27	34	___
9738	Illinois Terminal Boxcar, *82*	43	55	___
9739	D&RGW Boxcar (SSS), *74–76*	17	25	___
9740	Chessie System Boxcar, *74–75*	15	19	___
9742	M&StL Boxcar, *73 u*	17	19	___
9742	M&StL Season's Greetings Boxcar, *73 u*	85	105	___
9743	Sprite Boxcar, *74 u, 75*	17	24	___
9744	Tab Boxcar, *74 u, 75*	17	24	___
9745	Fanta Boxcar, *74 u, 75*	17	27	___
9747	Chessie System DD Boxcar, *75–76*	24	28	___
9748	CP Rail Boxcar, *75–76*	16	20	___
9749	Penn Central Boxcar, *75–76*	16	21	___
9750	DT&I Boxcar, *75–76*	13	18	___
9751	Frisco Boxcar, *75–76*	21	23	___
9752	L&N Boxcar, *75–76*	20	25	___
9753	Maine Central Boxcar, *75–76*	16	22	___
9754	NYC "Pacemaker" Boxcar (SSS), *75–77*	20	30	___
9755	Union Pacific Boxcar, *75–76*	20	24	___
9757	Central of Georgia Boxcar, *74 u*	16	19	___
9758	Alaska Boxcar (SSS), *75–77*	34	38	___
9759	Paul Revere Boxcar, *75 u*	36	43	___
9760	Liberty Bell Boxcar, *75 u*	40	49	___
9761	George Washington Boxcar, *75 u*	36	43	___
9762	Toy Fair Boxcar, *75 u*	125	170	___
9763	D&RGW Stock Car, *76–77*	15	20	___
9764	GTW DD Boxcar, *76–77*	40	55	___

		Exc	New	Cond/$
9767	Railbox Boxcar, *76–77*	15	20	___
9768	B&M Boxcar, *76–77*	18	27	___
9769	B&LE Boxcar, *76–77*	17	21	___
9770	Northern Pacific Boxcar, *76–77*	14	18	___
9771	Norfolk & Western Boxcar, *76–77*	16	24	___
9772	Great Northern Boxcar, *76*	60	85	___
9773	NYC Stock Car, *76*	32	39	___
9775	M&StL Boxcar (SSS), *76*	23	27	___
9776	SP "Overnight" Boxcar (SSS), *76*	34	40	___
9777	Virginian Boxcar, *76–77*	22	25	___
9778	Season's Greetings Boxcar, *75 u*	165	185	___
9780	Johnny Cash Boxcar, *76 u*	47	50	___
9781	Delaware & Hudson Boxcar, *77–78*	19	23	___
9782	Rock Island Boxcar, *77–78*	14	17	___
9783	B&O Timesaver Boxcar, *77–78*	25	27	___
9784	Santa Fe Boxcar, *77–78*	13	17	___
9785	Conrail Boxcar, *78*		NRS	___
9785	Conrail Boxcar, *77–78*	20	23	___
9786	C&NW Boxcar, *77–79*	18	27	___
9787	Jersey Central Boxcar, *77–79*	18	19	___
9788	Lehigh Valley Boxcar, *77–79*	17	21	___
9789	Pickens Boxcar, *77*	25	33	___
9801	B&O "Sentinel" Boxcar (Std. O), *73–75*	18	27	___
9802	Miller High Life Reefer (Std. O), *73–75*	35	40	___
9803	Johnson Wax Boxcar (Std. O), *73–75*	29	35	___
9805	Grand Trunk Reefer (Std. O), *73–75*	34	32	___
9806	Rock Island Boxcar (Std. O), *74–75*	40	47	___
9807	Stroh's Beer Reefer (Std. O), *74–76*	65	75	___
9808	Union Pacific Boxcar (Std. O), *75–76*	37	50	___
9809	Clark Reefer (Std. O), *75–76*	34	41	___
9811	Pacific Fruit Express Reefer (FARR #2), *80*	26	33	___
9812	Arm & Hammer Reefer, *80*	24	30	___
9813	Ruffles Reefer, *80*	18	26	___
9814	Perrier Reefer, *80*	21	30	___
9815	NYC "Early Bird" Reefer (Std. O), *84–85*	47	50	___
9816	Brach's Candy Reefer, *80*	21	26	___
9817	Bazooka Gum Reefer, *80*	24	31	___
9818	Western Maryland Reefer, *80*	18	23	___
9819	Western Fruit Express Reefer (FARR #3), *81*	22	29	___
9820	Wabash Gondola w/ coal load (Std. O), *73–74*	24	40	___

		Exc	New	Cond/$
9821	SP Gondola w/ coal load (Std. O), *73–75*	31	34	___
9822	Grand Trunk Gondola w/ coal load (Std. O), *74–75*	30	32	___
9823	Santa Fe Flatcar w/ crates (Std. O), *75–76*	37	47	___
9824	NYC Gondola w/ coal load (Std. O), *75–76*	44	60	___
9825	Schaefer Reefer (Std. O), *76–77*	49	65	___
9826	P&LE Boxcar (Std. O), *76–77*	42	43	___
9827	Cutty Sark Reefer, *84*	24	31	___
9828	J&B Reefer, *84*	25	31	___
9829	Dewar's White Label Reefer, *84*	24	29	___
9830	Johnnie Walker Red Label Reefer, *84*	24	31	___
9831	Pepsi Cola Reefer, *82*	60	70	___
9832	Cheerios Reefer, *82*	125	155	___
9833	Vlasic Pickles Reefer, *82*	23	29	___
9834	Southern Comfort Reefer, *83–84*	25	42	___
9835	Jim Beam Reefer, *83–84*	30	45	___
9836	Old Grand-Dad Reefer, *83–84*	27	39	___
9837	Wild Turkey Reefer, *83–84*	44	70	___
9840	Fleischmann's Gin Reefer, *85*	31	36	___
9841	Calvert Gin Reefer, *85*	31	36	___
9842	Seagram's Gin Reefer, *85*	30	34	___
9843	Tanqueray Gin Reefer, *85*	31	34	___
9844	Sambuca Reefer, *86*	31	40	___
9845	Baileys Irish Cream Reefer, *86*	40	70	___
9846	Seagram's Vodka Reefer, *86*	29	37	___
9847	Wolfschmidt Vodka Reefer, *86*	31	36	___
9849	Lionel Lines Reefer, *83 u*	30	32	___
9850	Budweiser Reefer, *72 u, 73–75*	46	55	___
9851	Schlitz Reefer, *72 u, 73–75*	26	32	___
9852	Miller Reefer, *72 u, 73–77*	29	35	___
9853	Cracker Jack Reefer, *72 u, 73–75*			
	(A) Caramel-colored body	29	34	___
	(B) White body, black logo border	23	28	___
9854	Baby Ruth Reefer, *72 u, 73–76*	22	26	___
9855	Swift Reefer, *72 u, 73–77*	23	28	___
9856	Old Milwaukee Reefer, *75–76*	28	36	___
9858	Butterfinger Reefer, *73 u, 74–76*	19	25	___
9859	Pabst Reefer, *73 u, 74–75*	32	39	___
9860	Gold Medal Reefer, *73 u, 74–76*	16	21	___
9861	Tropicana Reefer, *75–77*	23	35	___
9862	Hamm's Reefer, *75–76*	28	39	___

		Exc	New	Cond/$
9863	REA Reefer (SSS), *74–76*	24	28	___
9866	Coors Reefer, *76–77*	40	55	___
9867	Hershey's Reefer, *76–77*	60	70	___
9869	Santa Fe Reefer (SSS), *76*	33	39	___
9870	Old Dutch Cleanser Reefer, *77–78, 80*	15	21	___
9871	Carling Black Label Reefer, *77–78, 80*	33	45	___
9872	Pacific Fruit Express Reefer, *77–79*	24	28	___
9873	Ralston Purina Reefer, *78*	30	38	___
9874	Miller Lite Beer Reefer, *78–79*	40	50	___
9875	A&P Reefer, *78–79*	23	31	___
9876	Central Vermont Reefer, *78*	27	31	___
9877	Gerber Reefer, *79–80*	65	75	___
9878	Good and Plenty Reefer, *79*	24	31	___
9879	Hills Bros. Reefer, *79–80*	23	29	___
9879	Kraft Reefer, *79 u*		NM	___
9880	Santa Fe Reefer (FARR #1), *79*	27	31	___
9881	Rath Packing Reefer, *79 u*	23	27	___
9882	NYC "Early Bird" Reefer, *79*	27	33	___
9883	Nabisco Oreo Reefer, *79*	75	80	___
9884	Fritos Reefer, *81–82*	23	30	___
9885	Lipton Tea Reefer, *81–82*	27	35	___
9886	Mounds Reefer, *81–82*	20	25	___
9887	Fruit Growers Express Reefer (FARR #4), *83*	29	38	___
9888	Green Bay & Western Reefer, *83*	42	49	___
11004	NASCAR Diesel Freight Train Set, *06–07*		CP	___
11005	Dale Earnhardt Jr. Diesel Freight Train Set, *06–07*		240	___
11006	Kasey Kahne Expansion Pack, *06–07*		CP	___
11006	Lionel Lion Set, *03 u*		230	___
11007	Dale Earnhardt Sr. Expansion Pack, *06–07*		CP	___
11008	Dale Earnhardt Jr. Expansion Pack, *06–07*		CP	___
11009	Tony Stewart Expansion Pack, *06–07*		CP	___
11010	Jimmie Johnson Expansion Pack, *06–07*		CP	___
11011	Jeff Gordon Expansion Pack, *06–07*		CP	___
11025	Jimmie Johnson 2006 Champion Boxcar, *07*		CP	___
11100	PRR 2-8-2 Mikado Locomotive "9631", CC, *07*		CP	___
11101	Lionel Lines 2-8-4 Berkshire Steam Locomotive "737", CC, *06*		CP	___
11103	Southern PS-4 4-6-2 Pacific Steam Locomotive "1403", CC, *06*		CP	___
11104	UP Big Boy Steam Locomotive "4014", CC, *06*		CP	___

		Exc	New	Cond/$

MODERN ERA 1970-2008

		Exc	New	Cond/$
11105	NYC L-2A 4-8-2 Mohawk Steam Locomotive "2770", CC, 06		CP	___
11107	LionMaster SP Cab Forward Steam Locomotive "4276", w/ RailSounds, 06–07		CP	___
11108	C&O F-19 4-6-2 Pacific Steam Locomotive "494", CC, 06–07		CP	___
11109	C&O 0-8-0 Locomotive "79", w/ TrainSounds, 06		CP	___
11110	NYC 0-8-0 Locomotive "7805", w/ TrainSounds, 06		CP	___
11117	Santa Fe E6 4-4-2 Atlantic Steam Locomotive "1484", CC, 07		CP	___
11119	Southern 0-8-0 Steam Locomotive "6535" w/ TrainSounds, 07		CP	___
11122	UP Big Boy Steam Locomotive "4024", CC, 06		CP	___
11123	UP Big Boy Steam Locomotive "4023", CC, 06		CP	___
11127	SP GS-4 4-8-4 Northern Steam Locomotive "4436", CC, 07		CP	___
11128	C&O F-19 4-6-2 Pacific Steam Locomotive "490", CC, 07		CP	___
11650	Alderney Dairy General American Milk Car 2-pack (Std. O), 07		CP	___
11651	Freeport General American Milk Car 2-pack (Std. O), 07		CP	___
11652	BNSF Mechanical Refrigerator Car 2-pack (Std. O), 07		CP	___
11653	SPFE Mechanical Refrigerator Car 2-pack (Std. O), 07		CP	___
11654	UPFE Mechanical Refrigerator Car 2-pack (Std. O), 07		CP	___
11655	GN-WFE Mechanical Refrigerator Car 2-pack (Std. O), 07		CP	___
11657	PFE Wood-sided Refrigerator Car 3-pack (Std. O), 06		CP	___
11700	Conrail Limited Set, 87	320	370	___
11701	Rail Blazer Set, 87–88		60	___
11702	Black Diamond Set, 87	195	265	___
11703	Iron Horse Freight Set, 88–91	100	105	___
11704	Southern Freight Runner Set (SSS), 87	210	285	___
11705	Chessie System Unit Train Set, 88	360	450	___
11706	Dry Gulch Line Set (SSS), 88	190	260	___
11707	Silver Spike Set, 88–89	175	245	___
11708	Midnight Shift Set, 88 u, 89	60	75	___
11710	CP Rail Freight Set, 89	375	470	___
11711	Santa Fe F3 ABA Set	480	590	___

		Exc	New	Cond/$
	"8100", "8101", "8102", *91*			
11712	Great Lakes Express Set (SSS), *90*	260	280	___
11713	Santa Fe Dash 8-40B Set, *90*	395	480	___
11714	Badlands Express Set, *90–91*	49	60	___
11715	Lionel 90th Anniversary Set, *90*	275	285	___
11716	Lionelville Circus Special Set, *90–91*	155	190	___
11717	CSX Freight Set, *90*	240	230	___
11718	Norfolk Southern Dash 8-40C Unit Train Set, *92*	445	495	___
11719	Coastal Freight Set (SSS), *91*	165	215	___
11720	Santa Fe Special Set, *91*	49	60	___
11721	Mickey's World Tour Train Set, *91, 92 u*	115	155	___
11722	Girl's Train Set, *91*	540	810	___
11723	Amtrak Maintenance Train Set, *91, 92 u*	210	245	___
11724	Great Northern F3 ABA Set "366A", 370B", 351C", *92*	730	840	___
11726	Erie-Lackawanna Freight Set, *91 u*	225	275	___
11727	Coastal Limited Set, *92*	90	110	___
11728	High Plains Runner Set, *92*	120	130	___
11729	L&N Express Set, *92*		NM	___
11733	Feather River Set (SSS), *92*	285	330	___
11734	Erie Alco ABA Set "725A", "725B", "736A" (FF #7), *93*	250	305	___
11735	NYC Flyer Freight Set "1735WS", *93–99*	125	160	___
11736	Union Pacific Express Set, *93–95*	110	130	___
11738	Soo Line Set (SSS), *93*	250	280	___
11739	Super Chief Set, *93–94*	135	155	___
11740	Conrail Consolidated Set, *93*	200	240	___
11741	Northwest Express Set, *93*	130	155	___
11742	Coastal Limited Set, *93 u*	90	115	___
11743	Chesapeake & Ohio Freight Set, *94*	240	280	___
11744	NYC Passenger/Freight Set (SSS), *94*	295	335	___
11745	U.S. Navy Set, *94–95*	230	275	___
11746	Seaboard Freight Set, *94, 95 u*	90	115	___
11747	Lionel Lines Steam Set, *95*	310	340	___
11748	Amtrak Alco Passenger Set, *95–96*	130	185	___
11749	Western Maryland Set (SSS), *95*	275	300	___
11750	McDonald's Nickel Plate Special Set, *87 u*	135	145	___
11751	49C95171C Sears Pennsylvania Passenger Set, *87 u*	120	155	___
11752	JCPenney Timber Master Set, *87 u*	75	115	___

		Exc	New	Cond/$
11753	Kay Bee Toys Rail Blazer Set, *87 u*	80	100	___
11754	Key America Set, *87 u*	150	165	___
11755	Timber Master Set, *87 u*	150	165	___
11756	Hawthorne Freight Flyer Set, *87–88 u*	65	85	___
11757	Chrysler Mopar Express Set, *88 u*	260	300	___
11758	The Desert King Set (SSS), *89*	195	250	___
11759	JCPenney Silver Spike Set, *88 u*	175	250	___
11761	JCPenney Iron Horse Freight Set, *88 u*	120	125	___
11762	True Value Cannonball Express Set, *89 u*	95	145	___
11763	United Model Freight Hauler Set, *88 u*	135	145	___
11764	49N95178 Sears Iron Horse Freight Set, *88 u*	155	190	___
11765	Spiegel Silver Spike Set, *88 u*	175	250	___
11767	Shoprite Freight Flyer Set, *88 u*	80	125	___
11769	JCPenney Midnight Shift Set, *89 u*	100	175	___
11770	49GY95280 Sears Circus Set, *89 u*	185	220	___
11771	K-Mart Microracers Set, *89 u*	80	110	___
11772	Macy's Freight Flyer Set, *89 u*	170	220	___
11773	49GY95281 Sears NYC Passenger Set, *89 u*	175	200	___
11774	Ace Hardware Cannonball Express Set, *89 u*	145	175	___
11775	Anheuser-Busch Set, *89–92 u*	220	310	___
11776	Pace Iron Horse Freight Set, *89 u*	115	135	___
11777	49N95265 Sears Lionelville Circus Special Set, *90 u*	175	190	___
11778	49N95264 Sears Badlands Express Set, *90 u*	49	60	___
11779	49N95267 Sears CSX Freight Set, *90 u*	190	230	___
11780	49N95266 Sears NP Passenger Set, *90 u*	155	190	___
11781	True Value Cannonball Express Set, *90 u*	75	115	___
11783	Toys "R" Us Heavy Iron Set, *90–91 u*	135	160	___
11784	Pace Iron Horse Freight Set, *90 u*	115	135	___
11785	Costco Union Pacific Express Set, *90 u*	200	230	___
11789	Sears Illinois Central Passenger Set, *91 u*	170	200	___
11793	Santa Fe Set w/ mailer, *91 u*	49	60	___
11794	Mickey's World Tour Set w/ mailer, *91 u*	80	100	___
11796	Union Pacific Express Set, *91 u*	150	160	___
11797	Sears Coastal Limited Set w/ mailer, *92 u*	80	100	___
11800	Toys "R" Us Heavy Iron Thunder Limited Set, *92–93 u*	235	295	___
11803	Mall Promotion Nickel Plate Special Set, *92 u*	135	145	___
11804	K-Mart Coastal Limited Set, *92 u*	80	100	___
11809	Lionel Village Trolley Company Set "1809" (O), *95–97*	55	85	___

		Exc	New	Cond/$
11810	Budweiser Modern Era Set, *93–94 u*	190	195	___
11811	United Auto Workers Set, *93 u*	170	435	___
11812	Mall Promotion Coastal Limited Set, *93 u*	95	115	___
11813	Crayola Activity Train Set, *94 u, 95*	90	110	___
11814	Ford Limited Edition Set, *94 u*	185	230	___
11818	Chrysler Mopar Set, *94 u*	205	235	___
11819	Georgia Power Set, *95 u*	495	520	___
11820	Red Wing Shoes NYC Flyer Set, *95 u*	240	280	___
11821	Sears Zenith Set, *95 u*		700	___
11822	Chevrolet Set, *96 u*	265	295	___
11825	Bloomingdale's Set, *96 u*		310	___
11826	Sears Freight Set, *95–96 u*		700	___
11826	Sears Freight Set, *95–96 u*		700	___
11827	Zenith Employees Set, *96 u*		700	___
11827	Zenith Employees Set, *96 u*		700	___
11828	NJ Transit Passenger Set, *96 u*		180	___
11833	NJ Transit GP38 Passenger Set, *97*	275	300	___
11837	Union Pacific GP9 Unit Train Set, *97*		520	___
11838	AT&SF Warhorse Hudson Freight Set, *97*		810	___
11839	SP&S 4-6-2 Steam Freight Set, *97*		280	___
11841	Bloomingdale's Set, *97 u*		265	___
11843	Boston & Maine GP9 A-B-A Diesel Set, *98*		510	___
11844	Union Pacific Die-Cast Ore Cars 4-pack, *98*		225	___
11846	Kal Kan Pet Care Train Set, *01 u*		960	___
11849	1998 Lionel Centennial Series Reefer 4-pack, *98*		105	___
11850	Rice A Roni Trolley Set, *02 u*		260	___
11851	PFE Reefer 6-pack (Std. O), *02*	225	255	___
11852	Clinchfield PS-2 2-Bay Hopper, *04*		70	___
11853	B&M PS-2 2-Bay Hopper, 2-pack, *05*		CP	___
11854	N&W PS-2 Covered Hopper, 2-pack, *04*		70	___
11855	GN Offset Hopper w/ coal, 2-pack, *05*		CP	___
11856	Green Bay & Western Offset Hopper, 2-pack, *05*		CP	___
11857	Baltimore & Ohio Offset Hopper, 2-pack, *05*		CP	___
11858	Pennsylvania PS 4 FlatCar w/ piggyback trailers 2-pack, (Std. O), *05*		CP	___
11859	GN PS 4 FlatCar w/ piggyback trailers (Std. O), *05*		CP	___
11860	SP PS 4 FlatCar w/ piggyback trailers (Std. O), *05*		CP	___
11861	C&O PS 4 FlatCar w/ piggyback trailers (Std. O), *05*		CP	___
11863	Southern Pacific GP9 "2383", *98*		225	___
11864	New York Central GP9 "2383", *98*		275	___
11865	Alaska GP7 "1802", *98–99*		90	___

		Exc	New	Cond/$
11866	Government of Canada Cylindrical Hoppers 2-pack,(Std. O), *05*		CP	___
11867	CN Cylindrical Hoppers, 2-pack (Std. O), *05*		CP	___
11868	BN All-Purpose Husky Stack Car 2-pack (Std. O), *05*		CP	___
11869	SP All-Purpose Husky Stack Car, 2-pack (Std. O), *05*		CP	___
11870	CSX All-Purpose Husky Stack Car, 2-pack (Std. O), *05*		220	___
11871	TTX Trailer Train All-Purpose Stack Car 2-pack (Std. O), *05*		CP	___
11872	PFE Orange Steel-sided Refrigerator Car 3-pack (Std. O), *05*		CP	___
11873	C&O Offset Hopper, 3-pack (Std. O), *05*		CP	___
11874	PFE OrangeSteel-sided Refrigerator Car 3-pack (Std. O), *05*		CP	___
11875	NP Steel-Sided Refrigerator Car 3-pack (Std. O), *05*		CP	___
11876	PFE Silver Steel-Sided Refrigerator Car 3-pack (Std. O), *05*		CP	___
11877	NorthWestern Steel-Sided Refrigerator Car 3-pack (Std. O), *05*		CP	___
11878	Santa Fe PS-2 2-Bay Covered Hopper 3-pack (Std. O), *06*		CP	___
11879	MKT PS-2 2-Bay Covered Hopper 3-pack (Std. O), *06*		CP	___
11880	Boraxo PS-2 2-Bay Covered Hopper 3-pack (Std. O), *06*		CP	___
11881	Pennsylvania PS-2 2-Bay Covered Hopper 3-pack (Std. O), *06*		CP	___
11882	Rock Island Offset Hopper w/ gravel load 3-pack (Std. O), *06*		125	___
11883	CNJ Offset Hopper, 3-pack (Std. O), *06*		CP	___
11884	Maine Central Offset Hopper, 3-pack (Std. O), *06*		CP	___
11891	Pennsylvania ACF 3-Bay Hopper, 3-pack (Std. O), *06*		CP	___
11891	Pennsylvania 3-Bay Open Hopper 3-pack (Std. O), *06*		CP	___
11892	Conrail ACF 3-Bay Hopper 3-pack (Std. O), *06*		CP	___
11893	N&W 3-Bay Open Hopper 3-pack (Std. O), *06*		CP	___
11894	UP 3-Bay Open Hopper 3-pack (Std. O), *06*		CP	___
11895	GN Steel-Sided Refrigerator Car 3-pack (Std. O), *06*		CP	___
11896	Santa Fe Steel-Sided Refrigerator Car 3-pack (Std. O), *06*		CP	___

		Exc	New	Cond/$
11897	Pepper Packing Steel-Sided Refrigerator Car 3-pack (Std. O), *06*		CP	___
11900	SF Special Freight Set "1900WS" (O), *96–01*		130	___
11903	Atlantic Coast Line F3 ABA Set "342", "342B", "343", *96*		790	___
11905	U.S. Coast Guard Set, *96*	150	170	___
11906	Factory Selection Special Set, *95 u*		85	___
11909	N&W J 4-8-4 Warhorse Set, *96*	560	720	___
11910	Lionel Lines Set (O27), *96*	140	160	___
11912	"57" Switcher Service Exclusive, *96*		310	___
11913	SP GP9 Freight Set, *97*		440	___
11914	NYC GP9 Freight Set, *97*		370	___
11918	Conrail SD20 Service Exclusive "X1144" (SSS), *97*		255	___
11919	Lionel Docksider Set "1919" (O), *97*		70	___
11920	Port of Lionel City Dive Team Set "1920", *97*		185	___
11921	Lionel Lines Freight Set "1113WS", *97*		130	___
11929	AT&SF Warbonnet Passenger Set "1929W", *97–99*		165	___
11930	AT&SF Warbonnet Passenger, 2-pack "2404-05", *97–99*		80	___
11931	Chessie Flyer Freight Set "1931S" (O), *97–99*		165	___
11933	Dodge Motorsports Freight Set, *96 u*		250	___
11934	Virginian Rectifier Freight Set, *97–99*		260	___
11935	Lionel NYC Flyer Freight Set, *97*		155	___
11936	Little League Baseball Steam Set, *97*	205	265	___
11939	SP&S 4-6-2 Steam Freight Set, *97*		220	___
11940	Southern Pacific SD40 Warhorse Coal Set, *98*		600	___
11944	Lionel Lines 4-4-2 Steam Freight Set, *98*		175	___
11956	UP GP9 "2380", "2381" (powered & dummy), *97*	325	375	___
11957	Mobil Oil Steam Special Set, *97*		350	___
11971	D&H 4-4-2 Steam Freight Set, *98*	125	155	___
11972	Alaska GP7 Train Set, *98–99*	180	215	___
11974	Station Accessory Set, *98*		22	___
11975	Freight Accessory Pack, *98*		23	___
11977	NP 4-pack Freight Cars, *98*		170	___
11979	N&W 4-4-2 Steam Freight Set, *98*		75	___
11981	1998 Holiday Trolley Set, *98*		75	___
11982	New Jersey Transit Ore Car Set, *98*		250	___
11983	Farmrail Agricultural Set, *99*		425	___
11984	Corvette GP7 Set, *99*		420	___

		Exc	New	Cond/$
11988	NYC Firecar "18444" & Instruction Car "19853" Set, *99*		210	___
12014	Straight Track 10" (FasTrack), *03–07*		CP	___
12015	Curved Track 0-36 (FasTrack), *03–07*		CP	___
12016	Terminal Track 10" (FasTrack), *03–07*		CP	___
12017	Left Manual Switch 0-36 (FasTrack), *03–07*		CP	___
12018	Right Manual Switch 0-36 (FasTrack), *03–07*		CP	___
12019	90° Crossover (FasTrack), *03–07*		CP	___
12020	Uncoupling Track 5" (FasTrack), *03–07*		CP	___
12022	Half Curved Track 0-36 (FasTrack), *03–07*		CP	___
12023	Quarter Curved Track 0-36 (FasTrack), *03–07*		CP	___
12024	Half Straight Track (FasTrack), *03–07*		CP	___
12025	Straight Track 4½" (FasTrack), *03–07*		CP	___
12026	Straight Track 1¾" (FasTrack), *03–07*		CP	___
12027	Insulated Track 5" (FasTrack),, *03–07*		CP	___
12028	Inner Passing Loop Track Pack (FasTrack), *03–07*		CP	___
12029	Accessory Activator Pack (FasTrack), *03–07*		CP	___
12030	Figure 8 Track Pack (FasTrack), *03–07*		CP	___
12031	Outer Passing Loop Track Pack (FasTrack), *03–07*		CP	___
12032	Straight Track 10" 4-pack (FasTrack), *03–07*		CP	___
12033	Curved Track 0-36 4-pack (FasTrack), *03–07*		CP	___
12035	FasTrack Lighted Bumper 2-pack, *05–07*		CP	___
12036	Grade Crossing (FasTrack), *05–07*		CP	___
12037	Graduated Trestle Set (FasTrack), *05–07*		CP	___
12038	Elevated Trestle Set (FasTrack), *05–07*		CP	___
12039	Railer (FasTrack), *04–07*		CP	___
12040	O Gauge Transition Piece (FasTrack), *04–07*		CP	___
12041	Curved Track O-72 (FasTrack), *04–07*		CP	___
12042	Straight Track 30" (FasTrack), *04–07*		CP	___
12043	Curved Track O-48 (FasTrack), *04–07*		CP	___
12044	FasTrack Siding Track Add-on Track Plan, *04–07*		CP	___
12045	Left Remote Switch O-36 (FasTrack), *04–07*		CP	___
12046	Right Remote Switch O-36 (FasTrack), *04–07*		CP	___
12047	Wye Remote Switch O-72 (FasTrack), *04–07*		CP	___
12048	Left Remote Switch O-72 (FasTrack), *04–07*		CP	___
12048	Left Remote Switch O-72 (FasTrack), *04–07*		CP	___
12049	Right Remote Switch O-72 (FasTrack), *04–07*		CP	___
12050	22.5° Crossover (FasTrack), *04–07*		CP	___
12051	45° Crossover (FasTrack), *04–07*		CP	___
12052	Grade Crossing w/ flashers (FasTrack), *05–07*		CP	___
12053	Accessory Power Wire (FasTrack), *04–07*		CP	___

		Exc	New	Cond/$
12054	Operating Track w/ half straight (FasTrack), *05–07*		CP	___
12055	Half Curved Track O-72 (FasTrack), *04–07*		CP	___
12056	Curved Track O 60 (FasTrack), *05–07*		CP	___
12057	O-60 Remote Switch (Left Hand), *05–07*		CP	___
12058	Right Remote Switch O 60 (FasTrack), *05–07*		CP	___
12059	Earthen Bumper (FasTrack), *04–07*		CP	___
12060	Block Section (FasTrack), *05–07*		CP	___
12061	Curved Track O-84 (FasTrack), *05–07*		CP	___
12062	Grade Crossing w/ gates and flashers (FasTrack), *06–07*		CP	___
12065	Left Remote Switch O-48 (FasTrack), *07*		CP	___
12066	Right Remote Switch O-48 (FasTrack), *07*		CP	___
12073	1⅜" Track Section (FasTrack), *07*		CP	___
12074	1⅜" Track Section without roadbed (FasTrack), *07*		CP	___
12080	Left Remote Switch 72" Path, *07*		CP	___
12081	Right Remote Switch 72" Path, *07*		CP	___
12700	Erie Magnetic Gantry Crane, *87*	125	150	___
12701	Operating Fueling Station, *87*	60	70	___
12702	Control Tower, *87*	60	75	___
12703	Icing Station, *88–89*	60	65	___
12704	Dwarf Signal, *88–93*	9	11	___
12705	Lumber Shed Kit "832K", *88–99*		9	___
12706	Barrel Loader Building Kit, *87–99*		10	___
12707	Billboards (3), *87–99*		5	___
12708	Street Lamps (3), *88–93*	6	9	___
12709	Banjo Signal "140", *87–91, 95–00*		29	___
12710	Engine House Kit, *87–91*	21	25	___
12711	Water Tower Kit, *87–99*		13	___
12712	Automatic Ore Loader, *87–88*	17	21	___
12713	Automatic Gateman "145", *87–88, 94–00*	30	40	___
12714	Crossing Gate "252", *87–91, 93–07*		20	___
12715	Illuminated Bumpers "261", *87–07*		CP	___
12716	Searchlight Tower, *87–89, 91–92*	19	22	___
12717	Non-Illuminated Bumpers (3), *87–07*		5	___
12718	Barrel Shed Kit, *87–99*		10	___
12719	Animated Refreshment Stand, *88–89*	65	70	___
12720	Rotary Beacon, *88–89*	40	45	___
12721	Illuminated Extension Bridge w/ rock piers, *89*	26	38	___
12722	Roadside Diner w/ smoke, *88–89*	27	38	___
12723	Microwave Tower, *88–91, 94–95*	14	19	___
12724	Double Signal Bridge, *88–90*	39	50	___

		Exc	New	Cond/$
12725	Lionel Tractor and Trailer, *88–89*	16	18	___
12726	Grain Elevator Kit, *88–91, 94–99*		36	___
12727	Operating Semaphore "151", *89–99*		26	___
12728	Illuminated Freight Station, *89*	29	38	___
12729	Mail Pickup Set, *88–91, 95*	12	16	___
12730	Girder Bridge "314", *88–03*	10	10	___
12731	Station Platform "158", *88–00*		8	___
12732	Coal Bag "206", *88–07*		CP	___
12733	Watchman Shanty Kit, *88–99*		5	___
12734	Passenger/Freight Station, *89–99*		18	___
12735	Diesel Horn Shed, *88–91*	19	24	___
12736	Coaling Station Kit, *88–91*	21	31	___
12737	Whistling Freight Shed "118", *88–99*		28	___
12739	Lionel Gas Company Tractor and Tanker, *89*	20	25	___
12740	Genuine Wood Logs (3), *88–92, 94–95, 97–99*		5	___
12741	Union Pacific Intermodal Crane, *89*	165	185	___
12742	Gooseneck Lamps "58", *89–00*		23	___
12743	Track Clips (12) (O), *89–07*		CP	___
12744	Rock Piers (2) "920-5", *89–92, 94–05*		CP	___
12745	Barrel Pack (6), *89–07*		CP	___
12746	Operating/Uncoupling Track (O27), *89–07*		10	___
12748	Illuminated Passenger Platform "157", *89–99*		18	___
12749	Rotary Radar Antenna, *89–92, 95*	28	38	___
12750	Crane Kit, *89–91*	8	10	___
12751	Shovel Kit, *89–91*	8	10	___
12752	History of Lionel Trains Video, *89–92, 94*	19	21	___
12753	Ore Load (2), *89–91, 95*	1.50	2.50	___
12754	Graduated Trestle Set (22) "110", *89–07*		15	___
12755	Elevated Trestle Set (10) "111", *89–07*		15	___
12756	The Making of the Scale Hudson Video, *91–94*	20	22	___
12759	Floodlight Tower "195", *90–00*		25	___
12760	Automatic Highway Flasher, *90–91*	23	27	___
12761	Animated Billboard, *90–91, 93, 95*	22	23	___
12762	Freight Station w/ train control and sounds *90–91*		NM	___
12763	Single Signal Bridge, *90–91, 93*	31	35	___
12765	Die-Cast Auto Assortment (6), *90*		NM	___
12767	Steam Clean and Wheel Grind Shop *92–93, 95*	240	290	___
12768	Burning Switch Tower, *90, 93*	85	90	___
12770	Arch-Under Bridge "332", *90–03*		21	___

		Exc	New	Cond/$
12771	Mom's Roadside Diner w/ smoke, *90–91*	34	50	___
12772	Truss Bridge w/ flasher and piers "318", *90–07*		35	___
12773	Freight Platform Kit, *90–98*		32	___
12774	Lumber Loader Kit, *90–99*		19	___
12777	Chevron Tractor and Tanker, *90–91*	9	15	___
12778	Conrail Tractor and Trailer, *90*	9	16	___
12779	Lionelville Grain Company Tractor and Trailer, *90*	11	19	___
12780	RS-1 50-watt Transformer, *90–93*	95	130	___
12781	N&W Intermodal Crane, *90–91*	145	160	___
12782	Lift Bridge, *91–92*	425	510	___
12783	Monon Tractor and Trailer, *91*	11	19	___
12784	Intermodal Containers (3), *91*	12	17	___
12785	Lionel Gravel Company Tractor and Trailer, *91*	9	15	___
12786	Lionel Steel Company Tractor and Trailer, *91*	10	16	___
12790	ZW-II Transformer, *91*		NM	___
12791	Animated Passenger Station, *91*	65	75	___
12794	Lionel Tractor, *91*	7	13	___
12795	Lionel Cable Reels (2) "40-15", *91–98*	3	5	___
12797	Crossing Gate and Signal, *91*		NM	___
12798	Forklift Loader Station, *92–95*	33	38	___
12800	Scale Hudson Replacement Pilot Truck, *91 u*	13	17	___
12802	"Chat & Chew" Roadside Diner w/ smoke and lights, *92–95*	41	50	___
12804	Highway Lights "72", *92–99, 02–04*	9	13	___
12805	Intermodal Containers (3), *92*	10	14	___
12806	Lionel Lumber Company Tractor and Trailer, *92*	10	15	___
12807	Little Caesars Tractor and Trailer, *92*	9	14	___
12808	Mobil Tractor and Tanker, *92*	8	13	___
12809	Animated Billboard, *92–93*	20	22	___
12810	American Flyer Tractor and Trailer "DX26925", *94*	12	18	___
12811	Alka Seltzer Tractor and Trailer, *92*	11	19	___
12812	Illuminated Freight Station "133", *93–00*		27	___
12818	Animated Freight Station, *92, 94–95*	50	60	___
12819	Inland Steel Tractor and Trailer, *92*	9	16	___
12821	Lionel Catalog Video, *92*	13	17	___
12826	Intermodal Containers (3), *93*	10	16	___
12831	Rotary Beacon, *93–95*	22	32	___
12832	Block Target Signal "253", *93–98*		25	___
12833	RoadRailer Tractor and Trailer, *93*	9	15	___

		Exc	New	Cond/$
12834	Pennsylvania Magnetic Gantry Crane, *93*	130	170	___
12835	Operating Fueling Station, *93*	55	60	___
12836	Santa Fe Quantum Tractor and Trailer, *93*	8	14	___
12837	Humble Oil Tractor and Tanker, *93*	9	16	___
12838	Crate Load (2), *93–97*		3	___
12839	Grade Crossing (2), *93–07*		CP	___
12897	Engine House Kit, *96–98*		29	___
12840	Insulated Straight Track (O), *93–07*		CP	___
12841	Insulated Straight Track (O27), *93–07*		CP	___
12842	Dunkin' Donuts Tractor and Trailer, *92 u*	23	25	___
12843	Die-Cast Metal Sprung Trucks (2), *93–99*		10	___
12844	Coil Covers (2) (O), *93–98*		3	___
12847	Animated Ice Depot "352", *94–99*		65	___
12848	Lionel Oil Company Oil Derrick "2848", *94*	55	75	___
12849	Lionel Controller w/ wall pack, *94, 95 u*		NRS	___
12852	Die-Cast Intermodal Trailer Frame, *94–01*		6	___
12853	Coil Covers (2) (Std. O), *94–98*		7	___
12854	U.S. Navy Tractor and Tanker, *94–95*		33	___
12855	Intermodal Containers (3), *94–95*	9	13	___
12860	Lionel Visitor's Center Tractor and Trailer, *94 u*	10	14	___
12861	Lionel Leasing Company Tractor, *94*	8	13	___
12862	Oil Drum Loader, *94–95*	75	85	___
12864	Little Caesars Tractor and Trailer, *94*	8	14	___
12865	Wisk Tractor and Trailer, *94*	12	55	___
12866	TMCC 135-watt PowerHouse Power Supply *94 u, 95–03*		46	___
12867	TMCC 135 PowerMaster Power Distribution Center *94 u, 95–04*		49	___
12868	TMCC CAB-1 Remote Controller, *94 u, 95–07*		115	___
12869	Marathon Oil Tractor and Tanker, *94*	13	19	___
12873	Operating Sawmill "464", *95–97*		70	___
12874	Classic Street Lamps "71", *94–00*		13	___
12877	Operating Fueling Station, *95*	75	85	___
12878	Control Tower, *95*	49	60	___
12880	Power Station Transformer, *96*		NM	___
12881	Chrysler Mopar Tractor and Trailer, *94 u*	37	46	___
12882	Lighted Billboard, *95*	9	14	___
12883	Dwarf Signal "148", *95–07*		CP	___
12884	Truck Loading Dock Kit, *95–98*		16	___
12885	40-watt Control System, *94 u, 95–05*		35	___
12886	Floodlight Tower "395", *95–98*		31	___

		Exc	New	Cond/$
12887	Lionel Conductor Display, *95*		NM	___
12888	Railroad Crossing Flasher "154", *95–07*		CP	___
12889	Operating Windmill "453", *95–98*		34	___
12890	Big Red Control Button, *94 u, 95–00*		43	___
12891	LL Refrigerator Tractor and Trailer, *95*	12	16	___
12892	Automatic Flagman "1045", *92–98*		25	___
12893	TMCC PowerMaster Power Adapter Cable, *94 u, 95–07*		CP	___
12894	Signal Bridge "452", *95–01*		22	___
12895	Double-track Signal Bridge "450", *95–00*		44	___
12896	Tunnel Portals (2) "920-2", *95–06*		11	___
12898	Flagpole "89", *95–97*		8	___
12899	Searchlight Tower "496", *95–98*		25	___
12900	Crane Kit "6828-100", *95–98*		8	___
12901	Shovel Kit "6827-100", *95–98*		7	___
12902	Marathon Oil Derrick "2902", *94 u, 95*	105	190	___
12903	Diesel Horn Shed "114", *95–98*		29	___
12904	Coaling Station Kit, *95–98*		19	___
12905	Factory Kit, *95–98*		20	___
12906	Maintenance Shed Kit, *95–98*		20	___
12907	Intermodal Containers (3), *95*	9	14	___
12911	TMCC Command Base, *95–07*	75	CP	___
12912	Oil Pumping Station "457", *95–98*	38	65	___
12914	SC-1 Switch and Accessory Controller, *95–98*		35	___
12915	Log Loader "164", *96*		115	___
12916	Water Tower "138", *96–97*		60	___
12917	Animated Switch Tower "445", *96–98*		29	___
12922	NYC Operating Gantry Crane w/ coil covers, *96*	75	90	___
12923	Red Wing Shoes Tractor and Trailer "T-4", *95 u*	28	29	___
12925	Curved Track Section 42" (O), *96–07*		CP	___
12926	Globe Street Lamps "64", *96–03*		10	___
12927	Yard Light "65", *96–07*		10	___
12929	Rail-truck Loading Dock, *96*		44	___
12930	Lionelville Oil Company Oil Derrick "2930", *95 u, 96*	55	75	___
12931	Electrical Substation, *96*		22	___
12932	Laimbeer Packaging Tractor & Trailer Set, *96*		14	___
12933	GM Parts Tractor-Trailer Rig, *95*		NRS	___
12935	Zenith Tractor-Trailer Rig, *96*		22	___
12936	SP Intermodal Crane "292", *97*		195	___
12937	NS Intermodal Crane "292", *97*		200	___

		Exc	New	Cond/$
12938	PS PowerStationPowerHouse Set, *97–00*		150	___
12939	PG PowerGridPowerHouse Set, *97*		NM	___
12943	Illuminated Station Platform, *97–00*		24	___
12944	Sunoco Oil Derrick "455", *97*		85	___
12945	Sunoco Pumping Oil Station "457", *97*		80	___
12948	Bascule Bridge "313", *97*		315	___
12949	Billboard Set "310", *97–00*		7	___
12951	Airplane Hangar Kit "837K", *97–98*		29	___
12952	Big L Diner Kit "838K", *97*		24	___
12953	Linex Gas Tall Oil Tank "840K", *97*		9	___
12954	Linex Gas Wide Oil Tank "839K", *97*		10	___
12955	Road Runner & Wile E. Coyote Ambush Shack "145", *97*		90	___
12958	Industrial Water Tower "193", *97–98*		50	___
12960	Rotary Radar Antenna "197", *97*		26	___
12961	Lionel News Stand w/ diesel horn "114", *97*		30	___
12962	LL Passenger Service Train Whistle "118", *97–99*		30	___
12964	Donald Duck Radar Antenna "197", *97*		55	___
12965	Goofy Rotary Beacon "494", *97*		47	___
12966	Lionel Rotary Aicraft Beacon "494", *97–00*		35	___
12968	Girder Bridge Building Kit "841K", *97*		22	___
12969	TMCC Command Set, *97–07*		CP	___
12974	Blinking Light Billboard "410", *97–00*		15	___
12975	"Steiner" Victorian Building Kit "842K", *97–98*		33	___
12976	"Dobson" Victorian Building Kit "843K", *97–98*		24	___
12977	"Kindler" Victorian Building Kit "844K", *97–98*		35	___
12982	Culvert Loader, conventional, *98–00*		190	___
12982	Culvert Loader, conventional, *98–00*		190	___
12983	Culvert Unloader, conventional, *99*		185	___
12987	Intermodal 3-pack, *98*		15	___
12989	Lionel Logo Tractor-Trailer, *98*		16	___
12991	Linex Gas Tractor-Tanker, *98*		16	___
14000	Operating Forklift Platform "264", *00*		160	___
14001	Operating Belt Lumber Loader "364", *00*		95	___
14002	ZW Amp/Volt Meter, *00–04*		80	___
14003	80-watt Transformer/Controller, *00–03*		70	___
14004	Operating Coal Loader "397", *00*		135	___
14005	Operating Coal Ramp "456", *00*		130	___
14018	ElectroCoupler Kit for Command Upgradeable GP9s, *00*		20	___
14062	O31 Remote Switch (LH), *01–07*		55	___

		Exc	New	Cond/$
14063	O31 Remote Switch (RH), *01–07*		CP	___
14065	463 Nuclear Reactor, *00*		230	___
14071	#70 Yard Light, *00–07*		18	___
14072	Haunted House, *01*		175	___
14073	Video: History of Lionel, The First 90 Years, *00*		15	___
14075	Video: A Century of Lionel, 1900-1969, *00*		15	___
14076	Video: A Century of Lionel, 1970-2000, *00*		15	___
14077	ZW Amp/Volt Meter, *00–03*		70	___
14078	Die-Cast Sprung Trucks, *00–05*		CP	___
14079	Operating North Pole Pylon, *01*		70	___
14080	Hobo Hotel, *01*	30	65	___
14081	Shell Oil Derrick, *01*		100	___
14082	Pedestrian Walkover w/ speed sensor, *01–03*		50	___
14083	Pedestrian Walkover, *01–03*		30	___
14084	Lionel Heliport, *01*		85	___
14085	Newsstand, *01*		75	___
14086	Water Tower "38", *00*		105	___
14087	Lionel Lighthouse, *01*		95	___
14090	Banjo Signal, *01–07*		CP	___
14091	Automatic Gateman, *01–03*		45	___
14092	Floodlight Tower, *01–05*		35	___
14093	Single Signal Bridge, *01–04*		22	___
14094	Double Signal Bridge, *01–04*		30	___
14095	Illuminated Station Platform, *01–04*		20	___
14096	Station Platform, *01–04*		10	___
14097	Rotary Aircraft Beacon, *01–04*		40	___
14098	Auto Crossing Gate, *01–07*		CP	___
14099	Block Target Signal, *01–04*		22	___
14100	Blinking Light Billboard, *01–03*		23	___
14101	Red Baron Pylon, *01*		85	___
14102	Rocket Launcher "175", *01*		250	___
14104	Burning Switch Tower, *00*		70	___
14105	Lionel "505" Aquarium, *01*		175	___
14106	Operating Freight Station "356", *00*		70	___
14107	Lionel Postwar Coaling Station, "497", *01–03*		95	___
14109	Carousel, *01*		230	___
14110	Operating Ferris Wheel, *01–02*, *04*		170	___
14111	1531R Controller, *00–07*		CP	___
14112	Lighted Lockon, *01–07*		CP	___
14113	Engine Transfer Table, *01*		210	___
14114	Engine Transfer Table Extension, *01*		75	___

		Exc	New	Cond/$
14116	PRR Die-Cast Girder Bridge, *01*		20	___
14117	NYC Die-Cast Girder Bridge, *01*		20	___
14119	Gooseneck Lamps, Green, *01–04*		22	___
14121	Classic Billboard Set (3), *01–03*		10	___
14124	ZW Controller w/ two 135 W Packs, *01*		300	___
14125	Christmas Tree w/400E Train Set, *00*		65	___
14133	Madison Hobby Shop, *01*		290	___
14134	Triple Action Magnetic Crane, *01*		230	___
14135	NS Black Die-Cast Girder Bridge, *02*		15	___
14137	Generic Die-Cast Girder Bridge, *01–07*		CP	___
14138	Snap-On Tool Animated Billboard, *01 u*		NRS	___
14142	Industrial Smokestack, *02–04*		50	___
14143	Industrial Tank, *02–04*		40	___
14145	Operating Lumberjacks, *02–03*		65	___
14147	Die-Cast Old Style Clock Tower, *02–04*		42	___
14148	Operating Billboard Signmen, *02–03*		60	___
14149	Scale-sized Banjo Signal, *02–05*		CP	___
14151	Die-Cast Dwarf Signal, *02–07*		CP	___
14152	Passenger Station "133", *02–04*		37	___
14153	Lion Oil Derrick, *02–03*		50	___
14154	Water Tower "193", *01–02*		45	___
14155	Floodlight Tower "395", *02–03*		55	___
14156	Lion Oil Diesel Fueling Station "415", *02–03*		70	___
14157	Coal Loader "397", *01–03*		120	___
14158	Icing Station "352", *01–02*		75	___
14159	Animated Billboard, *02–04*		20	___
14160	Frank's Hotdog Stand, *03–04*		55	___
14161	Smoking Hobo Shack, *02*		60	___
14162	Missile Launching Platform "470", *02–03*		48	___
14163	Industrial Power Station "840", *02–03*		550	___
14164	Lionelville Bandstand, *02*		140	___
14166	Train Orders Building, *04–05*		49	___
14167	Operating Lift Bridge "213", *02*		380	___
14168	Operating Harry's Barber Shop, *02–04*		100	___
14170	Amusement Park Swing Ride, *03–04*		150	___
14171	Pirate Ship Ride, *02–04*		130	___
14172	NYC Railroad Tugboat, *02*		180	___
14173	Drawbridge, *02–04*		70	___
14175	Santa Fe Die-Cast Girder Bridge, *01–03*		17	___
14176	Norfolk Southern Die-Cast Girder Bridge, *02–03*		18	___

		Exc	New	Cond/$
14178	TMCC Direct Lockon, *02–03*		25	___
14179	TMCC Track Power Controller "400", *02–07*		130	___
14180	B&O Railroad Tugboat, *02–03*		155	___
14181	TMCC Action Recorder Controller, *02–07*		CP	___
14182	TMCC Accessory Switch Controller, *02–07*		CP	___
14183	TMCC Accessory Motor Controller, *02–07*		CP	___
14184	TMCC Block Power Controller, *02–07*		CP	___
14185	TMCC Operating Track Controller, *02–07*		CP	___
14186	TMCC Accessory Voltage Controller, *02–07*		CP	___
14187	TMCC How-To Video, *02–04*		11	___
14189	TMCC Track Power Controller "300", *02–07*		CP	___
14190	The Lionel Train Book, *04–07*		CP	___
14191	TMCC Command Base Cable (6 feet), *02–07*		CP	___
14192	TMCC 3-Wire Command Base Cable, *02–07*		CP	___
14193	TMCC Controller to Controller Cable (1 foot) *02–07*		CP	___
14194	TMCC TPC Cable Set, *02–07*		CP	___
14195	TMCC Command Base Cable (20 feet), *02–07*		CP	___
14196	TMCC Controller to Controller Cable (6 feet), *02–07*		CP	___
14197	TMCC Controller to Controller Cable (20 feet), *02–07*		CP	___
14198	CW-80 80-watt Transformer, *03–07*		55	___
14199	Playground Swings, *03–04*		50	___
14201	Burning Switch Tower, *05*		CP	___
14202	Postwar No. 38 Water Tower, *05*		CP	___
14203	Lionel Amusement Park Swing Ride, *06–07*		CP	___
14209	U.S. Steel Gantry Crane, *05*		CP	___
14210	Pony Ride, *06–07*		CP	___
14211	Road Crew, *07*		CP	___
14214	Lionelville Mini Golf, *06*		CP	___
14215	Tug-of-War, *06–07*		CP	___
14217	Helicopter Pylon, *06–07*		CP	___
14218	Downtown People Pack, *06–07*		CP	___
14219	Ice Rink, *06–07*		CP	___
14220	Lionelville Water Tower, *06*		CP	___
14221	Witches Cauldron, *06–07*		CP	___
14222	Die-Cast Metal Girder Bridge, *06*		CP	___
14225	Sunoco Industrial Tank, *06*		CP	___
14227	Yard Tower, *06–07*			
14229	Crossing Shanty, *06–07*		CP	___
14230	Milk Bottle Toss Midway Game, *06*		CP	___
14231	Cotton Candy Midway Booth, *06*		CP	___

		Exc	New	Cond/$
14236	No. 356 Operating Freight Station, *06–07*		CP	___
14237	Postwar No. 175 Rocket Launcher, *06–07*		CP	___
14240	Ice Block Pack, 06–*07*			
14241	Work Crew People Pack, *06–07*		CP	___
14242	Hard Rock Cafe, *06*		CP	___
14243	U.S. Army Water Tower, *06–07*			
14244	Ammo Loader, *06–07*		CP	___
14251	Die-Cast Metal Sprung Trucks w/ rotating bearing caps, *07*		CP	___
14255	Sand Tower, *06–07*		CP	___
14257	No. 133 Passenger Station, *06*		CP	___
14258	North Pole Passenger Station, *06*		CP	___
14259	Christmas People Pack, *06*		CP	___
14260	Christmas Tractor and Trailer, *06*		CP	___
14261	Christmas Tree Lot, *06*		70	___
14262	Elevated Tank, *07*		CP	___
14263	U.S. Army Water Tower, *06*		CP	___
14267	Sir Topham Hatt Gateman, *07*		CP	___
14273	Polar Express Add-on Figures, *06–07*		CP	___
14290	UPS Centennial Store, *06*		CP	___
14291	K-Line By Lionel Operating Milk Loading Depot, *06*		CP	___
14294	993 Legacy Expansion Set, *07*		CP	___
14295	990 Legacy Command Set, *07*		CP	___
14297	Halloween Witch Pylon, *07*		CP	___
14500	KCS F3 AA "2388" Passenger Set, *01*	380	660	___
14512	EMD F3 ABA "291", CC, *01*	360	425	___
14517	Santa Fe Powered F3 B Unit "2343C", *01*		280	___
14518	CP F3 B Unit w/ RailSounds "2373C", CC, *01*		345	___
14520	Texas Special F3 B-unit w/ RailSounds, *01*		360	___
14521	Rock Island E-6 AA, *01*		530	___
14524	Atlantic Coast Line E-6 AA, *01*		630	___
14536	Santa Fe F3 A-A Set w/ RailSounds, CC, *03–04*		800	___
14539	Santa Fe F3 B Unit, *03*		300	___
14540	D&RGW F3 B Unit w/ RailSounds, CC, *01*		315	___
14541	C&O F3 B Unit w/ RailSounds, CC, *01*		300	___
14542	KCS F3 B Unit w/ RailSounds "2388C", CC, *01*		375	___
14543	SP F3 B Unit w/ RailSounds, CC, *01*		250	___
14544	Southern EMD E6 AA Diesels, CC, *02*		560	___
14547	Burlington EMD E5 AA Diesels, CC, *02*		570	___
14552	NYC F3 A-A Set w/ RailSounds, CC, *03–04*		740	___
14555	NYC F3 B Unit, *03*		200	___

		Exc	New	Cond/$
14557	WP F3 B Unit (non-powered), *03–04*		190	___
14558	B&O F3 B Unit (non-powered), *03–04*		155	___
14559	D&RG F-3 AA, *01*		620	___
14560	NP F3 A Unit (freight) "2390B", *02*		175	___
14560	NP F3 A Unit (freight) "2390B", *02*		175	___
14561	NP F3 A Unit (passenger) "2390B", *02*		190	___
14561	NP F3 A Unit (passenger) "2390B", *02*		190	___
14562	Milwaukee Road F3 A Unit "75C", *02*		190	___
14562	Milwaukee Road F3 A Unit "75C", *02*		190	___
14563	Erie-Lackawanna F3 A Unit "7094", *02*		175	___
14563	Erie-Lackawanna F3 A Unit "7094", *02*		175	___
14564	CP F3 B Unit "237C", CC, *02*		350	___
14565	B&O F3 A-A Set, *03–04*		650	___
14568	WP F3 A-A Set, *03–04*		780	___
14571	Santa Fe PA A-A Set "51-51", CC, *03*		660	___
14574	D&H PA A-A Set " 18-19", CC, *03*		580	___
14584	Wabash F3 A Unit (non-powered), *03*		180	___
14586	D&H PB Unit, *03*		125	___
14587	Santa Fe PB Unit, *03*		125	___
14588	Santa Fe EMD F3 A-B-A Set "19" CC, *04–05*		980	___
14592	PRR EMD F3 A-B-A Set "9500/9501" CC, *04–05*		750	___
14596	NH Alco PA A-A Set "0767/0768", *04–05*		700	___
14599	NH Alco PB Unit "O767-B", *04–05*		CP	___
15000	D&RGW Waffle-sided Boxcar, *95*	16	18	___
15001	Seaboard Waffle-sided Boxcar, *95*	14	19	___
15002	Chesapeake & Ohio Waffle-sided Boxcar, *96*	16	20	___
15003	Green Bay & Western Waffle-sided Boxcar, *96*	16	20	___
15004	Bloomingdale's Boxcar, *97 u*		40	___
15005	I Love NY Boxcar, *97 u*		65	___
15008	CP Rail Boxcar		30	___
15013	L&N Waffle-sided Boxcar "102402", *00*		29	___
15014	Seaboard Waffle-sided Boxcar "125925", *00*		25	___
15015	C&NW Waffle-sided Boxcar "161013", *03*		18	___
15016	IC Waffle-sided Boxcar "12981", *04*		20	___
15017	CSX Waffle-Sided Boxcar, *05*		CP	___
15018	D&H Waffle-Sided Boxcar "24052", *06*		CP	___
15020	NH Waffle-Sided Boxcar, *07*		CP	___
15060	K-Line By Lionel Boxcar, *06*		CP	___
15100	Amtrak Passenger Car, *95–97*		35	___
15101	Reading Baggage Car (O27), *96*		34	___

		Exc	New	Cond/$
15102	Reading Combination Car (O27), *96*		23	___
15103	Reading Passenger Car (O27), *96*		23	___
15104	Reading Vista Dome Car (O27), *96*		26	___
15105	Reading Full Vista Dome Car (O27), *96*		26	___
15106	Reading Observation Car (O27), *96*		23	___
15107	Amtrak Vista Dome Car, *96*		38	___
15108	Northern Pacific Vista Dome Car, *96*		34	___
15109	AT&SF Combine Car "2407", *97*		35	___
15110	AT&SF Vista Dome Car 2404", *97*		35	___
15111	AT&SF Observation Car "2406", *97*		35	___
15112	AT&SF Coach "Albuquerque" "2405", *97*		34	___
15113	AT&SF Vista Dome "Culebra" "2404", *97*		34	___
15114	NJ Transit Coach "5610", *96 u*		45	___
15115	NJ Transit Coach "5611", *96 u*		45	___
15116	NJ Transit Coach "5612", *96 u*		45	___
15117	Annie Passenger Coach, surprised face, *97*		26	___
15118	Clarabel Passenger Coach, smiling face, *97*		26	___
15122	NJ Transit Passenger Coach "5613", *97 u*		45	___
15123	NJ Transit Passenger Coach "5614", *97 u*		45	___
15124	NJ Transit Passenger Coach "5615", *97 u*		45	___
15125	Amtrak Observation Car, *97 u*		50	___
15126	Stars & Stripes General Coach "Abraham Lincoln", *99*		60	___
15127	Stars & Stripes General Coach "Ulysses S. Grant", *99*		60	___
15128	Pride of Richmond General Coach "Robert E. Lee", *99*		60	___
15129	Pride of Richmond General Coach "Jefferson Davis", *99*		60	___
15136	Custom Series Short Observation, blue, *99*		40	___
15137	Custom Series Short Observation, red, *99*		34	___
15138	Pratt's Hollow Baggage Car, *98*		100	___
15139	Pratt's Hollow Vista Dome, *98*		100	___
15140	Pratt's Hollow Coach, *98*		100	___
15141	Pratt's Hollow Observation, *98*		100	___
15142	U.S. Army Baby Heavyweight Coach, *00*		50	___
15143	U.S. Army Baby Heavyweight Coach, *00*		50	___
15153	Pullman Baby Madison Set 4-pack, *01*		190	___
15163	T&P Baby Heavyweight Coach, *01*		30	___
15166	Union Pacific Whistling Baggage Car, *04*		30	___
15169	C&O Streamliner Passenger Car 4-pack, *03*		140	___
15170	L&N Streamliner Passenger Car 4-pack, *03*		140	___
15180	NYC Streamliner Passenger Car 4-pack, *04*		340	___
15185	UP Streamliner Passenger Car 4-pack, *04*		340	___

		Exc	New	Cond/$
15300	NYC Superliner Aluminum Passenger Car 4-pack, *02*	360		___
15301	NYC Superliner Passenger Car "Manhattan", *02*		90	___
15302	NYC Superliner Passenger Car "Queens", *02*		90	___
15304	NYC Superliner Passenger Car "Staten Island", *02*		90	___
15305	NYC Superliner Passenger Car "Brooklyn", *02*		90	___
15311	CB&Q California Zephyr Aluminum Passenger Car 4-pack, *03*	350		___
15312	Santa Fe Super Chief Aluminum Passenger Car 4-pack, *03*	275		___
15313	D&H Aluminum Passenger Car 4-pack, *05*	CP		___
15314	Amtrak Superliner 2-pack, *03*	220		___
15315	Santa Fe Superliner 2-pack, *03*	200		___
15316	NYC Superliner 2-pack, *03*	195		___
15317	Southern "The Southerner" Aluminum Passenger Car 4-pack, *03*	350		___
15318	Lionel Lines Aluminum Passenger Car 2-pack, *03*	125		___
15319	Santa Fe Superliner Aluminum Passenger Car 2-pack, *03*	145		___
15326	NYC 20th Century Limited Aluminum Passenger Car 6-pack, *02*	485		___
15333	N&W Powhatan Arrow Aluminum Passenger Car 6-pack, *02*	435		___
15340	Pennsylvania South Wind Aluminum Passenger Car 6-pack, *02*	435		___
15354	NYC Superliner Sleeper "The Bronx", *05*	CP		___
15355	NYC Superliner Lounge Car "Long Island", *05*	CP		___
15379	Lionel Lines Aluminum Combo Car "Silver Valley", *03*	100		___
15380	Lionel Lines Aluminum Dining Car "Silver Spoon", *03*	100		___
15381	Santa Fe Aluminum Baggage Car "2571", *03*	100		___
15382	Santa Fe Aluminum Vista Dome "Regal Dome", *03*	100		___
15383	NYC 20th Century Limited Diner w/ StationSounds, *03*	195		___
15384	N&W Powhattan Arrow Diner w/ StationSounds, *03*	190		___
15385	Pennsylvania South Wind Diner w/ StationSounds, *03*	190		___
15394	Amtrak Streamliner Passenger Car 4-pack, *03–04*	450		___
15395	Alaska Streamliner Passenger Car 4-pack, *03–04*	355		___
15396	Amtrak Superliner Diner w/ StationSounds, *03*	220		___
15397	Santa Fe Superliner Diner w/ StationSounds, *03*	200		___
15398	NYC Superliner Diner w/ StationSounds, *03*	200		___

		Exc	New	Cond/$
15405	50th Anniversary Heavyweight Diner "Hillside" w/ StationSounds, *02*		195	___
15406	Blue Comet Heavyweight Diner "Giacobini" w/ StationSounds, *02*		300	___
15504	Alton Limited Diner w/ StationSounds, *03*		230	___
15507	Phantom III Passenger Car 4-pack, *02* (15508 Baggage Car, 15509 Vista Dome Car, 15510 Coach Car, 15511 Observation Car)		245	___
15512	Phantom II Passenger Car 4-pack, *02*		250	___
15517	Southern Crescent Limited Heavyweight Passenger Car 2-pack, *03–04*		205	___
15520	Southern Crescent Limited Heavyweight Diner w/ StationSounds, *03–04*		220	___
15521	NYC "Twentieth Century Limited" Heavyweight Passenger Car 4-pack, *04*		345	___
15526	Santa Fe "The Chief" Heavyweight Passenger Car 4-pack, *04*		370	___
15538	NYC "Twentieth Century Limited" Heavyweight Passenger Car 2-pack, *04*		200	___
15541	NYC "Twentieth Century Limited" Heavyweight Diner w/ StationSounds, *04*		200	___
15542	Santa Fe "The Chief" Heavyweight Passenger Car 2-pack, *04*		195	___
15545	Santa Fe "The Chief" Heavyweight Diner w/ StationSounds, *04*		200	___
15546	Napa Valley Heavyweight 2-pack, *05*		CP	___
15549	Napa Valley Heavyweight w/ StationSounds Diner, *05*		CP	___
15554	Pennsylvania Heavyweight Car 3-pack (Std. O), *05*		375	___
15558	Pennsylvania Heavyweight Add-on Coach (Std. O), *05*		140	___
15559	Pennsylvania Reading Seashore Heavyweight Car 3-pack (Std. O), *05*		CP	___
15563	Pennsylvania Reading Seashore Heavyweight Add-on Coach (Std. O), *05*		CP	___
15564	LIRR Heavyweight Car 3-pack (Std. O), *05*		CP	___
15568	LIRR Heavyweight Add on Coach (Std. O), *05*		CP	___
15570	LIRR Heavyweight Car 3-pack (Std. O), *06*		230	___
15574	LIRR Heavyweight Car Add-on (Std. O), *06*		CP	___
15575	C&O Heavyweight Diner w/ StationSounds (Std. O), *06*		CP	___
15576	C&O Heavyweight Passenger Car 2-pack (Std. O), *06*		CP	___
15577	NYC Heavyweight 3-pack, (Std. O), *05–06*		CP	___
15581	NYC Heavyweight Add-on Coach "2381"		CP	___

Std. O, *05–06*

		Exc	New	Cond/$
15584	Amtrak Acela Passenger Car 3-pack (Std. O), *06*		580	___
15588	Southern Heavyweight Passenger Car 4-pack, *06*		CP	___
15593	Southern Heavyweight Passenger Car 2-pack, *06*		CP	___
15596	Southern Heavyweight Diner w/ StationSounds, *06*		CP	___
15597	C&O Heavyweight Passenger Car 4-pack (Std. O), *06*		CP	___
15906	RailSounds Trigger Button, *90–95*		12	___
16000	PRR Vista Dome Car (O27), *87–88*	37	55	___
16001	PRR Passenger Car (O27), *87–88*	33	41	___
16002	PRR Passenger Car (O27), *87–88*	24	29	___
16003	PRR Observation Car (O27), *87–88*	24	29	___
16009	PRR Combination Car (O27), *88*	36	38	___
16010	Virginia & Truckee Passenger Car (SSS), *88*	36	47	___
16011	Virginia & Truckee Passenger Car (SSS), *88*	36	47	___
16012	Virginia & Truckee Baggage Car (SSS), *88*	36	47	___
16013	Amtrak Combination Car (O27), *88–89*	21	34	___
16014	Amtrak Vista Dome Car (O27), *88–89*	21	34	___
16015	Amtrak Observation Car (O27), *88–89*	21	34	___
16016	NYC Baggage Car (O27), *89*	36	55	___
16017	NYC Combination Car (O27), *89*	21	29	___
16018	NYC Passenger Car (O27), *89*	21	29	___
16019	NYC Vista Dome Car (O27), *89*	21	29	___
16020	NYC Passenger Car (O27), *89*	23	33	___
16021	NYC Observation Car (O27), *89*	20	28	___
16022	Pennsylvania Baggage Car (O27), *89*	27	38	___
16023	Amtrak Passenger Car (O27), *89*	21	30	___
16024	NP Dining Car (O27), *92*	39	44	___
16027	LL Combination Car (O27) (SSS), *90*	39	48	___
16028	LL Passenger Car (O27) (SSS), *90*	35	42	___
16029	LL Passenger Car (O27) (SSS), *90*	35	42	___
16030	LL Observation Car (O27) (SSS), *90*	35	42	___
16031	Pennsylvania Dining Car (O27), *90*	35	39	___
16033	Amtrak Baggage Car (O27), *90*	28	38	___
16034	NP Baggage Car (O27), *90–91*	30	45	___
16035	NP Combination Car (O27), *90–91*	18	26	___
16036	NP Passenger Car (O27), *90–91*	21	30	___
16037	NP Vista Dome Car (O27), *90–91*	18	26	___
16038	NP Passenger Car (O27), *90–91*	17	25	___
16039	NP Observation Car (O27), *90–91*	21	30	___
16040	Southern Pacific Baggage Car, *90–91*	22	30	___

		Exc	New	Cond/$
16041	NYC Dining Car (O27), *91*	37	45	___
16042	Illinois Central Baggage Car (O27), *91*	24	34	___
16043	Illinois Central Combination Car (O27), *91*	22	30	___
16044	Illinois Central Passenger Car (O27), *91*	24	34	___
16045	Illinois Central Vista Dome Car (O27), *91*	22	30	___
16046	Illinois Central Passenger Car (O27), *91*	24	34	___
16047	Illinois Central Observation Car (O27), *91*	24	34	___
16048	Amtrak Dining Car (O27), *91–92*	33	40	___
16049	Illinois Central Dining Car (O27), *92*	27	38	___
16050	C&NW Baggage Car "6620", *93*	44	55	___
16051	C&NW Combination Car "6630", *93*	40	50	___
16052	C&NW Passenger Car "6616", *93*	34	42	___
16053	C&NW Passenger Car "6602", *93*	37	46	___
16054	C&NW Observation Car "6603", *93*	38	47	___
16055	Santa Fe Passenger Car (O27), *93–94*	29	38	___
16056	Santa Fe Vista Dome Car (O27), *93–94*	25	32	___
16057	Santa Fe Passenger Car (O27), *93–94*	30	40	___
16058	Santa Fe Combination Car (O27), *93–94*	27	35	___
16059	Santa Fe Vista Dome Car (O27), *93–94*	26	34	___
16060	Santa Fe Observation Car (O27), *93–94*	25	31	___
16061	N&W Baggage Car "6061", *94*	60	85	___
16062	N&W Combination Car "6062", *94*	38	50	___
16063	N&W Passenger Car "6063", *94*	43	55	___
16064	N&W Passenger Car "6064", *94*	43	55	___
16065	N&W Observation Car "6065", *94*	36	48	___
16066	NYC Combination Car "6066" (SSS), *94*	55	70	___
16067	NYC Passenger Car "6067" (SSS), *94*	38	47	___
16068	UP Baggage Car "6068" (O27), *94*	50	65	___
16069	UP Combination Car "6069" (O27), *94*	36	43	___
16070	UP Passenger Car "6070" (O27), *94*	36	43	___
16071	UP Dining Car "6071" (O27), *94*	36	46	___
16072	UP Vista Dome Car "6072" (O27), *94*	36	43	___
16073	UP Passenger Car "6073" (O27), *94*	36	42	___
16074	UP Observation Car "6074" (O27), *94*	36	43	___
16075	Missouri Pacific Baggage Car "6620", *95*	44	55	___
16076	Missouri Pacific Combination Car "6630", *95*	34	41	___
16077	Missouri Pacific Passenger Car "6616", *95*	34	41	___
16078	Missouri Pacific Passenger Car "7805", *95*	34	39	___
16079	Missouri Pacific Observation Car "6609", *95*	34	41	___
16080	New Haven Baggage Car "6080" (O27), *95*	35	44	___

		Exc	New	Cond/$
16081	New Haven Combination Car "6081" (O27), *95*	28	37	___
16082	New Haven Passenger Car "6082" (O27), *95*	28	37	___
16083	New Haven Vista Dome Car "6083" (O27), *95*	30	39	___
16084	New Haven Full Vista Dome Car "6084" (O27), *95*	33	39	___
16086	New Haven Observation Car "6086" (O27), *95*	31	40	___
16087	NYC Baggage Car "6087" (SSS), *95*	48	65	___
16088	NYC Passenger Car "6088" (SSS), *95*	36	43	___
16089	NYC Dining Car "6089" (SSS), *95*	36	43	___
16090	NYC Observation Car "6090" (SSS), *95*	38	46	___
16091	NYC Passenger Cars, set of 4 (SSS), *95*	140	165	___
16092	Santa Fe Full Vista Dome Car (O27), *95*	30	38	___
16093	Illinois Central Full Vista Dome Car (O27), *95*	29	38	___
16094	Pennsylvania Full Vista Dome Car (O27), *95*	30	39	___
16095	Amtrak Combination Car (O27), *95*	19	23	___
16096	Amtrak Vista Dome Car (O27), *95*	19	23	___
16097	Amtrak Observation Car (O27), *95*	19	23	___
16098	Amtrak Passenger Car, *95–97*	20	33	___
16099	Amtrak Vista Dome Car, *95–97*	20	33	___
16102	Southern 3-D Tank Car (SSS), *87*	23	30	___
16103	Lehigh Valley 2-D Tank Car (O27), *88*	19	25	___
16104	Santa Fe 2-D Tank Car (O27), *89*	19	23	___
16105	D&RGW 3-D Tank Car (SSS), *89*	48	65	___
16106	Mopar Express 3-D Tank Car, *88 u*	85	155	___
16107	Sunoco 2-D Tank Car (O27), *90*	16	20	___
16108	Racing Fuel 1-D Tank Car "6108" (O27), *89 u*, *92 u*	9	13	___
16109	B&O 1-D Tank Car (SSS), *91*	29	34	___
16110	Circus Animals Operating Stock Car "1989" (O27), *89 u*	24	34	___
16111	Alaska 1-D Tank Car (O27), *90–91*	22	27	___
16112	Dow Chemical 3-D Tank Car, *90*	20	26	___
16113	Diamond Shamrock 2-D Tank Car (O27), *91*	20	25	___
16114	Hooker Chemicals 1-D Tank Car (O27), *91*	13	17	___
16115	MKT 3-D Tank Car, *92*	13	16	___
16116	U.S. Army 1-D Tank Car, *91 u*	36	42	___
16119	MKT 2-D Tank Car (O27), *92*, *93 u*	14	19	___
16121	C&NW Stock Car (SSS), *92*	60	70	___
16123	Union Pacific 3-D Tank Car, *93–95*	16	22	___
16124	Penn Salt 3-D Tank Car, *93*	21	26	___
16125	Virginian Stock Car, *93*	19	24	___

		Exc	New	Cond/$
16126	Jefferson Lake 3-D Tank Car, *93*	22	26	___
16127	Mobil 1-D Tank Car, *93*	25	30	___
16128	Alaska 1-D Tank Car, *94*	24	29	___
16129	Alaska 1-D Tank Car (O27), *93 u*, *94*	21	28	___
16130	SP Stock Car (O27), *93 u*, *94*	10	13	___
16131	T&P Reefer, *94*	19	24	___
16132	Deep Rock 3-D Tank Car, *94*	25	30	___
16133	Santa Fe Reefer, *94*	22	28	___
16134	Reading Reefer, *94*	17	21	___
16135	C&O Stock Car, *94*	23	27	___
16136	B&O 1-D Tank Car, *94*	28	32	___
16137	Ford 1-D Tank Car "12", *94 u*	34	39	___
16138	Goodyear 1-D Tank Car, *95*	28	34	___
16140	Domino Sugar 1-D Tank Car, *95*	24	29	___
16141	Erie Stock Car, *95*	22	30	___
16142	Santa Fe 1-D Tank Car, *95*	26	30	___
16143	Reading Reefer, *95*	18	23	___
16144	San Angelo 3-D Tank Car, *95*	22	25	___
16146	Dairy Despatch Reefer, *95*	15	20	___
16147	Clearly Canadian 1-D Tank Car (O27), *94 u*	47	55	___
16149	Zep Chemical 1-D Tank Car (O27), *95 u*	42	55	___
16150	Sunoco 1-D Tank Car "6315", *97*	35	38	___
16152	Sunoco 3-D Tank Car "6415", *97*		26	___
16153	AEC Reactor Fluid "6515-1" SD Tank Car, *97*		80	___
16154	AEC Reactor Fluid "6515-2" SD Tank Car, *97*		85	___
16155	AEC Reactor Fluid "6515-3" SD Tank Car, *97*		85	___
16157	Gatorade Little League Baseball 1-D Tank Car "6315", *97 u*		48	___
16160	Atomic Energy Commission Tank Car w/ reactor fluid "6515", *98*		65	___
16162	Hooker 1-Dome Tank Car "6315-1", *97*		50	___
16163	Hooker 1-Dome Tank Car "6315-2", *97*		50	___
16164	Hooker 1-Dome Tank Car "6315-3", *97*		50	___
16165	Mobilfuel 3-Dome Tank Car "6415", *97 u*		50	___
16171	Alaska 1-Dome Tank Car "6171", *98–99*		33	___
16173	Harold the Helicopter Flatcar, *98*	45	60	___
16175	NJ Transit Ore Car "9125" Port Morris, *98*		45	___
16176	NJ Transit Ore Car "9126" Raritan Yard, *98 u*		45	___
16177	NJ Transit Ore Car "9127" Gladstone Yard, *98 u*		45	___
16178	NJ Transit Ore Car "9128" Bay Head Yard, *98 u*		45	___
16179	NJ Transit Ore Car "9129" Dover Yard, *98 u*		45	___

		Exc	New	Cond/$
16180	Tabasco 1-Dome Tank Car, *98*	55	70	___
16181	Biohazard Tank Car with Lights, *98*		65	___
16182	Gatorade 1-Dome Tank Car "6315", *98 u*		55	___
16187	Linex 3D Tank Car "6425", *99*		30	___
16188	Kodak SD Tank Car "6515", *99*	70	80	___
16196	Lava Lite SD Tank Car "9968", *99*		NM	___
16199	UP 1-D Tank Car "6035", *99–00*		25	___
16200	Rock Island Boxcar (O27), *87–88*	7	10	___
16201	Wabash Boxcar (O27), *88–91*	7	10	___
16203	Key America Boxcar (O27), *87 u*	45	65	___
16204	Hawthorne Boxcar (O27), *87 u*	50	85	___
16205	Mopar Express Boxcar "1987" (O27), *87–88 u*	50	60	___
16206	D&RGW Boxcar (SSS), *89*	37	42	___
16207	True Value Boxcar (O27), *88 u*	32	47	___
16208	PRR Auto Carrier w/ autos (3-tier), *89*	24	37	___
16209	Disney Magic Boxcar (O27), *88 u*	90	110	___
16211	Hawthorne Boxcar (O27), *88 u*	45	65	___
16213	Shoprite Boxcar (O27), *88 u*	55	80	___
16214	D&RGW Auto Carrier, *90*	24	32	___
16215	Conrail Auto Carrier, *90*	27	38	___
16217	Burlington Northern Auto Carrier, *92*	24	36	___
16219	True Value Boxcar (O27), *89 u*	55	75	___
16220	Ace Hardware Boxcar (O27), *89 u*	55	80	___
16221	Macy's Boxcar (O27), *89 u*	55	80	___
16222	Great Northern Boxcar (O27), *90–91*	8	15	___
16223	Budweiser Reefer, *89–92 u*	49	70	___
16224	True Value "Lawn Chief" Boxcar (O27), *90 u*	45	60	___
16225	Budweiser Vat Car, *90–91 u*	110	145	___
16226	Union Pacific Boxcar "6226" (O27), *90–91 u*	15	19	___
16227	Santa Fe Boxcar (O27), *91*	13	17	___
16228	Union Pacific Auto Carrier, *92*	26	33	___
16229	Erie-Lackawanna Auto Carrier, *91 u*	45	55	___
16232	Chessie System Boxcar, *92, 93 u, 94, 95 u*	25	30	___
16233	MKT DD Boxcar, *92*	20	29	___
16234	ACY Boxcar (SSS), *92*	34	41	___
16235	Railway Express Agency Reefer, *92*	19	23	___
16236	NYC "Pacemaker" Boxcar, *92 u*	25	27	___
16237	Railway Express Agency Boxcar, *92 u*	21	23	___
16238	NYNH&H Boxcar, *93–95*		3	___
16239	Union Pacific Boxcar, *93–95*	15	20	___

MODERN ERA 1970-2008

		Exc	New	Cond/$
16241	Toys "R" Us Boxcar, *92–93 u*	35	45	___
16242	Grand Trunk Auto Carrier, *93*	35	40	___
16243	Conrail Boxcar, *93*	26	34	___
16244	Duluth, South Shore & Atlantic Boxcar, *93*	20	24	___
16245	Contadina Boxcar, *93*	16	20	___
16247	ACL Boxcar, *94*	15	19	___
16248	Budweiser Boxcar, *93–94 u*	33	48	___
16249	United Auto Workers Boxcar, *93 u*		55	___
16250	Santa Fe Boxcar (O27), *93 u, 94*	8	10	___
16251	Columbus & Greenville Boxcar, *94*	14	15	___
16252	U.S. Navy Boxcar "6106888", *94–95*		30	___
16253	Santa Fe Auto Carrier, *94*	32	38	___
16255	Wabash DD Boxcar, *95*	20	26	___
16256	Ford DD Boxcar, *94 u*	30	34	___
16257	Crayola Boxcar, *94 u, 95*	17	23	___
16258	Lehigh Valley Boxcar, *95*	17	22	___
16259	Chrysler Mopar Boxcar, *97 u*	29	34	___
16260	Chrysler Mopar Auto Carrier, *96 u*	49	60	___
16261	Union Pacific DD Boxcar, *95*	26	29	___
16263	AT&SF Boxcar, *96–99*		25	___
16264	Red Wing Shoes Boxcar, *95*	22	27	___
16265	Georgia Power "Atlanta '96" Boxcar, *95 u*	165	215	___
16266	Crayola Boxcar, *95*	17	23	___
16267	Sears/Zenith Boxcar, *95–96 u*		49	___
16268	GM/AC Delco Boxcar, *95 u*		50	___
16269	Lionel Lines Boxcar "9700", *96*		NRS	___
16272	1997 Christmas Boxcar "9700", *97*		36	___
16274	Marvin the Martian Boxcar "9700", *97*		38	___
16279	Dodge Motorsports Boxcar, *96 u*	110	150	___
16284	Galveston Wharves Boxcar "9700", *98*		28	___
16285	Savannah State Docks Boxcar "9700", *98*		26	___
16291	1998 Christmas Boxcar, *98*		34	___
16292	Lionel Employee Christmas Boxcar "9700", *98*	280	350	___
16293	J.C. Penny Boxcar, *97*		100	___
16294	Pedigree Boxcar, *97*	120	140	___
16295	Kal Kan Boxcar, *97*	120	140	___
16296	Whiskas Boxcar, *97*	120	140	___
16297	Sheba Boxcar, *97*	120	140	___
16298	Mobil Boxcar "9700", *97*		45	___
16300	Rock Island Flatcar w/ fences (O27), *87–88*	8	10	___

		Exc	New	Cond/$
16301	Lionel Barrel Ramp Car, *87*	14	19	___
16303	PRR Flatcar w/ trailers, *87*	26	33	___
16304	RI Gondola w/ cable reels (O27), *87–88*	5	9	___
16305	Lehigh Valley Ore Car, *87*	80	130	___
16306	Santa Fe Barrel Ramp Car, *88*	12	16	___
16307	NKP Flatcar w/ trailers, *88*	30	44	___
16308	Burlington Northern Flatcar w/ trailer, *88–89*	20	25	___
16309	Wabash Gondola w/ canisters, *88–91*	9	13	___
16310	Mopar Express Gondola w/ canisters "1987", *87–88 u*	30	34	___
16311	Mopar Express Flatcar w/ trailers "1987", *87–88 u*	105	150	___
15313	D&H Aluminum Passenger Car 4-pack, *03*		350	___
16313	PRR Gondola w/ cable reels (O27), *88 u, 89*	9	10	___
16314	Wabash Flatcar w/ trailers, *89*	26	30	___
16315	PRR Flatcar w/ fences (O27), *88 u, 89*	7	9	___
16317	PRR Barrel Ramp Car, *89*	18	22	___
16318	LL Depressed Flatcar w/ cable reels, *89*	22	26	___
16320	Great Northern Barrel Ramp Car, *90*	13	19	___
16321/16322 Sealand TTUX Flatcar Set w/ trailers, *90*		65	85	___
16323	Lionel Lines Flatcar w/ trailers, *90*	21	25	___
16324	PRR Depressed Flatcar w/ cable reels, *90*	16	20	___
16325	Microracers Exhibition Ramp Car, *89 u*	20	27	___
16326	Santa Fe Depressed Flatcar w/ cable reels, *91*	16	21	___
16327	"The Big Top" Circus Gondola w/ canisters, *89 u*	19	24	___
16328	NKP Gondola w/ cable reels, *90–91*	17	23	___
16329	SP Flatcar w/ horses (O27), *90–91*	19	24	___
16330	MKT Flatcar w/ trailers, *91*	25	30	___
16331	Southern Barrel Ramp Car, *91*		NM	___
16332	LL Depressed Flatcar w/ transformer, *91*	28	33	___
16333	Frisco Bulkhead Flatcar w/ wood load, *91*	17	22	___
16334	C&NW TTUX Flatcar Set w/ trailers "16337" and "16338", *91*	55	60	___
16335	NYC "Pacemaker" Flatcar w/ trailer (SSS), *91*	46	65	___
16336	UP Gondola w/ canisters "6336", *90–91 u*	17	21	___
16339	Mickey's World Tour Gondola w/ canisters (O27), *91, 92 u*	17	21	___
16340	Amtrak Flatcar w/ stakes, *91*		NM	___
16341	NYC Depressed Flatcar w/ transformer, *92*	29	33	___
16342	CSX Gondola w/ coil covers, *92*	18	23	___

		Exc	New	Cond/$
16343	Burlington Gondola w/ coil covers, *92*	20	23	___
16345/16346	SP TTUX Flatcar Set w/ trailers, *92*	55	65	___
16347	Ontario Nortland Bulkhead Flatcar w/ pulp load, *92*	22	26	___
16348	Lionel-Erie Liquefied Gas Car, *92*	23	25	___
16349	Allis Chalmers Condenser Car, *92*	28	35	___
16350	CP Rail Bulkhead Flatcar w/ wood load, *91 u*	20	29	___
16351	Lionel Flatcar w/ U.S. Navy submarine, *92*	34	39	___
16352	U.S. Military Flatcar w/ cruise missile, *92*	33	49	___
16353	B&M Gondola w/ coil covers, *91 u*	33	39	___
16355	Burlington Gondola, *92, 93 u, 94–95*	11	17	___
16356	MKT Depressed Flatcar w/ cable reels, *92*	17	21	___
16357	L&N Flatcar w/ trailer, *92*	24	31	___
16358	L&N Gondola w/ coil covers, *92*	17	21	___
16359	Pacific Coast Gondola w/ coil covers (SSS), *92*	33	38	___
16360	N&W Maxi-Stack Flatcar Set w/ containers "16361" and "16362", *93*	44	55	___
16363	Southern TTUX Flatcar Set w/ trailers "16364" and "16365", *93*	38	49	___
16367	Clinchfield Gondola w/ coil covers, *93*	18	21	___
16368	MKT Liquid Oxygen Car, *93*	21	22	___
16369	Amtrak Flatcar w/ wheel load, *92 u*	19	28	___
16370	Amtrak Flatcar w/ rail load, *92 u*	19	28	___
16371	BN I-Beam Flatcar w/ load, *92 u*	24	29	___
16372	Southern I-Beam Flatcar w/ load, *92 u*	24	34	___
16373	Erie-Lackawanna Flatcar w/ stakes, *93*	19	23	___
16374	D&RGW Flatcar w/ trailer, *93*	25	30	___
16375	NYC Bulkhead Flatcar, *93–95*	21	25	___
16376	UP Flatcar w/ trailer, *93–95*	31	37	___
16378	Toys "R" Us Flatcar w/ trailer, *92–93 u*	60	95	___
16379	NP Bulkhead Flatcar w/ pulp load, *93*	16	23	___
16380	UP I-Beam Flatcar w/ load, *93*	28	31	___
16381	CSX I-Beam Flatcar w/ load, *93*	26	31	___
16382	Kansas City Southern Bulkhead Flatcar, *93*	14	18	___
16383	Conrail Flatcar w/ trailer, *93*	50	60	___
16384	Soo Line Gondola w/ cable reels, *93*	14	19	___
16385	Soo Line Ore Car, *93*	65	75	___
16386	SP Flatcar w/ wood load, *94*	15	19	___
16387	Kansas City Southern Gondola w/ coil covers, *94*	13	16	___

		Exc	New	Cond/$
16388	LV Gondola w/ canisters, *94*	16	20	___
16389	PRR Flatcar w/ wheel load, *94*	27	32	___
16390	Lionel Flatcar w/ water tank, *94*	24	27	___
16391	Lionel Lines Gondola, *93 u*		15	___
16392	Wabash Gondola w/ canisters (O27), *93 u, 94*	7	9	___
16393	Wisconsin Central Bulkhead Flatcar, *94*	13	19	___
16394	Central Vermont Bulkhead Flatcar, *94*	20	30	___
16395	CP Flatcar w/ rail load, *94*	18	23	___
16396	Alaska Bulkhead Flatcar, *94*	17	22	___
16397	Milwaukee Road I-Beam Flatcar w/ load, *94*	30	34	___
16398	C&O Flatcar w/ trailer, *94*	80	85	___
16399	Western Pacific I-Beam Flatcar w/ load, *94*	31	35	___
16400	PRR Hopper (O27), *88 u, 89*	15	18	___
16402	Southern Quad Hopper w/ coal load (SSS), *87*	30	42	___
16406	CSX Quad Hopper w/ coal load, *90*	29	34	___
16407	B&M Covered Quad Hopper (SSS), *91*	28	37	___
16408	UP Hopper "6408" (O27), *90–91 u*	17	21	___
16410	MKT Hopper (O27), *92, 93 u*	19	24	___
16411	L&N Quad Hopper w/ coal load, *92*	28	32	___
16412	C&NW Covered Quad Hopper, *94*	16	23	___
16413	Clinchfield Quad Hopper w/ coal load, *94*	16	22	___
16414	CCC&St L Hopper (O27), *94*	18	25	___
16416	D&RGW Covered Quad Hopper, *95*	16	20	___
16417	Wabash Quad Hopper w/ coal load, *95*	19	22	___
16418	C&NW Hopper w/ coal load (O27), *95*	15	21	___
16419	Tennessee Central Hopper, *96*		17	___
16420	Western Maryland Quad Hopper w/ coal load (SSS), *95*	30	34	___
16421	Western Maryland Quad Hopper w/ coal load (SSS), *95*	30	33	___
16422	Western Maryland Quad Hopper w/ coal load (SSS), *95*		33	___
16423	Western Maryland Quad Hopper w/ coal load (SSS), *95*		30	___
16424	Western Maryland Covered Quad Hopper (SSS), *95*	34	39	___
16425	Western Maryland Covered Quad Hopper (SSS), *95*	25	29	___
16426	Western Maryland Covered Quad Hopper (SSS), *95*	24	27	___
16427	Western Maryland Covered Quad Hopper (SSS), *95*	27	30	___

		Exc	New	Cond/$
16429	Western Maryland Quad Hopper w/ coal loads set of 2		70	___
16430	Georgia Power Quad Hopper w/ coal load "82947", *95 u*		105	___
16431	Lionel Corporation 2-Bay Hopper "6456-1", *96*		30	___
16432	Lionel Corporation 2-Bay Hopper "6456-2", *96*		17	___
16433	Lionel Corporation 2-Bay Hopper "6456-3", *96*		18	___
16434	LV 2-Bay Hopper "6456", "TLDX", *97*		25	___
16435	Virginian 2-Bay Hopper "6456-1", *97*		30	___
16436	N&W 2-Bay Hopper "6456-2", *97*		33	___
16437	C&O 2-Bay Hopper "6456-3", *97*		33	___
16438	Frisco 4-Bay Covered Hopper "87538", *98*		34	___
16439	Southern 4-Bay Covered Hopper "77836", *98*		34	___
16440	Alaska 2-Bay Hopper "7100", *98–99*		35	___
16441	New York Central 4-Bay Hopper 6446 "886888", *99*		26	___
16442	Bethlehem Gondola "6462" (SSS), *99*		40	___
16443	GN 2-Bay Hopper "172364", *99–00*		20	___
16444	CNJ 2-Bay Hopper "643", *00*		20	___
16445	Frisco 2-Bay Hopper "93108", *00*		20	___
16446	Burlington 2-Bay Hopper, *00*		20	___
16447	PRR Tuscan 2-Bay Hopper, *00 u*		30	___
16448	PRR Gray 2-Bay Hopper, *00 u*		30	___
16449	PRR Black 2-Bay Hopper, *00 u*		30	___
16450	PRR Green 2-Bay Hopper, *00 u*		30	___
16451	Lionel Mines 2-Bay Hopper, *00 u*		50	___
16453	SP 2-Bay Hopper "460604", *01*		15	___
16454	Bethlehem Steel Hopper "41025", *01*		37	___
16455	Pioneer Seed 2-Bay Hopper, *00 u*		50	___
16456	B&O 2-Bay Hopper, *01*		20	___
16459	LV 2-Bay Hopper "51102", *01*		23	___
16460	Reading 2-Bay Hopper "79636", *02*		25	___
16463	Rio Grande Icebreaker Tunnel Car "18936", *02*		32	___
16464	NYC Icebreaker Tunnel Car "X3200", *02*		32	___
16465	WP 2-Bay Hopper "100340", *03*		19	___
16466	Pennsylvania Icebreaker Tunnel Car "16466", *03*		33	___
16467	Naughty and Nice Hopper 2-pack, *02*		60	___
16469	B&O Hopper "435351", *02*		22	___
16470	Naughty & Nice Ore Car 2-pack, *03*		43	___
16473	Rock Island Ore Car "99122", *03*		18	___
16474	Alaska Ore Car "16474", *04*		21	___

		Exc	New	Cond/$
16475	Santa Fe Hopper "16475", *04*		18	___
16480	Lionelville Snow Transport Quad Hopper, *04*		45	___
16482	Norfolk Southern Hopper, traditional, *05*		CP	___
16489	BNSF Ore Car, traditional, *05*		15	___
16490	Sodor Mining Co. Hopper, *05*		CP	___
16491	CNJ Hopper "60714", *06*		CP	___
16492	C&NW Ore Car "114023", *06*		CP	___
16493	Christmas Ice Breaker Car, *06*		CP	___
16500	Rock Island Bobber Caboose, *87–88*	9	13	___
16501	Lehigh Valley SP-type Caboose, *87*	19	24	___
16503	NYC Transfer Caboose, *87*	16	22	___
16504	Southern N5C Caboose (SSS), *87*	17	30	___
16505	Wabash SP-type Caboose, *88–91*	10	15	___
16506	Santa Fe B/W Caboose, *88*	18	24	___
16507	Mopar Express SP-type Caboose "1987", *87–88 u*	41	50	___
16508	Lionel Lines SP-type Caboose "6508", *89 u*	13	17	___
16509	D&RGW SP-type Caboose (SSS), *89*	19	24	___
16510	New Haven B/W Caboose, *89*	25	30	___
16511	PRR Bobber Caboose, *88 u, 89*	9	13	___
16513	Union Pacific SP-type Caboose, *89*	14	21	___
16515	Lionel Lines RailScope SP-type Caboose, *89*	20	23	___
16516	Lehigh Valley SP-type Caboose, *90*	15	26	___
16517	Atlantic Coast Line B/W Caboose, *90*	22	26	___
16518	Chessie System B/W Caboose, *90*	41	50	___
16519	Rock Island Transfer Caboose, *90*	13	17	___
16520	"Welcome To The Show" Circus SP-type Caboose, *89 u*	13	21	___
16521	PRR SP-type Caboose, *90–91*	8	11	___
16522	"Chills & Thrills" Circus N5C Caboose, *90–91*	10	15	___
16523	Alaska SP-type Caboose, *91*	24	31	___
16524	Anheuser-Busch SP-type Caboose, *89–92 u*	30	39	___
16525	D&H B/W Caboose (SSS), *91*	30	39	___
16526	Kansas City Southern SP-type Caboose, *91*	17	21	___
16527	Western Pacific Work Caboose, *92*		NM	___
16528	UP SP-type Caboose "6528", *90–91 u*	17	21	___
16529	Santa Fe SP-type Caboose "16829", *91*	9	13	___
16530	Mickey's World Tour SP-type Caboose "16830", *91, 92 u*	13	17	___
16531	Texas &Pacific SP-type Caboose, *92*	18	23	___
16533	C&NW B/W Caboose, *92*	29	41	___

		Exc	New	Cond/$
16534	Delaware & Hudson SP-type Caboose, *92*	14	19	___
16535	Erie-Lackawanna B/W Caboose, *91 u*	42	50	___
16536	Chessie System SP-type Caboose *92*, *93 u*, *94*, *95 u*		23	___
16537	MKT SP-type Caboose, *92*, *93 u*	17	21	___
16538	L&N B/W Caboose "1041", *92 u*	29	33	___
16538	L&N/Family Lines Steelside Caboose w/ smoke (Std. O), *92*		NM	___
16539	WP Steelside Caboose w/ smoke "539" (Std. O) (SSS), *92*	50	55	___
16541	Montana Rail Link E/V Caboose w/ smoke "10131", *93*	55	65	___
16543	NYC SP-type Caboose, *93–95*		20	___
16544	Union Pacific SP-type Caboose, *93–95*	22	26	___
16546	Clinchfield SP-type Caboose, *93*	22	26	___
16547	Happy Holidays SP-type Caboose, *93–95*	46	55	___
16548	Conrail SP-type Caboose, *93*	15	20	___
16549	Soo Line Work Caboose, *93*	18	26	___
16550	U.S. Navy Searchlight Caboose, *94–95*	17	21	___
16551	Budweiser SP-type Caboose, *93–94 u*	24	29	___
16552	Frisco Searchlight Caboose, *94*	23	26	___
16553	United Auto Workers SP-type Caboose, *93 u*		40	___
16554	GT E/V Caboose w/ smoke "79052", *94*	40	47	___
16555	C&O SP-type Caboose, *94*	22	26	___
16557	Ford SP-type Caboose, *94 u*	19	24	___
16558	Crayola SP-type Caboose, *94 u*, *95*	17	21	___
16559	Seaboard CC Caboose "5658", *95*	23	24	___
16560	Chrysler Mopar Caboose, *94 u*	22	24	___
16561	Union Pacific CC Caboose "25766", *95*	27	31	___
16562	Reading CC Caboose, *95*	25	29	___
16563	Lionel Lines SP-type Caboose, *95*	22	26	___
16564	Western Maryland CC Caboose (SSS), *95*	30	34	___
16565	Milwaukee Road B/W Caboose, *95*	50	60	___
16566	U.S. Army SP-type Caboose "907", *95*		28	___
16568	AT&SF SP-type Caboose, *96–99*		23	___
16570	NdeM E/V Caboose, *96*		NM	___
16571	Georgia Power SP-type Caboose "52789", *95 u*		65	___
16575	Sears Zenith, SP-type Caboose, *95*		35	___
16577	U.S. Coast Guard Work Caboose, *96*		26	___
16578	Lionel Lines SP-type Caboose, *95 u*		20	___
16579	GM/AC Delco, SP-type Caboose, *95*		35	___

		Exc	New	Cond/$
16580	Lionel SP-type Caboose, *96–99*		11	___
16581	Union Pacific Illuminated Caboose, *96*		30	___
16585	LL Illuminated Caboose "6257", *97*		NM	___
16586	SP Illuminated Caboose "6357", *97*		30	___
16590	Dodge Motorsports SP-type Caboose, "6950", *96*		40	___
16591	Little League Baseball SP-type Caboose "6397", *97*		30	___
16593	Lionel Belt Line Caboose "6257", *98*		32	___
16594	Lionel Caboose "6357", *98*		34	___
16600	Illinois Central Coal Dump Car, *88*	14	23	___
16601	Canadian National Searchlight Car, *88*	19	24	___
16602	Erie-Lackawanna Coal Dump Car, *87*	16	26	___
16603	Detroit Zoo Giraffe Car (O27), *87*	40	49	___
16604	NYC Log Dump Car, *87*	15	27	___
16605	Bronx Zoo Giraffe Car (O27), *88*	39	44	___
16606	Southern Searchlight Car, *87*	13	21	___
16607	Southern Coal Dump Car "16707" (SSS), *87*	18	26	___
16608	Lehigh Valley Searchlight Car, *87*	22	30	___
16609	Lehigh Valley Derrick Car, *87*	22	30	___
16610	Lionel Track Maintenance Car, *87–88*	15	25	___
16611	Santa Fe Log Dump Car, *88*	15	23	___
16612	Soo Line Log Dump Car, *89*	14	24	___
16613	MKT Coal Dump Car, *89*	17	26	___
16614	Reading Cop and Hobo Car (O27), *89*	24	25	___
16615	Lionel Lines Extension Searchlight Car, *89*	20	28	___
16616	D&RGW Searchlight Car (SSS), *89*	22	30	___
16617	C&NW Boxcar w/ ETD, *89*	23	34	___
16618	Santa Fe Track Maintenance Car, *89*	11	19	___
16619	Wabash Coal Dump Car, *90*	14	25	___
16620	C&O Track Maintenance Car, *90–91*	16	19	___
16621	Alaska Log Dump Car, *90*	24	31	___
16622	CSX Boxcar w/ ETD, *90–91*	20	28	___
16623	MKT DD Boxcar w/ ETD, *91*	16	23	___
16624	NH Cop and Hobo Car (O27), *90–91*	23	31	___
16625	NYC Extension Searchlight Car, *90*	22	34	___
16626	CSX Searchlight Car, *90*	18	26	___
16627	CSX Log Dump Car, *90*	19	23	___
16628	"Laughter" Circus Animated Gondola, *90–91*	36	43	___
16629	"Animal Car" Circus Elephant Car (O27), *90–91*	38	50	___
16630	SP Operating Cowboy Car (O27), *90–91*	22	26	___
16631	RI Boxcar w/ Steam RailSounds, *90*	110	130	___

		Exc	New	Cond/$
16632	BN Boxcar w/ Diesel RailSounds, *90*	90	100	___
16633	Great Northern Cop and Hobo Car (O27), *91*		NM	___
16634	WM Coal Dump Car, *91*	26	32	___
16635	CP Rail Track Maintenance Car, *91*		NM	___
16636	D&RGW Log Dump Car, *91*	19	25	___
16637	WP Extension Searchlight Car, *91*	27	30	___
16638	Lionelville Circus Operating Animal Car (O27), *91*	50	55	___
16639	B&O Boxcar w/ Steam RailSounds, *91*	100	120	___
16640	Rutland Boxcar w/ Diesel RailSounds, *91*	100	120	___
16641	Toys "R" Us Giraffe Car (O27), *90–91 u*	45	65	___
16642	Mickey's World Tour Goofy Car (O27), *91, 92 u*	33	41	___
16643	Amtrak Coal Dump Car, *91*		NM	___
16644	Amtrak Crane Car, *91, 92 u*	36	42	___
16645	Amtrak Searchlight Caboose, *91, 92 u*	27	30	___
16646	Railbox Boxcar w/ ETD, *92*		NM	___
16649	Railway Express Agency Boxcar w/ Steam RailSounds, *92*	110	140	___
16650	NYC "Pacemaker" Boxcar w/ Diesel RailSounds, *92*	100	135	___
16651	Circus Operating Clown Car (O27), *92*	34	38	___
16652	Lionel Radar Car, *92*	25	29	___
16653	Western Pacific Crane Car (SSS), *92*	44	60	___
16655	Steam Tender w/ RailSounds "1993", *93*	115	140	___
16656	Burlington Log Dump Car, *92 u*	18	25	___
16657	Lehigh Valley Coal Dump Car, *92 u*	22	29	___
16658	Erie-Lackawanna Crane Car, *93*	47	65	___
16659	Union Pacific Searchlight Car, *93–95*	15	18	___
16660	Lionel Fire Car w/ ladders, *93–94*	28	33	___
16661	Lionel Flatcar w/ boat, *93*	20	21	___
16662	Looney Tunes Operating Bugs Bunny and Yosemite Sam Car (O27), *93–94*	27	28	___
16663	Missouri Pacific Searchlight Car, *93*	16	19	___
16664	L&N Coal Dump Car, *93*	22	25	___
16665	Maine Central Log Dump Car, *93*	23	27	___
16666	Lionel Toxic Waste Car, *93–94*	25	32	___
16667	Conrail Searchlight Car, *93*	27	30	___
16668	Ontario Northland Log Dump Car, *93*	20	24	___
16669	Soo Line Searchlight Car, *93*	17	21	___
16670	Lionel TV Car, *93–94*	20	21	___

		Exc	New	Cond/$
16673	Lionel Lines Tender w/ whistle, *94–97*	33	42	___
16674	Pinkerton Animated Gondola, *94*	28	32	___
16675	Great Northern Log Dump Car, *94*	21	25	___
16676	Burlington Coal Dump Car, *94*	23	28	___
16677	NATO Flatcar w/ Royal Navy submarine, *94*	34	44	___
16678	Rock Island Searchlight Car, *94*	21	23	___
16679	U.S. Mail Operating Boxcar, *94*	45	50	___
16680	Lionel Cherry Picker Car, *94*	25	29	___
16681	Aquarium Car, *95*	45	50	___
16682	Lionelville Farms Operating Stock Car (O27), *94*	23	27	___
16683	Los Angeles Zoo Elephant Car (O27), *94*	22	26	___
16684	U.S. Navy Crane Car, *94–95*	35	40	___
16685	Erie Extension Searchlight Car, *95*	30	34	___
16686	Mickey Mouse and Big Bad Pete Animated Boxcar, *95*	28	35	___
16687	U.S. Mail Operating Boxcar, *94*	29	37	___
16688	Lionel Fire Car w/ ladders, *94*	34	45	___
16689	Lionel Toxic Waste Car, *94*	29	32	___
16690	Looney Tunes Operating Bugs Bunny and Yosemite Sam Car (O27), *94*	30	34	___
16701	Southern Tool Car (SSS), *87*	43	55	___
16702	Amtrak Bunk Car, *91, 92 u*	25	27	___
16703	NYC Tool Car, *92*	24	31	___
16704	Lionel TV Car, *94*	27	29	___
16705	Chesapeake & Ohio Cop and Hobo Car, *95*	28	34	___
16706	Animal Transport Service Giraffe Car, *95*	27	30	___
16708	C&NW Track Maintenance Car, *95*	24	31	___
16709	New York Central Derrick Car, *95*	22	28	___
16710	U.S. Army Operating Missile Car, *95*	40	42	___
16711	Pennsylvania Searchlight Car, *95*	27	31	___
16712	Pinkerton Animated Gondola, *95*	34	39	___
16713	Great Northern Log Dump Car, *95*		NM	___
16714	Burlington Coal Dump Car, *95*		NM	___
16715	AT&SF Log Dump Car, *96–99*		24	___
16717	Jersey Central Crane Car, *96*		41	___
16718	USMC Missile Launching Flatcar, *96*	36	37	___
16719	Exploding Boxcar, *96*		38	___
16720	Lionel Lines Searchlight Car "3650", *96–97*		50	___
16724	Mickey and Friends Submarine Car, *96*		39	___
16725	Rhino Transport Car, *97*		31	___

		Exc	New	Cond/$
16726	U.S. Army Fire Ladder Car, *96*		43	___
16734	U.S. Coast Guard Searchlight Car, *96*		30	___
16735	U.S. Coast Guard Flatcar w/ radar, *96*	28	35	___
16736	U.S. Coast Guard Derrick Car, *96*		34	___
16737	Warner Bros. Road Runner & Wile E. Coyote ACME Gondola "3444", *96*		50	___
16738	Warner Bros. Pepe LePew & Penelope Boxcar "3370", *96*		38	___
16739	Warner Bros. Foghorn Leghorn Poultry Car "6434", *96*		41	___
16740	Lionel Corporation Mail Car "3428", *96*		37	___
16741	Union Pacific Illuminated Bunk Car, *97*		25	___
16742	Trout Ranch Aquarium Car "3435", *96*		32	___
16744	Port of Lionel City Searchlight Car, *97*		30	___
16745	Port of Lionel City Flatcar w/ Radar, *97*		30	___
16746	Port of Lionel City Derrick Car, *97*		30	___
16747	Breyer Animated Horsecar "6473", *97*		34	___
16748	US Forest Service Log-Dump Car "3361", *97*		30	___
16749	Midget Mines Ore-Dump Car "3479", *97*		36	___
16750	Lionel City Aquarium Car "3436", *97*		32	___
16751	WLNL Channel 7-AIREX Sports TV Car "3545", *97*		25	___
16752	Warner Bros. Marvin the Martian Missile-Launching Flatcar "6655", *97*	100	115	___
16754	Warner Bros. Porky Pig & Instant Martians "6805", *97*	110	150	___
16755	Warner Bros. Daffy Duck Animated Balloon Car "3470", *97*	95	130	___
16760	Pluto and Cats Animated Gondola "3444", *97*		55	___
16765	Bureau of Land Management Log Car "3351", *98*		30	___
16766	Bureau of Land Management Ore Car "3479", *98*		31	___
16767	New York Central Ice Docks Ice Car "6352", *98*		47	___
16776	Lionel Holiday RailSounds Boxcar, *98*		65	___
16777	Lionel Cola Animated Car & Platform, *98*		100	___
16782	Bethlehem Ore Dump Car "3479", *99*		95	___
16783	Westside Lumber Log Dump Car "3351", *99*		32	___
16784	Pratt's Hollow Seed Dump Car "3479", *99*		36	___
16785	Happy Holidays Music Reefer "5700", *99*		100	___
16789	Easter Operating Boxcar "9700", *99*		39	___
16790	UP Crowsounds Stock Car "3356", *99*		90	___
16791	NY City Lights Boxcar "9700", *99*		44	___
16792	Constellation Boxcar "9600", *99*		37	___

		Exc	New	Cond/$
16793	Animated Glow-in-the-Dark Alien Boxcar "9700", *99*		44	___
16794	Wicked Witch Halloween Boxcar "9700", *99*		46	___
16795	Elf Chasing Rudolph Gondola "6462", *99*		55	___
16796	Snowman Loading Ice Car "6352", *99*		55	___
16805	Budweiser Malt Nutrine Reefer "3285" *91–92 u*	65	90	___
16806	Toys "R" Us Boxcar, *92 u*	21	25	___
16807	H.J. Heinz Reefer "301", *93*	23	27	___
16808	Toys "R" Us Boxcar, *93 u*	28	30	___
16817	Ambassador 1-D Tank Car "1999", *00 u*		105	___
16818	Engineer Award Tank Car, *00 u*		680	___
16819	JLC Award Tank Car, *00 u*		750	___
16820	Ambassador Thank You Boxcar "2000", *00 u*	280	305	___
16901	Lionel Catalog Video, *91 u*	17	21	___
16903	CP Bulkhead Flatcar w/ pulp load (SSS), *94*	22	25	___
16904	NYC "Pacemaker" TTUX Flatcar Set w/ trailers "16905" and "16906", *94*	55	60	___
16907	Lionel Flatcar w/ farm tractors, *94*	27	33	___
16908	U.S. Navy Flatcar "04039" w/ submarine "930", *94–95*	39	46	___
16909	U.S. Navy Gondola w/ canisters "16556", *94–95*	16	22	___
16910	Missouri Pacific Flatcar w/ trailer, *94*	22	27	___
16911	B&M Flatcar w/ trailer, *94*	28	34	___
16912	CN Maxi-Stack Flatcar Set w/ containers "640000" and "640001", *94*	70	75	___
16915	Lionel Lines Gondola (O27), *93–94 u*	7	10	___
16916	Ford Flatcar w/ trailer, *94 u*	38	45	___
16917	Crayola Gondola w/ crayons, *94 u, 95*	8	9	___
16918	Budweiser Flatcar w/ trailer, *94*		NM	___
16919	Chrysler Mopar Gondola w/ coil covers, *94–96*	33	36	___
16920	Lionel Flatcar w/ construction block helicopter, *95*		NM	___
16922	Chesapeake &Ohio Flatcar w/ trailer, *95*	25	31	___
16923	Lionel Intermodal Service Flatcar w/ wheelchocks, *95*	15	22	___
16924	Lionel Corporation Flatcar w/ trailer "6424", *96*		24	___
16925	New York Central Flatcar w/ trailer, *95*	65	85	___
16926	Frisco Flatcar w/ trailers, *95*	24	31	___
16927	New York Central Flatcar w/ gondola, *95*	17	22	___
16928	Soo Line Flatcar w/ dump bin (O27), *95*	12	15	___

		Exc	New	Cond/$
16929	BCRail Gondola w/ cable reels, *95*	21	25	___
16930	Santa Fe Flatcar w/ wheel load, *95*	20	25	___
16932	Erie Flatcar w/ rail load, *95*	17	22	___
16933	Lionel Lines Flatcar w/ automobiles, *95*	23	25	___
16934	Pennsylvania Flatcar w/ Ertl road grader, *95*	28	39	___
16935	UP Depressed Flatcar w/ Ertl bulldozer, *95*	22	35	___
16936	Sealand Maxi-Stack Flatcar Set w/ containers "16937" and "16938", *95*	70	85	___
16939	U.S. Navy Flatcar w/ boat "04040", *95*	25	31	___
16940	AT&SF Flatcar w/ trailer, *96–99*		40	___
16941	AT&SF Flatcar w/ autos, *96–99*		25	___
16943	Jersey Central Gondola, *96*		18	___
16944	Georgia Power Depressed Flatcar w/ transformer "31438", *95 u*		50	___
16945	Georgia Power Depressed Flatcar w/ cable reels "31950", *95 u*		50	___
16946	C&O F9 Well Car "3840", *96*		31	___
16951	Southern I-Beam Flatcar w/ load "9823", *97*		25	___
16952	U.S. Navy Flatcar w/ Ertl helicopter, *96*		25	___
16953	NYC Flatcar w/ Red Wing Shoes trailer "1905-95", *95 u*	39	45	___
16954	NYC Flatcar w/ Ertl scraper "6424", *96*		30	___
16955	AT&SF Flatcar w/ Ertl Challenger, *96*		30	___
16956	Zenith Flatcar w/ trailer, *95 u*		130	___
16957	Lionel Depressed-Center Flatcar w/ Ertl Case 4WD tractor "6461", *96*		29	___
16958	Lionel Flatcar w/ Ertl New Hollandloader, *96*		26	___
16960	U.S.C.G Flatcar w/ boat, *96*		40	___
16961	GM/AC Delco Flatcar w/ trailer, *95*		70	___
16963	Lionel Corporation Flatcar "6411", *96–97*		34	___
16964	Lionel Corporation Gondola "6462", *97*		22	___
16965	Lionel Scout Flatcar w/ stakes "6424", *96–97*		20	___
16967	Lionel Depressed-Center Flatcar w/ transformer "6461", *96*		21	___
16968	Lionel Aviation Depressed-Center Flatcar w/ General Hospital LifeFlight Ertl Helicopter "6461", *96*		35	___
16969	Flatcar w/ Beechcraft Bonanza "6411", *96*		33	___
16970	LA County Flatcar w/ motorized LA County lifeguard powerboat "6424", *96*		20	___
16971	Port of Lionel City Flatcar w/ boat, *97*		35	___
16972	P&LE Gondola "6462", *97*		22	___
16975	Lionel Doublestack Set "6480", 2 well cars, *97*		75	___

		Exc	New	Cond/$
16978	MILW Flatcar "6424" w/ P&H shovel, *97*		43	___
16980	Warner Bros. Speedy Gonzales Missile Flatcar "6823", *97*		41	___
16982	BC Rail Bulkhead Flatcar w/ wood load "9823", *97*		28	___
16983	PRR F9 Well Car w/ cable reels "6983", *97*		39	___
16986	Sears Zenith Flatcar w/ bulkheads, *96 u*		45	___
16987	Musco Lighting Flatcar w/ bulkheads, *97 u*		35	___
16997	Lionel Lines Recovery Crane Car, *99*		50	___
17002	Conrail 2-Bay ACF Hopper (Std. O), *87*	42	47	___
17003	Du Pont 2-Bay ACF Hopper (Std. O), *90*	39	45	___
17004	MKT 2-Bay ACF Hopper (Std. O), *91*	23	27	___
17005	Cargill 2-Bay ACF Hopper (Std. O), *92*	29	37	___
17006	Soo Line 2-Bay ACF Hopper (Std. O) (SSS), *93*	31	36	___
17007	GN 2-Bay ACF Hopper "173872" (Std. O), *94*	26	31	___
17008	D&RGW 2-Bay ACF Hopper "10009" (Std. O), *95*		31	___
17009	New York Central 2-Bay ACF Hopper, *96*		37	___
17010	Government du Canada ACF 2-Bay Covered Hopper "7000", *98*		32	___
17011	NP ACF 2-Bay Covered Hoppers "75052", *98*		44	___
17012	Government du Canada ACF 2-Bay Covered Hopper "7001", *98*		30	___
17013	NYC Graffiti 2-Bay Covered Hopper "7000", *99*		55	___
17014	Graffiti 2-Bay Covered Hopper "7000" (Std. O), *99*		45	___
17015	Corning 2-Bay Hopper "90409" (Std. O), *01*		40	___
17016	C&NW 2-Bay Hopper "96644" (Std. O), *01* (Std. O), *02*		46	___
17017	Chessie System 2-Bay Hopper "605527"		32	___
17018	Nickel Plate Road Offset Hopper "33074", *02*		43	___
17019	Santa Fe Offset Hopper "78299", *02*		43	___
17020	Frisco Offset Hopper "92092", *02*		43	___
17021	NYC Offset Hopper "867999", *02*		43	___
17022	Burlington 2-Bay ACF Hopper "183925" (Std. O), *03*		30	___
17023	BNSF 2-Bay Hopper "409038" (Std. O), *04*		30	___
17024	Reading Offset Hopper "81089" (Std. O), *03–04*		43	___
17025	C&O Offset Hopper "300027" (Std. O), *03–04*		43	___
17026	D&H Offset Hopper "7215" (Std. O), *03–04*		41	___
17027	IC Offset Hopper "92142" (Std. O), *03–04*		49	___
17028	GE PS-2 2-Bay Covered Hopper "326" (Std. O), *03–04*		35	___
17029	CNJ PS-2 2-Bay Covered Hopper "803" (Std. O), *03–04*		35	___

		Exc	New	Cond/$
17030	Milwaukee Road PS-2 2-Bay Covered Hopper "99708" (Std. O), *03–04*		35	___
17031	SP PS-2 2-Bay Covered Hopper "401306" (Std. O), *03–04*		38	___
17038	Clinchfield PS-2 Covered Hopper, *05*		70	___
17039	Boston & Maine PS-2 Covered Hopper, *05*		CP	___
17040	Norfolk & Western PS-2 Covered Hopper, *05*		CP	___
17041	Great Northern Offset Hopper, *05*		CP	___
17042	Green Bay & Western Offset Hopper, *05*		CP	___
17043	Baltimore & Ohio Offset Hopper, *05*		CP	___
17063	Santa Fe PS-2 2-Bay Covered Hopper "82297" (Std. O), *06*		CP	___
17064	MKT PS-2 2-Bay Covered Hopper "1311" (Std. O), *06*		CP	___
17065	Boraxo PS-2 2-Bay Covered Hopper "31062" (Std. O), *06*		CP	___
17066	Pennsylvania PS-2 2-Bay Covered Hopper "256177" (Std. O), *06*		CP	___
17067	Rock Island Offset Hopper w/ gravel load "89500" (Std. O), *06*		CP	___
17068	CNJ Offset Hopper "61261" (Std. O), *06*		CP	___
17069	Maine Central Offset Hopper "3785" (Std. O), *06*		CP	___
17070	P&LE Offset Hopper "4990" (Std. O), *06*		CP	___
17083	C&O Offset Hopper "47386" (Std. O), *05*		40	___
17100	Chessie System 3-Bay ACF Hopper	49	85	___
17101	Chessie System 3-Bay ACF Hopper (Std. O), *88*	37	45	___
17102	Chessie System 3-Bay ACF Hopper (Std. O), *88*	35	41	___
17103	Chessie System 3-Bay ACF Hopper (Std. O), *88*	31	34	___
17104	Chessie System 3-Bay ACF Hopper (Std. O), *88*	38	46	___
17105	Chessie System 3-Bay ACF Hopper (Std. O), *95*	39	46	___
17107	Sclair 3-Bay ACF Hopper (Std. O), *89*	50	55	___
17108	Santa Fe 3-Bay ACF Hopper (Std. O), *90*	42	48	___
17109	N&W 3-Bay ACF Hopper (Std. O), *91*	24	31	___
17110	UP Hopper w/ coal load (Std. O), *91*	24	30	___
17111	Reading Hopper w/ coal load (Std. O), *91*	23	28	___
17112	Erie-Lack. 3-Bay ACF Hopper (Std. O), *92*	24	34	___
17113	LV Hopper w/ coal load (Std. O), *92–93*	25	32	___

		Exc	New	Cond/$
17114	Peabody Hopper w/ coal load (Std. O), *92–93*	26	30	___
17118	Archer Daniels Midland 3-Bay ACF Hopper "60029" (Std. O), *93*	28	35	___
17120	CSX Hopper w/ coal load "295110" (Std. O), *94*	28	33	___
17121	ICG Hopper w/ coal load "72867" (Std. O), *94*	26	33	___
17122	RI 3-Bay ACF Hopper "800200" (Std. O), *94*	32	39	___
17123	Cargill Covered Grain Hopper "844304" (Std. O), *95*	25	34	___
17124	Archer Daniels Midland 3-Bay ACF Hopper "50224" (Std. O), *95*	24	30	___
17125	Goodyear 3-Bay ACF Hopper (Std. O), *95*		NM	___
17127	Delaware & Hudson 3-Bay Hopper, *96*		34	___
17128	Chesapeake & Ohio 3-Bay hopper, *96*		30	___
17129	WM 3-Bay hopper w/ coal load "9300" (Std O), *97*		34	___
17132	PRR 3-Bay ACF Hopper "260815", *98*		40	___
17133	BNSF ACF 3-Bay Covered Hopper "403698", *98*		38	___
17134	BNSF 3-Bay Covered Hopper "403698" (Std. O), *01*		38	___
17135	BNSF ACF 3-Bay Covered Hopper w/ ETD, *98*		39	___
17137	Cargill 3-Bay Covered Hopper "1219" (Std. O), *99*		45	___
17138	Farmers Elevator 3-Bay Covered Hopper (Std. O), *99*		45	___
17139	Grain Train 3-Bay Hopper "BLMR 1025", *99–00*		39	___
17140	Virginian 3-Bay Hopper "5260-5265", 6-pack, *99*		230	___
17147	C&O 3-Bay Hopper "156330-156335", 6-pack, *99*		230	___
17154	Alberta Cylindrical Hopper "628373" (Std. O), *01*		40	___
17155	Shell Cylindrical Hopper "3527" (Std. O), *01*		40	___
17155	Shell Cylindrical Hopper "3527" (Std. O), *01*		40	___
17156	ACF Pressureaide 3-Bay Hopper "59267" (Std. O), *01*		27	___
17157	Wonder Bread "56670" 3-Bay Hopper (Std. O), *01*		40	___
17158	Conrail Coal Hopper "487739" (Std. O), *01*		42	___
17159	N&W Coal Hopper "1776" (Std. O), *01*		45	___
17170	General Mills 3-Bay Covered Hopper (Std. O), *00 u*		60	___
17171	Lionel Lion Cylindrical Hopper (Std. O), *01*		45	___
17172	CP Rail Cylindrical Hopper "385206" (Std. O), *02*		37	___
17173	Government of Canada Cylindrical Hopper "111031" (Std. O), *02*		33	___
17174	GN 3-Bay Hopper "171250" (Std. O), *02*		33	___

		Exc	New	Cond/$
17175	IC PS-2CD 4427 Covered Hopper "57031" (Std. O), *02*		40	___
17176	Cargill PS-2CD 4427 Covered Hopper "2514" (Std. O), *02*		46	___
17177	Demonstrator PS-2CD 4427 Covered Hopper 2500 (Std. O), *02*		40	___
17178	Santa Fe PS-2CD 4427 Covered Hopper 304774 (Std. O), *02*		40	___
17179	Indianapolis Power & Light Coal Hopper "10074", Std. O, *02*		40	___
17180	Rock Island Coal Hopper "700665" (Std. O), *02*		40	___
17181	NYC 4-Bay ACF Centerflow Hopper " 892138" (Std. O), *03*		45	___
17182	Sigco, Hybrids 4-Bay ACF Centerflow Hopper "1100" (Std. O), *03*		46	___
17183	C&O Hopper "156341" (Std. O), *01*		30	___
17184	Virginian Hopper "5271" (Std. O), *01*		30	___
17185	LLCX Bathtub Gondola "877900" (Std. O), *01*		36	___
17186	Cannonaide 4-Bay ACF Centerflow Hopper "96169" (Std. O), *03*		40	___
17187	Rio Grande 4-Bay ACF Centerflow Hopper "15521" (Std. O), *03*		40	___
17188	Govt. of Canada 3-Bay Cylindrical Hopper "106068" (Std. O), *03*		48	___
17189	Saskatchewan Grain 3-Bay Cylindrical Hopper "1625338" (Std. O), *03*		48	___
17190	Soo/CP 3-Bay ACF Hopper "119303" (Std. O), *03*		37	___
17191	BN PS-2CD 4427 Hopper "450669" (Std. O), *03–04*		45	___
17192	Lehigh Valley PS-2CD 4427 Hopper "51118"(Std. O), *03–04*		40	___
17193	Chessie System/WM PS-2CD 4427 Hopper "4673" (Std. O), *03–04*		30	___
17194	MKT PS-2CD 4427 Hopper "1122" (Std. O), *03–04*		40	___
17195	L&N 3-Bay Hopper "240850" (Std. O), *04*		40	___
17196	Firestone 4-Bay Hopper "53240" (Std. O), *04*		40	___
17197	Diamond Chemicals 4-Bay Hopper "53286" (Std. O), *04*		40	___
17198	Hercules 4-Bay Hopper "50503" (Std. O), *04*		40	___
17199	Conrail 4-Bay Hopper "888367" (Std. O), *04*		46	___
17200	Canadian Pacific Boxcar (Std. O), *89*	46	47	___
17201	Conrail Boxcar (Std. O), *87*	33	38	___
17202	Santa Fe Boxcar w/ Diesel RailSounds (Std. O), *90*	80	85	___

		Exc	New	Cond/$
17203	Cotton Belt DD Boxcar (Std. O), *91*	33	38	___
17204	Missouri Pacific DD Boxcar (Std. O), *91*	27	30	___
17207	C&IM DD Boxcar (Std. O), *92*	36	42	___
17208	Union Pacific DD Boxcar (Std. O), *92*	35	40	___
17209	B&O DD Boxcar "296000" (Std. O), *93*	37	43	___
17210	Chicago & Illinois Midland Boxcar "16021" (Std. O), *92 u*	30	39	___
17211	Chicago & Illinois Midland Boxcar "16022" (Std. O), *92 u*	30	39	___
17212	Chicago & Illinois Midland Boxcar "16023" (Std. O), *92 u*	24	31	___
17213	Susquehanna Boxcar "501" (Std. O), *93*	28	31	___
17214	Railbox Boxcar w/ Diesel RailSounds (Std. O), *93*	75	85	___
17216	PRR DD Boxcar "60155" (Std. O), *94*	34	38	___
17217	New Haven "State of Maine" Boxcar " 45003" (Std. O), *95*	28	39	___
17218	BAR "State of Maine" Boxcar "2184" (Std. O), *95*	23	36	___
17219	Tazmanian Devil 40th Birthday Boxcar (Std. O), *95*	37	48	___
17220	Pennsylvania Boxcar (Std. O), *96*		23	___
17221	NYCBoxcar (Std. O), *96*		34	___
17222	Western Pacific Boxcar (Std. O), *96*	28	34	___
17223	Milwaukee Road DD Boxcar Std. 0, *96*		34	___
17224	Central of Georgia Boxcar "9464-197" (Std O), *97*	15	29	___
17225	Penn Central Boxcar "9464-297" (Std O), *97*	13	26	___
17226	Milwaukee Road Boxcar "9464-397" (Std O), *97*		23	___
17227	UP DD Boxcar "9200" (Std O), *97*		35	___
17231	Wisconsin Central Double-Door Boxcar w/ auto frames "9200", *98*		40	___
17232	Southern Pacific/Union Pacific Merger Double-Door Boxcar "9200", *98*		33	___
17233	Western Pacific Boxcar "9464-198", *98*		27	___
17234	Port Huron & Detroit Boxcar "9464-298", *98*		33	___
17235	Boston & Maine Boxcar "9464-398", *98*		41	___
17239	AT&SF Texas Chief Boxcar "9464-1", *97*		50	___
17240	AT&SF Super Chief Boxcar "9464-2", *97*		50	___
17241	AT&SF El Capitan Boxcar "9464-3", *97*		50	___
17242	AT&SF Grand Canyon Boxcar "9464-4", *97*		60	___
17243	NP Boxcar "8722", *98*		48	___

		Exc	New	Cond/$
17244	Santa Fe Chief Boxcar, *98*		37	___
17245	C&O Boxcar with Chessie kitten, *98*		44	___
17246	NYC Pacemaker Rolling Stock 4-pack, *98*		200	___
17247	NYC 9464 Boxcar "174940", *98*		135	___
17248	NYC 9464 Boxcar "174945", *98*		115	___
17249	NYC 9464 Boxcar "174949", *98*		100	___
17250	UP Boxcar "507406" (Std. O), *99*		45	___
17251	BNSF Modern Boxcar "103277", *99*		41	___
17252	NS Modern Boxcar "564824" (Std O), *99*		41	___
17253	CSX Modern Boxcar "141756" (Std O), *99*		35	___
17254	UP Modern Boxcar "551967" (Std O), *99*		42	___
17255	Chevy Modern Double-Door Boxcar "9200" (Std O), *99*		38	___
17257	Atlantic Coast Line Boxcar 9464 "28809" (Std. O), *99*		36	___
17258	D&H 9464 Boxcar "29055" Std. O, *99*		41	___
17259	MKT 9464 Boxcar "1422" (Std. O), *99*		34	___
17260	CP Rail 9464 Boxcar "286138" (Std. O), silver, *00*		45	___
17261	CP Rail 9464 Boxcar "85154", green, *00*		44	___
17262	CP Rail 9464 Boxcar "56776" (Std. O), red, *00*		48	___
17263	NYC Modern Boxcar "45725" (Std O), *00*		46	___
17264	C&O Modern Boxcar "6054" (Std O), *00*		44	___
17265	U.S. Army Modern Boxcar, (Std O), *00*		35	___
17266	Monon Modern Boxcar "911" (Std O), *00*		45	___
17268	C&O 9464 Boxcar "12700" (Std.O), *01*		44	___
17269	Western Maryland 9464 Boxcar "29140" (Std. O), *01*		44	___
17270	B&O Timesaver 9464 Boxcar "467439" (Std. O), *01*		42	___
17271	The Rock Modern Boxcar "300324" (Std. O), *01*		37	___
17272	Railbox Modern Boxcar "15150" (Std. O), *01*		27	___
17273	DT&I DD Boxcar "26852" (Std. O), *01*		44	___
17274	Soo Line DD Boxcar "177587" (Std. O), *01*		42	___
17275	NYC PS-1 Boxcar "175008" (Std. O), *02*		43	___
17276	SSW (Cotton Belt) PS-1 Boxcar "75000" (Std. O), *02*		44	___
17277	Rio Grande PS-1 Boxcar "69676" (Std. O), *02*		40	___
17278	WP PS-1 Boxcar "1953" (Std. O), *02*		44	___
17279	Ontario Northland Modern Boxcar "7428" (Std. O), *02*		40	___
17280	Santa Fe 2-Door Boxcar w/ automobile		45	___

frames, "600194" (Std. O), *02*

		Exc	New	Cond/$
17281	PRR Double-Door Boxcar "83158" (Std. O), *04*		42	___
17282	UP Double-Door Boxcar "160300" (Std. O), *04*		42	___
17283	GM&O Double-Door Boxcar "9077" (Std. O), *04*		41	___
17284	Erie Double-Door Boxcar "66000" (Std. O), *04*		41	___
17285	CSX Big Blue Modern Boxcar "151296" (Std. O), *03*		36	___
17287	BAR Modern Boxcar "5976" (Std. O), *03*		35	___
17288	NYC PS-1 Boxcar "175012" (Std. O), *03–04*		38	___
17289	GN PS-1 Boxcar "18485" (Std. O), *03*		40	___
17290	Seaboard PS-1 Boxcar "24452" (Std. O), *03–04*		42	___
17291	RI PS-1 Boxcar "21110" (Std. O), *03–04*		42	___
17292	B&M PS-1 Boxcar "76182" (Std. O), *04*		34	___
17293	IC PS-1 Boxcar "400666" (Std. O), *04*		40	___
17294	TP&W PS-1 Boxcar "5036" (Std. O), *04*		36	___
17295	Santa Fe PS-1 Boxcar "276749" (Std. O), *04*		40	___
17297	UP PS-1 Boxcar, *03*		100	___
17300	Canadian Pacific Reefer (Std. O), *89*	28	33	___
17301	Conrail Reefer (Std. O), *87*	35	42	___
17302	Santa Fe Reefer w/ ETD (Std. O), *90*	35	41	___
17303	C&O Reefer "7890" (Std. O), *93*	23	30	___
17304	Wabash Reefer "26269" (Std. O), *94*	29	37	___
17305	Pacific Fruit Express Reefer "459400" (Std. O), *94*	27	40	___
17306	Pacific Fruit Express Reefer "459401" (Std. O), *94*	19	27	___
17307	Tropicana Reefer "300" (Std. O), *95*	44	65	___
17308	Tropicana Reefer "301" (Std. O), *95*	22	35	___
17309	Tropicana Reefer "302" (Std. O), *95*	21	29	___
17310	Tropicana Reefer "303" (Std. O), *95*	20	27	___
17311	REA Reefer (Std. O), *96*	28	30	___
17314	PFE Reefer "9800-198", *98*		42	___
17315	PFE Reefer "9800-298", *98*		39	___
17316	NP Reefer "98583", *98*		50	___
17317	PRR Reefer FGE "91904", *98*		36	___
17318	UP Refrigerator Car "170650" (Std. O), *99*		47	___
17319	PFE Standard O Reefer 6-pack, *01*		300	___
17331	Hood's General American Milk Car "802" (Std. O), *02*		100	___
17332	Pfaudler General American Milk Car "501" (Std. O), *02*		70	___

		Exc	New	Cond/$
17334	REA General American Milk Car "1741" (Std. O), *02*		100	___
17335	New Haven General American Milk Car "102" (Std. O), *02*		75	___
17336	PFE Steel-sided Refrigerator Car "17760" (Std. O), *03*		45	___
17337	CN Steel-sided Refrigerator Car "209712" (Std. O), *03*		38	___
17338	Merchants Dispatch Transit Steel-sided Refrigerator Car "12322" (Std. O), *03*		39	___
17339	Burlington Steel-sided Refrigerator Car "74825" (Std. O), *03*		45	___
17340	White Bros. General American Milk Car "891" (Std. O), *03*		44	___
17341	Dairymen's League General American Milk Car "779" (Std. O), *03*		43	___
17342	Miller Beer Steel-sided Refrigerator Car (Std. O), *03 u*		50	___
17343	Miller Beer Steel-sided Refrigerator Car (Std. O), *03 u*		55	___
17349	NYC General American Milk Car "6581" (Std. O), *03 u*		42	___
17350	Hood's General American Milk Car "503" (Std. O), *03 u*		45	___
17351	Santa Fe Steel-sided Refrigerator Car "3526" (Std. O), *04*		43	___
17352	Pacific Fruit Express Steel-sided Refrigerator Car "20043" (Std. O), *04*		40	___
17353	Needham Packing Co. Steel-sided Refrigerator Car "60507" (Std. O), *04*		44	___
17354	Swift Steel-sided Refrigerator Car "15392" (Std. O), *04*		42	___
17355	Hood's Steel-sided Refrigerator Car "550" (Std. O), *04*		43	___
17356	Nestle Nesquik Steel-sided Refrigerator Car (Std. O), *04*		44	___
17357	Borden's Steel-sided Refrigerator Car "522" (Std. O), *04*		47	___
17358	Fairfield Farms Steel-sided Refrigerator Car (Std. O), *04*		44	___
17360	Hood's General American Milk Car "810" (Std. O), *03*		46	___
17361	Hood's General American Milk Car "811" (Std. O), *03*		43	___

		Exc	New	Cond/$
17362	Pfaudler General American Milk Car "502" (Std. O), *03*		47	___
17363	Pfaudler General American Milk Car "503" (Std. O), *03*		40	___
17364	REA General American Milk Car "1742" (Std. O), *03*		38	___
17365	REA General American Milk Car "1743" (Std. O), *03*		44	___
17366	NH General American Milk Car "103" (Std. O), *03*		43	___
17367	NH General American Milk Car "104" (Std. O), *03*		47	___
17368	White Brothers General American Milk Car "892" (Std. O), *03*		43	___
17369	White Brothers General American Milk Car "893" (Std. O), *03*		47	___
17370	Dairymen's League General American Milk Car "780" (Std. O), *03*		47	___
17371	Dairymen's League General American Milk Car "781" (Std. O), *03*		47	___
17372	NYC General American Milk Car "6582" (Std. O), *03*		47	___
17373	NYC General American Milk Car "6583" (Std. O), *03*		40	___
17374	Hood's General American Milk Car (2nd version) "504" (Std. O), *03*		43	___
17375	Hood's General American Milk Car (2nd version) "505" (Std. O), *03*		47	___
17377	American Railway Express Milk Car "302" (Std. O), *05*		260	___
17378	Supplee Wills Jones Milk Car (Std. O), *05*		CP	___
17379	NP Steel-sided Refrigerator Car "91353" (Std. O), *05*		CP	___
17380	PFE Silver Steel-sided Refrigerator Car "45698" (Std. O), *05*		CP	___
17381	NorthWestern Steel-sided Refrigerator Car "751" (Std. O), *05*		40	___
17397	PFE Steel-sided Refrigerator Car "47767" (Std. O), *05*		45	___
17398	A&P Milk Car "737" (Std. O), *06*		CP	___
17399	Bowman Dairy Milk Car "117" (Std. O), *06*		CP	___
17400	CP Rail Gondola w/ coal load (Std. O), *89*	30	34	___
17401	Conrail Gondola w/ coal load (Std. O), *87*	24	26	___
17402	Santa Fe Gondola w/ coal load (Std. O), *90*	19	25	___

		Exc	New	Cond/$
17403	Chessie System Gondola w/ coil covers "371629" (Std. O), *93*	24	25	___
17404	Illinois Central Gulf Gondola w/ coil covers "245998" (Std. O), *93*	34	39	___
17405	Reading Gondola w/ coil covers "24876" (Std. O), *94*	27	31	___
17406	PRR Gondola w/ coil covers "385405" (Std. O), *95*	37	42	___
17407	NKP Gondola w/ scrap load, *96*		24	___
17408	Cotton Belt Gondola w/ scrap load "9820" (Std O), *97*		32	___
17410	UP Gondola w/ scrap "903004" (Std. O), *99*		30	___
17413	Service Center Gondola w/ parts load (SSS), *00*		24	___
17414	Nickel Plate PS-5 Gondola "44801" (Std. O), *01–02*		40	___
17415	Frisco PS-5 Gondola "61878" (Std. O), *01–02*		35	___
17416	D&H Gondola w/ scrap "14011" (Std. O), *01*		33	___
17417	BN Rotary Bathtub Gondola 3-pack, *01*		140	___
17421	CSX Rotary Bathtub Gondola 3-pack, *01*		135	___
17425	Western Maryland PS-5 Gondola "354903" (Std. O), *01–02*		36	___
17426	Maine Central PS-5 Gondola "1116" (Std. O), *01–02*		40	___
17427	CSX Rotary Bathtub Gondola Single Unit Add-on (Std. O), *02*		47	___
17428	BN Rotary Bathtub Gondola Single Unit Add-on (Std. O), *02*		42	___
17429	Conrail Rotary Bathtub Gondola 3-pack (Std. O), *02–03*		115	___
17433	BNSF Rotary Bathtub Gondola 3-pack (Std. O), *02–03*		145	___
17439	UP PS-5 Gondola "229606" (Std. O), *03*		35	___
17440	Algoma Central PS-5 Gondola "801" (Std. O), *03*		32	___
17441	Conrail Rotary Bathtub Gondola "507673" (Std. O), *03*		39	___
17442	BNSF Rotary Bathtub Gondola "668330" (Std. O), *03*		46	___
17443	NS Rotary Bathtub Gondola 3-pack (Std. O), *03*		90	___
17447	UP Rotary Bathtub Gondola 3-pack (Std. O), *03*		100	___
17457	GN PS-5 Gondola "72839" (Std. O), *03*		35	___
17458	Reading PS-5 Gondola "33267" (Std. O), *03*		35	___
17459	CP Rail PS-5 Gondola "338966" (Std. O), *04*		35	___
17460	NYC PS-5 Gondola "749592" (Std. O), *04*		40	___

		Exc	New	Cond/$
17461	Pennsylvania PS-5 Gondola "374256" (Std. O), *04*		36	___
17462	Santa Fe PS-5 Gondola "167340" (Std. O), *04*		35	___
17463	NS Bathtub Gondola "10303" (Std. O), *04*		40	___
17464	UP Bathtub Gondola "28100" (Std. O), *04*		35	___
17465	CP Rail Bathtub Gondola 3-pack (Std. O), *04*		105	___
17470	CP Rail Bathtub Gondola, *05*		CP	___
17471	Burlington PS-5 Gondola w/ covers (Std. O), *05*		44	___
17472	New Haven PS-5 Gondola w/ covers (Std. O), *05*		CP	___
17473	NYC PS-5 Gondola "502351" (Std. O), *06–07*		CP	___
17474	D&H PS-5 Gondola "13816" (Std. O), *06–07*		CP	___
17475	Koppers PS-5 Gondola "213" (Std. O), *06–07*		CP	___
17477	L&N PS-5 Gondola "170012" (Std. O), *06–07*		CP	___
17500	CP Flatcar w/ logs (Std. O), *89*	27	29	___
17501	Conrail Flatcar w/ stakes (Std. O), *87*	37	45	___
17502	Santa Fe Flatcar w/ trailer (Std. O), *90*	70	75	___
17503	NS Flatcar w/ trailer (Std. O), *92*	55	65	___
17504	NS Flatcar w/ trailer (Std. O), *92*	55	65	___
17505	NS Flatcar w/ trailer (Std. O), *92*	50	55	___
17506	NS Flatcar w/ trailer (Std. O), *92*	46	55	___
17507	NS Flatcar w/ trailer (Std. O), *92*	50	55	___
17508	BN I-Beam Flatcar w/ load (Std. O), *92*		NM	___
17509	Southern Flatcar w/ load (Std. O), *92*		NM	___
17510	NP Flatcar w/ logs "61200" (Std. O), *94*	31	36	___
17511	WM Flatcar w/ logs, set of 3 (Std. O), *95*		145	___
17512	WM Flatcar w/ logs (Std. O), *95*	35	41	___
17513	WM Flatcar w/ logs (Std. O), *95*	43	50	___
17514	WM Flatcar w/ logs (Std. O), *95*	39	45	___
17515	Norfolk Southern Flatcar w/ tractors (Std. O), *95*	24	42	___
17516	T&P Flatcar w/ 2 Beechcraft Bonanzas "9823" (Std O), *97*		50	___
17517	WP Flatcar w/ Ertl Caterpillar frontloader "9823" (Std O), *97*		39	___
17518	PRR Flatcar w/ 2 Corgi Mack trucks "9823" (Std O), *97*	49	50	___
17522	Flatcar with Plymouth Prowler, *98*		41	___
17527	Flatcar with Pair of Dodge Vipers, *98*		38	___
17529	AT&SF Flatcar w/ Ford milk truck "90010", *99*		55	___
17533	MTTX Ford Flatcar w/ auto frames, *99*		38	___
17534	Diamond T Flatcar w/ Mack trucks "9823", *99*		55	___

		Exc	New	Cond/$
17536	Route 66 Flatcar w/2 luxury coupes "9823-3", *99*		37	___
17537	Route 66 Flatcar w/2 touring coupes "9823-4", *99*		32	___
17538	NYC Flatcar w /Ford tow truck, *99*		43	___
17539	Flatcar with 2 Corvettes "9823" (Std. O), *99*		70	___
17540	Flatcar with 2 Corvettes "9823" (Std. O), *99*		70	___
17546	Lionel Lines Recovery Flatcar w/ rails "6424", *99*		50	___
17547	Lionel Lines Recovery Flatcar w/ machinery "6429", *99*		50	___
17548	Route 66 Flatcar w/ 2 luxury coupes "9823-6", *99*		42	___
17549	Route 66 Flatcar w/ station wagon, trailer "9823-5", *99*		42	___
17550	B&N Center Beam Flatcar w/ lumber load "6216" (Std O), *99*		39	___
17551	NYC Flatcar with NYC pickups "499", *99*		49	___
17553	Trailer Train Flatcar with combine "98102" (Std. O), *99*		125	___
17554	GN Flatcar w/ logs "61042", *00*		32	___
17555	Ford Mustang Flatcar w/ 2 cars (Std. O), *01*		NRS	___
17556	Ford Mustang Flatcar w/ 2 cars (Std. O), *01*		NRS	___
17557	Route 66 Flatcar w/ black sedans "9823-7", *99–00*		39	___
17558	Route 66 Flatcar w/ brown sedans "9823-8", *99*		39	___
17559	Route 66 Flatcar w/ 2 wagons "9823-9" (Std. O), *01*		40	___
17560	Route 66 Flatcar w/ 2 sedans "9823-10" (Std. O), *01*		40	___
17563	Santa Fe Flatcar w/ railroad pickup trucks "90011" (Std. O), *01*		49	___
17564	West Side Lumber Shay Log Car 3-pack #2 (Std. O), *01*		95	___
17568	PRR Flatcar w/ M.O.W. pickup trucks "470333" (Std. O), *02*		50	___
17571	UP Flatcar w/ M.O.W. pickup trucks "909231" (Std. O), *03*		50	___
17572	Pioneer Seed Flatcar w/ peddle cars, *02 u*		180	___
17573	WM PS-4 Flatcar "2631" (Std. O), *03*		35	___
17574	Santa Fe PS-4 Flatcar "90081" (Std. O), *03*		35	___
17575	NYC PS-4 Flatcar "506098" (Std. O), *03*		40	___
17576	Ontario Northland PS-4 Flatcar "2020" (Std. O), *03*		35	___
17577	B&O PS-4 Flatcar "8651" (Std. O), *04*		35	___
17578	B&M PS-4 Flatcar "34007" (Std. O), *04*		35	___

		Exc	New	Cond/$
17579	Milwaukee Road PS-4 Flatcar "64073" (Std. O), *04*		35	___
17580	UP PS-4 Flatcar "54603" (Std. O), *04*		35	___
17581	GN Flatcar w/ pickup trucks "X4168" (Std. O), *04*		42	___
17582	Pennsylvania PS-4 Flatcar w/ piggyback trailers "469617" (Std. O), *05*		110	___
17583	GN PS-4 Flatcar w/ piggyback trailers, *05*		CP	___
17584	SP PS-4 Flatcar w/ piggyback trailers, *05*		CP	___
17585	C&O PS-4 Flatcar w/ piggyback trailers "81000" (Std. O), *05*		CP	___
17586	BN All-Purpose Husky Stack Car "63322" (Std. O), *05*		CP	___
17587	SP All-Purpose Husky Stack Car "513915" (Std. O), *05*		CP	___
17588	CSX All-Purpose Husky Stack Car "620350" (Std. O), *05*		CP	___
17589	TTX Trailer Train All-Purpose Stack Car "456249" (Std. O), *05*		65	___
17600	NYC Wood-sided Caboose (Std. O), *87 u*	46	55	___
17601	Southern Wood-sided Caboose (Std. O), *88*	35	42	___
17602	Conrail Wood-sided Caboose (Std. O), *87*	65	75	___
17603	RI Wood-sided Caboose (Std. O), *88*	19	38	___
17604	Lackawanna Wood-sided Caboose (Std. O), *88*	42	55	___
17605	Reading Wood-sided Caboose (Std. O), *89*	34	37	___
17606	NYC Steel-sided Caboose w/ smoke (Std. O), *90*	49	65	___
17607	Reading Steel-sided Caboose w/ smoke (Std. O), *90*	55	65	___
17608	C&O Steel-sided Caboose w/ smoke (Std. O), *91*	46	55	___
17610	Wabash Steel-sided Caboose w/ smoke (Std. O), *91*	39	55	___
17611	NYC Wood-sided Caboose "6003" (Std. O), *90 u, 91*	40	55	___
17612	NKP Steel-sided Caboose w/ smoke (FF #6) (Std. O), *92*	60	65	___
17613	Southern Steel-sided Caboose w/ smoke "7613" (Std. O), *92*	60	65	___
17615	NP Wood-sided Caboose w/ smoke (Std. O), *92*	65	70	___
17617	D&RGW Steel-sided Caboose (Std. O), *95*	50	55	___
17618	Frisco Wood-sided Caboose (Std. O), *95*	65	75	___
17620	NP Wood-sided Caboose "1746", *98*		70	___
17623	Farmrail E/V Caboose, *99*		65	___
17624	Conrail E/V Caboose "6900", *99*		43	___

		Exc	New	Cond/$
17625	Burlington Northern Steel-sided Caboose "7606", *99*		65	___
17626	Service Center E/V Caboose (SSS), *00*		29	___
17627	C&O E/V Caboose, *01*		65	___
17628	BNSF E/V Caboose, *01*		65	___
17629	Santa Fe E/V Caboose, *01*		80	___
17630	UP E/V Caboose, *01*		85	___
17631	Virginian B/W Caboose, *01*		85	___
17632	CSX B/W Caboose, *01*		75	___
17633	NYC B/W Caboose, *01*		90	___
17634	Delaware & Hudson B/W Caboose, *01*		75	___
17635	100th Anniversary Die-Cast Gold Caboose "2000", *00*		345	___
17636	NYC Die-Cast Semi-Scale Caboose "18096", *00–01*		100	___
17637	NYC/P&LE Die-Cast Semi-Scale Caboose "21", *00*		135	___
17638	Rock Island E/V Caboose "17011", Std. O, *02*		55	___
17639	Chessie System E/V Caboose "3322", Std. O, *02*		55	___
17640	CP Rail E/V Caboose "434604", (Std. O), *02*		57	___
17641	Soo Line E/V Caboose "2", (Std. O), *02*		55	___
17642	Conrail Bay Window Caboose "21023", (Std. O), *02*		65	___
17643	Nickel Plate Road Bay Window Caboose "480" (Std. O), *02*		60	___
17644	Erie Bay Window Caboose "C307", (Std. O), *02*		55	___
17645	N&W Bay Window Caboose "C-6", (Std. O), *02*		55	___
17646	UP Bay Window Caboose "24555", (Std. O), *02*		65	___
17647	B&O Caboose "C-2820" (Std. O), *03–04*		65	___
17648	Chessie System Caboose "C-2800" (Std. O), *03–04*		75	___
17649	Lionel Lines Caboose "7649" (Std. O), *03–04*		65	___
17650	Rio Grande E/V Caboose "01500" (Std. O), *03*		65	___
17651	BN E/V Caboose "10531" (Std. O), *03–05*		CP	___
17652	NYC Bay Window Caboose "20200" (Std. O), *03*		75	___
17653	SP Bay Window Caboose "1337" (Std. O), *03*		65	___
17654	Alaska E/V Caboose "989" (Std. O), *03*		75	___
17655	WP Bay Window Caboose "448" (Std. O), *03–04*		75	___
17658	Burlington E/V Caboose "13611" (Std. O), *04*		70	___
17659	CN E/V Caboose "79646" (Std. O), *04*		70	___
17660	Seaboard E/V Caboose "5700" (Std. O), *04*		65	___
17661	C&NW B/W Caboose "10871" (Std.O), *04*		65	___
17662	PC B/W Caboose "21001" (Std. O), *04*		65	___

		Exc	New	Cond/$
17663	Southern B/W Caboose "X546" (Std. O), *04*		65	___
17664	B&O Caboose "C-2824" (Std. O), *03–04*		65	___
17665	Chessie System Caboose "C-2802" (Std. O), *03–04*		75	___
17669	NYC Smoking B/W Caboose, *05*		CP	___
17670	CP Rail Smoking B/W Caboose, *05*		CP	___
17671	Burlington Northern E/V Caboose, *05*		CP	___
17672	GN E/V Caboose "X-106" (Std. O), *05*		CP	___
17673	Santa Fe E/V Caboose, *05*		CP	___
17674	Reading E/V Caboose "94119" (Std. O), *05*		75	___
17675	Rio Grande E/V Caboose "01507" (Std. O), *06*		CP	___
17676	NYC B/W Caboose "20300", *07*			
17677	Erie-Lackawanna B/W Caboose "C359" (Std. O), *06*		CP	___
17678	B&O I-12 Caboose "C2421" (Std. O), *06*		CP	___
17679	Long Island B/W Caboose "C-62" (Std. O), *06*		CP	___
17682	Reading Northeastern Caboose "92841" (Std. O), *06*		CP	___
17683	Chessie System Northeastern Caboose "1893" (Std. O), *07*		CP	___
17684	Conrail Northeastern Caboose "18873" (Std. O), *07*		CP	___
17685	Jersey Central Northeastern Caboose "91533" (Std. O), *07*		CP	___
17690	UP CA-4 Caboose "3826" (Std. O), *06*		CP	___
17691	UP CA-4 Caboose "25103" (Std. O), *06*		CP	___
17692	LL CA-4 B22 Caboose "7629" (Std. O), *06*		CP	___
17693	Chessie System E/V Caboose "3285" (Std. O), *06*		CP	___
17694	NS E/V Caboose "555582" (Std. O), *06*		CP	___
17695	Alaska RR I-12 Caboose "1001" (Std. O), *06*		CP	___
17696	CP B/W Caboose "437266" (Std. O), *06*		CP	___
17697	CN E/V Caboose "78128" (Std. O), *06*		CP	___
17700	UP ACF 40-ton Stock Car "47456" (Std. O), *01–02*		85	___
17701	Rio Grande ACF 40-ton Stock Car "39269" (Std. O), *01–02*		60	___
17702	CP ACF 40-ton Stock Car "277083" (Std. O), *01–02*		75	___
17703	NYC ACF 40-ton Stock Car "23334" (Std. O), *01–02*		85	___
17704	B&O ACF 40-ton Stock Car "110234", Std. O, *02*		40	___
17705	CB&Q ACF 40-ton Stock Car "52886", Std. O, *02*		40	___
17707	Pennsylvania ARF 40-ton Stock Car "128994" (Std. O), *03*		35	___
17708	CP Rail ACF 40-ton Stock Car "277313" (Std. O), *03*		38	___

		Exc	New	Cond/$
17709	UP Stock Car "48154" (Std. O), *04*		45	___
17710	Great Northern Stock Car "56385" (Std. O), *04*		40	___
17711	C&O ACF 40-ton Stock Car "95237" (Std. O), *06*		CP	___
17712	N&W ACF 40-ton Stock Car "33000" (Std. O), *06*		CP	___
17713	MKT ACF 40-ton Stock Car "47150" (Std. O), *06*		CP	___
17714	CN 40-ton Stock Car "172755" (Std. O), *06*		CP	___
17715	MP 40-ton Stock Car "52428" (Std. O), *06*		CP	___
17800	Ontario Northland Ore Car "6126/6021", *00*		30	___
17801	CN Ore Car "6126/345165", *00*		37	___
17802	CP Ore Car "377249", *00*		28	___
17803	DMIR Ore Car "51456", *00*		30	___
17804	UP Ore Car "8023", *01*		29	___
17805	CP Rail Ore Car "377238", *01*		29	___
17806	UP Ore Car "27250", *03*		30	___
17807	BN Ore Car "95887", *02*		28	___
17900	Santa Fe Unibody Tank Car (Std. O), *90*	37	46	___
17901	Chevron Unibody Tank Car (Std. O), *90*	22	26	___
17902	NJ Zinc Unibody Tank Car (Std. O), *91*	26	34	___
17903	Conoco Unibody Tank Car (Std. O), *91*	24	29	___
17904	Texaco Unibody Tank Car (Std. O), *92*	29	37	___
17905	Archer Daniels Midland Unibody Tank Car (Std. O), *92*	26	32	___
17906	SCM Unibody Tank Car "78286" (Std. O), *93*	47	55	___
17908	Marathon Oil Unibody Tank Car (Std. O), *95*	44	50	___
17909	Hooker Chemicals Unibody Tank Car (Std. O), *96*		55	___
17910	Sunoco Unibody Tank Car "7900", *97*		37	___
17913	J.M. Huber Tank Car, *98*		29	___
17914	Englehard Tank Car, *98*		36	___
17915	Gulf Uni-Body Tank Car "8438", *00*		43	___
17916	Burlington Unibody Tank Car "130000", *00*	24	38	___
17918	Southern Unibody Tank Car, *01*		32	___
17919	Koppers Unibody Tank Car, *01*		39	___
17924	Safety Kleen Unibody Tank Car "77603", (Std. O), *02*		40	___
17925	Beefmaster Unibody Tank Car "120021", Std. O, *02*		38	___
17926	Cargill Unibody 1-D Tank Car "5836" (Std. O), *03*		40	___
17927	Union Starch Unibody 1-D Tank Car "59137" (Std. O), *03*		35	___
17928	Merck 1-D Tank Car "25421" (Std. O), *03*		35	___
17929	Wyandotte Chemicals 1-D Tank Car "1325" (Std. O), *03*		34	___

		Exc	New	Cond/$
17930	CSX Unibody Tank Car "993369" (Std. O), *04*		35	___
17931	UP Unibody Tank Car "6" (Std. O), *04*		35	___
17932	CIBRO Tank Train Intermediate Car "26263" (Std. O), *04*		35	___
17933	GATX Tank Train Intermediate Car 3-pack (Std. O), *04*		100	___
17946	Candy Cane Unibody Tank Car, *04*		60	___
17948	Philadelphia Quartz 1-D Tank Car "806" (Std. O), *06*		CP	___
17949	Skelly Oil 1-D Tank Car "2293" (Std. O), *06*		CP	___
17950	ADM Unibody Tank Car "19020" (Std. O), *06*		CP	___
17951	Cerestar Unibody Tank Car "190177" (Std. O), *06*		CP	___
17959	Dow 1-D Tank Car "310101" (Std. O), *07*		CP	___
17960	Amaizo 1-Dome Tank Car "15440" (Std. O), *07*		CP	___
17962	Domino Sugar 1-D Tank Car "3008" (Std. O), *07*		CP	___
17966	Procor 1-D Tank Car "82607" (Std. O), *07*		CP	___
18000	PRR 0-6-0 "8977" 89, *91*	380	485	___
18001	Rock Island 4-8-4 "5100", *87*	305	370	___
18002	NYC 4-6-4 "785", *87 u*	510	570	___
18003	DL&W 4-8-4 "1501", *88*	235	305	___
18004	Reading 4-6-2 "8004", *89*	215	255	___
18005	NYC 4-6-4 "5340" w/ display case, *90*	860	900	___
18006	Reading 4-8-4 "2100", *89 u*	490	560	___
18007	Southern Pacific 4-8-4 "4410", *91*	415	420	___
18008	Disneyland 35th Anniversary 4-4-0 "4" w/ display case, *90*	225	275	___
18009	NYC 4-8-2 "3000", *90 u, 91*	370	560	___
18010	PRR 6-8-6 Steam Turbine "6200", *91–92*	900	1150	___
18011	Chessie System 4-8-4 "2101", *91*	440	550	___
18012	NYC 4-6-4 "5340", *90*	710	1000	___
18013	Disneyland 35th Anniversary 4-4-0 "4", *90*	210	265	___
18014	Lionel Lines 2-6-4 "8014", *91*	145	190	___
18016	Northern Pacific 4-8-4 "2626", *92*	385	440	___
18018	Southern 2-8-2 "4501", *92*	640	650	___
18022	Pere Marquette 2-8-4 "1201", *93*	550	650	___
18023	Western Maryland Shay "6", *92*	1050	1350	___
18024	Sears T&P 4-8-2 "907", *92 u* w/ display case	750	790	___
18025	T&P 4-8-2 "907", *92 u*		640	___
18026	Smithsonian NYC Dreyfuss 4-6-4 "5450" (2-rail), *92 u*		2300	___
18027	NYC Dreyfuss 4-6-4 "5450" (3-rail), *93 u*		1450	___

		Exc	New	Cond/$
18028	Smithsonian Pennsylvania 4-6-2 "3768" (2-rail), *93 u*		2150	___
18029	NYC Dreyfuss 4-6-4 "5454" (3-rail) w/ operating roller base, *93 u*	1900	2150	___
18030	Frisco 2-8-2 "4100", *93 u*	530	630	___
18031	Bundesbahn BR-50 2-10-0 (2-rail), *93 u*		NRS	___
18034	Santa Fe 2-8-2 "3158", *94*	540	620	___
18035	Reichsbahn BR-50 2-10-0 (2-rail), *93 u*		NRS	___
18036	French BR-50 2-10-0 (2-rail), *93 u*		NRS	___
18040	N&W 4-8-4 "612", *95*	640	710	___
18041	Boston & Albany 4-6-4 "619", *95*		NM	___
18042	Boston & Albany 4-6-4 "618", *95*		250	___
18043	Chesapeake & Ohio 4-6-4 "490", *95*	680	750	___
18044	Southern 4-6-2 "1390", *96*		255	___
18045	"777" Commodore Vanderbilt, *96*		710	___
18046	Wabash 4-6-4 "700", *96*	190	375	___
18049	N&W Warhorse 4-8-2 "600", *96*		490	___
18050	JCPenney 4-6-2 Locomotive "2055", *96*	235	245	___
18052	Pennsylvania Torpedo "238E", *97*		455	___
18054	NYC Switcher 0-4-0 "1665", black, *97*		145	___
18056	NYC J1-e Hudson "763E" w/ Vanderbilt Tender, *97*		740	___
18059	WM Pacific 4-6-2 Deluxe "209", *98*		NM	___
18062	AT&SF 4-6-4 Hudson L/T "3447", *97*		680	___
18063	NYC Commodore Vanderbilt 4-6-4, *99*		980	___
18064	NYC 4-8-2 Mohawk L-3A Locomotive w/ Tender "3000", *98*	540	740	___
18067	Commodore Vanderbilt Special Edition, *97*		830	___
18068	Pennsylvania Century Club Steam Turbine Tender, *99*		290	___
18070	WM Pacific 4-6-2 Locomotive "208", *98*		NM	___
18071	Southern Pacific Daylight Locomotive "4449", *98*		680	___
18072	Lionel Lines Torpedo Engine w/ tender, *98*		360	___
18079	NYC Mikado 2-8-2 "1967", *99*		710	___
18080	D&RG Mikado 2-8-2 "1210", *99*		720	___
18082	NYC Hudson 4-6-4 "5404", *99*		230	___
18083	C&O Hudson 4-6-4 "305", *99*		205	___
18084	Santa Fe Hudson 4-6-4 "305", *99*		225	___
18085	NH Pacific 4-6-2 "1334", *99*		275	___
18086	NYC Pacific 4-6-2 "4929", *99*		235	___
18087	Santa Fe Pacific 4-6-2 "3448", *99*		265	___
18088	SP Pacific 4-6-2 "1407", *99*		350	___

		Exc	New	Cond/$
18089	CNJ Camelback 4-6-0 "771", *99*		405	___
18091	PRR Camelback 4-6-0 "821", *99*		405	___
18092	SP Camelback 4-6-0 "2283", *99*		395	___
18093	C&NW Camelback 4-6-0 "3006", *99*		285	___
18094	B&O E6 4-4-2 Atlantic Locomotive, CC, *99–00*		345	___
18095	Pennsylvania E6 4-4-2 Atlantic, CC, *99–00*	275	455	___
18096	AT&SF E6 4-4-2 Atlantic Locomotive, CC, *99–00*		370	___
18097	CNJ Camelback 4-6-0 "770", *99*		330	___
18098	PRR Camelback 4-6-0 "820", *99*		355	___
18099	SP Camelback 4-6-0 "2282", *99*		360	___
18100	Santa Fe F-3 A Unit "8100" (see 11711)		NRS	___
18101	Santa Fe F-3 B Unit "8101" (see 11711)		NRS	___
18102	Santa Fe F-3 A Unit Dummy "8102" (see 11711)		NRS	___
18103	Santa Fe F-3 B Unit Dummy "8103", *91 u*	180	190	___
18104	GN F-3 A Unit Dummy "366A" (see 11724)		500	___
18105	GN F-3 B Unit Dummy "370B" (see 11724)		NRS	___
18106	GN F-3 A Unit Dummy "351C" (see 11724)		NRS	___
18107	D&RGW Alco PA-1 ABA Set "6001" and "6002", *92*	640	740	___
18108	Great Northern F-3 B Unit "371B", *93*	85	105	___
18109	Erie Alco A Unit "725A" (see 11734)		NRS	___
18110	Erie Alco B Unit "725B" (see 11734)		160	___
18111	Erie Alco A Unit Dummy "736A" (see 11734)		NRS	___
18115	Santa Fe F-3 B Unit, *93*	90	115	___
18116	Erie-Lackawanna Alco PA-1 AA Set "858" and "859", *93*	550	600	___
18117/18118	Santa Fe F-3 AA Set "200", *93*	330	410	___
18119/18120	UP Alco AA Set "8119" and "8120", *94*	200	235	___
18121	Santa Fe F-3 B Unit "200A", *94*	75	95	___
18122	Santa Fe F-3 B Unit "200B", *95*	140	150	___
18123	ACL F-3 A Unit "342" (see 11903)		NRS	___
18124	ACL F-3 B Unit "342B" (see 11903)		NRS	___
18125	ACL F-3 A Unit Dummy "343" (see 11903)		NRS	___
18128	Santa Fe F-3 A Unit "2343", *96*		435	___
18130	Santa Fe F-3 Diesel Locomotive AB Set, *96*		580	___
18131	NP F-3 AB Set, "2390A", "2390C", *97*	295	360	___
18132	Santa Fe F-3 A Powered (see 18130)		NRS	___
18133	Santa Fe F-3 A Dummy (see 18130)		NRS	___
18134	Santa Fe F-3 A Unit Dummy "2343", *97*		195	___
18136	AT&SF F-3 B Unit w/ RailSounds "2343C", *97*	135	240	___

		Exc	New	Cond/$
18138	Milwaukee Road F3 A, "75A", *98*		400	___
18139	Milwaukee Road F3 B, "2378B", *98*		250	___
18140	Milwaukee Road F3 A-B Diesel "75A", *98*	390	600	___
18145	NP F-3 A Unit "2390A", *97*	300	360	___
18146	NP F-3 B Unit "2390C", *97*		170	___
18147	NP F-3 AB Units "2390A", "2390C", *97*	450	580	___
18149	UP Veranda Gas Turbine "61", *98*	860	900	___
18154	Deluxe Santa Fe FT AA "168", *98–00*		375	___
18155	Deluxe Santa Fe FT A Powered (see 18154)		NRS	___
18156	Deluxe Santa Fe FT A Dummy (see 18154)		NRS	___
18157	Santa Fe FT AA "158", *98–00*		240	___
18158	Santa Fe FT A Powered (see 18157)		NRS	___
18159	Santa Fe FT A Dummy (see 18157)		NRS	___
18160	NYC Deluxe FT AA "1602", "1603", *98–00*		500	___
18163	NYC FT AA Unit, "1600", "2400", *98–00*		300	___
18166	B&O FT AA, Command Control, *99–00*		340	___
18169	B&O FT AA, traditional, *99–00*		240	___
18189	Army of Potomoc Operating Stock Car, *99*		45	___
18190	McNeil's Rangers Operating Stock Car "2", *99*		45	___
18191	WP F-3 A-A, *98*		570	___
18192	WP F3 A Powered (see 18191)		485	___
18193	WP F-3 A Dummy (see 18191)		495	___
18197	WP F3 B-Unit "2355C", *99*		255	___
18198	WP F3 B-Unit "2345C" CC, *99*		360	___
18200	Conrail SD-40 "8200", *87*	180	200	___
18201	Chessie System SD-40 "8201", *88*	245	340	___
18202	Erie-Lack. SD-40 Dummy "8459", *89 u*	90	140	___
18203	CP Rail SD-40 "8203", *89*	195	250	___
18204	Chessie SD-40 Dummy "8204", *90 u*	135	190	___
18205	Union Pacific Dash 8-40C "9100", *89*	275	335	___
18206	Santa Fe Dash 8-40B "8206", *90*	195	235	___
18207	Norfolk Southern Dash 8-40C "8689", *92*	230	270	___
18208	BN SD-40 Dummy "8586", *91 u*	115	165	___
18209	CP Rail SD-40 Dummy "8209", *92 u*	135	165	___
18210	Illinois Central SD-40 "6006", *93*	220	250	___
18211	Susquehanna Dash 8-40B "4002", *93*	145	165	___
18212	Santa Fe Dash 8-40B Dummy "8212", *93*	155	180	___
18213	Norfolk Southern Dash 8-40C "8688", *94*	225	240	___
18214	CSX Dash 8-40C "7500", *94*	235	255	___
18215	CSX Dash 8-40C "7643", *94*	240	260	___

		Exc	New	Cond/$
18228	SP Dash 9 "8228", gray, red nose, *97*		335	___
18229	SP SD40 Diesel Warhorse "7333", *98*	300	425	___
18231	BNSF Dash 9 Diesel Deluxe "739", *98*		435	___
18232	SOO Line SD-60 Diesel "5500", *97*		350	___
18233	BNSF Dash 9 Diesel Locomotive "745", *98*		330	___
18234	BNSF Dash 9 "740" Command Control, *98–99*		405	___
18235	BNSF Dash 9 Diesel 2-pack "739, "740", *98*		710	___
18238	Conrail SD70 "4145", *99–00*		300	___
18240	Conrail Dash 8-40B "5065" CC, *98*		260	___
18241	BN SD70 "9413", *99–00*		345	___
18245	PRR Alco PA-1 AA "5750", *99*		495	___
18248	PRR Alco PB-1 "5750B", *99*		215	___
18249	Erie Alco PB-1 "850B", *00*		250	___
18250	BNSF SD70 "9870", *99–00*		365	___
18251	CSX SD60 "8701", *99–00*		300	___
18252	Amtrak Dash 9, Command Control, *99*		285	___
18253	BNSF Dash 9, Command Control, *99*		305	___
18254	AT&SF Dash 9, Command Control, *99*		340	___
18255	NS Dash 9, Commmand Control, *99*		315	___
18256	Amtrak Dash 9, traditional, *99*		200	___
18257	BNSF Dash 9, traditional, *99*		190	___
18258	AT&SF Dash 9, traditional, *99*		205	___
18259	NS Dash 9, traditional, *99*		215	___
18260	Conrail SD70 "4144", *99–00*		280	___
18261	BN SD60 "9412", *99–00*		255	___
18262	BNSF SD70 "9869", *99–00*		250	___
18263	CSX SD60 "8700", *99–00*		255	___
18264	Southern Pacific SD70M "8238", *99–00*		245	___
18265	Southern Pacific SD70M "9803", *99–00*		340	___
18266	Norfolk Southern SD60 "6552", CC, *01–02*		400	___
18268	Lionel Centennial SD90MAC "2000", CC, *00*		355	___
18269	UP SD90MAC "8006", Command Control, *00*		405	___
18270	UP SD90MAC "8007", traditional, *00*		NM	___
18271	CP SD90MAC "9129", Command Control, *00*		440	___
18272	CP SD90MAC "9130", traditional, *00*		NM	___
18273	UP SD40MAC "8071", *99–00*		330	___
18274	Burlington U30C "891", CC, *01*		370	___
18276	Seaboard U30C "7274", CC, *01*		325	___
18278	UP U30C "2938", CC, *01*		330	___
18280	Maersk SD70, CC, *00*		345	___

		Exc	New	Cond/$
18281	BNSF Dash 9-44CW "788", CC, *00*		340	___
18282	BNSF Dash 9-44CW "789", traditional, *00*		225	___
18283	CSX Dash 9-44CW "9019", CC, *00*		340	___
18284	CSX Dash 9-44CW "9020", traditional, *00*		300	___
18285	UP Dash 9-44C "9659", CC, *01*		325	___
18286	UP Dash 9-44CW "9717", CC, *01*		355	___
18286	UP Dash 9-44CW "9717", CC, *01*		355	___
18287	CN Dash 9-44C "2529", CC, *01*		460	___
18288	Odyssey System SD70, CC, *00 u*		400	___
18290	Amtrak Dash 8-32BWH "509", CC, *01*		325	___
18291	BNSF Dash 8-32BWH "580", CC, *02*		340	___
18292	Chessie GE U30C Diesel "3312", CC, *02*		340	___
18293	Santa Fe U30C, CC, *03*		395	___
18294	Alaska SD70MAC "4005", CC, *01–02*		435	___
18295	Conrail SD80MAC "7200", CC, *02–03*		365	___
18296	CSX SD80MAC "801", CC, *02–03*		405	___
18297	NYC SD80MAC "9914", CC, *02–03*		405	___
18298	UP Desert Victory SD40-2 "3593", CC, *02–03*		380	___
18299	CP Rail SD40-2 "5420", CC, *02–03*		375	___
18300	PRR GG-1 "8300", *87*	365	410	___
18301	Southern FM Train Master "8301", *88*	225	260	___
18302	GN EP-5 "8302" (FF #3), *88*	190	250	___
18303	Amtrak GG-1 "8303", *89*	275	490	___
18304	Lackawanna MU Car Set, powered and dummy, "2401" and "2402", *91*	380	435	___
18305	Lackawanna MU Car Set, dummies "2400" and "2403", *92*	230	255	___
18306	PRR MU Car Set, powered and dummy, "4574" and "483", *92*	260	330	___
18307	PRR FM Train Master "8699", *94*	230	255	___
18308	PRR GG-1 "4866", *92*	235	260	___
18309	Reading FM Train Master "863", *93*	240	270	___
18310	PRR MU Car Set, dummies "484" and "485", *93*	265	345	___
18311	Disney EP-5 "8311", *94*	285	485	___
18313	Pennsylvania GG-1 "4907", *96*		350	___
18314	PRR GG-1 "2332", 5 gold stripes, *97*	500	570	___
18315	Virginian E33 Recifier Electric "2329", *97*		240	___
18319	New Haven EP-5 Rectifier, *99*	300	365	___
18321	CNJ Train Master "2341", *99*		405	___
18322	Lackawanna Train Master "2321", *99*		465	___

		Exc	New	Cond/$
18326	PRR GG-1 Congressional, *00*		600	___
18327	Virginian "2331" FM Train Master, *99–00*		410	___
18328	NH MU Commuter Set "4082/4083", CC, *00*		385	___
18331	Reading MU Commuter Set "9109/10", CC, *00*		460	___
18334	NH MU Dummy Set "4084/5", CC, *01*		180	___
18337	Reading MU Dummy Set "9111/2", CC, *01*		200	___
118343	PRR GG-1 "2332", black, CC, *01*		610	___
18344	LIRR MU Powered Set"1163/4", CC, *01*		470	___
18347	IC MU Powered Set "1204/5", CC, *01*		470	___
18350	Archive Lionel EP-5 "2350", CC, *01*		NM	___
18353	Pennsylvania E-33 Rectifier "4403", CC, *02*		280	___
18354	PRR GG1 "4918", tuscan, CC, *04*		790	___
18355	PRR GG1 "4876", Brunswick green, CC, *04*		900	___
18356	Penn Central GG1 "4901", CC, *04*		1050	___
18364	PRR BB1 Electric Locomotive "3900", CC, *05–07*		530	___
18367	LIRR BB3 Electric Locomotive "328 A", CC, *05*		530	___
18371	Pennsylvania GG1 Electric "4912", tuscan 5 stripes, CC, *05–07*		780	___
18372	Pennsylvania GG1 Electric "4925", green 1 stripe, CC, *05–07*		780	___
18373	NYC S-2 Electric Locomotive "125", CC, *05–07*		410	___
18374	PRR GG1 Electric "4866, silver, CC, *06–07*		CP	___
18375	Lackawanna Train Master Diesel "850", CC, *06*		400	___
18376	Lackawanna Non-Powered Train Master Diesel "851" (Std. O), *06*		130	___
18378	New York City Transit Authority R27 Subway Car 2-pack, *07*		CP	___
18384	Milwaukee Road EP-2 "Bipolar" Electric Locomotive "E-2", CC, *07*		CP	___
18385	NYC H-16-44 Diesel Locomotive "7001", *07*		CP	___
18386	NYC Non-Powered H-16-44 Diesel "7002" (Std. O), *07*		CP	___
18389	Milwaukee Road EP-2 "Bipolar" Electric Locomotive "E-1", CC, *07*		CP	___
18400	Santa Fe Vulcan Rotary Snowplow "8400", *87*	135	170	___
18401	Workmen Handcar, *87–88*	38	44	___
18402	Lionel Lines Burro Crane, *88*	65	80	___
18403	Santa Claus Handcar, *88*	26	32	___
18404	San Francisco Trolley "8404", *88*	55	85	___
18405	Santa Fe Burro Crane, *89*	70	90	___
18406	Lionel Track Maintenance Car, *89*, *91*	34	49	___
18407	Snoopy and Woodstock Handcar, *90–91*	75	115	___

		Exc	New	Cond/$
18408	Santa Claus Handcar, *89*	26	35	___
18410	PRR Burro Crane, *90*	100	115	___
18411	Canadian Pacific Fire Car, *90*	70	90	___
18412	Union Pacific Fire Car, *91*		NM	___
18413	Charlie Brown and Lucy Handcar, *91*	32	60	___
18416	Bugs Bunny and Daffy Duck Handcar, *92–93*	95	135	___
18417	Lionel Gang Car, *93*	65	80	___
18419	Lionelville Electric Trolley "8419", *94*	75	90	___
18421	Sylvester and Tweety Handcar, *94*	44	60	___
18422	Santa and Snowman Handcar, *94*	32	37	___
18423	On-Track Step Van, *95*	23	28	___
18424	On-Track Pickup Truck, *95*	20	25	___
18425	Goofy and Pluto Handcar, *95*	28	44	___
18426	Santa and Snowman Handcar, *95*	25	30	___
18427	Tie-Jector "55", *97*		60	___
18429	Workmen Handcar, *96*	41	47	___
18430	Crew Car, *96*		30	___
18431	Trolley Car, *96–97*		50	___
18433	Mickey and Minnie Handcar, *96–97*	36	50	___
18434	Porky and Petunia Handcar, *96*		32	___
18436	Dodge Ram Track Inspection Vehicle, *97*		39	___
18438	Pennsylvania High Rail Vehicle "49", *98*		50	___
18439	Union Pacific High Rail Maintenance Vehicle, *98*		42	___
18440	NJ Transit High Rail Inspection Vehicle, *98*		50	___
18444	Lionelville Fire Car (SSS), *98*		150	___
18445	NYC Fire Car, *98*		90	___
18446	Postwar GN Rotary Snowplow "58", *99*		190	___
18447	Executive Inspection Vehicle, *99*		125	___
18452	Boston Trolley "3321", *99–00*		65	___
18454	Blue Executive Inspection Car (#68), *00*		105	___
18455	NYC Tie-Jector "X-2", *00–01*		70	___
18456	Postwar Minuteman Motorized Unit "59", *01–02*		280	___
18457	Postwar Handcar "65", *00–01*		45	___
18458	Postwar D&RGW Snowplow "53", *00*		160	___
18459	Christmas Handcar, *01*		35	___
18461	Lionel Track Cleaner, *02–03*		90	___
18463	Hot Rod Inspection Vehicle, *01–02*		100	___
18464	Postwar Track Ballast Tamper "54", *02–03*		170	___
18465	Postwar Gang Car "50", *03*		85	___
18466	UP Rotary Snow Plow, *01–02*		150	___

		Exc	New	Cond/$
18468	CN Railroad Speeder, *03–04*		49	___
18469	Chessie System Railroad Speeder, *03–04*		49	___
18470	Lionel Postwar Fire Car "52", *02*		105	___
18471	UP GP20 "1977", *03*		105	___
18473	Lehigh Valley GP20 "310", *03*		160	___
18474	Postwar U.S. Army Switcher "41", *03–04*		145	___
18476	Mickey and Minnie Mouse Handcar, *03–04*		55	___
18475	Toy Story Handcar, *03*		55	___
18481	Christmas Yuletide Trolley, *03*		50	___
18482	New Haven Rail Bonder "16", *04*		35	___
18483	C&O Ballast Tamper "48", *04*		55	___
18484	NS Dodge Inspection Vehicle, *04–05*		50	___
18485	NYC Gang Car, *04–05*		CP	___
18486	Donald and Daisy Duck Handcar, *04–05*		50	___
18487	Postwar M&StL Mine Transport "56", *04–05*		230	___
18489	Great Northern Rail Bonder "HR-73", *04*		35	___
18490	UP Ballast Tamper, *04–05*		150	___
18491	M.O.W. Ballast Tamper "325", *04*		44	___
18492	M.O.W. Rail Bonder "58", *04*		35	___
18493	Santa's Speeder, *05*		CP	___
18497	N&W Speeder "541005", traditional, *05*		CP	___
18498	New York Central Rotary Snowplow, *05*		CP	___
18500	Milwaukee Road GP-9 "8500" (FF #2), *87*	275	315	___
18501	WM NW-2 "8501" (FF #4), *89*	230	250	___
18502	LL 90th Anniversary GP-9 "1900", *90*	145	170	___
18503	Southern Pacific NW-2 "8503", *90*	250	280	___
18504	Frisco GP-7 "504" (FF #5), *91*	155	240	___
18505	NKP GP-7 Powered and Dummy Set "400" and "401" (FF #6), *92*	295	365	___
18506	CN Budd RDC Powered and Dummy Set "D202" and "D203", *92*	300	345	___
18507	CN Budd RDC Baggage, powered, "D202", *92*	50	75	___
18508	CN Budd RDC Passenger Dummy "D203", *92*	125	150	___
18510	CN Budd RDC Passenger Dummy "D200"	50	75	___
18511	CN Budd RDC Passenger Dummy "D250"	50	75	___
18512	CN Budd RDC Dummies Set, "D200" and "D250", *93*	125	195	___
18513	NYC GP-7 "7420", *94*	90	125	___
18514	Missouri Pacific GP-7 "4124", *95*	245	310	___
18515	Lionel Steel Vulcan Diesel "57" (SSS), *96*		190	___
18516	Phantom III Locomotive, CC, *02*		345	___

MODERN ERA 1970-2008

		Exc	New	Cond/$
18550	JCPenney MILW GP-9 "8500" w/ display case, *87 u*	180	245	___
18551	JCPenney Susquehanna RS-3 "8809" w/ display case, *89 u*	180	195	___
18552	JCPenney DM&IR SD-18 "8813" w/ display case, *90 u*	170	195	___
18553	Sears UP GP-9 "150" w/ display case, *91 u*	150	180	___
18554	JCPenney GM&O RS-3 "721" w/ display case, *92–93 u*	160	180	___
18555	Sears C&IM SD-9 "52", *92 u*	165	190	___
18556	Sears Chicago & Illinois Midland Caboose and Freight Car Set, *92 u*	110	120	___
18557	Chessie System 4-8-4 "2101" w/ display case for export, *92 u*		NRS	___
18558	JCPenney MKT GP-9 "91" w/ display case *94 u*	160	180	___
18562	SP GP-9 "2380", *96*		195	___
18563	NYC GP-9 "2380", *96*		230	___
18564	CP GP-9 "2380", *97*		265	___
18565	Milwaukee GP-9 "2338", *97*		220	___
18566	CR SD-20 "8495" (SSS), *97*		150	___
18567	PRR GP-9 "2028", *97*		225	___
18569	CB&Q GP9 Diesel "2380", *98*		190	___
18573	Santa Fe GP9 Diesel Freight "2380", *98*		155	___
18574	Milwaukee Road GP20 "975", *98*		250	___
18575	Custom Series I GP9 "2398", *98*		350	___
18576	SP GP9 Non-Powered B Unit "2385", *98*		135	___
18577	NYC GP9 Non-Powered B Unit "2385", *98*		145	___
18579	Milwaukee GP9 Non-Powered "2384", *99*		135	___
18580	Pennsylvania GP-9 B-Unit "2027", *98*		165	___
18582	Seaboard NW-2 Switcher, *98*	450	455	___
18583	AEC-57 Switcher, *98*		200	___
18585	Centennial SD40 "1999", *99*		435	___
18587	Nickel Plate C-420 "577", CC, *99–01*	215	255	___
18588	D&H C-420 "412", CC, *99–01*	250	275	___
18589	LV C-420 "409", CC, *99–01*	255	300	___
18590	Nickel Plate C-420 "578", traditional, *99–01*		170	___
18591	D&H C-420 "411", traditional, *99–01*		215	___
18592	LV C-420 "410", traditional, *99–01*		175	___
18595	D&H RS-11, traditional "5002", *99–00*		NM	___
18596	D&H RS-11 "5001", CC, *99–01*		370	___
18597	NYC RS-1, traditional, "8011", *99–00*		NM	___

		Exc	New	Cond/$
18598	NYC RS-11 "8010", CC, *99–01*		380	___
18599	C&O GP-38 "3855", *99–00*		145	___
18600	ACL 4-4-2 "8600", *87 u*	65	75	___
18601	Great Northern 4-4-2 "8601", *88*	80	95	___
18602	PRR 4-4-2 "8602", *87*	75	85	___
18604	Wabash 4-4-2 "8604", *88–91*	65	75	___
18605	Mopar Express 4-4-2 "1987", *87–88 u*	75	120	___
18606	NYC 2-6-4 "8606", *89*	170	190	___
18607	Union Pacific 2-6-4 "8607", *89*	130	155	___
18608	D&RGW 2-6-4 "8608" (SSS), *89*	90	105	___
18609	Northern Pacific 2-6-4 "8609", *90*	170	195	___
18610	Rock Island 0-4-0 "8610", *90*	105	115	___
18611	Lionel Lines 2-6-4 "8611" (SSS), *90*	125	140	___
18612	C&NW 4-4-2 "8612", *89*	75	100	___
18613	NYC 4-4-2 "8613", *89 u*	75	95	___
18614	Circus Train 4-4-2 "1989", *89 u*	95	125	___
18615	GTW 4-4-2 "8615", *90*	70	85	___
18616	Northern Pacific 4-4-2 "8616", *90 u*	85	110	___
18617	Adolphus III 4-4-2, *89–92 u*	100	125	___
18618	B&O 4-4-2 "8618", *91*		NM	___
18620	Illinois Central 2-6-2 "8620", *91*	165	190	___
18621	Western Pacific 0-4-0 "8621", *92*		NM	___
18622	Union Pacific 4-4-2 "8622", *90–91 u*	65	80	___
18623	Texas & Pacific 4-4-2 "8623", *92*	80	110	___
18625	Illinois Central 4-4-2 "8625", *91 u*	70	95	___
18626	Delaware & Hudson 2-6-2 "8626", *92*	105	115	___
18627	C&O 4-4-2 "8627" or "8633" *92, 93 u, 94, 95 u*	75	95	___
18628	MKT 4-4-2 "8628", *92, 93 u*	70	85	___
18630	C&NW 4-6-2 "2903", *93*	325	370	___
18632	NYC 4-4-2 "8632", *93–95*	75	95	___
18632	C&O 4-4-2 Columbia Locomotive "8632" *97–99*	75	95	___
18633	C&O 4-4-2 "8633", *94–95*	65	85	___
18633	Union Pacific 4-4-2 "8633", *93–95*	65	85	___
18635	Santa Fe 2-6-4 "8625", *93*	135	155	___
18636	B&O 4-6-2 "5300", *94*	295	315	___
18637	United Auto Workers 4-4-2 "8633", *93 u*		90	___
18638	Norfolk & Western 2-6-4 "638", *94*	170	220	___
18639	Reading 4-6-2 "639", *95*	145	170	___
18640	Union Pacific 4-6-2 "8640", *95*	110	130	___

		Exc	New	Cond/$
18641	Ford 4-4-2 "8641", *94 u*	65	85	___
18642	Lionel Lines 4-6-2 "8642", *95*	110	130	___
18644	AT&SF 4-4-2 Columbia Locomotive "8644" *96–99*	75	90	___
18648	Sears Zenith 4-4-2 "8632", *96 u*		100	___
18649	Chevrolet 4-4-2 "USA-1", *96 u*		100	___
18650	Lionel Lines 4-4-2 Columbia Locomotive "X-1110", *96–99*	95	120	___
18653	B&A 4-6-2 Pacific "2044", *97*		140	___
18654	SP 4-6-2 Pacific "2044", *97*		140	___
18656	Bloomingdale's 4-4-2 Columbia Locomotive "8632", *96*		105	___
18657	Sears Zenith 4-4-2 Columbia Locomotive "8632", *96*		105	___
18658	LL Little League 4-4-2 Columbia Locomotive "X-1110", *97*		90	___
18660	Canadian National 4-2 Locomotive w/ tender "2044", *98*		175	___
18661	Norfolk & Western 4-2 Steam Locomotive w/ tender "2044", *98*		160	___
18662	Pennsylvania 0-4-0 Switcher, *98*	165	230	___
18666	SP&S 4-6-2 Pacific "2044", *97*		200	___
18668	Bloomingdale's 4-4-2 Columbia Locomotive "8632", *97*		130	___
18669	JCPenney IC 4-6-2 Pacific "2099", *98*		205	___
18670	D&H 4-4-2 Columbia Locomotive "1400", *98*		80	___
18671	N&W 4-4-2 Columbia Locomotive "1201", *98*		70	___
18678	Quaker Oats 4-4-2 Columbia Locomotive "8632", *98*		150	___
18679	JCPenney T&P 4-6-2, 99 "2000", traditional, *00 u*		250	___
18681	PRR 4-4-2 Steam Engine "460", *99*		75	___
18682	Santa Fe 4-4-2 Columbia "524" Locomotive traditional, *00–01*		70	___
18696	ACL 4-6-4 "1800", *01*		120	___
18697	Santa Fe 4-6-4 "3465", *01*		100	___
18699	Alaska 4-4-2 "64", *01*		105	___
18700	Rock Island 0-4-0T "8700", *87–88*	36	43	___
18702	V&TRR 4-4-0 "8702" (SSS), *88*	160	195	___
18704	Lionel Lines 2-4-0 "8704", *89 u*	36	43	___
18705	Neptune 0-4-0T "8705", *90–91*	35	42	___
18706	Santa Fe 2-4-0 "8706", *91*	36	43	___
18707	Mickey's World Tour 2-4-0 "8707", *91, 92 u*	55	65	___

		Exc	New	Cond/S
18709	Lionel Employee Learning Center "Blue Engine" 0-4-0T, *92 u*		135	___
18710	SP 2-4-0 "2000", *93*	30	38	___
18711	Southern 2-4-0 "2000", *93*	30	38	___
18712	Jersey Central 2-4-0 "2000", *93*	30	38	___
18713	Chessie System 2-4-0 "1993", *94–95*	30	38	___
18716	Lionelville Circus 4-4-0 "8716", *90–91*	90	110	___
18718	LL 0-4-0 Dockside Switcher "8200", *97–98*		40	___
18719	Thomas the Tank Engine 0-6-0 "1", *97*		155	___
18720	Union Cavalry 4-4-0 General "1865", *99*		175	___
18721	Confederate States 4-4-0 General "1861", *99*		175	___
18722	Percy the Tank Engine "6", *99*		170	___
18723	Union Pacific 4-4-0 General, *05*		100	___
18730	Transylvania RR 4-4-0 Locomotive "13" traditional, *05*		CP	___
18732	North Pole Central 4-4-0 Steam Locomotive "25", *06*		CP	___
18733	Percy the Tank Engine "6", *05–07*		CP	___
18734	James the Tank Engine "5", *06–07*		CP	___
18799	Bethlehem Steel Diesel Switcher "44", *99*		100	___
18800	Lehigh Valley GP-9 "8800", *87*	80	95	___
18801	Santa Fe U36B "8801", *87*	100	120	___
18802	Southern GP-9 "8802" (SSS), *87*	100	115	___
18803	Santa Fe RS-3 "8803", *88*	90	105	___
18804	Soo Line RS-3 "8804", *88*	95	115	___
18805	Union Pacific RS-3 "8805", *89*	100	125	___
18806	New Haven SD-18 "8806", *89*	100	115	___
18807	Lehigh Valley RS-3 "8807", *90*	90	120	___
18808	ACL SD-18 "8808", *90*	85	105	___
18809	Susquehanna RS-3 "8809", *89 u*		130	___
18810	CSX SD-18 "8810", *90*	95	130	___
18811	Alaska SD-9 "8811", *91*	95	135	___
18812	Kansas City Southern GP-38 "4000", *91*	120	140	___
18813	DM&IR SD-18 "8813", *90 u*	90	145	___
18814	D&H RS-3 "8814" (SSS), *91*	90	120	___
18815	Amtrak RS-3 "1815", *91, 92 u*	100	130	___
18816	C&NW GP-38-2 "4600", *92*	105	130	___
18817	UP GP-9 "150" (see 18553), *91 u*		135	___
18819	L&N GP-38-2 "4136", *92*	115	145	___
18820	WP GP-9 "8820" (SSS), *92*	120	140	___
18821	Clinchfield GP-38-2 "6005", *93*	125	150	___

		Exc	New	Cond/$
18822	Gulf, Mobile & Ohio RS-3 "721", *92–93* u		NRS	___
18823	Chicago & Illinois Midland SD-9 "52", *92 u*		235	___
18824	Montana Rail Link SD-9 "600", *93*	185	230	___
18825	Soo Line GP-38-2 "4000" (SSS), *93*	120	145	___
18826	Conrail GP-7 "5808", *93*	100	120	___
18827	"Happy Holidays" RS-3 "8827", *93*	165	220	___
18830	Budweiser GP-9 "1947", *93–94 u*	115	155	___
18831	SP GP-20 "4060", *94*	105	120	___
18832	PRR RSD-4 "8446", *95*	110	135	___
18833	Milwaukee Road RS-3 "2487", *94*	100	110	___
18834	C&O SD-28 "8834", *94*	110	140	___
18835	NYC RS-3 "8223" (SSS), *94*	135	195	___
18836	CN/Grand Trunk GP-38-2 "5800", *94*	135	160	___
18837	"Happy Holidays" RS-3 "8837", *94–95*	150	190	___
18838	Seaboard RSC-3 "1538", *95*	110	140	___
18840	U.S.Army GP-7 "1821", *95*	85	125	___
18841	Western Maryland GP-20 "27" (SSS), *95*	120	150	___
18842	JCPenney/B&LE SD-38 "868", *95 u*		265	___
18843	Great Northern RS-3 "197", *96*		145	___
18844	NdeM GP-38 "9288", *96*		NM	___
18845	D&RGW RS-3 "5204", *97*		100	___
18846	1997 Lionel Centennial Series GP-9 Diesel, *98*		370	___
18847	Santa Fe H-12-44 Switcher "602", *99*		385	___
18848	PRR H-12-44 Switcher "9087", *99*		420	___
18853	Santa Fe JCPenney GP-9 "2370", *97 u*		150	___
18854	UP GP-9 Set, "2380", "2387" Dummy, *97*		450	___
18856	NJ Transit GP-38-2 "4303", *99*		315	___
18857	Union Pacific GP-9 "2397", *97*		240	___
18858	1998 Lionel Centennial GP20 Diesel "1998", *98*		400	___
18859	The Phantom II, *99*		360	___
18860	Pratt's Hollow Collection I: The Phantom, *98*		400	___
18864	Southern Pacific GP-9 B-Unit, *98*		140	___
18865	New York Central GP-9 B-Unit, *98*		170	___
18866	Milwaukee Road GP7 "2383", *98*		205	___
18868	NJ Transit GP-38-2 "4300", *98 u*		140	___
18870	Pennsylvania GP-9 Diesel "2029", *98*		180	___
18872	Wabash GP7 3-Unit Set "453, 454, 455", *99*		560	___
18876	C&NW H-12-44 Switcher "1053", *99*		425	___
18877	Union Pacific GP9 Non-Powered "2399", *99*		175	___
18878	Alaska GP7 "1803", *99*		115	___

		Exc	New	Cond/$
18879	B&O GP9 "5616", *99*		260	___
18881	Custom GP9 "5616", *99*		350	___
18892	Burlington GP9 "2328", *99*		205	___
18897	Christmas GP7 "1999", *99*		200	___
18900	PRR Diesel Switcher "8900", *88 u, 89*	26	34	___
18901/18902	PRR Alco AA Set "8901" and "8902", *88*	110	130	___
18903/18904	Amtrak Alco AA Set "8903" and "8904" *88–89*	90	130	___
18903	Amtrak "Mopar Express", *99*		500	___
18905	PRR 44-tonner "9312", *92*	80	120	___
18906	Erie-Lackawanna RS-3 "8906", *91 u*	70	90	___
18907	Rock Island 44-tonner "371", *93*	95	110	___
18908/18909	NYC Alco AA Set "8908" and "8909", *93*	105	115	___
18910	CSX Diesel Switcher "8910", *93*	40	46	___
18911	UP Diesel Switcher "8911", *93*	33	37	___
18912	Amtrak Diesel Switcher "8912", *93*	37	43	___
18913	Santa Fe Alco A Unit "8913", *93–94*	55	65	___
18915	WM Alco A Unit "8915", *93*	65	80	___
18916	WM Alco A Unit Dummy "8916", *93*	38	42	___
18917	Soo Line NW-2, *93*	65	75	___
18918	B&M NW-2 "8918", *93*	75	90	___
18919	Santa Fe Alco A Unit Dummy "8919", *93–94*	36	55	___
18920	Frisco NW-2 "254", *94*	70	75	___
18921	C&NW NW-2 "1017", *94*	60	80	___
18922	New Haven Alco A Unit "8922", *94*	75	105	___
18923	New Haven Alco A Unit Dummy "8923", *94*	50	55	___
18924	IC Diesel Switcher "8924", *94–95*	37	44	___
18925	D&RGW Diesel Switcher "8925", *94–95*	32	37	___
18926	Reading Diesel Switcher "8926", *94–95*	31	39	___
18927	U.S. Navy NW-2 "65-00637", *94–95*	65	85	___
18928	C&NW NW-2 Calf, *95*	50	55	___
18929	B&M NW-2 Calf, *95*	44	49	___
18930	Crayola Diesel Switcher, *94 u, 95*	27	30	___
18931	Chrysler Mopar NW-2 "1818", *94 u*	70	85	___
18932	Jersey Central NW-2 "8932", *96*		65	___
18933	Jersey Central NW-2 Calf "8933", *96*		55	___
18934/18935	Reading Alco AA Set "300" and "304", *95*	75	95	___
18936	Amtrak Alco A Unit "8936", *95*		65	___
18937	Non-Powered Amtrak FA-2 ALCO, *95–97*		50	___
18938	U.S. Navy NW-2 Calf, *95*	55	65	___

		Exc	New	Cond/$
18939	Union Pacific NW-2 Diesel Switcher Set, *96*		145	___
18943	Georgia Power NW-2 "1960", *95 u*		170	___
18946	U.S. Coast Guard NW-2 Switcher "8946", *96*		80	___
18947	Port of Lionel City Alco FA-2 "2030", *97*		70	___
18948	Port of Lionel City Alco FB-2 "2030B", *97*		45	___
18949	NYC NW-2 "622", black, *97*		NM	___
18951	Erie NW-2 "6220", black, *97*		NM	___
18952	AT&SF Alco PA-1 "2000", *97*		345	___
18953	NYC Alco PA-1 "2000", *97*		260	___
18954	AT&SF Alco FA-2 "212" Powered, *97–99*		80	___
18955	NJ Transit NW-2 Switcher "500", *96 u*		110	___
18956	Dodge Motorsports "8956" NW-2, *96 u*		155	___
18959	NYC NW-2 Switcher "622", *97*		475	___
18961	Erie Alco PA-1"850", *98*		315	___
18965	Santa Fe Alco PB1, *98*		255	___
18966	New York Central Alco BP1 "2008", *98*		250	___
18971	Alco A-Unit (non-powered), *98*		60	___
18972	Rock Island Alco FA AA, *98*		NM	___
18973	RI Alco FA-2 "2031" Powered, *98–99*		NRS	___
18974	RI Alco FA-2 Dummy, *98–99*		NRS	___
18975	Southern 44-Ton Switcher "1955", *99*		190	___
18978	C&O NW-2 Switcher "624", *99–00*		410	___
18981	Pennsylvania Railroad Speeder "16", *04*		45	___
18982	Santa Fe Railroad Speeder "122", *04–05*		CP	___
18988	K-Line By Lionel MP15 Diesel, *06*		CP	___
18989	K-Line By Lionel Bethlehem Steel Plymouth Diesel Switcher, traditional, *06*		CP	___
19000	Blue Comet Dining Car, *87 u*	60	75	___
19001	Southern Dining Car, *87 u*	55	65	___
19002	Pennsylvania Dining Car, *88 u*	29	45	___
19003	Milwaukee Road Dining Car, *88 u*	29	44	___
19010	B&O Dining Car, *89 u*	36	55	___
19011	Lionel Lines Baggage Car "9011", *93*	335	495	___
19015	Lionel Lines Passenger Car "9015", *91*	150	210	___
19016	Lionel Lines Passenger Car "9016", *91*	100	135	___
19017	Lionel Lines Passenger Car "9017", *91*	70	95	___
19018	Lionel Lines Observation Car "9018", *91*	90	115	___
19019	SP Baggage Car "9019", *93*	120	170	___
19023	SP Passenger Car "9023", *92*	125	160	___
19024	SP Passenger Car "9024", *92*	85	100	___
19025	SP Passenger Car "9025", *92*	100	115	___

		Exc	New	Cond/$
19026	SP Observation Car "9026", *92*	85	100	___
19027	Reading Baggage Car "9027", *92*		NM	___
19031	Reading Passenger Car "9031", *92*		NM	___
19032	Reading Passenger Car "9032", *92*		NM	___
19033	Reading Observation Car "9033", *92*		NM	___
19038	Adolphus Busch Observation Car, *92–93 u*		85	___
19039	Pere Marquette Baggage Car, *93*		75	___
19040	Pere Marquette Passenger Car "1115", *93*		75	___
19041	Pere Marquette Passenger Car "1116", *93*		75	___
19042	Pere Marquette Observation Car "36", *93*		75	___
19047	Baltimore & Ohio Combination Car "9047", *96*		55	___
19048	Baltimore & Ohio Passenger Car "9048", *96*		50	___
19049	Baltimore & Ohio Dining Car "9049", *96*		42	___
19050	Baltimore & Ohio Observation Car "9050", *96*		42	___
19056	NYC Heavyweight Baggage Car, *96*		105	___
19057	NYC Heavyweight "Willow Run" Coach, *96*		95	___
19058	NYC Heavyweight "Willow Trail" Coach, *96*		90	___
19059	NYC Heavyweight "Seneca Valley" Observation, *96*		100	___
19060	Pullman Heavyweight Set, *96*		470	___
19061	Wabash Passenger Set, *97*		235	___
19062	Wabash "City of Columbia" Coach "2361", *97*		90	___
19063	Wabash "City of Danville" Coach "2362", *97*		75	___
19064	Wabash REA Baggage Car "2360", *97*		47	___
19065	Wabash "Windy City" Observation "2363", *97*		90	___
19066	Commodore Vanderbilt Pullman Heavyweight 2-pack, *97*		190	___
19067	Commodore Vanderbilt "Willow River" Pullman "2543", *97*		115	___
19068	Commodore Vanderbilt "Willow Valley" Pullman "2544", *97*		100	___
19069	Pullman Baby Madison Set "9500-02", *97*		155	___
19070	Baby Madison REA/Combo "9501", *97*		40	___
19071	Baby Madison "Laurel Gap" Coach "9500", *97*		34	___
19072	Baby Madison "Laurel Summit" Coach "9500", *97*		40	___
19073	Baby Madison "Catskill Valley" Observation "9502", *97*		34	___
19074	Legends of Lionel Madison Set, *97*		385	___
19075	Lionel Legends "Mazzone" Coach "2621", *97*		105	___
19076	Lionel Legends "Caruso" Coach "2624", *97*		90	___
19077	Lionel Legends "Raphael" Coach "2652", *97*		90	___
19078	Lionel Legends "Cowen" Observation "2600", *97*		95	___
19079	NYC Heavyweight Passenger Car Set, *97*		275	___

		Exc	New	Cond/$
19080	NYC Heavyweight REA Baggage Car "2564", *97*		100	___
19081	NYC Heavyweight "Park Place" Coach "2565", *97*		100	___
19082	NYC Heavyweight "Star Beam" Coach "2566", *97*		100	___
19083	NYC Heavyweight "Hudson Valley" Observation "2566", *97*		100	___
19087	C&O Heavyweight Passenger Car 4-pack "2571-74", *97*		290	___
19088	C&O Heavyweight Baggage Car "2571", *97*		100	___
19089	C&O Heavyweight Sleeper Car "2572", *97*		100	___
19090	C&O Heavyweight Diner Car "2573", *97*		110	___
19091	C&O Heavyweight Observation Car "2574", *97*		100	___
19093	Commodore Vanderbilt Heavyweight Sleeper Car 2-pack, *98*		170	___
19094	Commodore Vanderbilt "Niagara Falls" Sleeper, *98*		75	___
19095	Commodore Vanderbilt "Highland Falls" Sleeper, *98*		75	___
19096	Legends of Lionel Madison Cars 2-pack, *98*		130	___
19097	Lionel Legends "Bonnano" Coach "2653", *98*		80	___
19098	Lionel Legends "Pagano" Coach "2654", *98*		105	___
19099	PRR "Liberty Gap" Baggage Car "2623", *99*		80	___
19100	Amtrak Baggage Car "9100", *89*	125	165	___
19101	Amtrak Combination Car "9101", *89*	75	85	___
19102	Amtrak Passenger Car "9102", *89*	75	85	___
19103	Amtrak Vista Dome Car "9103", *89*	70	90	___
19104	Amtrak Dining Car "9104", *89*	65	80	___
19105	Amtrak Full Vista Dome Car "9105", *89 u*	70	75	___
19106	Amtrak Observation Car "9106", *89*	75	90	___
19107	SP Full Vista Dome Car, *90 u*	70	75	___
19108	N&W Full Vista Dome Car "576", *91 u*	75	85	___
19109	Santa Fe Baggage Car "3400", *91*	225	300	___
19110	Santa Fe Combination Car "3500", *91*	80	110	___
19111	Santa Fe Dining Car "601", *91*	100	135	___
19112	Santa Fe Passenger Car, *91*	125	175	___
19113	Santa Fe Vista Dome Observation Car, *91*	100	135	___
19116	Great Northern Baggage Car "1200", *92*	135	165	___
19117	Great Northern Combination Car "1240", *92*	65	80	___
19118	Great Northern Passenger Car "1212", *92*	75	95	___
19119	Great Northern Vista Dome Car "1322", *92*	75	95	___
19120	Great Northern Observation Car "1192", *92*	75	95	___
19121	Union Pacific Vista Dome Car "9121", *92 u*	90	100	___
19122	D&RGW California Zephyr Baggage Car, *93*	170	210	___
19123	D&RGW California Zephyr "Silver Bronco"	95	115	___

		Exc	New	Cond/$
	Vista Dome Car, *93*			
19124	D&RGW California Zephyr "Silver Colt" Vista Dome Car, *93*	95	115	___
19125	D&RGW California Zephyr "Silver Mustang" Vista Dome Car, *93*	100	125	___
19126	D&RGW California Zephyr "Silver Pony" Vista Dome Car, *93*	95	115	___
19127	D&RGW California Zephyr Vista Dome Observation Car, *93*	85	100	___
19128	Santa Fe Full Vista Dome Car "507", *92 u*	175	185	___
19129	IC Full Vista Dome Car "9129", *93*	75	85	___
19130	Lackawanna Passenger Cars, set of 4, *94*	280	350	___
19131	Lackawanna Baggage Car "2000" (see 19130)		150	___
19132	Lackawanna Dining Car "469" (see 19130)		100	___
19133	Lackawanna Passenger Car "260" (see 19130)		100	___
19134	Lackawanna Observation Car "789" (see 19130)		85	___
19135	Lackawanna Combination Car "425", *94*	85	100	___
19136	Lackawanna Passenger Car "211", *94*	65	75	___
19137	New York Central Roomette Car, *95*	90	105	___
19138	Santa Fe Roomette Car, *95*	75	95	___
19139	N&W Baggage Car "577", *95*	150	200	___
19140	N&W Combination Car "494", *95*	60	80	___
19141	N&W Dining Car "495", *95*	105	135	___
19142	N&W Passenger Car "538", *95*	75	95	___
19143	N&W Passenger Car "537", *95*	75	95	___
19144	N&W Observation Car "582", *95*	80	95	___
19145	C&O Combination Car "1403", *96*		95	___
19146	C&O Passenger Car "1623", *96*		85	___
19147	C&O Passenger Car "1803", *96*		75	___
19148	C&O Chessie Club Coach "1903", *96*		75	___
19149	C&O Gadsby Kitchen Passenger/Diner "1950", *96*		65	___
19150	C&O Observation Car "2504", *96*		75	___
19151	Norfolk & Western Duplex Roomette car, *96*		105	___
19152	Union Pacific Duplex Roomette Car, *96*		75	___
19153	C&O Passenger Cars, set of 4, *96*		340	___
19154	Atlantic Coast Line Passenger Cars Set, *96*		340	___
19155	ACL Passenger/Combo "101", *96*		90	___
19156	ACL "Talladega" Diner, *96*		90	___
19157	ACL "Moultrie" Coach, *96*		95	___
19158	ACL Observation "256", *96*		90	___

		Exc	New	Cond/$
19159	N&W Passenger Cars, set of 4, *95 u*	300	385	___
19160	AT&SF Super Chief REA Baggage Car, *96*		90	___
19161	AT&SF Super Chief Silver Sky Coach, *96*		80	___
19162	AT&SF Super Chief "Silver Mesa" Vista Dome, *96*		75	___
19163	AT&SF Super Chief "Silver Rail" Observation, *96*		75	___
19164	Chesapeake & Ohio Passenger Cars, *96*		160	___
19165	AT&SF Super Chief Set, *96*		305	___
19166	NP Vista Dome Set, *97*		305	___
19167	NP Pullman "2571", *97*		105	___
19168	NP Pullman "2571", *97*		105	___
19169	NP Pullman "2570", *97*		95	___
19170	NP Pullman "2571", *97*		100	___
19171	NYC Streamlined Passenger Set "2570-75", *97*		285	___
19172	NYC Aluminum Passenger Baggage "2570", *97*		95	___
19173	NYC Aluminum Passenger Diner "Manhattan Island", *97*		100	___
19174	NYC Aluminum Passenger Coach "Queensboro Bridge", *97*		100	___
19175	NYC Aluminum Passenger Observation "Windgate Brook", *97*		90	___
19176	AT&SF "Indian Arrow" Diner "2572", *97*		90	___
19177	AT&SF "Grass Valley" Coach "2573", *97*		90	___
19178	AT&SF "Citrus Valley" Coach "2574", *97*		90	___
19179	AT&SF "Vista Heights" "2575", *97*		90	___
19180	AT&SF Surfliner Passenger Set "2572-75", *97*		250	___
19181	GN Empire Builder "Prairie View" Full Vista Dome, *98*		75	___
19182	GN Empire Builder "River View" Full Vista Dome, *98*		75	___
19183	Great Northern Empire Builder Vista Dome Cars 2-pack, *98*		125	___
19184	Milwaukee Passenger Set 4-pack, *99*		390	___
19185	Milwaukee Road Aluminum Passenger Coach "194 Red River Valley", *99*		125	___
19186	Milwaukee Road Aluminum Passenger Diner "170", *99*		110	___
19187	Milwaukee Road Aluminum Passenger Observation "186 Cedar Rapids", *99*		120	___
19188	Milwaukee Road Aluminum Passenger Baggage "1336", REA, *99*		95	___
19194	KCS Aluminum Passenger Car 4-pack, *00*		380	___
19200	Tidewater Southern Boxcar, *87*	13	21	___

		Exc	New	Cond/$
19201	Lancaster & Chester Boxcar, *87*	23	37	___
19202	PRR Boxcar, *87*	22	26	___
19203	D&TS Boxcar, *87*	11	18	___
19204	Milwaukee Road Boxcar (FF #2), *87*	29	41	___
19205	Great Northern DD Boxcar (FF #3), *88*	20	24	___
19206	Seaboard System Boxcar, *88*	18	23	___
19207	CP Rail DD Boxcar, *88*	17	22	___
19208	Southern DD Boxcar, *88*	11	13	___
19209	Florida East Coast Boxcar, *88*	15	19	___
19210	Soo Line Boxcar, *89*	19	23	___
19211	Vermont Railway Boxcar, *89*	18	21	___
19212	PRR Boxcar, *89*	21	25	___
19213	SP&S DD Boxcar, *89*	16	19	___
19214	Western Maryland Boxcar (FF #4), *89*	23	27	___
19215	Union Pacific DD Boxcar, *90*	17	21	___
19216	Santa Fe Boxcar, *90*	17	22	___
19217	Burlington Boxcar, *90*	16	21	___
19218	New Haven Boxcar, *90*	16	20	___
19219	Lionel Lines 1900-1906 Boxcar w/ Diesel RailSounds, *90*	120	145	___
19220	Lionel Lines 1926-1934 Boxcar, *90*	27	30	___
19221	Lionel Lines 1935-1937 Boxcar, *90*	27	30	___
19222	Lionel Lines 1948-1950 Boxcar, *90*	27	30	___
19223	Lionel Lines 1979-1989 Boxcar, *90*	23	25	___
19228	Cotton Belt Boxcar, *91*	21	22	___
19229	Frisco Boxcar w/ Diesel RailSounds (FF #5), *91*	75	90	___
19230	Frisco DD Boxcar (FF #5), *91*	21	26	___
19231	TA&G DD Boxcar, *91*	13	16	___
19232	Rock Island DD Boxcar, *91*	17	20	___
19233	Southern Pacific Boxcar, *91*	15	19	___
19234	NYC Boxcar, *91*	60	65	___
19235	MKT Boxcar, *91*	55	65	___
19236	NKP DD Boxcar (FF #6), *92*	22	30	___
19237	C&IM Boxcar, *92*	17	24	___
19238	Kansas City Southern Boxcar, *92*	18	23	___
19239	Toronto, Hamilton & Buffalo DD Boxcar, *92*	15	20	___
19240	Great Northern DD Boxcar, *92*	15	20	___
19241	Mickey Mouse 60th Anniversary Hi-Cube Boxcar, *91 u*	125	165	___
19242	Donald Duck 50th Anniversary Hi-Cube	120	150	___

		Exc	New	Cond/$
	Boxcar, *91 u*			
19243	Clinchfield Boxcar "9790", *91 u*	35	41	___
19244	L&N Boxcar "9791", *92*	35	38	___
19245	Mickey's World Tour Hi-Cube Boxcar, *92 u*	35	40	___
19246	Disney World 20th Anniversary Hi-Cube Boxcar, *92 u*	33	40	___
19247	6464 Series Boxcars, 1st Edition set of 3, *93*	445	610	___
19248	Western Pacific Boxcar "6464", *93*	75	95	___
19249	Great Northern Boxcar "6464", *93*	75	95	___
19250	M&StL Boxcar "6464", *93*	80	105	___
19251	Montana Rail Link DD Boxcar "10001", *93*	21	27	___
19254	Erie Boxcar (FF #7), *93*	21	25	___
19255	Erie DD Boxcar (FF #7), *93*	22	26	___
19256	Goofy Hi-Cube Boxcar, *93*	23	27	___
19257	6464 Series Boxcars, 2nd Edition set of 3, *94*	115	125	___
19258	Rock Island Boxcar "6464", *94*	25	34	___
19259	Western Pacific Boxcar "6464100", *94*	33	46	___
19260	Western Pacific Boxcar "6464100", *94*	35	49	___
19261	Perils of Mickey Hi-Cube Boxcar #1, *93*	28	30	___
19262	Perils of Mickey Hi-Cube Boxcar #2, *93*	31	33	___
19263	NYC DD Boxcar (SSS), *94*	36	42	___
19264	Perils of Mickey Hi-Cube Boxcar #3, *94*	28	31	___
19265	Mickey Mouse 65th Anniversary Hi-Cube Boxcar, *94*	42	44	___
19266	6464 Series Boxcars, 3rd Edition (3), *95*	75	90	___
19267	NYC "Pacemaker" Boxcar "6464125", *95*	37	42	___
19268	Missouri Pacific Boxcar "6464150", *95*	30	33	___
19269	Rock Island Boxcar "6464", *95*	25	26	___
19270	Donald Duck 60th Anniversary Hi-Cube Boxcar, *95*	30	34	___
19271	Minnie Mouse Hi-Cube Boxcar, *95*	41	43	___
19272	6464 Series Boxcars, 4th edition (3), *96*	70	85	___
19273	BAR "State of Maine" Boxcar "6464275", *96*		35	___
19274	SP "Overnight" Boxcar "6464225", *96*		28	___
19275	Pennsylvania Boxcar "6464", *96*		44	___
19276	"6464" Boxcar (Series V) "19277-79", *96*	65	85	___
19277	Rutland Boxcar "6464-300" (Series V), *96*		26	___
19278	B&O Boxcar "6464-325" (Series V), *96*		30	___
19279	Central of Georgia "6464-375" (Series V), *96*		29	___

		Exc	New	Cond/$
19280	Mickey's Wheat Hi-Cube Boxcar, *96*		32	___
19281	Mickey's Carrots Hi-Cube Boxcar, *96*		40	___
19282	Santa Fe "Super Chief" Boxcar "6464-196", *96*		24	___
19283	Erie Boxcar "6464-296", *96*		27	___
19284	Northern Pacific Boxcar "6464-396", *96*		29	___
19285	Bangor and Aroostook "State of Maine" Boxcar "6464-275", *96*		27	___
19286	Warner Bros. "All Abirrrrd" Boxcar, *96*		41	___
19287	NYC/PC Merger Boxcar "6464-125X" (SSS), *97*	50	75	___
19288	PRR/CR Merger Boxcar "6464-200X" (SSS), *97*	43	65	___
19289	Monon "Hoosier Line" Boxcar "6464", *97*		27	___
19290	Seaboard "Silver Meteor" Boxcar "6464", *97*		26	___
19291	GN Boxcar "6464-397", dark green, *97*		26	___
19292	"6464" Boxcar Series VI "19293-95", *97*		90	___
19293	MKT Boxcar "6464-350" (Series VI), *97*	28	32	___
19294	B&O Boxcar "6464-400" (Series VI), *97*	27	34	___
19295	NH Boxcar "6464-425" (Series VI), *97*	25	34	___
19300	PRR Ore Car, *87*	15	23	___
19301	Milwaukee Road Ore Car, *87*	20	25	___
19302	Milwaukee Road Quad Hopper w/ coal load (FF #2), *87*	24	35	___
19303	Lionel Lines Quad Hopper w/ coal load, *87 u*	20	29	___
19304	GN Covered Quad Hopper (FF #3), *88*	24	25	___
19305	Chessie System Ore Car, *88*	18	23	___
19307	B&LE Ore Car w/ load, *89*	19	25	___
19308	GN Ore Car w/ load, *89*	18	23	___
19309	Seaboard Covered Quad Hopper, *89*	16	20	___
19310	L&C Quad Hopper w/ coal load, *89*	16	23	___
19311	SP Covered Quad Hopper, *90*	14	19	___
19312	Reading Quad Hopper w/ coal load, *90*	21	32	___
19313	B&O Ore Car w/ load, *90–91*	20	25	___
19315	Amtrak Ore Car w/ load, *91*	22	30	___
19316	Wabash Covered Quad Hopper, *91*	18	25	___
19317	Lehigh Valley Quad Hopper w/ coal load, *91*	47	55	___
19318	NKP Quad Hopper w/ coal load (FF #6), *92*	30	34	___
19319	Union Pacific Covered Quad Hopper, *92*	19	23	___
19320	PRR Ore Car w/ load, *92*	21	30	___
19321	B&LE Ore Car w/ load, *92*	21	30	___
19322	C&NW Ore Car w/ load, *93*	27	34	___

		Exc	New	Cond/$
19323	Detroit & Mackinac Ore Car w/ load, *93*	20	29	___
19324	Erie Quad Hopper w/ coal load (FF #7), *93*	25	33	___
19325	N&W 4-Bay Hopper w/ coal "6446-1", *97*		65	___
19326	N&W 4-Bay Hopper w/ coal "6446-2", *96*		60	___
19327	N&W 4-Bay Hopper w/ coal "6446-3", *96*		60	___
19328	N&W 4-Bay Hopper w/ coal "6446-4", *96*		60	___
19329	N&W 4-Bay Hopper w/ coal "6436", *97*		55	___
19330	Cotton Belt 4-Bay Hopper w/ coal "64661", *98*		45	___
19331	Cotton Belt 4-Bay Hopper w/ coal "64662", *98*		45	___
19332	Cotton Belt 4-Bay Hopper w/ coal "64663", *98*		45	___
19333	Cotton Belt 4-Bay Hopper w/ coal "64664", *98*		45	___
19338	Cotton Belt 4-Bay Hopper 2-pack, *99*		120	___
19339	Cotton Belt 4-Bay Hopper "64469", *99*		NRS	___
19340	Cotton Belt 4-Bay Hopper "64470", *99*		NRS	___
19341	LV 2-Bay Hopper "6456", *99*		30	___
19344	D&RGW 3-Bay Cylindrical Hopper "15990", *99–00*		42	___
19345	CN 3-Bay Cylindrical Hopper "370708", *99–00*		95	___
19346	PRR 4-Bay Hopper w/ coal load "744433", *01*		40	___
19347	LV 2-Bay Hopper "643657", *01*		40	___
19348	Duluth, Missabe & Iron Range Ore Car "28000", *03*		25	___
19349	US Steel Ore Car "19349", *03*		29	___
19350	Postwar Alaska Quad Hopper "6636", *03*		34	___
19357	Postwar Archive No. 6446-25 N&W Hopper, *07*		CP	___
19371	Burlington Northern I-Beam Car, *04*		60	___
19400	Milwaukee Road Gondola w/ cable reels (FF #2), *87*	23	31	___
19401	GN Gondola w/ coal load (FF #3), *88*	14	16	___
19402	GN Crane Car (FF #3), *88*	47	65	___
19403	WM Gondola w/ coal load (FF #4), *89*	20	25	___
19404	Trailer Train Flatcar w/ WM trailers (FF #4), *89*	29	33	___
19405	Southern Crane Car, *91*	42	65	___
19406	West Point Mint Car, *91 u*	38	55	___
19408	Frisco Gondola w/ coil covers (FF #5), *91*	26	31	___
19409	Southern Flatcar w/ stakes, *91*	18	22	___
19410	NYC Gondola w/ canisters, *91*	47	55	___
19411	NKP Flatcar w/ Sears trailer (FF #6), *92*	50	65	___
19412	Frisco Crane Car, *92*	49	65	___
19413	Frisco Flatcar w/ stakes, *92*	16	21	___
19414	Union Pacific Flatcar w/ stakes (SSS), *92*	19	26	___

		Exc	New	Cond/$
19415	Erie Flatcar w/ trailer "7200" (FF #7), *93*	28	39	___
19416	ICG TTUX Flatcar Set w/ trailers "19417" and "19418" (SSS), *93*	70	75	___
19419	Charlotte Mint Car, *93*	25	32	___
19420	Lionel Lines Vat Car, *94*	24	25	___
19421	Hirsch Brothers Vat Car, *95*	20	24	___
19423	Circle-L Racing Flatcar w/ stock cars "6424", *96*		27	___
19424	Edison Electric Depressed Center Flatcar w/ transformer "6461", *97*		31	___
119427	Evans Auto Loader "6414", *99*		55	___
19428	Evans Boat Loader "6414", *99*		70	___
19429	Culvert Gondola "6342", *98–99*		48	___
19430	AT&SF Flatcar w/ Beechcraft Bonanza "6411", *98*		47	___
19438	Standard O Christmas Gondola, *98*		44	___
19439	Flatcar with safes, *98*		35	___
19440	Flatcar with FedEx trailer, *98*		34	___
19441	Lobster Vat Car, *98*		32	___
19442	Water Supply Flatcar w/ tank (SSS), *98*		31	___
19444	Flatcar with VW Bug, *98*		38	___
19445	Borden Milk Tank Car "520", *99*		38	___
19446	Pittsburg Paint Vat Car, *99*		43	___
19447	Mama's Baked Beans Vat Car, *99*		35	___
19448	Easter Gondola w/ candy "6462", *99*		27	___
19449	Liquified Gas Tank Car "6469", *99*		31	___
19450	Barrel Ramp Car "6343", *99*		34	___
19451	Wheel Car "6262", *99*		32	___
19454	PRR Flatcar with gondola "6424", *99*		25	___
19455	Lionel Lines Flatcar w/ Cooper-Jarrett trailers "6430", *99*		60	___
19457	Lionel Lines Extension Searchlight Car, *99*		40	___
19459	Valentine Gondola w/ candy "6462", *99*		50	___
19471	Mobil Flatcar w/ 2 trailers, *00 u*		90	___
19472	Mobil Bulkhead Flatcar w/ tank, *00 u*		65	___
19474	L&N Flatcar w/ die-cast trailer frames 6424, *99*		26	___
19476	Lionel Zoo Gondola w/ animals "6462", *99–00*		43	___
19477	Monday Night Football Flatcar w/ trailer, *01*		30	___
19478	Culvert Gondola "6342", *99*		45	___
19479	Borden's Milk Car "521", *00*		38	___
19480	Valentine's Vat Car "6475", *99–00*		30	___
19481	Easter Vat Car "2000", *99–00*		38	___

		Exc	New	Cond/$
19482	NYC Flat with trailer "6424", *00*		50	___
19483	VW Beetle Flatcar "2000", *00*		48	___
19484	Lionel Flatcar w/ timbers "6264", *00*		34	___
19485	PRR Culvert Gondola "347004", *01*		49	___
19486	NYC Lumber Flatcar, *01*		34	___
19487	Flatcar w/ airplane "6800", *00*		37	___
19489	Evans Auto Loader "500085", *00*		50	___
19490	Postwar Libby's Vat Car "6475", *01–02*		32	___
19491	Christmas Vat Car, *01*		30	___
19492	WM Skeleton Log Car 3-pack, *01*		95	___
19496	Westside Lumber Skeleton Log Car 3-pack, *01*		125	___
19500	Milwaukee Road Reefer (FF #2), *87*	30	39	___
19502	C&NW Reefer, *87*	30	37	___
19503	Bangor & Aroostook Reefer, *87*	22	25	___
19504	Northern Pacific Reefer, *87*	20	24	___
19505	Great Northern Reefer (FF #3), *88*	29	35	___
19506	Thomas Newcomen Reefer, *88*	18	23	___
19507	Thomas Edison Reefer, *88*	21	27	___
19508	Leonardo da Vinci Reefer, *89*	19	27	___
19509	Alexander Graham Bell Reefer, *89*	17	20	___
19510	PRR Stockcar (FARR #5), *89 u*	25	26	___
19511	WM Reefer (FF #4), *89*	22	26	___
19512	Wright Brothers Reefer, *90*	17	21	___
19513	Ben Franklin Reefer, *90*	17	20	___
19515	Milwaukee Road Stock Car (FF #2), *90 u*	33	41	___
19516	George Washington Reefer, *89 u*, *91*	14	19	___
19517	Civil War Reefer, *89 u*, *91*	14	19	___
19518	Man on the Moon Reefer, *89 u*, *91*	13	17	___
19519	Frisco Stock Car (FF #5), *91*	26	31	___
19520	CSX Reefer, *91*	18	23	___
19522	Guglielmo Marconi Reefer, *91*	19	23	___
19523	Dr. Robert Goddard Reefer, *91*	19	23	___
19524	Delaware & Hudson Reefer (SSS), *91*	29	32	___
19525	Speedy Alka Seltzer Reefer, *91 u*	31	38	___
19526	Jolly Green Giant Reefer, *91 u*	21	33	___
19527	Nickel Plate Road Reefer (FF #6), *92*	20	29	___
19528	Joshua L. Cowen Reefer, *92*	23	28	___
19529	A.C. Gilbert Reefer, *92*	18	23	___
19530	Rock Island Stock Car, *92 u*	34	38	___
19531	Rice Krispies Reefer, *92 u*	23	33	___

		Exc	New	Cond/$
19532	Hormel Reefer "901", *92 u*	18	24	___
19535	Erie Reefer (FF #7), *93*	23	26	___
19536	Soo Line REA Reefer (SSS), *93*	29	35	___
19537	Kellogg's Corn Flakes Reefer, *93*		NM	___
19538	Hormel Reefer "102", *94*	22	25	___
19539	Heinz Reefer, *94*	37	46	___
19540	Broken Arrow Ranch Stock Car "3356", *97*		28	___
19552	Rutland Reefer "395" (Std O), *00*		32	___
19553	AT&SF Stock Car "23003", *00*		37	___
19554	Milk Car "36621", *00*		125	___
19555	Swift Reefer "5839", red, *01*		33	___
19556	Swift Reefer "1020", silver, *01*		31	___
19557	Circus Stock Car "6376", *00*		32	___
19558	Postwar MKT Stock Car "6556", *02*		27	___
19560	Lionel Archives NP 2-Door Stock Car "6356", *02*		33	___
19564	Postwar Santa Fe Refrigerator Car "6672", *03*		35	___
19565	Archive Burlington Refrigerator Car "6672", *03*		35	___
19567	#6572 Railway Express Agency Reefer, *05*		CP	___
19568	GN Reefer-Archive, *05*		CP	___
19569	Pillsbury Refrigerator Car, traditional, *05*		CP	___
19570	Nestle Nesquik Refrigerator Car, traditional, *05*		CP	___
19572	Archive No. 6672 NYC Refrigerator Car, *06*		CP	___
19573	Postwar No. 6356 NYC Stock Car, *06–07*		CP	___
19599	Old Glory Reefers, set of 3, *89 u, 91*	37	43	___
19600	Milwaukee Road 1-D Tank Car (FF # 2), *87*	33	40	___
19601	North American 1-D Tank Car (FF #4), *89*	27	29	___
19602	Johnson 1-D Tank Car (FF #5), *91*	24	30	___
19603	GATX 1-D Tank Car (FF #6), *92*	32	41	___
19604	Goodyear 1-D Tank Car (SSS), *93*	33	36	___
19605	Hudson's Bay 1-D Tank Car (SSS), *94*	25	29	___
19607	Sunoco 1-D Tank Car "6315", *96*		23	___
19608	Sunoco Aviation Services 1-Dome Tank Car "6315" (SSS), *97*		38	___
19611	Gulf Oil 1-D Tank Car "6315", *98*		33	___
19612	Gulf Oil 3-D Tank Car "6425", *98*		30	___
19614	BASF SD Tank Car "UTLX 78252", *99–00*		25	___
19615	Vulcan Chemicals SD Tank Car, *99–00*		25	___
19621	Centennial SD Tank Car "6015-1", *99*		44	___
19622	Centennial SD Tank Car "6015-2", *99*		48	___
19623	Centennial SD Tank Car "6015-3", *99*		46	___
19624	Centennial SD Tank Car "6015-4", *99*		44	___

		Exc	New	Cond/$
19625	Ethyl Tank Car " 6236", *01*		31	___
19626	Diamond Chemical Tank Car "19419", *01*		29	___
19627	Shell SD Tank Car "1227", *01*		37	___
19628	Lion Oil SD Tank Car"2256", *01*		35	___
19629	Lifesaver SD Tank Car, *01*		NM	___
19634	General American 1-D Tank Car, *01*		30	___
19635	U.S. Army 1-Dome Tank Car "10936", *01*		31	___
19636	Hooker Chemicals 1-Dome Tank Car "6180", *01*		36	___
19637	GATX TankTrain Tank Car "44589" (Std. O), *02*		55	___
19638	CN TankTrain Tank Car "75571" (Std. O), *02*		65	___
19639	GATX TankTrain Tank Car 3-pack (Std. O), *02*		140	___
19644	Union Texas 1-Dome Tank Car "9922", *02*		33	___
19645	Penn Salt 1-Dome Tank Car "4730", *02*		33	___
19646	CN Intermediate TankTrain Tank Car "75571"(Std. O), *03*		45	___
19647	GATX Intermediate TankTrain Tank Car "44589" (Std. O), *03*		45	___
19649	Scrooge/MC Duck Mint Car, *05*		175	___
19651	Santa Fe Tool Car, *87*	30	35	___
19652	Jersey Central Bunk Car, *88*	25	33	___
19653	Jersey Central Tool Car, *88*	26	32	___
19654	Amtrak Bunk Car, *89*	22	25	___
19655	Amtrak Tool Car, *90–91*	23	30	___
19656	Milwaukee Road Bunk Car w/ smoke, *90*	40	50	___
19657	Wabash Bunk Car w/ smoke, *91–92*	36	42	___
19658	Norfolk & Western Tool Car, *91*	24	29	___
19660	Lionel Mint Car, *98*		40	___
19663	Pratt's Hollow Bunk Car "5717", *99*		40	___
19664	Ambassador Award Bunk Car "1998", bronze, *99 u*		355	___
19665	Ambassador Engineer Bunk Car "1998", silver, *99 u*		550	___
19666	Ambassador Cowen Bunk Car "1998", gold, *99 u*		385	___
19667	Wellspring Gold Bullion Car, *99*		49	___
19669	King Tut Museum Car "9660", *99*		65	___
19670	NY Federal Reserve Bullion Car "6445", *00*		44	___
19671	Lionel Model Shop Display Car "6445-01", *99–00*		50	___
19672	Lionel Mines Mint Car, *00 u*		250	___
19673	Wellspring Capital Management Mint Car, *99 u*		200	___
19674	Lionel Lines Platinum Car, *00*		43	___
19675	Lionel Model Shop Display "6445-2", *01*		42	___
19676	Philadelphia Mint Car, *01*		40	___
19677	Fort Knox Mint Car "6445", *00*		50	___

		Exc	New	Cond/$
19678	U.S. Army Bunk Car, *02*		45	___
19679	St. Louis Federal Reserve Mint Car, *02*		38	___
19681	Area 51 Alien Suspension Car, *02*		47	___
19682	Alaska Klondike Mining Co. Mint Car, *02*		40	___
19683	Pony Express Mint Car, *02*		50	___
19686	Chicago Federal Reserve Mint Car "6445", *03–04*		45	___
19687	UP Bunk Car w/ smoke "3887", *03*		40	___
19688	Postwar Fort Knox Mint Car "6445", *02–03*		39	___
19689	CIBRO TankTrain Tank Car 3-pack (Std. O), *03*		100	___
19694	Pony Express Mint Car, *03*		50	___
19696	U.S. Savings Bond Mint Car, *00*		150	___
19697	U.S. Bureau of Engraving and Printing Mint Car "19697", *04*		40	___
19698	San Francisco Federal Reserve Mint Car, *04*		40	___
19700	Chessie System E/V Caboose, *88*	43	50	___
19701	Milwaukee Road N5C Caboose (FF #2), *88*	50	65	___
19702	PRR N5C Caboose, *87*	44	55	___
19703	Great Northern E/V Caboose (FF #3), *88*	42	49	___
19704	WM E/V Caboose w/ smoke (FF #4), *89*	42	49	___
19705	CP Rail E/V Caboose w/ smoke, *89*	43	47	___
19706	UP E/V Caboose w/ smoke "9706", *89*	40	43	___
19707	SP Work Caboose w/ searchlight and smoke, *90*	55	60	___
19708	Lionel Lines B/W Caboose "1990", *90*	43	46	___
19709	PRR Work Caboose w/ smoke, *89, 91*	55	70	___
19710	Frisco E/V Caboose w/ smoke (FF #5), *91*	43	47	___
19711	Norfolk Southern E/V Caboose w/ smoke, *92*	47	65	___
19712	PRR N5C Caboose, *91*	44	47	___
19714	NYC Work Caboose w/ searchlight and smoke, *92*	100	130	___
19715	DM&IR E/V Caboose "C-217", *92 u*	50	60	___
19716	IC E/V Caboose w/ smoke "9405", *93*	105	135	___
19717	Susquehanna B/W Caboose "0121", *93*	44	55	___
19718	Chicago & Illinois Midland E/V Caboose "74", *92 u*	38	45	___
19719	Erie B/W Caboose "C-300" (FF #7), *93*	47	55	___
19720	Soo Line E/V Caboose (SSS), *93*	39	47	___
19721	GM&O E/V Caboose "2956", *93 u*	47	50	___
19723	Disney E/V Caboose, *94*	36	45	___
19724	JCPenney/MKT E/V Caboose "125", *94 u*	38	43	___
19726	NYC B/W Caboose (SSS), *95*	50	60	___

		Exc	New	Cond/$
19727	Pennsylvania N5C Caboose "477938", *96*		30	___
19728	N&W Bay Window Caboose, *96*		70	___
19732	AT&SF B/W Caboose "6517", *96*		49	___
19733	New York Central Caboose "6357", *96*		30	___
19734	Southern Pacific Caboose "6357", *96*		26	___
19736	PRR N5c Caboose "6417" "Buffalo Zone" tuscan, *97*		27	___
19737	Lackawanna Searchlight Caboose "2420", *97*		75	___
19738	Conrail N5c Caboose "6417" (SSS), *97*		55	___
19739	NYC Wood-sided Caboose "6907", *97*		60	___
19740	Virginian N5c Caboose "6427", *97 u*		65	___
19741	Pennsylvania N5C Caboose "6417", *98*		50	___
19742	Erie B/W Caboose w/ Caboose Talk "C301", *98*		95	___
19748	SP&S B/W Caboose "6517", *97 u*		50	___
19749	SP Bay Window Caboose "6517", *98*		100	___
19750	1998 Holiday Music Bay Window Caboose, *98*		160	___
19751	PRR N5C Caboose PRR "492418", *98*		30	___
19752	NP Bay Window Caboose "407", *98*		50	___
19753	UP E/V Caboose "25641", *98*		55	___
19754	NYC Caboose "20112", *98*		55	___
19755	Centennial Porthole Caboose, *99*		50	___
19756	Lionel Lines Bay Window Caboose, *99*		50	___
19758	DL&W Work Caboose "6419", *99*		55	___
19759	Corvette N5C Caboose, *99*		60	___
19772	Lionel Visitor's Center Vat Car, *99 u*		40	___
19773	Lionel Kids Club Barrel Ramp Car "6343", *96 u*		45	___
19778	Southern/Case Cutlery Wood-sided Caboose "1889" (Std. O), *99 u*		NRS	___
19779	SP Bay Window Caboose "1908", *99*		65	___
19780	LV Porthole Caboose "641751", *99–00*		43	___
19781	Vapor Records Holiday Porthole Caboose "6417", *99–00*		36	___
19782	NYC Bay Window Caboose "21719", *00*		65	___
19783	Ford Mustang E/V Caboose, *01*		50	___
19785	SP Bay Window Caboose "6517", *00*		55	___
19786	Pennsylvania RR E/V Caboose, *00 u*		40	___
19787	Pennsylvania RR E/V Caboose "477927", *01*		40	___
19790	Postwar Lehigh Valley Caboose "6417", *02*		41	___
19792	Postwar Erie Bay Window Caboose "C301", *03*		45	___
19800	Circle L Ranch Operating Cattle Car, *88*	75	95	___
19801	Poultry Dispatch Chicken Car, *87*	20	27	___

		Exc	New	Cond/$
19802	Carnation Milk Car, *87*	85	100	___
19803	Reading Ice Car, *87*	38	45	___
19804	Wabash Operating Hopper, *87*	25	33	___
19805	Santa Fe Operating Boxcar, *87*	28	38	___
19806	PRR Operating Hopper, *88*	28	32	___
19807	PRR E/V Caboose w/ smoke, *88*	39	47	___
19808	NYC Ice Car, *88*	38	49	___
19809	Erie-Lackawanna Operating Boxcar, *88*	27	35	___
19810	Bosco Milk Car, *88*	80	100	___
19811	Monon Brakeman Car, *90*	50	55	___
19813	Northern Pacific Ice Car, *89 u*	41	46	___
19815	Delaware & Hudson Brakeman Car, *92*	49	60	___
19816	Madison Hardware Operating Boxcar "190991", *91 u*	120	135	___
19817	Virginian Ice Car, *94*	31	41	___
19818	Dairymen's League Milk Car "788", *94*	65	80	___
19819	Poultry Dispatch Car (SSS), *94*	36	43	___
19820	Die-Cast Metal Tender w/ RailSounds II *95–96*		175	___
19821	UP Opera, *95*	31	36	___
19822	Pork Dispatch Car, *95*	29	39	___
19823	Burlington Ice Car, *94 u*, *95*	39	49	___
19824	US Army Target Launcher, *96*		30	___
19825	EMD Generator Car, *96*		50	___
19827	NYC Operating Boxcar, *97*		37	___
19828	C&NW Animated Stock Car and Stockyard "3356", *96–97*		100	___
19830	US Mail Operating Boxcar "3428", *97*		39	___
19831	GM Generator Car w/ power pole and wire "3530", *97*		46	___
19832	Lionel Cola Ice Car "6352", *97*		47	___
19833	RailSounds II Tender "2426RS", *97*		240	___
19834	LL 6-Wheel Crane Car "2460", *97*		60	___
19835	FedEx Animated Boxcar "3464X", *97*		38	___
19837	Bucyrus 6-Wheel Crane Car "2460", *99*		49	___
19845	Command Control Aquarium Car "3435", *98*		155	___
19846	Animated Giraffe Car "3376C", *98*		105	___
19850	Lionel RailSounds Stock Car "33760", *00*		130	___
19853	Firefighting Instruction Generator Car (SSS), *98*		60	___
19854	Lionelville Fire Car #1 (SSS), *98*		55	___

		Exc	New	Cond/$
19855	Christmas Aquarium Car, *98*		60	___
19856	Mermaid Transport, *98*		65	___
19857	NYC Fire Instruction Car "19853", *98–99*		175	___
19858	Lionelville Operational Searchlight Car "19854", *99*		65	___
19859	REA Steam R/S Boxcar "6267", *99*		170	___
19860	Conrail Diesel R/S Boxcar "169671", *99*		140	___
19864	Animated Ostrich Boxcar "9700", *99*		37	___
19867	Operational Poultry Dispatch Car "3434", *99*		48	___
19868	Shark Aquarium Car "3435", *99*		190	___
19869	Alien Aquarium Car "3435", *99*		49	___
19877	AT&SF Operating Barrel Car, *99*		55	___
19878	Operating Helium Tank Flatcar "3362", *99*		40	___
19880	Lionel Lines Extended Searchlight Car, *00*		50	___
19882	Sanderson Farms Poultry Car "3434", *99*		41	___
19883	LL Bucyrus Erie Crane Car "64608", *99*		45	___
19884	Atlantis Travel Aquarium Car, *00 u*		95	___
19885	3456 N&W Operating Hopper Car "22000", *00*		31	___
19886	Seaboard Boxcar w/ Steam RailSounds "16126", *00*		140	___
19887	SP Boxcar w/ Diesel RailSounds "651663", *00*		140	___
19888	Christmas Music Boxcar, *01*		65	___
19889	PRR B/W Caboose w/ Crewtalk "477719", *00*		140	___
19890	Santa Fe B/W Caboose w/ Crewtalk "999211", *00*		100	___
19894	Pony Express Mint Car, *03*		50	___
19894	Hood's Milk Car w/ platform, *03–04*		95	___
19895	3356 Santa Fe Horse Car w/ corral, *04*		120	___
19896	USMC Missile Launch Sound Car "45", *03–04*		165	___
19897	NYC Crane Car w/ TMCC "X-13", *04*		255	___
19898	Nestle Nesquik Operating Milk Car, *04*		95	___
19899	Pennsylvania Crane Car "19899" CC, *03–05*		260	___
19900	Toy Fair Boxcar, *87 u*	65	80	___
19901	"I Love Virginia" Boxcar, *87*	25	35	___
19902	Toy Fair Boxcar, *88 u*	55	80	___
19903	Christmas Boxcar, *87 u*	32	47	___
19904	Christmas Boxcar, *88 u*	32	43	___
19905	"I Love California" Boxcar, *88*	20	24	___
19906	"I Love Pennsylvania" Boxcar, *89*	26	32	___
19907	Toy Fair Boxcar, *89 u*	38	55	___
19908	Christmas Boxcar, *89 u*	30	47	___
19909	"I Love New Jersey" Boxcar, *90*	19	25	___

		Exc	New	Cond/$
19910	Christmas Boxcar, *90 u*	35	38	___
19911	Toy Fair Boxcar, *90 u*	75	95	___
19912	"I Love Ohio" Boxcar, *91*	21	28	___
19913	Christmas Boxcar, regular issue, *91*	34	41	___
19913	Christmas Boxcar for Lionel Employees, *91 u*	150	200	___
19914	Toy Fair Boxcar, *91 u*	38	50	___
19915	"I Love Texas" Boxcar, *92*	35	60	___
19916	Christmas Boxcar for Lionel Employees, *92 u*	190	220	___
19917	Toy Fair Boxcar, *92 u*	55	60	___
19918	Christmas Boxcar, *92 u*	49	70	___
19919	"I Love Minnesota" Boxcar, *93*	40	60	___
19920	Lionel Visitor's Center Boxcar, *92 u*	26	32	___
19921	Christmas Boxcar for Lionel Employees, *93 u*	140	185	___
19922	Christmas Boxcar, *93*	33	41	___
19923	Toy Fair Boxcar, *93 u*	65	95	___
19924	Lionel Railroader Club Boxcar, *93 u*	18	22	___
19925	Learning Center Boxcar for Lionel Employees, *93 u*	80	85	___
19926	"I Love Nevada" Boxcar, *94*	21	26	___
19927	Lionel Visitor's Center Boxcar "1993", *93 u*	26	33	___
19928	Christmas Boxcar for Lionel Employees *94 u*	205	230	___
19929	Christmas Boxcar, *94*	30	40	___
19931	Toy Fair Boxcar, *94 u*	49	65	___
19932	Lionel Visitor's Center Boxcar, *94 u*	26	33	___
19933	"I Love Illinois" Boxcar, *95*	21	27	___
19934	Lionel Visitor's Center Boxcar "1995", *95 u*	18	22	___
19937	Toy Fair Boxcar, *95 u*	55	75	___
19938	Christmas Boxcar, *95*	26	34	___
19939	Christmas Boxcar for Lionel Employees, *95 u*	230	240	___
19940	Lionel Railroad Vat Car, *96 u*		38	___
19941	"I Love Colorado" Boxcar, *95*	23	30	___
19942	"I Love Florida" Boxcar, *96*	19	27	___
19943	"I Love Arizona" Boxcar, *96*	20	25	___
19944	Lionel Visitor's Center Tank Car, *96 u*		35	___
19945	Holiday Boxcar, *96*		33	___
19946	Christmas Boxcar for Lionel Employees, *96 u*		195	___
19947	Lionel Toy Fair Boxcar "9700", *96 u*		200	___
19948	Visitor's Center Flatcar w/ trailer, *96 u*		34	___
19949	"I Love NY" Boxcar "9700", *97*		50	___
19950	"I Love Montana" Boxcar "9700", *97*		30	___

		Exc	New	Cond/$
19951	"I Love Massachusetts" Boxcar "9700", *98*		26	___
19952	"I Love Indiana" Boxcar, "9700", *98*		31	___
19955	Lionel Visitor's Center Gondola w/ coil covers, *98 u*		20	___
19956	Toy Fair Boxcar "777", *98 u*		65	___
19957	Ambassador Caboose "1997", *97 u*		385	___
19958	Ambassador Silver Caboose, "1998" (Std. O), *98 u*		530	___
19959	Ambassador Gold Caboose, "1998" (Std O), *98 u*		710	___
19964	U.S. JCI Senate Boxcar, *92 u*	55	70	___
19968	"I Love Maine" Boxcar "9700", *99*		40	___
19969	"I Love Vermont" Boxcar "9700", *99*		40	___
19970	"I Love New Hampshire" Boxcar "9700", *99*		34	___
19971	"I Love Rhode Island" Boxcar "9700", *99*		34	___
19976	Lionel Employee Holiday Boxcar "1999", *99 u*		150	___
19977	Toy Fair Boxcar "9700", *99 u*		50	___
19978	"Gold" Boxcar "1900-2000", *99–00*		43	___
19981	Lionel Centennial Boxcar "1998-1", *99*		30	___
19982	Lionel Centennial Boxcar "1998-2", *99*		30	___
19983	Lionel Centennial Boxcar "1998-3", *99*		30	___
19984	Lionel Centennial Boxcar "1998-4", *99*		30	___
19985	"I Love Georgia" Boxcar 9700, *99–00*		45	___
19986	"I Love North Carolina" Boxcar 9700, *99–00*		40	___
19987	"I Love South Carolina" Boxcar 9700, *99–00*		40	___
19988	"I Love Tennessee" Boxcar 9700, *99–00*		55	___
19989	Toy Fair Boxcar, *00 u*		55	___
19996	Toy Fair 2001 Boxcar, *01 u*		50	___
19997	Lionel Employee 2001 Boxcar, *01 u*		120	___
19998	Christmas Boxcar, *01*		33	___
19999	Lionel Visitor's Center 4-Bay Hopper "19999", *02 u*		150	___
21029	World of Little Choo Choo Set, *94 u, 95*	36	43	___
21750	Nickel Plate Rolling Stock 4-pack, *98*		160	___
21751	PRR Rolling Stock 4-pack, *98*		145	___
21752	Conrail Unit Trailer Train Set, *98*		285	___
21753	1998 Service Station Fire Rescue Train Set, *98*	490	570	___
21754	BNSF 3-Bay Covered Hopper 2-pack (Std. O), *98*		65	___
21755	4-Bay Covered Hoppers 2-pack, *98*		65	___
21756	Overstamped 6464 Style Boxcars, 2-pack, *98*		65	___
21757	UP Freight Car Set, *98*		185	___
21758	Bethlehem Steel "44" (SSS), *99*		375	___

		Exc	New	Cond/$
21759	Canadian Pacific F3 Passenger Set, *99*		930	___
21761	B&M Boxcar Set, 4-pack, *99*		180	___
21763	New Haven Freight Set, *99*		265	___
21766	ACL Passenger Car Set, 2-pack, *99*		385	___
21769	Centennial SD Tank Car Set, 4-pack, *99*		190	___
21770	NYC Reefer Set, 4-pack, *99*		225	___
21771	D&RGW Stock Car Set, 4-pack, *99*		230	___
21774	Custom Series Consist I "6424", 3-pack, *99*		150	___
21775	Lionel Train Wreck Recovery Set, *99*		190	___
21778	AT&SF Trainmaster Freight Set, *99*		NRS	___
21779	Seaboard Freight Car Set, *99*		280	___
21780	NYC Aluminum Passenger Car Set, 2-pack, *99*		160	___
21781	Case Cutlery Freight Set, *99 u*		900	___
21782	PRR Congressional Set, *00*		930	___
21783	Monday Night Football 2-pack, *01–02*		50	___
21784	QVC PRR Coal Freight Steam Set, *00 u*		345	___
21785	QVC Gold Mine Freight Steam Set, *00 u*		370	___
21786	Santa Fe F3 ABBA Passenger Set "200", *00*		1500	___
21787	Blue Comet Steam Passenger Set, *01–02*		1050	___
21788	Postwar Missile Launch Freight Set, *02–03*		350	___
21789	NS GP9 Flatcar Set "102", SSS, CC, *01*		370	___
21790	CN TankTrain Dash 9 Diesel Freight Set, *02*		630	___
21791	Freedom Train Diesel Passenger Set w/ RailSounds, *03*		540	___
21792	C&O Coal Hopper 6-pack #2 (Std. O), *01*		145	___
21793	Virginian Coal Hopper 6-pack #2 (Std. O), *01*		160	___
21794	Pioneer Seed GP7 Freight Set, *01 u*		820	___
21795	Case Farmall Freight Set, *01 u*		930	___
21796	NJ Medical Steam Freight Set (NJMSAA), *01 u*		445	___
21797	SP Daylight Passenger Set, *01*		670	___
21852	Milwaukee Road PS-2CD Hopper 3-pack (Std. O), *06*		CP	___
21853	BNSF PS2-CD Hopper 3-pack (Std. O), *06*		CP	___
21854	N&W PS2-CD Hopper 3-pack (Std. O), *06*		CP	___
21855	A&P Milk Car 3-pack V, *06*		CP	___
21856	Bowman Dairy Milk Car 3-pack (Std. O), *06*		CP	___
21857	Western Dairy Milk Car 3-pack (Std. O), *06*		CP	___
21858	NP PS-4 Flatcar w/ pggyback trailers 2-pack (Std. O), *06*		CP	___
21859	C&NW PS-4 Flatcar w/ pggyback trailers 2-pack (Std. O), *06*		CP	___

		Exc	New	Cond/$
21860	UP PS-4 Flatcar w/ pggyback trailers 2-pack (Std. O), *06*		CP	___
21861	Pennsylvania PS-4 Flatcar w/ pggyback trailers (Std. O), *06*		CP	___
21863	ADM Unibody Tank Car 3-pack (Std. O), *06*		CP	___
21864	Cerestar Unibody Tank Car 3-pack (Std. O), *06*		CP	___
21865	Coe Rail Husky Stack 2-pack (Std. O), *06*		CP	___
21866	Santa Fe Husky Stack 2-pack (Std. O), *06*		CP	___
21872	C&O Offset Hopper 3-pack 2 (Std. O), *05*		CP	___
21873	P&LE Offset Hopper 3-pack (Std. O), *06*		CP	___
21874	TTX Trailer Train 2-pack (Std. O), *06*		CP	___
21875	CSX Husky Stack 2-pack (Std. O), *06*		CP	___
21876	Disney Villain Hi-Cube Boxcar 3-pack, *05–06*		CP	___
21877	Domino Sugar 1-D Tank Car 3-pack (Std. O), *07*		CP	___
21878	Procor 1-D Tank Car 3-pack (Std. O), *07*		CP	___
21879	C&EI Offset Hopper 3-pack (Std. O), *07*		CP	___
21880	Erie Offset Hopper 3-pack (Std. O), *07*		CP	___
21881	Frisco Offset Hopper 3-pack (Std. O), *07*		CP	___
21882	Chessie System Offset Hopper 3-pack (Std. O), *07*		CP	___
21883	C&O 3-Bay Open Hopper 2-pack (Std. O), *07*		CP	___
21884	Pennsylvania Power & Light 3-Bay Open Hopper 2-pack (Std. O), *07*		CP	___
21885	Santa Fe 3-Bay Open Hopper 2-pack (Std. O), *07*		CP	___
21886	C&NW 3-Bay Open Hopper 2-pack (Std. O), *07*		CP	___
21888	IMC Canada Cylindrical Hopper 2-pack, *06*		CP	___
21893	Greenbrier (GBRX) All-Purpose Husky Stack 2-pack (Std. O), *07*		CP	___
21894	CSX All-Purpose Husky Stack 2-pack (Std. O), *07*		CP	___
21895	BN All-Purpose Husky Stack 2-pack (Std. O), *07*		CP	___
21896	Arizona & California (ARCZ) All-Purpose Husky Stack 2-pack (Std. O), *07*		CP	___
21897	REA PS-4 Flatcar w/ piggyback trailers 2-pack (Std. O), *07*		CP	___
21898	NYC PS-4 Flatcar w/ piggyback trailers 2-pack (Std. O), *07*		CP	___
21899	Lackawanna PS-4 Flatcar w/ piggyback trailers 2-pack (Std. O), *07*		CP	___
21900	Union Civil War Train Set, *99*		375	___
21901	Confederate Civil War Train Set, *99*		375	___
21902	Milwaukee Road PS-4 Flatcar w/ piggyback trailers 2-pack (Std. O), *07*		CP	___
21902	Construction Zone Set, *99 u*		87	___

		Exc	New	Cond/$
21904	UP PS-2 Covered Hopper 2-pack (Std. O), *07*		CP	___
21904	Safari Adventure Set, *99 u*		90	___
21905	NYC Flyer for Mass Merchants Set, *99 u*		100	___
21909	AGFA Film Steam Freight Set, *98 u*		1100	___
21914	Lionel Lines Freight Set, *99*		120	___
21916	Lionel Village Trolley, *99*		75	___
21917	N&W Freight Set, *99*		70	___
21918	PC PS-2 Covered Hopper 2-pack (Std. O), *07*		CP	___
21918	Thomas Circus Play Set, *00*		100	___
21920	Amtrak "Talgo" Passenger Set, *99*		NM	___
21921	Imco PS-2 Covered Hopper 2-pack (Std. O), *07*		CP	___
21924	Holiday Trolley Set, *99*		65	___
21925	Thomas Tank Engine Island of Sodor Train Set, *99–00*		150	___
21930	NYC PS-2 Covered Hopper 2-pack (Std. O), *07*		CP	___
21932	JCPenney NYC Freight Flyer Steam Set, *00 u*		170	___
21934	Custom Series Consist II 3-pack "6424", *99*		140	___
21936	WB Looney Tunes Set, *00 u*		340	___
21937	NYC Steel-sided Refrigerator Car 2-pack (Std. O), *07*		CP	___
21939	Dubuque Steel-sided Refrigerator Car 2-pack (Std. O), *07*		CP	___
21940	ADM Steel-sided Refrigerator Car 2-pack (Std. O), *07*		CP	___
21941	National Car Steel-sided Refrigerator Car 2-pack (Std. O), *07*		CP	___
21944	"Celebrate a Lionel Christmas" Steam Set, *00–01*		165	___
21945	Christmas Trolley Set, *00*		100	___
21948	NYC Freight Flyer Set w/ air whistle, *00*		240	___
21950	Maersk SD70 Maxi-Stack Set, *00*	560	700	___
21951	World War II Troop Train Set, *00*		410	___
21952	2000 Lionel Lines Service Station Special Set, *00*		275	___
21953	Ford Mustang GP7 Set, CC, *01*		340	___
21955	D&RGW F3 AA Passenger Set "5521", CC, *01*		740	___
21956	New York Central Freight Set "5412", *99–00*		355	___
21969	Lionel Village Trolley Set, *00*		85	___
21970	SP RS-3 Diesel Freight Set w/ horn, *00–01*		110	___
21971	Pennsylvania Flyer Steam Set, *00*		150	___
21972	Frisco GP7 Diesel Freight Set w/ horn, *00*		150	___
21973	AT&SF Passenger Set w/ RailSounds, *00–01*		375	___
21974	AT&SF Passenger Set w/ SignalSounds, *00–01*		240	___

		Exc	New	Cond/$
21975	Burlington Steam Freight Set w/ SignalSounds, *00*		275	___
21976	Centennial Steam Freight Starter Set, *00*		530	___
21977	NYC Trainmaster Freight Set, *99–00*		620	___
21978	AT&SF Trainmaster Freight Set, *99–00*		500	___
21981	JCPenney NYC Flyer Set, *00 u*		150	___
21988	NYC Freight Set w/ RailSounds, *00*		325	___
21989	Burlington Steam Freight Set w/ RailSounds, *00*		300	___
21990	NYC Flyer Freight Set w/ RailSounds, *00*		175	___
21999	Whirlpool Steam Freight Set, *00 u*		680	___
22902	Quonset Hut, *98–99*		22	___
22907	Die-Cast Girder Bridge, *98–01*		10	___
22910	Gilbert Tractor trailer, *98*		20	___
22914	PowerHouse Lockon, *98–01*		24	___
22915	Municipal Building, *98–99*		28	___
22916	190-watt Power Accessory System, *98*		425	___
22918	The Lionel Locomotive Backshop, *98*	300	460	___
22919	ElectroCouplers Kit for GP9, *98–00*		20	___
22920	Steam Service Siding, *98*		NM	___
22922	Intermodal Crane, *98*		195	___
22929	Lionel Factory, *98*		NM	___
22931	Die-Cast Cantilever Signal Bridge, *98–06*		35	___
22932	High Tension Metal Wire Tower, *98*		NM	___
22933	Section Gang House, *98*		NM	___
22934	Walkout Cantilever Signal, *98–03*		42	___
22935	Hot Box Detector, *98*		NM	___
22936	3-Piece Coaling Tower, *98*		85	___
22938	High Tension Plastic Tower, *98*		NM	___
22939	Transformer Substation, *98*		NM	___
22940	Mast Signal, *98–00*		37	___
22942	Accessories Box, *98–01*		20	___
22944	Automatic Operating Semaphore, *98–03*		3	___
22945	Block Target Signal, *98–00*		39	___
22946	Automatic Crossing Gate and Railroad Crossing Signal, *98–99*		45	___
22947	Auto Crossing Gate, *98–00*		36	___
22948	Gooseneck Street Lamps (2), *98–00*		165	___
22949	Highway Lights (4), *98–99*		20	___
22950	Classic Street Lamps (3), *98–02*		20	___
22951	Dwarf Signal, *98–00*		24	___
22952	Classic Billboards (3) , *98–00*		15	___
22953	Linex Gasoline Tall Oil Tank, *98–99*		6	___

		Exc	New	Cond/$
22954	Linex Gasoline Wide Oil Tank, *98–99*		6	___
22955	ElectroCouplers Kit for J Class Tender and B&A Tender, *98–00*		20	___
22956	ElectroCouplers Kit for Switcher/NW2, *98*		20	___
22957	ElectroCouplers Kit for F3, *98–01*		20	___
22958	ElectroCouplers Kit for Dash 9, *98–01*		20	___
22959	ElectroCoupler Conversion Kit for Atlantic Steamer, *98–01*		13	___
22960	TrainMaster Command Basic Upgrade Kit, *98–01*		34	___
22961	Standard GP9 B Unit Upgrade Kit, *98–01*		30	___
22962	Deluxe GP9 B Unit Upgrade Kit w/ black trucks, *98–01*		44	___
22963	RailSounds Upgrade Kit w/ Steam RailSounds, *98–01*		55	___
22964	RailSounds Upgrade Kit w/ Diesel RailSounds, *98–01*		55	___
22965	Command Control Culvert Loader, *98–01*		255	___
22966	Figure-8 Add-On Track Pack (O-27), *98–07*		CP	___
22967	Double-Loop Add-On Track Pack (O-27), *98–07*		CP	___
22968	Double-Loop Complete Track Pack (O-27), *98–03*		65	___
22969	Deluxe Complete Track Pack (O), *98–07*		CP	___
22972	Bascule Bridge, *98–99*		360	___
22973	Lionel Corp Tractor trailer, *98*		15	___
22975	Culvert Unloader, CC, *99–00*		225	___
22979	GP9 B-Unit Deluxe Upgrade Kit w/ silver trucks, *98–01*		34	___
22980	TMCC SC-2 Switch Controller, *99–07*		CP	___
22982	ZW Postwar Celebration Series Controller and Transformer Set, *98*		265	___
22983	180-watt PowerHouse Power Supply, *99–07*		CP	___
22990	Route 66 Autos on Flatcar 4-pack, *99*		37	___
22991	Christmas Tree w/ Blue Comet Train, *99–00*		60	___
22993	Route 66 Sinclair/Dino Cafe, *99–00*		210	___
22997	Oil Drum Loader, *99–00*		100	___
22998	Triple Action Magnetic Crane, *99*		220	___
22999	Sound Dispatching Station, *99–00*		90	___
23000	Operating Base Smithsonian NYC Dreyfuss Hudson (2-rail), *92 u*		190	___
23001	Operating Base NYC Dreyfuss Hudson (3-rail), *93 u*		190	___
23002	Operating Base NYC Hudson, *92 u, 93–94*		190	___
23003	Operating Base PRR B-6 Switcher, *92 u, 93–94*		190	___

		Exc	New	Cond/$
23004	Operating Base NP 4-8-4, *92 u, 93–94*		190	___
23005	Operating Base Reading T-1, *92 u, 93–94*		190	___
23006	Operating Base Chessie System T-1, *92 u, 93–94*		190	___
23007	Operating Base SP Daylight, *92 u, 93–94*		190	___
23008	Operating Base NYC L-3 Mohawk, *92 u, 93–94*		190	___
23009	Operating Base PRR S-2 Turbine, *92 u, 93–94*		190	___
23010	Left Remote Switch 31" "3010" (O), *95–99*	30	37	___
23011	Right Remote Switch 31" "3011" (O), *95–99*	28	30	___
23012	Operating Base F3 ABA Diesels, *92 u, 93–94*		190	___
24101	Mainline Color Position Signal, *04–07*		CP	___
24102	Industrial Water Tower, *03*		55	___
24103	Double Floodlight Tower, *03, 05–07*		CP	___
24104	Hobo Tower, *03–05*		CP	___
24105	Track Gang, *03–06*		70	___
24106	Exploding Ammunition Dump, *02*		25	___
24107	Missile Firing Range Set, *02*		60	___
24108	World War II Pylon, *03*		80	___
24109	Santa Fe Railroad Tugboat, *03*		125	___
24110	Pennsylvania Railroad Tugboat, *03*		135	___
24111	Swing Bridge, *03*		215	___
24112	Oil Field w/ bubble tubes, *03*		44	___
24113	Lionelville Ford Auto Dealership, *03*		225	___
24114	AMC/ARC Gantry Crane, CC, *03*		195	___
24115	AMC/ARC Log Loader, CC, *03, 06–07*		CP	___
24117	Covered Bridge, *02–07*		CP	___
24119	Big Bay Lighthouse, *04–05*		CP	___
24122	Lionelville People Pack, *03*		15	___
24123	Passenger Station People Pack, *03*		15	___
24124	Carnival People Pack, *03*	5	15	___
24130	TMCC 135/180 PowerMaster, *04–07*		CP	___
24131	Dumbo Pylon, *03*		70	___
24134	Bethlehem Steel Gantry Crane, *02*		200	___
24135	Lionel Lighthouse, *02–03*		100	___
24137	Mr. Spiff and Puddles Historic Layout, *03*		34	___
24138	Playtime Playground Historic Layout, *03*		50	___
24139	Duck Shooting Gallery Historic Layout, *03*		110	___
24140	Charles Bowdish Homestead Historic Layout, *03*		60	___
24147	Lionel Sawmill, *03*		90	___
24148	Coal Tipple Coal Pack, *02*		20	___
24149	NYC Hobo Hotel, *02*		42	___

		Exc	New	Cond/$
24151	Hobo Campfire, *03*		25	___
24152	Conveyor Lumber Loader, *03*		65	___
24153	Railroad Control Tower, *03*		40	___
24154	Maiden Rescue, *03*		35	___
24155	Blinking Light Billboard, *04–07*		CP	___
24156	Lionelville Street Lamps, *04–05*		CP	___
24159	Illuminated Station Platform, *04–07*		CP	___
24160	Rub-a-Dub-Dub Historic Layout, *04*		42	___
24161	Test O-Strength Historic Layout, *04–06*		CP	___
24164	Summer Vacation, *04–05*		CP	___
24168	Tire Swing Historic Layout, *04–05*		CP	___
24170	Rover's Revenge, *04–05*		CP	___
24171	Campbell's Soup Water Tower, *04*		45	___
24172	Balancing Man Historic Layout, *04–05*		CP	___
24173	Derrick Platform "462", *03–05*		CP	___
24197	City Accessory Pack, *04*		20	___
24174	Icing Station, *04–06*		CP	___
24176	Irene's Diner, *06–07*		CP	___
24177	Hot Air Balloon Ride, *04, 06*		95	___
24179	Scrambler Amusement Ride Historic Layout, *04–07*		165	___
24180	Choo Choo Barn Lionelville Zoo, *04–05*		105	___
24182	Lionelville Firehouse, *04*		100	___
24183	Lionelville Gas Station, *04, 06*		115	___
24187	Classic Billboard Set, *04–07*		CP	___
24190	Station Platform, *05–07*		CP	___
24191	Park People Pack, *04–07*		CP	___
24192	Park Benches People Pack, *04–07*		CP	___
24193	Railroad Yard People Pack, *04–07*		CP	___
24194	Civil Servants People Pack, *04–07*		CP	___
24196	Farm People Pack, *04–07*		CP	___
24197	City Accessory Pack, *05–07*		CP	___
24200	Lionel FasTrack Book, *07*		CP	___
24201	UPS Centennial Operating Billboard Signmen, *07*		CP	___
24500	D&RGW Alco PA A-A Set "601", *04*		530	___
24503	D&RGW Alco PB Unit, *04*		150	___
24504	Santa Fe E6 A-A "14-15", CC, *03*		530	___
24507	Milwaukee Road E6 A-A "15-16", CC, *03*		530	___
24511	Burlington FT A-A Set "113-A/D" w/ RailSounds, *03*		225	___
24516	Santa Fe F3 B Unit, *03*		235	___
24517	NYC F3 B Unit "2404", powered, CC, *03*		250	___

		Exc	New	Cond/$
24518	WP F3 B Unit, *03*		275	___
24519	B&O F3 B Unit, *03*		270	___
24520	Alaska F3 A-A Set, *03*		650	___
24521	Alaska F3 B Unit, non-powered, *03*		200	___
24522	Alaska F3 B Unit "1519", powered, CC, *03*		300	___
24528	Postwar Rio Grande F3 A Unit "2379T", non-powered, *04*		175	___
24529	Santa Fe F3 A-A Set "18", CC, *04*		690	___
24532	Santa Fe F3 B Unit "18A", non-powered, *04*		150	___
24533	Santa Fe F3 B Unit "18B", *04*		200	___
24534	Erie-Lack. F3 A-B-A Set "8031/32/34", CC, *05*		CP	___
24538	Erie-Lack. F3 Powered B Unit "8042", CC, *05*		225	___
24544	NYC FA-2 A-A Set "1046/47", CC, *05*		CP	___
24547	NYC FB-2 Unit "3330" (Std. O), *05*		CP	___
24548	CN FPA-4 A-A Set "6765/67", CC, *05*		CP	___
24551	CN FPB-4 Unit "6865" (Std. O), *05*		CP	___
24552	UP F3 A-B-A Set "900/900B/901", CC, *05*		680	___
24556	UP F3 Powered B Unit "900C", CC, *05*		285	___
24562	Santa Fe Powered EMD F3 B Unit, *04–05*		CP	___
24563	PRR Powered EMD F3 B Unit, *04–05*		195	___
24570	Santa Fe Non-Powered FT B Unit, *05*		CP	___
24573	Postwar No. 2383C Santa Fe Non-Powered F3 B Unit, *05*		180	___
24574	UP E7 Diesel A-A "988/989", CC, *06*		CP	___
24577	UP Non-Powered E7 Diesel B Unit "990" (Std. O), *06*		CP	___
24578	UP Powered E7 Diesel B Unit "988", *06*		CP	___
24579	NYC E7 Diesel A-A "4008/4009", CC, *06*		CP	___
24582	NYC Non-Powered E7 Diesel B Unit "4105" (Std. O), *06*		CP	___
24583	NYC Powered E7 Diesel B Unit "4104", *06*		CP	___
24584	Pennsylvania F7 Diesel A-B-A "9642/9643B/9643" CC, *06*		CP	___
24588	Pennsylvania Powered F7 B Unit "9643B", *06–07*		CP	___
24589	Santa Fe F7 A-B-A "332/332B/333", CC, *06–07*		CP	___
24593	Santa Fe Powered F7 B Unit "332B", *06–07*		CP	___
24594	Pennsylvania F7 Diesel Breakdown B Unit "9644B" w/ RailSounds, *06–07*		160	___
24595	Santa Fe F7 Diesel Breakdown B Unit "333B" w/ RailSounds, *06–07*		CP	___
24596	UP E7 Diesel Breakdown B Unit "994B" w/ RailSounds, *06*		CP	___

		Exc	New	Cond/$
24597	NYC E7 Diesel Breakdown B Unit "4106" w/ RailSounds, *06*		CP	___
25008	Holiday Boxcar, *06*		CP	___
25009	Santa Fe Hi-Cube Boxcar "14064", *06*		CP	___
25010	NP Boxcar "48189", *06*		CP	___
25011	Angela Trotta Thomas "Santa's Break" Boxcar, *06*		CP	___
25025	Reading Boxcar "106502", *07*		CP	___
25026	RI Hi-Cube Boxcar, *07*		CP	___
25041	UPS Centennial Boxcar #1, *06*		CP	___
25042	UPS Centennial Boxcar #2, *07*		CP	___
25043	Macy's Boxcar, *07*		CP	___
25103	Chessie Steam Special Madison Car 2-pack, *05*		100	___
25106	Pennsylvania Madison Car 4-pack, *05*		CP	___
25111	Pennsylvania Madison Car 2-pack, *05*		CP	___
25114	Lionel Lines Passenger Car 3-pack, *05*		CP	___
25118	Lionel Lines Passenger Car 2-pack, *05*		CP	___
25121	Southern Streamliner Car 4-pack, *05*		CP	___
25126	Southern Streamliner Car 2-pack, *05–06*		CP	___
25134	Polar Express Diner, *05–07*		47	___
25135	Polar Express Baggage Car, *05–07*		CP	___
25148	B&O Madison Car 4-pack, *06–07*		CP	___
25153	B&O Madison Car 2-pack, *06–07*		CP	___
25156	California Zephyr Streamliner 4-pack (Std. O), *06*		CP	___
25156	California Zephyr B313, *06–07*		CP	___
25161	California Zephyr Streamliner 2-pack, *06–07*		CP	___
25164	UP Madison Car 4-pack, *06–07*		CP	___
25169	UP Madison Car 2-pack, *06–07*		CP	___
25176	B&O Baggage Car w/ TrainSounds, *06–07*		CP	___
25177	UP Baggage Car w/ TrainSounds, *06–07*		CP	___
25178	California Zephyr Streamlined Baggage Car w/ TrainSounds, *06–07*		CP	___
25186	Polar Express Add-on Hot Chocolate Car, *06–07*		CP	___
25187	GN Streamlined Passenger Car 4-pack, *07*		CP	___
25188	GN Streamlined Passenger Car 2-pack, *07*		CP	___
25189	GN Streamlined Baggage Car w/ TrainSounds, *07*		CP	___
25196	North Pole Central Vista Dome, *07*		CP	___
25197	North Pole Central Baggage Car, *07*		CP	___
25198	PRR Vista Dome "4058", *07*		CP	___
25199	PRR Baggage Car "9359", *07*		CP	___
25404	FEC "The Champion" Aluminum Passenger Car 2-pack, *04–05*		CP	___

		Exc	New	Cond/$
25407	FEC "The Champion" Aluminum Diner w/ StationSounds, *04–05*		CP	___
25408	Santa Fe "El Capitan" 18" Aluminum Passenger Car 2-pack, *05*		CP	___
25411	Santa Fe "El Capitan" 18" Aluminum Diner w/ StationSounds, *05*		CP	___
25412	B&O "The Columbian" 18" Aluminum Passenger Car 2-pack, *05*		275	___
25415	B&O "The Columbian" 18" Aluminum Diner w/ StationSounds, *05*		CP	___
25416	SP "Daylight" Aluminum Passenger Car 2-pack, *04–05*		CP	___
25419	SP "Daylight" Aluminum Diner w/ StationSounds, *04–05*		CP	___
25420	PRR "The Trail Blazer" Aluminum Passenger Car 2-pack, *04–05*		CP	___
25423	PRR "The Trail Blazer" Aluminum Diner w/ StationSounds, *04–05*		CP	___
25433	UP "City of Denver" 18" Aluminum Passenger Car 4-pack (Std. O), *05*		1000	___
25438	Union Pacific 18" Aluminum 2-pack, *05*		250	___
25441	UP "City of Denver" 18" Aluminum Diner w/ StationSounds, *05*		CP	___
25446	Santa Fe Super Chief Streamlined Car 2-pack, *05*		150	___
25450	Pennsylvania Congressional Aluminum Passenger Car 4-pack (Std. O), *06–07*		CP	___
25455	Pennsylvania Congressional Aluminum Passenger Car 2-pack (Std. O), *06–07*		CP	___
25458	Pennsylvania Congressional B146 Diner w/ StationSounds (Std. O), *06–07*		CP	___
25473	NYC Commodore Vanderbilt Aluminum Passenger Car 2-pack (Std. O), *06*		CP	___
25476	NYC Commodore Vanderbilt Diner w/ StationSounds (Std. O), *06*		CP	___
25496	Texas Special 21" Streamlined Diner w/ StationSounds (Std. O), *07*		CP	___
25503	Santa Fe Heavyweight Passenger Car 4-pack (Std. O), *07*		CP	___
25504	Santa Fe Heavyweight Passenger Car 2-pack (Std. O), *07*		CP	___
25505	Santa Fe Heavyweight Diner w/ StationSounds (Std. O), *07*		CP	___
25506	SP Heavyweight Passenger Car 4-pack (Std. O), *07*		CP	___
25515	Milwaukee Road Heavyweight Passenger Car		CP	___

		Exc	New	Cond/$
	4-pack (Std. O), *07*			
25507	SP Heavyweight Passenger Car 2-pack (Std. O), *07*		CP	___
25507	SP Daylight Heavyweight Passenger Car 2-pack, *07*		CP	___
25508	SP Heavyweight Diner w/ StationSounds (Std. O), *07*		CP	___
25508	SP Daylight Heavyweight Passenger Diner w/ StationSounds, *07*		CP	___
25512	Texas Special Streamlined Passenger Car 2-pack (Std. O), *07*		CP	___
25516	Milwaukee Road Heavyweight Passenger Car 2-pack (Std. O), *07*		CP	___
25517	Milwaukee Road Heavyweight Diner w/ StationSounds (Std. O), *07*		CP	___
25518	PRR Heavyweight Passenger Car 4-pack (Std. O), *07*		CP	___
25519	PRR Heavyweight Passenger Car 2-pack (Std. O), *07*		CP	___
25520	PRR Heavyweight Diner w/ StationSounds (Std. O), *07*		CP	___
25521	B&O Heavyweight Passenger Car 4-pack (Std. O), *07*		CP	___
25522	B&O Heavyweight Passenger Car 2-pack (Std. O), *07*		CP	___
25523	B&O Heavyweight Diner w/ StationSounds (Std. O), *07*		CP	___
25743	Santa Fe 40-foot Flatcar w/ covered loads "191549" (Std. O), *07*		CP	___
26000	C&O Flatcar with pipes, *01*		20	___
26001	BP Flatcar with trailers "6424", *01 u*		150	___
26002	Monopoly Flatcar with airplane, *00 u*		NRS	___
26003	Lackawanna Flatcar with NH trailer, *01*		60	___
26004	Conrail Flatcar with trailer "71693", *01*		50	___
26005	Nickel Plate Flatcar with trailer, *01*		55	___
26006	Southern Flatcar with trailer "50126", *01*		50	___
26007	NW Flatcar with trailer "203029", *01*		50	___
26008	Farmall Flatcar, *01 u*		NRS	___
26011	B&M Flatcar with bulkheads, *01 u*		NRS	___
26013	CN Flatcar w/ Zamboni "26013", *01*		48	___
26014	JCPenney Flatcar, *01 u*		145	___
26016	Soo Line Flatcar with trucks, *01 u*		NRS	___
26017	Soo Line Flatcar with trailer, *01 u*		NRS	___
26018	Soo Line Flatcar with trailer, *01 u*		NRS	___

		Exc	New	Cond/$
26019	Alaska Gondola "13801", *02*		30	___
26020	Postwar Flatcar w/ submarine "3830", *02*		46	___
26021	CN Flatcar w/ trailer features "685965", *02*		44	___
26022	PFE Flatcar w/ trailer features "26022", *02*		32	___
26023	Postwar Flatcar w/ bulldozer "6816", *02*		65	___
26024	Postwar Flatcar w/ scraper "6817", *02*		65	___
26025	Postwar Flatcar w/ rocket "6407", *02*		42	___
26026	Postwar Flatcar w/ Mercury capsules "6413", *02*		95	___
26027	Flatcar w/ U.S. Army boat "6425", *02*		30	___
26028	Conrail Well Car "768121", *02*		40	___
26030	NYC Flatcar "601172" w/ stakes and bulkheads, *02*		22	___
26033	NYC Gondola "6462", *01*		30	___
26035	Lionel Lines Flatcar w/ traffic helicopter, *01*		50	___
26039	Lionel Lions Flatcar w/ Zamboni ice machines, *02*		39	___
26041	NP Ore Car "78540", *07*			___
26042	B&O Gondola w/ canisters "601272", *03*		19	___
26043	Seaboard Flatcar w/ trailer "48109", *03*		30	___
26044	NYC Flatcar w/ trailers "506089", *03*		35	___
26045	Postwar Flatcar w/ pipes "2411", *03*		40	___
26046	Postwar Flatcar w/ cable reels "6561", *03*		30	___
26047	Postwar Flatcar w/ transformer "2461", *03*		25	___
26048	Postwar Flatcar w/ boat "6801", *02*		29	___
26049	Steamboat Willie Flatcar w/ boat, *03*		29	___
26056	Southern Flatcar w/ bulkheads "50125", *02*		19	___
26057	SP Flatcar w/ tractors "599365", *02*		37	___
26058	SP Flatcar w/ trailer frames "599366", *02*		35	___
26061	Lionelville Tree Transport Gondola, *03*		40	___
26062	NYC Gondola w/ cable reels "26062", *03*		19	___
26063	Pennsylvania Flatcar w/ bulkheads "26063", *03*		19	___
26064	Rock Island Flatcar w/ trailer "90088", *04*		34	___
26065	REA Flatcar w/ piggyback trailers "TLCX2", *04*		35	___
26066	Great Northern Flatcar w/ bulkheads "26066", *04*		20	___
26067	Southern Gondola w/ cable reels "60141", *04*		20	___
26070	Nestle Nesquik Flatcar w/ trailer "26070", *03*		41	___
26077	Girl's Lionel Lines Flatcar w/ autos "6424", *03*		44	___
26078	Boy's Lionel Lines Flatcar w/ boat "6801", *03*		40	___
26082	Frisco Two-tier Auto Carrier "26082", *04*		20	___
26085	New York Two-Tier Auto Carrier, *05*		CP	___
26086	Alaska Flatcar w/ bulkheads, traditional, *05*		CP	___
26087	Rock Island Gondola w/ canisters, traditional, *05*		CP	___
26091	Elvis Flatcar w/ tractor and trailer, traditional, *05*		CP	___

		Exc	New	Cond/$
26099	PRR 3-Tier Auto Carrier "500423", *07*		CP	___
26100	PRR 1-D Tank Car, *00*		27	___
26101	Lenoil 1-D Tank Car "6015", *00*		34	___
26102	AEC Glow-in-Dark 1-D Tank Car, *00*		39	___
26103	GATX Tank Train 1-D Tank Car "44588", *00*		34	___
26107	BP Petroleum 3-D Tank Car, *00 u*		95	___
26108	Lionel Visitor's Center Reefer "206482", *00 u*		30	___
26109	NYC/P&LE SD Tank Car, *00*		42	___
26110	SP 3-Dome Tank Car "6415", *00–01*		15	___
26111	Frisco Tank Car, *00*		29	___
26112	Gulf Oil Tank Car, *00*		40	___
26113	U.S. Army Tank Car, *00*		35	___
26114	Service Station Ltd. 1-Dome Tank Car (SSS), *00*		28	___
26115	Lionel Celebrate SD Tank Car, *00 u*		75	___
26116	Pepe LePew SD Tank Car, *00 u*		90	___
26118	NYC Tank Car "101900", *01*		23	___
26119	Protex 3D Tank Car "1054", *00*		29	___
26120	KCS Tank Car "1229", *00*		32	___
26122	Pioneer Seed Tank Car, *00 u*		NRS	___
26123	Santa Fe Stock Car "23002", *01*		35	___
26124	C&O 1-Dome Tank Car "X1019", *01*		30	___
26126	Cheerios Boxcar, *98*		46	___
26127	Wellspring Capital Management Clear 1-D Tank Car w/ confetti, *00 u*		195	___
26131	Santa Fe 1-Dome Tank Car "335268", *02*		22	___
26132	UP 1-Dome Tank Car "69015, *02*		40	___
26133	Tootsie Roll 1-Dome Tank Car "26133", *02*		36	___
26135	Whirlpool Tank Car, *01*		NRS	___
26136	Southern 1-Dome Tank Car "8790011", *03*		20	___
26137	Jack Frost 1-Dome Tank Car "106", *03*		32	___
26138	Nestle Nesquik 1-Dome Tank Car "26138", *03*		40	___
26139	Lionel Lines Stockcar with horses "26139", *03*		39	___
26141	Whirlpool 1-Dome Tank Car, *03 u*		85	___
26144	Chessie System 1-Dome Tank Car "2233", *02*		22	___
26145	Do It Best 1-Dome Tank Car, *03 u*		80	___
26146	Do It Best 1-Dome Tank Car, *03 u*		95	___
26147	Lionel Archives Diamond Chemicals 1-Dome Tank Car "6315", *02*		33	___
26149	Egg Nog 1-Dome Tank Car, *03*		43	___
26150	Alaska 3-Dome Tank Car "26150", *03*		23	___
26151	NP Wood-sided Refrigerator Car "26151", *03*		19	___

		Exc	New	Cond/$
26152	Morton Salt 1-Dome Tank Car "26152", *04*		40	___
26153	Pillsbury 1-Dome Tank Car "26153", *04*		40	___
26154	NYC 3-Dome Tank Car "26154", *04*		25	___
26155	Pennsylvania 1-Dome Tank Car "26155", *04*		20	___
26156	North Western Wood-sided Refrigerator Car "15356", *04*		20	___
26157	Ballyhoo Brothers Circus Stock Car "26157", *04*		35	___
26158	Campbell's Soup 1-Dome Tank Car, *04*		35	___
26164	Girl's Lionel Lines I-Dome Tank Car "6315", *03*		43	___
26167	New Haven 1-D Tank Car, traditional, *05*		CP	___
26168	Conrail 3-D Tank Car, traditional, *05*		CP	___
26169	Santa Fe Wood-sided Refrigerator Car traditional, *05*		CP	___
26176	Tidmouth Milk 1-D Tank Car, *05*		CP	___
26179	GN 3-Dome Tank Car, *06*		CP	___
26180	DM&IR 1-Dome Tank Car "S15", *06*		CP	___
26181	NYC Wood-sided Refrigerator Car, *06*		CP	___
26196	Candy Cane 1-Dome Tank Car, *06*		CP	___
26197	D&H 1-Dome Tank Car "55", *07*		CP	___
26198	D&RGW 3-Dome Tank Car, *07*		CP	___
26199	WP-PFE Wood-sided Refrigerator Car "55327", *07*		CP	___
26200	NKP Boxcar "18211", *98*		35	___
26201	Operation Lifesaver Boxcar, *98*		29	___
26203	D&H Boxcar "1829", *98*		25	___
26204	Alaska Boxcar "10806", *98–99*		35	___
26205	Rocky & Bullwinkle Boxcar "9700", *99*		36	___
26206	Curious George Boxcar "9700", *99*		40	___
26208	Vapor Records Boxcar #2, *98*		37	___
26214	Celebrate the Century Stamp Boxcar, *98 u*		90	___
26215	AEC Glow-in-the-Dark Boxcar, *98*		70	___
26216	Cheerios Boxcar "9700", *98 u*		60	___
26218	Quaker Oats Boxcar, *98 u*		380	___
26219	Ace Hardware Boxcar, *98 u*		NRS	___
26220	Smuckers Boxcar "9700", *98 u*		75	___
26222	Penn Central Boxcar "125962", *99*		31	___
26223	FEC Boxcar "5027", *99*		31	___
26224	D&H Boxcar "9700", *99*		24	___
26228	Vapor Records Holiday Boxcar "9700", *99 u*		90	___
26230	AEC Glow-in-the-Dark Boxcar #2 "9700", *99*		39	___
26232	Martin Guitar Lumber Boxcar "9823", *99*		40	___
26234	NYC Boxcar "9700", *99*		29	___

		Exc	New	Cond/$
26235	Valentine Boxcar "9700", *99*		40	___
26236	Aircraft Boxcar "9700", *99*		28	___
26237	Boy Scout Boxcar "9700", *99*		85	___
26238	Detroit Historical Museum Boxcar "9700", *99*		29	___
26239	M.A.D.D Boxcar "9700", *99*		19	___
26240	Starter Set RailBox Boxcar "9700", *99–00*		28	___
26241	Starter Set Norfolk & Western "9700", *99–00*		17	___
26242	D.A.R.E Boxcar "9700", *99*		30	___
26243	Lionel Christmas Boxcar "9700", *99*		35	___
26244	Woody Woodpecker Box Car "9700", *99*		43	___
26247	Lionel Lines Boxcar "9700", *99*		38	___
26253	Acme Explosives Boxcar "9700", *99 u*		NRS	___
26254	Keebler Boxcar "9700", *99 u*		NRS	___
26255	NYC Boxcar "200495", *99 u*		30	___
26256	Salvation Army Charity Boxcar "9700", *99*		29	___
26257	Wheaties Boxcar "9700", *99*		70	___
26264	Lionel Station Boxcar, *99*		44	___
26265	NYC Pacemaker Boxcar "9700", *00*		30	___
26271	AEC Glow-in-the-Dark Boxcar "9700-glo", *99*		40	___
26272	Christmas Boxcar, *00*		44	___
26275	Boy Scout Boxcar "9700", *00*		55	___
26276	C&O 9700 Boxcar "23296", *99–00*		23	___
26277	UP Boxcar "491050", *00*		20	___
26278	Cap'n Crunch Christmas Boxcar, *99*		550	___
26280	Tinsel Town Express Boxcar w/ music, *00*		50	___
26284	NY Toy Fair Preview Boxcar, *99 u*		725	___
26285	NYC Pacemaker Boxcar "9700", *00*		40	___
26288	AEC Glow-in-Dark "9700" Boxcar, *99*		39	___
26290	SP Boxcar, *00*		20	___
26291	Pennsylvania Boxcar "47158", *00*		20	___
26292	Frisco Boxcar "22015", *00*		20	___
26293	Burlington Boxcar, *00*		30	___
26294	Centennial Express Boxcar, *00*		NRS	___
26295	TrainMaster Boxcar, *99 u*		55	___
26296	Service Station Ltd. Boxcar Set (SSS), *00*		100	___
26298	Taz Bobbing Boxcar, *00*		65	___
26300	UPS Flatcar w/ trailers, *04*		50	___
26301	UPS Flatcar w/ airplane, traditional, *05*		CP	___
26302	Troublesome Truck #1, *05*		CP	___
26303	Troublesome Truck #2, *05*		CP	___

		Exc	New	Cond/$
26305	SP 2-Tier Auto Carrier, *06*		CP	___
26306	D&RGW Gondola w/ canisters "56135", *06*		CP	___
26307	Chessie System Flatcar w/ bulkheads, *06*		CP	___
26308	Hard Rock Cafè Flatcar w/ billboards, *06*		CP	___
26309	Alaska Flatcar w/ cable reels, *06*		CP	___
26310	CGW Flatcar w/ trailer "3707", *06*		CP	___
26311	Santa Fe Flatcar w/ pickups, *06*		CP	___
26330	Gondola w/ trees and presents, *06*		CP	___
26331	Lionel Lines Flatcar w/ bulkheads, *07*		CP	___
26332	CP Rail Gondola w/ canisters "337061", *07*		CP	___
26335	Domino Sugar Flatcar w/ trailer, *07*		CP	___
26357	CSX Flatcar w/ pipes "600514", *07*		CP	___
26366	REA Flatcar w/ piggyback trailers "TLCX3", *07*		CP	___
26400	C&NW Hopper, *07*		CP	___
26502	UP Bay Window Caboose "6517", *97*		47	___
26503	AT&SF High-Cupola Caboose "7606R", *97*		85	___
26504	Mobil Oil Square Window Caboose "6257", *97 u*		30	___
26505	Lionelville Fire Co. Work Caboose, *98*		50	___
26506	N&W Square Window Caboose "562748", *98*		15	___
26507	D&H Square Window Caboose "35707", *98*		20	___
26508	Alaska RR Square Window Caboose "1081", *98*		28	___
26511	Quaker Oats NP Square Window Caboose, *98 u*		43	___
26513	NYC Emergency Caboose "26505", *99*		47	___
26515	Lionel Lines Bobber Caboose, *99*		10	___
26516	Safari RR Bobber Caboose, *99 u*		10	___
26519	Christmas Work Caboose "6496", *99*		41	___
26520	Bethlehem Steel Work Caboose "6130" (SSS), *99*		55	___
26523	Keebler Cheezit S/W Caboose, *99 u*		NRS	___
26524	NYC Square Window Caboose "295", *99 u*		20	___
26526	Santa Fe S/W Caboose "999471", *01*		30	___
26527	Christmas Work Caboose w/ presents, *02*		27	___
26528	PRR Square Window Caboose "6257", *99*		21	___
26530	LL Square Window Caboose "6257", *99*		22	___
26532	NYC Square Window Caboose "296", *00*		20	___
26533	SP Square Window Caboose, *00*		20	___
26534	PRR Square Window Caboose "6257", *00*		20	___
26535	Frisco Square Window Caboose "1700", *00*		20	___
26536	Centennial Express S/W Caboose, *00*		NRS	___
26537	Lionel Mines Square Window Caboose, *00 u*		45	___
26539	Whirlpool Square Window Caboose, *00 u*		NRS	___

		Exc	New	Cond/$
26542	ACL S/W Caboose "069", *01*		31	___
26543	GN Square Window Caboose "X66", *00–01*		28	___
26544	Alaska S/W Caboose "1084", *01*		25	___
26545	Snap-On Square Window Caboose, *00 u*		NRS	___
26548	Pioneer Seed Square Window Caboose, *00 u*		NRS	___
26549	PRR Square Window Caboose "4977947", *01*		20	___
26550	NYC Square Window Caboose "19293", *01*		20	___
26551	Chessie System Center Cupola Caboose, *01*		25	___
26552	Santa Fe S/W Caboose "999472", *01*		25	___
26553	C&O Center Cupola Caboose "A918", *01*		30	___
26554	Monopoly Short Line S/W Caboose, *00 u*		NRS	___
26556	NH Center Cupola Caboose, *01*		35	___
26557	Farmall Square Window Caboose, *01 u*		NRS	___
26559	N&W Center Cupola Caboose "518408", *01*		20	___
26560	B&M Square Window Caboose, *01 u*		20	___
26564	Soo Line Center Cupola Caboose, *01 u*		20	___
26565	Lionel Employee S/W Caboose "2001", *01 u*		170	___
26566	WP Square Window Caboose "731", *02*		25	___
26568	Nickel Plate S/W Caboose "1155", *02*		25	___
26569	Southern Square Window Caboose "252", *02*		25	___
26570	B&O Square Window Caboose "295", *02*		25	___
26572	Lionel 20th Century Square Window Caboose, *00 u*		25	___
26580	Wabash Square Window Caboose "2805", *03*		22	___
26581	C&O Square Window Caboose "C-1831", *03*		20	___
26582	L&N Square Window Caboose "318", *03*		20	___
26583	Pennsylvania S/W Caboose"477814", *03*		25	___
26594	Ontario Northland Work Caboose "26594", *03*		25	___
26595	UP Caboose "26595", *03*		18	___
26596	NYC Caboose "17716", *04*		25	___
26597	Great Northern Caboose "X295", *04*		25	___
26598	UP Caboose "26598", *04*		25	___
26599	DM&IR Work Caboose "26599", *04*		25	___
26706	Lighted Christmas Boxcar, *00*		47	___
26707	Lionel Steel Operating Welding Flatcar "1108", *00*		90	___
26709	Flatcar w/ psychedelic submarine "6511", *99*		32	___
26710	Southern Railroad Carsounds Stockcar, *99*		95	___
26712	Churchill Downs Horse Car "6473", *99–00*		38	___
26713	Shay Log Car 3-pack "9823", *99*		90	___
26714	Westside Lumber Flatcar w/ logs (Std O), *99*		45	___
26715	Westside Lumber Flatcar w/ logs (Std O), *99*		45	___

		Exc	New	Cond/$
26716	Westside Lumber Flatcar w/ llogs (Std O), *99*		45	___
26717	Orion Star Boxcar 9600, *00*		30	___
26718	Christmas RailSounds Boxcar, *00*		160	___
26719	Bobbing Ghost Halloween Boxcar "9700", *00*		46	___
26721	Lionel Lines Coal Dump Car "3379", *00*		31	___
26722	Lionel Lines Log Dump Car "3351", *00*		31	___
26723	Lion Chasing Trainer Gondola "3444", *00*		49	___
26724	Veterans Day Boxcar "9700", *00*		70	___
26725	NYC Jumping Hobo Boxcar "88160", *00*		38	___
26726	T. Rex Bobbing Boxcar "9700", *00*		41	___
26727	San Francisco City Lights Boxcar, *00*		50	___
26736	Lionel Birthday Boxcar, *02 u*		40	___
26737	Chasing Santa Operating Gondola "6462", *00 u*		65	___
26738	Lionel Mines Gondola, *00 u*		NRS	___
26739	Santa & Snowman Boxcar, *00*		46	___
26740	Reindeer Car, *00*		43	___
26741	Operating Santa Boxcar, *00*		50	___
26743	Christmas Reindeer Car, *01*		55	___
26745	Lionel Traveling Aquarium Car "506", *01*		70	___
26746	Bobbing Vampire Boxcar, *01*		46	___
26747	Halloween Bats Aquarium Car, *01*		75	___
26748	T&P Operating Hopper Car "9699", *01*		38	___
26749	Alaska Log Dump Car, *01*		29	___
26751	Chessie Coal Dump Car, *01*		27	___
26752	Christmas Aquarium Car, *01*		55	___
26753	Christmas Operating Dump Car, *01*		43	___
26757	Operating Barrel Car "35621", *00*		55	___
26758	AEC Nuclear Gondola "719766", *01*		80	___
26759	Lionel Postwar Coal Dump Car "3459", *02*		60	___
26760	Lionel Postwar Log Dump Car "3461", *02*		60	___
26761	AEC Security Caboose 3535, *01*		60	___
26762	Postwar Minuteman Car "3665", *01*		55	___
26763	Postwar Exploding Boxcar "6448", *01*		40	___
26764	Bethlehem Steel Operating Welding Car, *01*		75	___
26765	Postwar Sheriff and Outlaw Car "3370" *01–02*	40	49	___
26766	Priority Mail Operating Boxcar, *01–02*		32	___
26768	Postwar Searchlight Car "6520", *02*		49	___
26769	Santa Fe Crane Car "199793", CC, *03*		255	___
26770	Wabash Brakeman Car "3424", *01*		70	___
26773	Chessie Searchlight Car, *01*		20	___

		Exc	New	Cond/$
26774	Santa Fe Log Dump Car, *01*		25	___
26775	US Army Searchlight Car, *00*		50	___
26776	US Army Operating Boxcar "26413", *00*		55	___
26777	United States Flag Boxcar, *01 u*		250	___
26779	Burlington Operating Hopper "189312", *02*		40	___
26780	Postwar Bronx Zoo Giraffe Car "3376", *02*	35	36	___
26781	Postwar Operating Radar Car "3540", *02*		35	___
26782	Lenny the Lion Bobbing Head Car, *02*		38	___
26784	Stingray Express Aquarium Car, *02*		35	___
26785	Flatcar with powerboat, *02*		31	___
26786	Lionelville Operating Parade Car, *02*		40	___
26787	Erie Jumping Hobo Boxcar, *01–02*		43	___
26788	Christmas Music Boxcar, *02*		46	___
26789	Kiss Kringle Chase Gondola, *02*		35	___
26790	Christmas Lighted Boxcar, *02*		34	___
26791	UP Animated Gondola, *02*	40	46	___
26792	REA Operating Boxcar "6299", *03*		39	___
26793	Alaska Extension Searchlight Car, *01*		44	___
26794	Postwar PFE Ice Car "6352", *01–02*		60	___
26795	NYC Stock Car w/ Cattle Sounds "3121", *02*		50	___
26796	Lionel Farms Poultry Dispatch Car "26796", *01*		55	___
26797	GN Log Dump Car "60011", *02*		48	___
26798	Bethlehem Steel Coal Dump Car "26798", *02*		70	___
26801	Jumping Bart Simpson Boxcar, *04*		44	___
26802	Simpsons Animated Gondola, *04*		46	___
26803	Santa Fe Derrick Car "26803", *04*		25	___
26804	NYC Coal Dump Car "26804", *04*		22	___
26805	Pennsylvania Log Dump Car "26805", *04*		24	___
26806	Archive Pillsbury Operating Boxcar "3428", *04*		40	___
26807	Blue Chip Line Motorized Animated Gondola, *04*		40	___
26808	Egg Nog Barrel Car, *04*		55	___
26809	Santa's Mobile Lighting Service Extension Searchlight Car, *04*		42	___
26810	NYC Operating Searchlight Car, *05*		CP	___
26811	Pennsylvania Coal Dump Car, *05*		CP	___
26812	Santa Fe Log Dump Car, *05*		CP	___
26813	Lionel Lines Derrick Car, *05*		CP	___
26814	NYC Walking Brakeman Car "174226", *05*		40	___
26815	Pennsylvania "Workin' on the Railroad" Boxcar "24255", *05*		42	___
26816	REA Boxcar w/ Steam TrainSounds, *05*		CP	___

		Exc	New	Cond/$
26817	Alaska Boxcar w/ Diesel TrainSounds, *05*		145	___
26818	Christmas Music Boxcar, *05*		CP	___
26819	Holiday Animated Gondola, *05*		55	___
26820	Penguin Transport Aquarium Car, *05*		60	___
26821	NP Moe & Joe Lumber Flatcar, *05*		CP	___
26827	Archive UPS Operating Boxcar "9237", *05*		CP	___
26828	Tornado Chaser Radar Tracking Car, *05*		CP	___
26829	UPS Holiday Operating Boxcar, *05*		CP	___
26832	Lionel Lines Steam TrainSounds Tender, *07*		CP	___
26834	PFE Ice Car "20042" (Std. O), *05–06*		CP	___
26835	M.O.W. Track Cleaning Car, *05*		CP	___
26836	Halloween Boxcar w/ SpookySounds, *05*		CP	___
26845	Southern Derrick Car, *06*		CP	___
26846	GN Coal Dump Car, *06*		38	___
26847	C&O Coal Dump Car, *06–07*		CP	___
26848	Lionel Lines Moe & Joe Flatcar, *06*		CP	___
26849	SP Log Dump Car, *06–07*		CP	___
26850	D&RGW Searchlight Car, *06*		CP	___
26851	WM Log Dump Car, *06*		CP	___
26852	Postwar No. 3562-25 Santa Fe Barrel Car, *06*		CP	___
26853	SeaWorld Aquarium Car, *06*		CP	___
26854	UP Walking Brakeman Car, *06*		CP	___
26855	Halloween Animated Gondola, *06*		CP	___
26856	Christmas Chase Gondola, *06*		CP	___
26857	Alien Radar Tracking Car, *06*		CP	___
26858	Christmas Music Boxcar, *06*		CP	___
26859	Christmas Parade Boxcar, *06*		CP	___
26860	B&O Boxcar w/ Steam TrainSounds "466035" (Std. O), *06–07*		75	___
26861	Santa Fe Boxcar w/ Diesel TrainSounds (Std. O), *06–07*		CP	___
26863	American Railway Express Operating Milk Car "308", *06*		CP	___
26864	Domino Sugar Operating Boxcar, *06–07*		40	___
26865	CP Animated Caboose, *06–07*		CP	___
26867	AlienSounds Boxcar, *06–07*		CP	___
26868	U.S. Steel Operating Welding Car, *06*		CP	___
26869	REA Jumping Hobo Boxcar, *06–07*		CP	___
26870	Christmas Dump Car w/ presents, *06*		CP	___
26871	Pennsylvania Tender w/ Steam TrainSounds (Std. O), *06*		CP	___

		Exc	New	Cond/$
26872	U.S. Army Security Car, *06*		CP	___
26876	Postwar No. 6544 Missile Firing Trail Car, *06*		CP	___
26877	U.S. Army Missile Launch Sound Car, *06–07*		CP	___
26905	Bethlehem Steel Gondola w/ canisters "6462", *98*		29	___
26906	SP Flatcar w/ Corgi `57 Chevy "9823", *98*		40	___
26908	TTUX w/ Apple trailers "6300", *98*		70	___
26913	E. St. Louis Gondola "9820", *98*		29	___
26920	UP Die-Cast Ore Car "64861", *97*		70	___
26921	UP Die-Cast Ore Car "64862", *97*		55	___
26922	UP Die-Cast Ore Car "64863", *97*		65	___
26923	UP Die-Cast Ore Car "64864", *97*		55	___
26924	UP Die-Cast Ore Car "64865", *97*		55	___
26925	UP Die-Cast Ore Car "64866", *97*		60	___
26926	Union Pacific Die-Cast Ore Car, *98*		55	___
26927	Union Pacific Die-Cast Ore Car, *98*		55	___
26928	Union Pacific Die-Cast Ore Car, *98*		55	___
26929	Union Pacific Die-Cast Ore Car, *98*		50	___
26936	Die-Cast Tank Car 4-pack, *98*		335	___
26937	Die-Cast Hopper 4-pack, *98*		325	___
26938	NYC Reefer, *99*		80	___
26940	Rio Grande Stock Car "37710", *99*		80	___
26946	D&H Semi-Scale Hopper "9642"		85	___
26947	Gulf Die-Cast Tank Car, *98*		120	___
26948	P&LE Die-Cast Hopper, *98*		65	___
26949	NP Flatcar w/ trailer "6424-2017", *98*		47	___
26950	NP Flatcar w/ trailer "6424-2016", *98*		47	___
26951	TTX Flatcar w/ PRR trailer "475185', *98*		55	___
26952	J.B. Hunt Flatcar w/ trailer, *98*		40	___
26953	J.B. Hunt Flatcar w/ trailer, *98*		40	___
26954	J.B. Hunt Flatcar w/ trailer, *98*		40	___
26955	J.B. Hunt Flatcar w/ trailer, *98*		40	___
26956	C&O Gondola (O27), *98–99*		15	___
26957	Delaware & Hudson Flatcar w/ stakes, *98*		20	___
26971	Lionel Steel 16-wheel Depressed Flatcar, *98*		135	___
26972	Animated Pony Express Gondola, *98*		36	___
26973	Getty Die-Cast Tank Cars 3-pack, *98*		270	___
26974	Getty Die-Cast SD Tank Car "4003", *98*		80	___
26975	Getty Die-Cast SD Tank Car "4004", *98*		90	___
26976	Getty Die-Cast SD Tank Car "4005", *98*		80	___
26977	Sinclair Die-Cast Tank Cars 3-pack, *98*		275	___

		Exc	New	Cond/$
26978	Sinclair Tank Car UTLX "64026", *98*		105	___
26979	Sinclair Tank Car UTLX "64027", *98*		85	___
26980	Sinclair Tank UTLX "64028", *98*		90	___
26981	Gulf Die-Cast Tank Car 2-pack, *99*		165	___
26985	B&O Die-Cast Hoppers 2-pack, *99*		160	___
26987	Chessie System B&O Die-Cast 4-Bay Hopper "235154", *99*		90	___
26991	Lionelville Ladder Firecar, Dept. #2, *99*		47	___
26992	NYC Reefer, *99*		75	___
26993	NYC Reefer, *99*		85	___
26994	NYC Reefer, *99*		135	___
26995	Rio Grande Stock Car "37714", *99*		80	___
26996	Rio Grande Stock Car "37715", *99*		80	___
26997	Rio Grande Stock Car "37716", *99*		80	___
27000	C&EI Offset Hopper "97393" (Std. O), *07*		CP	___
27001	Erie Offset Hopper "28001" (Std. O), *07*		CP	___
27002	Frisco Offset Hopper "92399" (Std. O), *07*		CP	___
27003	Chessie System Offset Hopper "234355" (Std. O), *07*		CP	___
27016	UP PS-2 Covered Hopper "1312" (Std. O), *07*		CP	___
27019	Imco PS-2 Covered Hopper "41001" (Std. O), *07*		CP	___
27022	PC PS-2 Covered Hopper "74217" (Std. O), *07*		CP	___
27025	NYC PS-2 Covered Hopper "883180" (Std. O), *07*		CP	___
27100	C&NW PS-2CD 4427 Hopper "450669" (Std. O), *04*		40	___
27101	Morton Salt PS-2CD 4427 Hopper "504" (Std. O), *04*		43	___
27102	Pillsbury PS-2CD 4427 Hopper "3980" (Std. O), *04*		42	___
27103	Soo Line PS-2CD 4427 Hopper "70207" (Std. O), *04*		49	___
27104	Wabash Cylindrical Hopper "33007" (Std. O), *03*		43	___
27105	PC Cylindrical Hopper "884312" (Std. O), *03*		42	___
27113	Gov't. of Canada Cylindrical Hopper, *04–05*		CP	___
27114	Canadian National Cylindrical Hopper, *04–05*		CP	___
27115	D&H 3-Bay ACF Hopper "3454" (Std. O), *05–06*		CP	___
27116	NYC 3-Bay ACF Hopper "886270" (Std. O), *05–06*		CP	___
27117	DM&IR 3-Bay ACF Hopper "5017" (Std. O), *05*		CP	___
27118	WP 3-Bay ACF Hopper "11774" (Std. O), *05–06*		CP	___
27130	Pennsylvania ACF 3-Bay Hopper "180658" (Std. O), *06*		CP	___
27129	N&W 3-Bay Open Hopper "10717" (Std. O), *06*		CP	___
27130	Pennsylvania 3-Bay Open Hopper "180658" (Std. O), *06*		CP	___
27131	Conrail ACF 3-Bay Hopper "473877" (Std. O), *06*		CP	___
27132	UP 3-Bay Open Hopper "18137" (Std. O), *06*		CP	___

		Exc	New	Cond/$
27133	Milwaukee Road PS-2CD Hopper "98606" (Std. O), *06*		CP	___
27134	BNSF PS2-CD Hopper "414367" (Std. O), *06*		CP	___
27135	N&W PS2-CD Hopper "71573" (Std. O), *06*		CP	___
27165	C&O 3-Bay Open Hopper "86912" (Std. O), *07*		CP	___
27166	Pennsylvania Power & Light 3-Bay Open Hopper "347" (Std. O), *07*		CP	___
27167	Santa Fe 3-Bay Open Hopper "178558" (Std. O), *07*		CP	___
27168	C&NW 3-Bay Open Hopper "135000" (Std. O), *07*		CP	___
27169	CN Cylindrical Hopper "370708" (Std. O), *06*		CP	___
27172	IMC Canada Cylindrical Hopper "45726" (Std. O), *06*		CP	___
27203	NYC Double-Door Boxcar "75509" (Std. O), *05*		CP	___
27204	Grand Trunk Western Double-Door Boxcar "596377" (Std. O), *05*		CP / CP	___
27205	D&RGW Double-Door Boxcar "63798" (Std. O), *05*		40	___
27210	Pennsylvania PS-1 Boxcar "47009" (Std. O), *05*		CP	___
27211	Missouri Kansas Texas PS 1 Boxcar "948" (Std. O), *05*		CP	___
27212	Rutland PS 1 Boxcar "358" (Std. O), *05*		CP	___
27214	Chessie System PS-1 Boxcar "23770" (Std. O), *06*		CP	___
27215	Rock Island PS-1 Boxcar "57607" (Std. O), *06*		CP	___
27216	Erie-Lackawanna PS-1 Boxcar "84433" (Std. O), *06*		CP	___
27217	Frisco PS-1 Boxcar "17826" (Std. O), *06*		19	___
27218	Santa Fe Double-Door Boxcar "9870" (Std. O), *06–07*		CP	___
27219	GN Double-Door Boxcar "35449" (Std. O), *06–07*		CP	___
27220	L&N Double-Door Boxcar "41237" (Std. O), *06–07*		CP	___
27221	CB&Q Double-Door Boxcar "48500" (Std. O), *06–07*		CP	___
27224	CGW PS-1 Boxcar "5180" (Std. O), *06*		CP	___
27225	WP PS-1 Boxcar "19528" (Std. O), *06*		CP	___
27226	NH PS-1 Boxcar "32196" (Std. O), *06*		CP	___
27227	UP PS-1 Boxcar "100306" (Std. O), *06*		CP	___
27231	GN USRA Double-Sheathed Boxcar "24872" (Std. O), *07*		CP	___
27232	UP USRA Double-Sheathed Boxcar "100101" (Std. O), *07*		CP	___
27233	Cotton Belt USRA Double-Sheathed Boxcar "32493" (Std. O), *07*		CP	___
27234	C&NW USRA Double-Sheathed Boxcar "142204" (Std. O), *07*		CP	___
27235	Railbox Modern Boxcar "10011" (Std. O), *07*		CP	___

		Exc	New	Cond/$
27238	SPFE Mechanical Refrigerator Car "456465" (Std. O), *07*		CP	___
27300	Western Dairy Milk Car "M705" (Std. O), *06*		CP	___
27305	GN Steel-sided Refrigerator Car "70290" (Std. O), *06*		CP	___
27306	Santa Fe Steel-sided Refrigerator Car "3494" (Std. O), *06*		42	___
27307	Pepper Packing Steel-sided Refrigerator Car "2330" (Std. O), *06*		CP	___
27327	BNSF Mechanical Refrigerator Car "798870" (Std. O), *07*		CP	___
27329	UPFE Mechanical Refrigerator Car "55962" (Std. O), *07*		CP	___
27330	GN-WFE Mechanical Refrigerator Car "8873" (Std. O), *07*		CP	___
27331	Alderney Dairy General American Milk Car "106" (Std. O), *07*		CP	___
27332	Freeport General American Milk Car "1003" (Std. O), *07*		CP	___
27349	ADM Steel-sided Refrigerator Car "7019" (Std. O), *07*		CP	___
27350	National Car Steel-sided Refrigerator Car "2430" (Std. O), *07*		CP	___
27355	NYC Steel-sided Refrigerator Car "2570" (Std. O), *07*		CP	___
27358	Dubuque Steel-sided Refrigerator Car "63648" (Std. O), *07*		CP	___
27510	WP PS 4 Flatcar "2001" (Std. O), *05–06*		CP	___
27511	P&LE PS-4 Flatcar "1154" (Std. O), *05–06*		35	___
27512	Reading PS 4 Flatcar "9314" (Std. O), *05*		CP	___
27513	UP 40-foot Flatcar "51219" (Std. O), *06*		CP	___
27514	CP 40-foot Flatcar "307401" (Std. O), *06*		CP	___
27515	Pennsylvania 40-foot Flatcar "473567" (Std. O), *06*		CP	___
27516	N&W 40-foot Flatcar "32900" (Std. O), *06*		CP	___
27517	NP PS-4 Flatcar w/ pggyback trailers "62829" (Std. O), *06*		CP	___
27518	C&NW PS-4 Flatcar w/ pggyback trailers "44503" (Std. O), *06*		CP	___
27519	UP PS-4 Flatcar w/ pggyback trailers "53007" (Std. O), *06*		CP	___
27520	Coe Rail Husky Stack "5540" (Std. O), *06*		CP	___
27521	Santa Fe Husky Stack "254220" (Std. O), *06*		CP	___
27541	NYC 40-foot Flatcar w/ covered loads "496299"		CP	___

		Exc	New	Cond/$
	(Std. O), *07*			
27542	NH 40-foot Flatcar w/ covered loads "17808" (Std. O), *07*		CP	___
27544	GT 40-foot Flatcar w/ covered loads "64301" (Std. O), *07*		CP	___
27545	REA PS-4 Flatcar w/ piggyback trailers "81003" (Std. O), *07*		CP	___
27546	Greenbrier (All-Purpose Husky Stack "1993" (Std. O), *07*		CP	___
27552	Arizona & California All-Purpose Husky Stack "100010" (Std. O), *07*		CP	___
27562	NYC PS-4 Flatcar w/ piggyback trailers "506075" (Std. O), *07*		CP	___
27563	Lackawanna PS-4 Flatcar w/ piggyback trailers "16540" (Std. O), *07*		CP	___
27564	Milwaukee Road PS-4 Flatcar w/ piggyback trailers "64074" (Std. O), *07*		CP	___
27600	RI B/W Caboose "17070" (Std. O), *07*		CP	___
27601	Milwaukee Road E/V Caboose "992300" (Std. O), *07*		CP	___
17699	UP CA-4 Caboose "25193" (Std. O), *07*		CP	___
27631	PFE Wood-sided Refrigerator Car "97680" (Std. O), *06*		CP	___
28000	C&NW Hudson 4-6-4 "3005", *99*		205	___
28004	B&O E6 4-4-2 Atlantic Steam Locomotive traditional, *99–00*		410	___
28005	PRR E6 4-4-2 Atlantic Steam Locomotive traditional, *99–00*		345	___
28006	AT&SF E6 4-4-2 Atlantic Steam Locomotive traditional, *99–00*		285	___
28007	NYC Hudson 4-6-4 "5406", *99*		380	___
28008	C&O Hudson 4-6-4 "306", *99*		345	___
28009	Santa Fe Hudson 4-6-4 "3463", *99*		330	___
28011	C&O 2-6-6-6 Allegheny Steam "1601", *99*		1800	___
28012	Commodore Vanderbilt 4-6-4 Hudson Steam Locomotive, red, *00 u*		1700	___
28013	NH Pacific 4-6-2 "1335", *99*		325	___
28014	NYC Pacific 4-6-2 "4930", *99*		305	___
28015	Santa Fe Pacific 4-6-2 "3449", *99*		340	___
28016	Southern Railway Pacific 4-6-2 "1407", *99*		345	___
28017	Case Cutlery 4-6-2 Steamer, *99 u*		300	___
28018	Reading Camelback "571", CC, *01*		495	___
28020	Lionel Lines Pacific 4-6-2 "3344", *99*		250	___
28022	West Side Lumber Shay "800", *99*		810	___

		Exc	New	Cond/$
28023	PRR K4 4-6-2 Pacific, "3755", CC, *99*		375	___
28024	Commodore Vanderbilt 4-6-4 Hudson Steam Locomotive, blue, *00 u*		2000	___
28025	PRR K4 4-6-2 Pacific Steam Locomotive traditional, *99*		330	___
28026	LL 4-6-2 Pacific Locomotive, "1999", CC, *99*		325	___
28027	NYC 4-6-4 Hudson Locomotive "5413", *00*		590	___
28028	Virginian 2-6-6-6 Allegheny Locomotive "1601", *99*		980	___
28029	UP Big Boy 4-8-8-4 Articulated Steam Locomotive "4006", *99–00*		1500	___
28030	NYC 4-6-4 Hudson "5450", Gray, CC, *00*		315	___
28031	NYC 4-6-4 Hudson "5451" gray, *00*		NM	___
28032	B&O 4-6-2 Pacific Steam Locomotive, CC, *00*		315	___
28033	B&O 4-6-2 Pacific Locomotive, traditional, *00*		195	___
28034	UP 4-6-2 Pacific Steam Locomotive, CC, *00*		310	___
28035	UP 4-6-2 Pacific Locomotive, traditional, *00*		210	___
28036	SP 2-8-0 Consolidation "2685" Steam Locomotive, CC, *00–01*		270	___
28037	SP 2-8-0 Consolidation "2686" Locomotive traditional, *00–01*		295	___
28038	UP 2-8-0 Consolidation "324" Steam Locomotive CC, *00–01*		315	___
28039	UP 2-8-0 Consolidation "326" Steam Locomotive traditional, *00–01*		240	___
28051	B&O EM-1 2-8-8-4 Articulated Steam Locomotive "7617", *00*		970	___
28052	N&W Class A 2-6-6-4 Articulated Locomotive "1218", *00*		870	___
28055	GN 4-6-4 Hudson "1725" Steam Locomotive traditional, *00–01*		170	___
28057	SRR 4-8-2 Mountain "1491", CC, *00*		690	___
28058	NH 4-8-2 Mountain "3310", CC, *00*		670	___
28059	WP 4-8-2 Mountain "179", CC, *00*		630	___
28062	LL Gold-plated 700E J-1E 4-6-4 Hudson "1900" w/ case, *00*		1050	___
28063	PRR T-1 4-4-4-4 Duplex "5511", CC, *00*		910	___
28064	UP Challenger Coal Tender "3985", CC, *00 u*	1350	1800	___
28065	NYC 4-6-4 Hudson w/ RailSounds "5412", *00*		290	___
28066	B&O 4-6-2 President Polk, CC, *01*		750	___
28067	Erie 4-6-2 "2934", CC, *01*		570	___
28068	D&RG 4-6-4 Hudson "2001" Steam Locomotive, traditional, *01 u*		300	___

		Exc	New	Cond/$
28070	SP Daylight 4-4-2 Atlantic "3000", CC, *01*		425	___
28071	NP 4-4-2 Atlantic "604", CC, *01*		415	___
28072	NYC 4-6-4 Hudson J3a "5444", CC, *01*		790	___
28074	NP 2-8-4 Berkshire "759", CC, *01*		640	___
28075	C&O 2-6-6-2 "1521", CC, *01*		930	___
28076	NKP 2-6-6-2 "921", CC, *01*		960	___
28077	UP Lionmaster Challenger 4-6-6-4 "3983", CC, *01*		680	___
28078	PRR J1a 2-10-4 "6496", CC, *01*		880	___
28079	C&O Class T 2-10-4 "3004", CC, *01*		900	___
28080	NYC 0-8-0 Yard Goat "7745" Steam Locomotive CC, *01–02*		540	___
28081	C&O 0-8-0 Yard Goat "75" Steam Locomotive CC, *01–02*		520	___
28084	NYC Dreyfuss 4-6-4 Hudson "5452" Steam Locomotive, CC, *01–02*		790	___
28085	N&W 2-8-8-2 Class Y6b Articulated "2200" Steam Locomotive, CC, *03*		1300	___
28086	PRR H9 Consolidation "1111", CC, *01*		480	___
28087	UP Auxiliary Tender Yellow, CC, *01*		210	___
28088	N&W Auxiliary Water Tender, CC, *01–02*		200	___
28089	PRR T-1 4-4-4-4 Duplex "5511", 2-rail, *00*		1150	___
28090	UP Challenger Oil Tender "3977", 2-rail, *00 u*		1800	___
28098	NYC 4-6-0 10-wheeler "1916" Steam Locomotive, CC, *01–02*		520	___
28099	UP Challenger Oil Tender "3977", CC, *00 u*		1700	___
28200	D&H U30C "702", CC, (SSS), *02*		375	___
28201	UP SD90MAC "8049", *03*		345	___
28202	Conrail SD80MAC "7203", *03*		325	___
28203	CSX SD80MAC "803", *03*		325	___
28204	NS SD80MAC "7201", *03*		345	___
28205	Chessie System SD9 "1833", CC, *03*		230	___
28207	Erie-Lackawanna U33C Diesel "3304", CC, *02*		355	___
28208	BN U33C Diesel "5734", CC, *02*		355	___
28211	CP SD90MAC "9107", *03*		300	___
28213	Amtrak GE Dash 8 Diesel "516", CC, *02*		300	___
28214	BNSF GE Dash 8 Diesel "582", CC, *02*		325	___
28215	B&O EMD GP30 Diesel "6939", CC, *02*		315	___
28216	Reading EMD GP30 Diesel "5518", CC, *02*		315	___
28217	Rio Grande EMD GP30 Diesel "3013", CC, *02*		315	___
28218	Lehigh Valley C-420 "407", CC, *04*		325	___
28219	Seaboard C-420 "136", CC, *04*		300	___

		Exc	New	Cond/$
26220	Smuckers Boxcar		NRS	___
28222	Santa Fe Dash 9 "605" CC, *05*		CP	___
28223	BNSF SD70MAC "9433", CC, *05*		CP	___
28224	Jersey Central SD40-2 "3067", CC, *04*		350	___
28225	UP SD40T-2 Diesel "4551", traditional, *07*		CP	___
28225	SPSF SD40T-2 "8521", CC, *04–05*		CP	___
28226	NS SD80MAC "7204", CC, *04–05*		CP	___
28227	UP SD70MAC "4979", CC, *04*		375	___
28228	C&NW Dash 9-44CW "8669", CC, *03*		350	___
28229	SP Dash 9-44CW "8132", CC, *03*		350	___
28230	Amtrak Dash 8 "505", CC, *04*		295	___
28235	Great Northern U33C "2543", CC, *05*		CP	___
28237	Reading U30C "6301", CC, *05*		CP	___
28238	CP Dash 9-TMCC, *05*		CP	___
28239	Union Pacific SD-70-TMCC, *04*		360	___
28241	C&NW U30C Diesel "935", CC, *06*		CP	___
28242	SP U33C Diesel "8773", CC, *06*		475	___
28243	LIRR Hi-Nose Alco C-420 Diesel "206", CC, *06*		CP	___
28244	N&W Hi-Nose Alco C-420 Diesel "417", CC, *06–07*		CP	___
28245	Chessie System SD40T-2 Diesel "7617" w/ RailSounds, *06*		CP	___
28246	Chessie System Non-Powered SD40T-2 Diesel "7618" (Std. O), *06*		CP	___
28247	Rio Grande SD40T-2 Diesel "5348" w/ RailSounds, *06*		CP	___
28248	Rio Grande Non-Powered SD40T-2 Diesel "5349" (Std. O), *06*		CP	___
28250	N&W Non-Powered HI-Nose Alco C-420 Diesel "416" (Std. O), *06–07*		CP	___
28251	Long Island Non-Powered Hi-Nose Alco C-420 "206" (Std. O), *06*		CP	___
28252	SP Non-Powered U33C Diesel "8774" (Std. O), *06*		CP	___
28253	C&NW Non-Powered U30C Diesel "936" (Std. O), *06*		CP	___
28256	UP Non-Powered SD40T-2 Diesel "4596" (Std. O), *07*		CP	___
28257	NS SD40-2 Diesel "3340", CC, *06*		CP	___
28258	NS Non-Powered SD40-2 Diesel "3341" (Std. O), *06*		CP	___
28259	CN SD40-2 Diesel "5383", CC, *06*		CP	___
28260	CN Non-Powered SD40-2 Diesel "5384" (Std. O), *06*		CP	___
28261	UP-MP SD70ACe Diesel "1982", CC, *07*		CP	___
28262	UP-WP SD70ACe Diesel "1983", CC, *07*		CP	___
28263	UP-MKT SD70ACe Diesel "1988", CC, *07*		CP	___

		Exc	New	Cond/$
28264	UP "Building America" SD70ACe Diesel "8348" CC, *07*		CP	___
28265	Milwaukee Road U30C Diesel "5657", CC, *07*		CP	___
28266	Milwaukee Road Non-Powered U30C Diesel "5657" (Std. O), *07*		CP	___
28267	Conrail U30C Diesel Locomotive "6837", CC, *07*		CP	___
28268	Conrail Non-Powered U30C Diesel "6838" (Std. O), *07*		CP	___
28272	"I Love U.S.A." SD60 Diesel "1776", traditional, *06*		CP	___
28292	Chessie System U30C "3312", CC, *02*		300	___
28293	Santa Fe U28CG "354", CC, *02*		375	___
28400	Amtrak Rail Bonder, *05*		CP	___
28403	Pennsylvania Ballast Tamper "18", traditional, *05–06*		CP	___
28404	Postwar No. 69 Maintenance Car, *05*		CP	___
28405	Postwar No. 42 Picatinny Arsenal Switcher, CC, *05*		CP	___
28406	CSX Rail Bonder "92794", traditional, *05*		CP	___
28407	UP Speeder, *05*		CP	___
28408	CNJ Speeder "MW840", traditional, *06*		CP	___
28409	Conrail Rail Bonder "X409", traditional, *06*		CP	___
28411	U.S. Army Missile Launcher Locomotive, *06–07*		CP	___
28412	Santa's Speeder, *06*		CP	___
28413	Milwaukee Road Snowplow "X903", traditional, *06*		CP	___
28414	Postwar No. 3360 Lionel Lines Burro Crane traditional, *06*		CP	___
28415	Third Avenue Trolley "1651, traditional, *06*		CP	___
28416	Hobo Handcar, traditional, *06*		CP	___
28417	Christmas Rotary Snowplow, *06*		180	___
28418	Christmas Trolley, *06*		CP	___
28419	Lionel Lines Speeder, *07*		CP	___
28420	D&RGW Handcar, *07*		CP	___
28422	PRR Burro Crane Motorized Unit, *07*		CP	___
28425	Polar Express Elf Handcar, *06*		CP	___
28426	UP Tie-Jector Motorized Unit "TC-2", *07*		CP	___
28428	Halloween Handcar, *07*		CP	___
28432	Bethlehem Steel Diesel Switcher, traditional, *07*		CP	___
28500	Mopac GP20 "2274", *99–00*		205	___
28501	AT&SF Merger GP9 "2924", traditional, *99*		200	___
28502	AT&SF Merger GP9 "2925", CC, *99–00*		255	___
28503	ACL GP7, CC, *00*		245	___
28504	ACL GP7, traditional, *00*		170	___
28505	Monon C-420 "505", CC, *00–01*		230	___

		Exc	New	Cond/$
28506	Monon C-420 "506", traditional, *00–01*		170	___
28507	NH C-420 "2556", CC, *00–01*		275	___
28508	NH C-420 "2557", traditional, *00–01*		290	___
28509	FEC GP7 Triple Lashup "607/608/609", *99*		560	___
28514	B&O GP9 "6590", *00*		85	___
28515	Lionel Service Station C-420, CC, *00*		205	___
28517	C&NW GP7 "1518", CC, *00–01*		275	___
28518	PRR EP-5 Electric "2352", CC, *00*		410	___
28519	NP GP9 "2349", CC, *01*		295	___
28521	SP RS-11"5725", CC, *01–02*		280	___
28522	MP RS-11"4611", CC, *01–02*		305	___
28523	SOO SD-40-2 "6622", CC, *01*		375	___
28524	Chessie SD-40-2 "7616", CC, *01*		355	___
28527	AEC GP-9 "2001", CC, *01*		345	___
28529	Norfolk Southern GP9, CC, *02*		200	___
28530	NP Alco S-4 Diesel "722", CC, *02*		285	___
28531	Santa Fe Alco S-2 Diesel "2337", CC, *02*		285	___
28532	LV Alco S-2 Diesel "150", CC, *02*		280	___
28533	SAL Alco S-4 Diesel "1489", CC, *02*		290	___
28534	Archive GTW GP9 "4134", CC, *01*		NM	___
28535	U.S. Army Transportation Corps GP9, *02*		NM	___
28536	Rock Island GP7 "1274", CC, *02–03*		230	___
28538	WP S-2 "553", CC, *03*		340	___
28539	B&O S-2 "9045", CC, *03*		320	___
28540	UP SD40T-2 "4455", CC, *03*		390	___
28541	SP SD40T-2 "8239", CC, *03*		400	___
28542	Rio Grande SD40T-2 "5350", CC, *03*		400	___
28543	Ontario Northland RS-3 "1308", *03*		70	___
28544	PRR Non-Powered RS-11 Diesel "8621" (Std. O), *07*		CP	___
28544	Pennsylvania RS-11 "8618", CC, *04*		350	___
28545	NP RS-11 "900", CC, *03*		325	___
28548	Chessie System S-4 "9009", CC, *05*		CP	___
28553	PRR RS-11 Diesel "8620", traditional, *07*		CP	___
28555	Alaska RR GP38-2 Diesel "2001", CC, *06*		CP	___
28556	Alaska RR Non-Powered GP38-2 Diesel "2002" (Std. O), *06*		CP	___
28557	CP GP30 Diesel "5000", CC, *06–07*		CP	___
28558	CP Non-Powered GP30 Diesel "5001" (Std. O), *06–07*		CP	___
28559	Chessie System GP30 Diesel "3044", CC, *06–07*		CP	___

		Exc	New	Cond/$
28560	Chessie System Non-Powered GP30 Diesel "3045" (Std. O), *06–07*		CP	___
28561	NYC GP7 Diesel Locomotive "5628", CC, *07*		CP	___
28562	NYC Non-Powered GP7 Diesel "5629" (Std. O), *07*		CP	___
28563	GN GP7 Diesel Locomotive "626", CC, *07*		CP	___
28564	GN Non-Powered GP7 Diesel "627" (Std. O), *07*		CP	___
28565	RI GP7 Diesel Locomotive "1265", CC, *07*		CP	___
28566	RI Non-Powered GP7 Diesel "1266" (Std. O), *07*		CP	___
28567	UP GP7 Diesel Locomotive "105", CC, *07*		CP	___
28568	UP Non-Powered GP7 Diesel "106" (Std. O), *07*		CP	___
28612	WP 4-4-2 Atlantic Locomotive, traditional, *02*		80	___
28613	Reading 0-6-0 Docksider "1251", traditional, *04*		100	___
28615	B&O 4-6-4 Hudson Locomotive, traditional, *02*		225	___
28616	Nickel Plate 2-8-4 Berkshire Locomotive, traditional, *02*		190	___
28617	Southern 2-8-4 Berkshire Locomotive, traditional, *02*		235	___
28619	Century Express 4-4-2, *05*		CP	___
28624	Santa Fe 0-6-0 Docksider "2174", traditional, *04*		175	___
28625	Wabash 4-4-2 Atlantic Steam Locomotive "8625" traditional, *03*		85	___
28626	Pennsylvania 4-6-4 Hudson Steam Locomotive "626", traditional, *03*		175	___
28627	C&O 2-8-4 Berkshire Steam Locomotive "2755" traditional, *03*		200	___
28628	L&N 2-8-4 Berkshire Locomotive "1970" traditional, *03*	150	200	___
28636	D&RGW 4-4-2 Atlantic "8636", traditional, *04*		95	___
28637	UP 4-6-4 Hudson "673", traditional, *04*		160	___
28638	Great Northern 2-8-4 Berkshire "3414" traditional, *04*		200	___
28639	NYC 2-8-4 Berkshire "9401", traditional, *04*		200	___
28646	North Pole Central Lines 2-8-4 Berkshire "1900" traditional, *04*		230	___
28650	New York Central 0-6-0 Dockside Switcher "X 8688", traditional, *05*		80	___
28651	Bethlehem Steel 0-6-0 Dockside Switcher "72" traditional, *05*		80	___
28652	LL 4-4-2 Locomotive "8652", traditional, *05*		CP	___
28655	Erie 2-8-4 Berkshire "3338", traditional, *05*		CP	___
28656	Pennsylvania 2-8-4 Berkshire "56", traditional, *05*		CP	___
28660	North Pole Central Lines 0-6-0 Dockside Switcher "25", traditional, *05*		CP	___

		Exc	New	Cond/$
28661	Santa Fe 0-4-0 Locomotive "2300" traditional, *05*		CP	___
28662	C&O 0-4-0 Locomotive "39", traditional, *05*		CP	___
28674	C&O 0-6-0 Docksider "67", traditional, *06–07*		CP	___
28675	SP 0-6-0 Docksider "675", traditional, *06–07*		CP	___
28676	U.S. Steel 0-6-0 Docksider "76", traditional, *06–07*		CP	___
28677	WM 4-4-2 Atlantic Locomotive "103", traditional, *06*		CP	___
28678	Rio Grande 0-4-0 Steam Locomotive "55" traditional, *06–07*		CP	___
28679	Army Transportation 0-4-0 Steam Locomotive "40", traditional, *06*		CP	___
28680	Reading 0-4-0 Locomotive "1152", traditional, *06*		CP	___
28681	Virginian 2-8-4 Berkshire Steam Locomotive "509" traditional, *06*		CP	___
28683	B&O 2-8-2 Mikado Steam Locomotive "1520" w/ TrainSounds, *06–07*		CP	___
28684	UP 2-8-2 Mikado Steam Locomotive "2498" w/ TrainSounds, *06–07*		CP	___
28693	B&O 4-4-2 "28" Locomotive, traditional, *05*		CP	___
28694	NYC 4-4-2 Atlantic Steam Locomotive "8637" traditional, *06*		CP	___
28695	Halloween 0-6-0 Docksider "X-131", traditional *06–07*		85	___
28700	CB&Q 0-8-0 Locomotive "543", w/ RailSounds, *05*		CP	___
28701	NP 0-8-0 Locomotive "1178", w/ RailSounds, *05*		CP	___
28702	Boston & Albany 0-8-0 Steam Locomotive "53" w/ RailSounds, *05*		CP	___
28704	Pennsylvania 4-4-2 Atlantic "68", CC, *05*		CP	___
28706	Pennsylvania Reading Seashore 4-4-2 Atlantic "6064", CC, *05*		CP	___
28742	B&O 4-6-0 Camelback "1630" Locomotive, CC, *03*		335	___
28743	B&O 4-6-0 Camelback "1632" Locomotive traditional, *03*		300	___
28744	D&H 4-6-0 Camelback "548" Locomotive, CC, *03*		325	___
28745	D&H 4-6-0 Camelback "555" Locomotive traditional, *03*		300	___
28746	Erie 4-6-0 Camelback "860" Locomotive, CC, *03*		375	___
28747	Erie 4-6-0 Camelback "878" Locomotive traditional, *03*		300	___
28748	Jersey Central 4-6-0 Camelback "772" Locomotive, CC, *03*		300	___
28749	Jersey Central 4-6-0 Camelback "773" Locomotive, traditional, *03*		300	___
28750	Lackawanna 4-6-0 Camelback "690" Locomotive		375	___

		Exc	New	Cond/$
	CC, *03*			
28751	Lackawanna 4-6-0 Camelback "1031" Locomotive traditional, *03*		300	___
28752	LIRR 4-6-0 Camelback "126" Locomotive, CC, *03*		300	___
28753	LIRR 4-6-0 Camelback "127" Locomotive traditional, *03*		300	___
28754	NYO&W 4-6-0 Camelback "249" Locomotive CC, *03*		300	___
28755	NYO&W 4-6-0 Camelback "253" Locomotive traditional, *03*		300	___
28756	Pennsylvania-Reading 4-6-0 Camelback "6000" Locomotive, CC, *03*		325	___
28757	Pennsylvania-Reading 4-6-0 Camelback "6001" Locomotive, traditional, *03*		300	___
28758	Susquehanna 4-6-0 Camelback "30" Locomotive CC, *03*		305	___
28759	Susquehanna 4-6-0 Camelback "36" Locomotive traditional, *03*		300	___
28800	N&W GP7 "507", *99–00*		80	___
28801	Lionel Lines 44-ton Switcher, *99*		135	___
28806	Jersey Central Baby TrainMaster "1516", CC, *01*		335	___
28811	Santa Fe Baby TrainMaster "3003", CC, *01*		290	___
28813	Milwaukee Road Baby TrainMaster "406", CC, *01*		280	___
28815	B&O GP30 "6935", CC, *02*		295	___
28817	Reading GP30 "5513", CC, *02*		310	___
28819	Rio Grande GP30 "3013", CC, *02*		310	___
28821	GT GP-7 "4438", *01*		100	___
28822	SRR RS-3 "2127", *01*		70	___
28823	Virginian Rectifier "234", *01*		140	___
28824	Santa Fe FT Non-Powered "172", *00*		NM	___
28826	Pioneer Seed GP7 "2001", traditional, *00 u*		NRS	___
28827	Chessie GP38, traditional, *01*		100	___
28830	Soo Line GP9, traditional, *01 u*		NRS	___
28831	Conrail U36B "2971", traditional, *02*		100	___
28832	Santa Fe RS-3 "2099", traditional, *02*		70	___
28836	NYC F-M H-16-44 Diesel "7000", CC, *02*		330	___
28837	NH F-M H-16-44 Diesel "591", CC, *02*		325	___
28838	UP F-M H-16-44 Diesel "1340", CC, *02*		325	___
28839	Alaska GP 30 "2000", CC, *04*		315	___
28840	Burlington GP30 "945", CC, *03*		325	___
28841	Seaboard GP30 "1315", CC, *03*		220	___
28842	C&O GP-9 w/ horn, *04*		160	___

		Exc	New	Cond/$
28843	Southern GP-38 w/ horn, *04*		140	___
28845	Amtrak RS-3 "106", *03*		70	___
28846	Western Pacific U36B "3067", traditional, *04*		100	___
28847	DM & IR GP38 "203", traditional, *04*		170	___
28849	Western Maryland GP-7 w/ horn, *04*		170	___
28850	NYC GP30 "6115" CC, *04*		360	___
28851	Pennsylvania RS-3, *04*		75	___
28852	CSX U36B "1976", traditional, *05*		CP	___
28853	Santa Fe GP38 "2371", traditional, *05*		CP	___
28859	Pennsylvania Non-Powered GP30 "2206", *06*		CP	___
28860	UP GP30 Diesel "844", CC, *06*		360	___
28861	UP Non-Powered GP30 Diesel "845" (Std. O), *06*		CP	___
28862	CSX GP30 Diesel "4249", CC, *06*		CP	___
28863	CSX Non-Powered GP30 Diesel "4250" (Std. O), *06*		CP	___
28864	UP RS-3 Diesel "1195", traditional, *06*		CP	___
28865	GN GP9 Diesel "688", traditional, *06*		CP	___
28866	NYC GP20 Diesel "6110", traditional, *06*		CP	___
28873	NYC RS-3 Diesel Locomotive "8226" traditional, *06*		CP	___
28874	UP GP9 Diesel "178", traditional, *06–07*		CP	___
28875	Santa Fe GP20 "1107", traditional, *06*		CP	___
28876	GN FT Diesel "418", traditional, *07*		CP	___
28879	UPS Centennial GP38 Diesel "07", traditional, *06*		CP	___
28880	Mavis the Diesel Engine, *07*		CP	___
28881	Conrail GP20 Diesel "2107", traditional, *07*		CP	___
28882	Alaska RR RS-3 Diesel "1079", traditional, *07*		CP	___
29000	PRR Madison Coach "2622 Caleb Strong", *99*		80	___
29001	PRR Madison Coach "2621 Villa Royal", *99*		80	___
29002	PRR Madison Coach "2624 Philadelphia", *99*		80	___
29003	PRR Madison Cars 4-pack, *98*		220	___
29004	NYC Heavyweight Passenger Set 2-pack, *99*		170	___
29007	NYC Pullman Passenger Car 2-pack, *98 u*		95	___
29008	NYC Heavyweight Diner "383", *98*		95	___
29009	NYC Heavyweight Combo Car "Van Twiller", *98*		95	___
29010	C&O Heavyweight Passenger Set, 2-pack, *99* (29011 and 29012 Passenger Cars)		150	___
29039	Lionel Lines Recovery Combo Car "9501", *99*		NRS	___
29041	Alaska Streamline Passenger 4-pack, *99–00*		230	___
29042	Alaska Streamline Baggage "6310", *99–00*		50	___
29043	Alaska Streamline Coach "5408", *99–00*		65	___

		Exc	New	Cond/$
29044	Alaska Streamline Vista Dome "7014", *99–00*		65	___
29046	B&O Streamline Passenger 4-pack, *99–00*		165	___
29047	B&O Streamline Baggage, *99–00*		35	___
29048	B&O Streamline Coach, *99–00*		50	___
29049	B&O Streamline Vista Dome, *99–00*		50	___
29050	B&O Streamline Observation, *99–00*		40	___
29051	AT&SF Streamline Passenger 4-pack, *99–00*		200	___
29052	AT&SF Streamline Baggage, *99–00*		40	___
29053	AT&SF Streamline Coach, *99–00*		60	___
29054	AT&SF Streamline Vista Dome, *99–00*		60	___
29055	AT&SF Streamline Obsevation, *99–00*		40	___
29056	NYC Streamline Passenger 4-pack, *99–00*		180	___
29057	NYC Streamline Baggage, *99–00*		40	___
29058	NYC Streamline Coach, *99–00*		50	___
29059	NYC Streamline Vista Dome, *99–00*		50	___
29060	NYC Streamline Observation, *99–00*		45	___
29061	PRR Madison Passenger 4-pack, *99–00*		190	___
29062	PRR Madison Baggage "Indian Point", *99–00*		50	___
29063	PRR Madison Coach "Christopher Columbus" *99–00*		50	___
29064	PRR Madison Coach "Andrew Jackson", *99–00*		50	___
29065	PRR Madison Obsevation "Broussard", *99–00*		50	___
29066	CNJ Madison Passenger 4-pack, *99–00*		210	___
29067	CNJ Madison Baggage "420", *99–00*		50	___
29068	CNJ Madison Coach "Beachcomber", *99–00*		50	___
29069	CNJ Madison Coach "Echo Lake", *99–00*		50	___
29070	CNJ Madison Observation "1178", *99–00*		50	___
29071	NYC Baby Madison 4-pack, *00*		155	___
29072	NYC Baby Madison Baggage "1001", *00*		50	___
29073	NYC Baby Madison Coach "1005", *00*		50	___
29074	NYC Baby Madison Coach "1006", *00*		50	___
29075	NYC Baby Madison Observation "1019 Detroit", *00*		40	___
29076	Southern Baby Madison 4-pack, *00*		155	___
29077	Southern Madison Baggage "702 Deleware", *00*		30	___
29078	Southern Madison Coach "800 North Carolina", *00*		50	___
29079	Southern Madison Coach "801 Maryland", *00*		50	___
29080	Southern Madison Observation "1100", *00*		40	___
29081	AT&SF Baby Madison, 4-pack, *00*		160	___
29082	AT&SF Baby Madison Baggage/RPO "1765", *00*		30	___
29083	AT&SF Baby Madison Coach "3040" Chair, *00*		50	___
29084	AT&SF Baby Madison Coach "1535 Coach Club", *00*		50	___

		Exc	New	Cond/$
29085	AT&SF Baby Madison Observation "10", *00*		45	___
29086	Madison Set, 3-pack, *99*		280	___
29090	Lionel Liontech Madison Car "2656", *99*		75	___
29091	Cowen Legends Madison Passenger "2657" *99–00*		75	___
29105	PRR "The Trail Blazer" Aluminum Passenger Car 4-pack, *04–05*		CP	___
29108	Searchlight Car, *00*		30	___
29110	B&O "The Columbian" Aluminum Passenger Car 4-pack, *04*		425	___
29115	SP "Daylight" Aluminum Passenger Car 4-pack, *04–05*		CP	___
29122	Erie-Lackawanna F3 A-B Passenger Set, *99*		840	___
29123	Erie-Lackawanna Aluminum Passenger Baggage "203", *99*		100	___
29124	Erie-Lackawanna Aluminum Passenger Diner "770", *99*		100	___
29125	Erie-Lackawanna Aluminum Passenger Coach "Eleanor Lord", *99*		100	___
29126	Erie-Lackawanna Aluminum Passenger Observation "789 Tavern Lounge", *99*		125	___
29127	ACL Aluminum Baggage "152", *99*		NRS	___
29128	ACL Aluminum Coach "North Hampton", *99*		NRS	___
29129	Texas Special Passenger Set, 4-pack, *99*	650	700	___
29130	Texas Special Aluminum "1200 Edward Burleson", *99*		115	___
29131	Texas Special Aluminum "1201 David G. Burnett", *99*		115	___
29132	Texas Special Aluminum "1202 J. Pinckney Henderson", *99*		115	___
29133	Texas Special Aluminum "1203", *99*		100	___
29134	WP Passenger Set, 4-pack, *99*		495	___
29135	California Zephyr Aluminum Vista "Silver Poplar", *99*		150	___
29136	California Zephyr Aluminum Vista "Silver Palm", *99*		150	___
29137	California Zephyr Aluminum Vista "Silver Tavern", *99*		150	___
29138	California Zephyr Aluminum Vista "Silver Planet", *99*		150	___
29139	Lionel Kughn Madison Car "2655", *99*		105	___
29140	NYC Aluminum Sleeper "Castleton Bridge", *99*		120	___
29141	NYC Aluminum Combine "Martin Van Buren", *99*		120	___
29142	CP Aluminum Vista "Skyline 596", *99*		125	___
29143	CP Aluminum Observation "Banff Park", *99*		125	___
29144	Santa Fe "El Capitan" Aluminum Passenger Car		400	___

		Exc	New	Cond/$
	4-pack, *04*			
29149	CB&Q California Zephyr Aluminum Passenger Car 2-pack, *03*		300	___
29152	Santa Fe Super Chief Aluminum Passenger Car 2-pack, *03*		190	___
29155	D&H Aluminum Passenger Car 2-pack, *03*		190	___
29158	Southern "The Southerner" Aluminum Passenger Car 2-pack, *03*		205	___
29165	Amtrak "Phase IV" Superliner Passenger Car 2-pack, *04*		195	___
29168	Amtrak "Phase IV" Superliner Diner w/ StationSounds, *04*		200	___
29169	Alaska Superliner Passenger Car 2-pack, *04*		200	___
29172	Alaska Superliner Diner w/ StationSounds, *04*		200	___
29182	N&W Powhattan Arrow 18" Aluminum Passenger Car 4-pack (Std. O), *05*		CP	___
29187	N&W Powhattan Arrow 18" Aluminum Passenger Car 2-pack (Std. O), *05*		CP	___
29190	N&W Powhattan Arrow 18" Aluminum Diner w/ StationSounds, *05*		CP	___
29191	Milwaukee Road Hiawatha 18" Passenger Car 4-pack, *06*		370	___
29196	Milwaukee Road Hiawatha 18" Passenger Car 2-pack, *06*		190	___
29199	Milwaukee Road Hiawatha Diner w/ StationSounds, *06*		190	___
29202	Santa Fe Map Boxcar "6464", *97 u*		60	___
29203	Maine Central Boxcar "6464-597", *97 u*		30	___
29205	MM Railroad Hi-Cube Boxcar "9555", *97*		65	___
29206	Vapor Records Boxcar #1, *97*		75	___
29209	6464 Boxcar Series VII 3-pack, *98*		90	___
29210	GN Boxcar "6464-450", *98*		33	___
29211	B&M Boxcar "6464-475", *98*		27	___
29212	Timken Boxcar "6464-500", *98*		28	___
29213	AT&SF Grand Canyon Route 6464 Boxcar "6464-198", *98*		26	___
29214	Southern Railway 6464 Boxcar "6464-298", *98*		27	___
29215	Canadian Pacific 6464 Boxcar "6464-398", *98*		26	___
29217	Airex Boxcar, *97 u*		55	___
29218	Vapor Records Boxcar "6464-496", *97 u*		80	___
29220	1997 Lionel Centennial Series Hi-Cube Boxcar 4-Car Set, *97*		180	___
29221	1997 Centennial Series Hi-Cube Boxcar		41	___

		Exc	New	Cond/$
	"9697-1", *97*			
29222	1997 Centennial Series Hi-Cube Boxcar "9697-2", *97*		50	___
29223	1997 Centennial Series Hi-Cube Boxcar "9697-3", *97*		45	___
29224	1997 Centennial Series Hi-Cube Boxcar "9697-4", *97*		50	___
29225	H.O.R.D.E. Music Festival Boxcar, *97*	48	55	___
29229	Vapor Records Holiday Car, *98*		135	___
29231	Animated Halloween Boxcar, *98*		42	___
29233	CR Overstamp PC Boxcar "6464-598", *98*		38	___
29234	CR Overstamp Erie Boxcar "6464-698", *98*		32	___
29235	NYC Boxcar "6464-510", *99*		47	___
29236	Katy Boxcar "6464-515", *99*		40	___
29237	M&StL Boxcar "6464-525", *99*		25	___
29250	Phoebe Snow Boxcar "6464-199", *99*		41	___
29251	BN Boxcar "6464-299", *99*		31	___
29252	CP Boxcar "6464-399", *99*		33	___
29253	B&M Boxcar 6565 "76032", *99*		50	___
29254	B&M Boxcar 6565 "76033", *99*		50	___
29255	B&M Boxcar 6565 "76034", *99*		50	___
29256	B&M Boxcar 6565 "76035", *99*		50	___
29257	Southern Boxcar "9464-199", *99*		38	___
29258	Reading Boxcar "9464-299", *99*		36	___
29259	NP Bicentennial Boxcar "9464-399", *99*		34	___
29265	Maine Central Boxcar 6565 "8661", *99*		36	___
29266	Frisco Boxcar 6565 "8722", *99*		36	___
29267	6464 Boxcar Series VIII 3-pack, *99*		105	___
29268	Rio Grande Boxcar 6565 "63067", *99*		40	___
29271	Lionel Cola Tractor Trailer, *98*		12	___
29279	JC/CR Boxcar "6464-28X", *99*		40	___
29280	LV/CR Boxcar "6464-31X", *99*		41	___
29281	Post-Merger Boxcar Conrail Overstamped CNJ & LV 2-pack Set, *99*		70	___
29282	Archive 3-pack "6464", *99*		130	___
29283	NYC Boxcar "6464-900", *99*		55	___
29284	GN Boxcar "6464/0000", *99*		40	___
29285	Seaboard Boxcar, *99*		36	___
29286	Overstamp Boxcars, 2-pack, *99*		70	___
29287	NH/PC Boxcar "6464-29X", *99*	18	34	___
29288	RDG/CR Boxcar "6464-32X", *99*		38	___

		Exc	New	Cond/$
29289	6464- Boxcar Series IX, 3-pack, *99–00*		70	___
29290	D&RGW Boxcar "6464-650", *00*		41	___
29291	AT&SF Boxcar "6464-700", *00*		38	___
29292	NH Boxcar "6464-725", *00*		39	___
29293	NH Boxcar "6464-425", *99*		95	___
29294	Hellgate Bridge Boxcar "1900-2000", *99 u*		45	___
29295	PRR 6565 "Don't Stand Me Still" Boxcar "24018", *99–00*		65	___
29296	PRR 6565 "Merchandise" Boxcar "29296", *99–00*		65	___
29297	PRR 6565 "No Damage" Boxcar "47158", *99–00*		65	___
29298	Lionel Boxcar "6464-2000", *00*		43	___
29400	Bethlehem Steel Slag Car 3-pack (Std. O), *03*		185	___
29404	Bethlehem Steel Hot Metal Car 3-pack (Std. O), *03*		210	___
29408	PRR Coil Car, *01*		40	___
29411	Sherwin-Williams Vat Car, *02*		34	___
29412	Tabasco Brand Vat Car, *02*		35	___
29413	Airex Boat Loader Car "29413", *02*		42	___
29414	PRR Evans Auto Loader "480123", *01*		50	___
29415	WM Skeleton Log Car 3-pack #2 (Std. O), *02*		90	___
29419	West Side Lumber Skeleton Log Car 3-pack #2 (Std. O), *02*		90	___
29423	Wellspring Capital Management Happy Holidays Vat Car, *03 u*		245	___
29424	Meadow River Lumber Skeleton Log Car 3-pack (Std. O), *03*		90	___
29429	Campbell's Soup Vat Car "29429", *03*		38	___
29430	Meadow River Lumber Skeleton Log Car 3-pack #2 (Std. O), *03*		90	___
29434	Weyerhauser Skeleton Log Car 3-pack, *05*		100	___
29438	UP TTUX Car, *03*		60	___
29439	Lionel Postwar Evans Auto Loader "6414", *02*		43	___
29441	UP Flatcar w/ grader "53471", *02*		43	___
29442	CSX Flatcar w/ backhoe "600513", *02*		43	___
29445	Elk River Lumber Skeleton Log Car 3-pack, *05*		CP	___
29453	Elk River Lumber Skeleton Log Car 3-pack #2 (Std. O), *03*		90	___
29457	NS Flatcar w/ Caterpillar load "157590", *03*		42	___
29458	BNSF Flatcar w/ Caterpillar load "922268", *03*		44	___
29459	Archive Water Barrel Car "1878", *03*		40	___
29460	Archive Lionel Lines Flatcar w/ piggyback trailers "3460", *03*		39	___
29461	Postwar Flatcar w/ red-and-white airplane		32	___

		Exc	New	Cond/$
	"6500", *03*			
29462	Postwar Flatcar w/ white-and-red airplane "6500", *03*		31	___
29463	Postwar Evans Auto Loader "6414", *03*		30	___
29464	U.S. Army Vat Car "29464", *04*		35	___
29465	U.S. Steel Slag Car 3-pack (Std. O), *04–05*		CP	___
29469	U.S. Steel Hot Metal Car 3-pack (Std. O), *04–05*		CP	___
29473	Youngstown Sheet & Tube Slag Car 3-pack (Std. O), *03*		150	___
29477	Youngstown Sheet & Tube Hot Metal Car 3-pack (Std. O), *03*		170	___
29481	Cass Scenic Railroad Skeleton Log Car 3-pack (Std. O), *03*		80	___
29488	Cass Scenic Railroad Skeleton Log Car 3-pack #2 (Std. O), *04*		90	___
29492	Pickering Lumber Skeleton Log Car 3-pack #1 (Std. O), *04*		100	___
29496	Pickering Lumber Skeleton Log Car 3-pack #2 (Std. O), *04*		90	___
29602	Postwar No. 6315 Celanese Chemicals 1-D Tank Car, *05*		CP	___
29603	Comet 1-D Tank Car, traditional, *05*		CP	___
29604	Meadow Brook Molasses 1-D Tank Car traditional, *05*		CP	___
29607	Las Vegas Mint Car, traditional, *05*		CP	___
29609	Alien Suspension Car, *06*		CP	___
29610	Dixie Honey 1-Dome Tank Car, *06*		CP	___
29611	Sunoco 1-Dome Tank Car, *06*		CP	___
29612	Las Vegas Poker Chip Car, *06*		40	___
29613	Postwar No. 6463 Rocket Fuel 2-D Tank Car, *06*		75	___
29617	Postwar No. 6465 Cities Service Tank Car, *06–07*		CP	___
29618	Hooker Chemicals 3-Dome Tank Car, *07*		CP	___
29619	Grave's Formaldehyde 1-Dome Tank Car, *07*		CP	___
29622	Postwar Archive No. 6445 Fort Knox Mint Car, *07*		CP	___
29703	PRR Porthole Caboose, *01*		45	___
29708	C&O B/W Caboose "8315", *04*		45	___
29709	Pennsylvania N5C Caboose "477938", *04*		40	___
29711	Postwar No. 6516 Santa Fe B/W Caboose, *05*		CP	___
29712	#2420 Lionel Lines Searchlight Caboose, *04*		50	___
29717	Norfolk Southern E/V Caboose, *05*		CP	___
29718	Postwar No. 6419-100 N&W Work Caboose, *06*		CP	___
29719	Archive No. 6427 Santa Fe Caboose, *06*		CP	___

		Exc	New	Cond/$
29726	Postwar No. 6427-60 Virginian Caboose, *06–07*		CP	___
29727	"I Love U.S.A." B/W Caboose "1985", *06*		CP	___
29729	Bethlehem Steel Searchlight Caboose, *06*		CP	___
29800	M.O.W. Crane Car w/ TMCC "X-800", *04*		250	___
29804	UP Crane Car "JPX 250", CC, *05*		CP	___
29805	Conrail Boom Car "50202", CC, *05*		CP	___
29806	Weyerhaeuser Log Dump Car, *05*		CP	___
29807	DM&IR Coal Dump Car, *05*		CP	___
29808	Candy Cane Dump Car, *05*		55	___
29809	Dump Car w/ presents, *05*		60	___
29810	Operating Egg Nog Car, *05*		CP	___
29811	Merchant's Despatch Transit Hot Box Refrigerator Car "12425", *05*		85	___
29812	Santa Fe Hot Box Refrigerator Car "20699", *05*		90	___
29813	Santa Fe Boom Car "19144" w/ Crane Sounds, *05*		CP	___
29814	Pennsylvania Boom Car "491063" w/ Crane Sounds, *05*		CP	___
29815	NYC Boom Car "X923" w/ Crane Sounds, *05*		CP	___
29816	M.O.W. Boom Car "X-816" w/ Crane Sounds, *05*		CP	___
29817	UP Boom Car "909438 w/ Crane Sounds, *05*		CP	___
29818	Conrail Boom Car w/ Crane Sounds, *05*		CP	___
29821	Lionel Lines Crane P/W #2460, *05*		43	___
29822	Postwar No. 773W NYC Tender w/ whistle, *05*		48	___
29823	#3484 Pennsylvania Operating Boxcar, *05*		38	___
29827	Postwar No. 3419 LL Helicopter Launching Car, *06*		49	___
29828	Postwar No. 3666 Minuteman Car w/ cannon, *06*		85	___
29829	Postwar No. 6905 Radioactive Waste Car, *06*		85	___
29830	PFE Hot Box Refrigerator Car "5890" (Std. O), *06*		105	___
29831	Swift Hot Box Refrigerator Car "15342" (Std. O), *06*		CP	___
29832	Chessie System Crane Car "940504", CC, *06*		CP	___
29833	Chessie System Boom Car "940561", CC, *06*		CP	___
29834	Lionel Lines B/W Caboose w/ TrainSounds "834" (Std. O), *06–07*		110	___
29835	SP B/W Caboose w/ TrainSounds "4667" (Std. O) *06–07*		CP	___
29839	Postwar No. 6512 Cherry Picker Car, *06*		CP	___
29839	#6512 Cherry Picker Car, *06*		CP	___
29849	Postwar No. 2460 Lionel Lines Crane Car, *06*		CP	___
29850	N&W Air Whistle Tender, *06–07*		CP	___
29850	N&W Air Whistle Tender, *06–07*		CP	___
29854	Postwar No. 3510 Satellite Launching Car, *07*		CP	___

		Exc	New	Cond/$
29855	Lionel Lines Operating Milk Car, *07*		CP	___
29856	Postwar No. 3494-550 Monon Operating Boxcar *06–07*		CP	___
29857	Postwar No. 6660 Lionel Lines Boom Car, *06–07*		CP	___
29858	CP Rail Crane Car "414475",CC, *07*		CP	___
29859	CP Rail Boom Car "412567", CC, *07*		CP	___
29865	Southern Operating Barrel Car, *07*		CP	___
29866	Pirates Aquarium Car, *07*		CP	___
29867	NYC Jet Snow Blower "X27207", *07*		CP	___
29868	Alaska RR Jet Snow Blower, *07*		CP	___
29869	Bethlehem Steel Crane Car, *06*		CP	___
29870	Maintenance-of-Way Jet Snow Blower "MWX-16", *07*		CP	___
29900	"I Love Wisconsin" Boxcar "9700", *01*		35	___
29901	"I Love Kentucky" Boxcar "9700", *01*		30	___
29902	"I Love Iowa" Boxcar "9700", *01*		31	___
29903	"I Love Missouri" Boxcar "9700", *01*		31	___
29906	"I Love Connecticut" Boxcar "9700", *02*		33	___
29907	"I Love West Virginia" Boxcar "9700", *02*		33	___
29908	"I Love Delaware" Boxcar "9700", *02*		33	___
29909	"I Love Maryland" Boxcar "9700", *02*		65	___
29910	Toy Fair Centennial Boxcar "9700", *03*		40	___
29912	"I Love Alabama" Boxcar "9700", *03*		30	___
29913	"I Love Mississippi" Boxcar "9700", *03*		35	___
29914	"I Love Louisiana" Boxcar "9700", *03*		35	___
29915	"I Love Arkansas" Boxcar "9700", *03*		30	___
29920	"I Love North Dakota" Boxcar "9700", *03*		35	___
29921	"I Love South Dakota" Boxcar "9700", *03*		40	___
29922	"I Love Nebraska" Boxcar "9700", *03*		30	___
29923	"I Love Kansas" Boxcar "9700", *03*		30	___
29927	"I Love Washington" Boxcar, *05*		CP	___
29928	"I Love Oregon" Boxcar, *05*		40	___
29929	"I Love Idaho" Boxcar, *05*		CP	___
29930	"I Love Utah" Boxcar, *05*		CP	___
29932	"I Love Oklahoma" Boxcar, *06*		CP	___
29933	"I Love New Mexico" Boxcar, *06*		CP	___
29934	"I Love Hawaii" Boxcar, *06*		CP	___
29935	"I Love Alaska" Boxcar, *06*		CP	___
29936	"I Love Wyoming" Boxcar, *06*		CP	___
29942	Santa Fe Railroad Art Boxcar, *06*		CP	___
29943	Texas Special Railroad Art Boxcar, *06*		CP	___

		Exc	New	Cond/$
29944	1957 Lionel Art Boxcar, *06*		CP	___
29945	1947 Lionel Art Boxcar, *06*		CP	___
29949	Weyerhaeuser Timber Skeleton Log Car 3-pack #2 (Std. O), *03*		90	___
30000	Pennsylvania Keystone Steam Super Freight Set w/ TMCC, *05*		CP	___
30001	Santa Fe El Capitan Diesel Passenger Set w/ TrainSounds, *05–07*		CP	___
30002	Neil Young's Greendale Diesel Freight Set, *04*		420	___
30003	Pennsylvania Flyer Operating Freight Expansion Pack, *05*		CP	___
30004	Pennsylvania Flyer Passenger Expansion Pack *05–07*		CP	___
30007	NYC Flyer Operating Freight Expansion Pack, *05*		CP	___
30008	NYC Flyer Passenger Expansion Pack, *05–07*		CP	___
30011	Holiday Expansion Pack, *05*		CP	___
30012	Thomas the Tank Engine Expansion Pack, *05–07*		CP	___
30016	NYC Flyer Steam Freight Set, *06–07*		CP	___
30018	Pennsylvania Flyer Steam Freight Set, *06–07*		CP	___
30020	North Pole Central Christmas Steam Train Set *06–07*		CP	___
30021	Cascade Range Steam Logging Train Set, *06–07*		CP	___
30022	Southwest Diesel Freight Train Set w/ TrainSounds, *06*		CP	___
30024	UP Fast Freight Steam Train Set w/ TrainSounds, *06–07*		CP	___
30025	Chesapeake Super Freight Train Set w/ TMCC, *06–07*		CP	___
30026	CP Diesel Freight Train Set w/ TMCC, *06*		CP	___
30034	Great Western Steam Freight Train Set w/ Lincoln Logs, *07*		CP	___
30035	Sodor Freight Expansion Pack, *06–07*		CP	___
30036	Great Western Expansion Pack, *07*		CP	___
30037	Pennsylvania Flyer Operating Freight Expansion Pack, *06–07*		CP	___
30038	NYC Flyer Operating Freight Expansion Pack, *06–07*		CP	___
30039	North Pole Central Passenger Expansion Pack, *06–07*		CP	___
30040	North Pole Central Freight Expansion Pack, *06–07*		CP	___
30041	Southwest Diesel Freight Expansion Pack, *06*		CP	___
30042	Cascade Range Expansion Pack, *06*		CP	___
30044	NYC Empire Builder Steam Freight Train Set w/ TMCC, *06*		CP	___

		Exc	New	Cond/$
30045	Alaska RR Steam Work Train Set, *07*		CP	___
30046	Alaska RR Work Train Expansion Pack, *07*		CP	___
30047	Northwest Special Diesel Freight Set w/ TrainSounds, *07*		CP	___
30048	Northwest Special Freight Expansion Pack, *07*		CP	___
30051	UP Diesel Freight Train Set w/ TMCC, *07*		CP	___
30056	Halloween Steam Freight Train Set, *07*		CP	___
30061	UPS Centennial Stream Freight Train Set, *07*		CP	___
30064	K-Line By Lionel Pennsylvania Speeder Set traditional, *06*		CP	___
30066	C&O Empire Builder Steam Freight Set w/ CC, *07*		CP	___
31700	Postwar Girl's Train Freight Set, *01*		570	___
31701	Postwar Boy's Train Freight Set, *02*		345	___
31704	Alton Limited Steam Passenger Set, *02*		870	___
31705	50th Anniversary Hudson Passenger Set, *02*		900	___
31706	UP Burro Crane Set, *02*		210	___
31707	C&O Diesel Freight Set, *03*		280	___
31708	Postwar No. 1805 Land-Sea-Air Marines Missile Launch Set, *03*		400	___
31710	BN Coal Train Diesel Freight Set w/ RailSounds, *03*		690	___
31711	Postwar No. 1563W Wabash Diesel Freight Set w/ RailSounds, *03*		570	___
31712	UP Alco PA Diesel Passenger Set w/ RailSounds, *03*		1495	___
31713	Southern Crescent Limited Steam Passenger Set w/ RailSounds, *03*		1195	___
31714	Amtrak Acela Diesel Passenger Set w/ RailSounds *04–05*		CP	___
31715	Fire Rescue Steam Freight Set, *02*		285	___
31716	Century Club 2 Niagrara Milk Train Set		730	___
31716	Fire Rescue Steam Freight Set, *03*		250	___
31717	CP Rail Snow Removal Train Set, *03*		255	___
31718	SP "Oil Can" TankTrain Freight Set, *03*		1600	___
31719	Western Maryland Fireball Diesel Freight Set, *04*		290	___
31720	FEC "The Champion" Diesel Passenger Set w/ RailSounds, *04*		900	___
31721	Postwar No. 13138 "Majestic" Electric Freight Set w/ RailSounds, *04*		580	___
31727	Postwar No. 2291W Rio Grande Diesel Freight Set w/ RailSounds, *04*		640	___
31728	Elvis "He Dared to Rock" Steam Freight Set, *04*		325	___
31730	Norman Rockwell Cars, 4-pack, *05*		95	___
31733	Jones & Laughlin Steel Slag Train Set, *05*		CP	___

		Exc	New	Cond/$
31734	Chessie Steam Special Passenger Set w/ TMCC, *05*		405	___
31735	Chessie Diesel Freight Set w/ TMCC, *05–06*		670	___
31736	CP Diesel Grain Train Freight Set w/ TMCC, *05*		CP	___
31737	Napa Valley Diesel Wine Train Passenger Set w/ diner, TMCC, *05*		900	___
31739	Postwar No. 13150 Super O Hudson Steam Freight Set, *05*		940	___
31740	Postwar No. 2519W Virginian Diesel Freight Train Set w/ TMCC, *05–07*		620	___
31742	Postwar No. 2544W Santa Fe Super Chief Diesel Passenger Set, *05*		700	___
31747	Pennsylvania Electric Ballast Train Set w/ TMCC, *06*		550	___
31748	Santa Fe U28CG Standard O Diesel Freight Train Set w/ TMCC, *06–07*		CP	___
31749	Pennsylvania Coal Diesel Freight Train Set w/ TMCC, *06*		CP	___
31750	NYC Hotbox Reefer Steam Freight Train Set w/ TMCC, *06–07*		CP	___
31752	Postwar No. 2369W B&O Diesel Freight Train Set w/ TMCC, *06–07*		CP	___
31753	Postwar No. 2551W GN Diesel Freight Train Set w/ TMCC, *06–07*		CP	___
31754	Postwar No. 2545WS N&W Space-Freight Train Set w/ TMCC, *06–07*		960	___
31755	Texas Special Diesel Passenger Train Set, CC, *07*		CP	___
31760	CSX SD40-2 Diesel Husky Stack Train Set, CC, *07*		CP	___
31767	K-Line By Lionel Bethlehem Steel Rolling Stock Set, *06*		CP	___
31768	K-Line By Lionel B&O Rolling Stock Set, *06*		CP	___
31901	Christmas Steam Freight Set, *02*		145	___
31902	PRR K4 Freight Set, *01–02*		580	___
31904	C&O Steam Freight Set w/ RailSounds, *01*		400	___
31905	NH RS-11 Freight Set, CC, *01*		660	___
31907	PRR Atlantic Freight Set, *01 u*		400	___
31908	Reading Hobo Express Freight Set, *01 u*		365	___
31909	Santa Fe Shell Tank Car Freight Set, *01 u*		320	___
31910	Soo Line Diesel Freight Set, *01 u*		350	___
31911	Snap-On Anniversary Steam Freight Set, *00 u*		530	___
31913	PRR Steam Freight Flyer Set, *01*		145	___
31914	NYC Steam Freight Flyer Set w/ RailSounds, *01–02*		170	___
31915	Chessie GP-38 Freight Set, *01–02*		155	___
31916	Santa Fe Steam Freight Set, *01*		300	___

		Exc	New	Cond/$
31918	C&O Steam Freight Set w/ SignalSounds, *01*		315	___
31919	T&P Steam Passenger Set w/ RailSounds, *01*		210	___
31920	LL Bean Freight Set, *01 u*		240	___
31922	Snap-On Tool Diesel Freight Set, *01 u*		340	___
31923	PRR Flyer Freight Set, *01 u*		130	___
31924	UP RS-3 Freight Set, *02*		95	___
31926	Area 51 FA Freight Set, *02*		160	___
31931	Ballyhoo Circus Freight Set, *02*		190	___
31932	NYC FT Passenger Set w/ RailSounds, *02*		285	___
31933	Santa Fe Steam Freight Set w/ RailSounds, *02*		320	___
31934	Lionel 20th Century Express Steam Freight Set, *00 u*		275	___
31936	Pennsylvania Flyer Steam Freight Set, *03–05*		CP	___
31938	Southern Diesel Freight Set, *03–04*		160	___
31939	Great Train Robbery Steam Freight Set, *03*		185	___
31940	NYC Flyer Steam Freight Set w/ RailSounds, *03*		225	___
31941	Winter Wonderland Railroad Christmas Train Steam Freight Set, *03*		150	___
31942	Norman Rockwell Christmas Train, *03*		330	___
31944	NYC Limited Diesel Passenger Set w/ RailSounds, *03*		250	___
31945	Santa Fe Super Steam Freight Set w/ RailSounds, *03*		350	___
31946	Disney Christmas Steam Train Set, *04–05*		CP	___
31947	World of Disney Steam Freight Set, *03*		215	___
31950	Kraft Holiday UP RS-3 Freight Set, *02 u*		145	___
31952	Great Northern Glacier Route Diesel Freight Set *03–04*		110	___
31953	"Riding the Rails" Hobo Train Steam Freight Set *03–04*		225	___
31956	Thomas the Tank Engine Set, *04–07*		195	___
31958	Santa Fe Flyer Steam Freight Set w/ RailSounds, *04*		205	___
31960	Polar Express Steam Passenger Set, *04–07*		270	___
31961	Bloomingdale's Pennsylvania Flyer Steam Freight Set, *02 u*		155	___
31962	Nickel Plate Road Super Freight Set w/ RailSounds, *04*		350	___
31962	GN Glacier Route Freight Set, *03*		100	___
31963	Southern Pacific Overnight Steam Freight Set, *04*		340	___
31963	Riding the Rails Hobo Steam Freight Set, *03*		NRS	___
31966	Holiday Tradition Steam Freight Set, *04–05*		CP	___
31969	NYC Flyer Steam Freight Set w/ RailSounds, *04*		205	___

		Exc	New	Cond/$
31976	Yukon Special Diesel Freight Set, *05*		225	___
31977	New York Central Flyer Steam Freight Set, *05*		CP	___
31985	Santa Fe Steam Fast Freight Set w/ TrainSounds, *05*		CP	___
31989	Overland Freight Express UP Set, *04*		880	___
31990	Copper Range Steam Freight Mine Set, *05*		175	___
31993	Norfolk Southern Diesel Black Diamond Freight Set w/ TMCC, *05*		CP	___
32900	DC Billboard Lionel, *99*		24	___
32902	Construction Zone Signs (6), *99–07*		CP	___
32904	Lionel Hellgate Bridge, *99*	235	415	___
32905	Lionel Irvington Factory, *99–00*		295	___
32910	Rotary Coal Dumper w/ rotary bathtub gondola, *02*		425	___
32919	Animated Maiden Rescue, *99*		65	___
32920	Animated Pylon w/ airplane, *99*	25	130	___
32921	Electric Coaling Station "97", *99–01*		125	___
32922	Highway Barrels (6), *99–07*		CP	___
32923	36-watt Accessory Transformer, *99–03, 06–07*		CP	___
32929	Icing Station with Santa, *99*		90	___
32930	ZW Controller w/ two 180-watt transformers *99–02, 06–07*		CP	___
32933	Christmas Stocking Hanger Set, 4-piece, *99–00*		50	___
32934	Stocking Hanger, Gondola, *99–00*		15	___
32935	Stocking Hanger, Boxcar, *99–00*		15	___
32960	Hindenburger Cafe, *99*		195	___
32961	Route *66* U.F.O. Cafe, *99*		200	___
32987	Hobo Campfire, *99–00*	25	45	___
32988	#192 Railroad Control Tower, *99–00*		75	___
32989	#464 Sawmill, *99–00*		75	___
32990	Linex Oil Derrick, *99–00*		55	___
32991	WLLC Radio Station, *99*		65	___
32996	362 Barrel Loader, *00*		125	___
32997	Aluminum Rico Station, *00*		300	___
32998	Lionel Hobby Shop, *99–00*		300	___
32999	Hellgate Bridge, *99–00*		350	___
33000	LL RailScope GP-9 "3000", *88–90*	125	170	___
33002	RailScope B&W TV, *88–90*	45	70	___
33004	NYC RailScope GP-9 "3004", *90*		NM	___
33005	Union Pacific RailScope GP-9 "3005", *90*		NM	___
34102	Amtrak Shelter, *04–07*		CP	___
34108	Lionelville Suburban House, *03*		20	___

		Exc	New	Cond/$
34109	Lionelville Large Suburban House, *03*		15	___
34110	Lionelville Estate House, *03*		30	___
34111	Lionelville Deluxe Fieldstone House, *03*		17	___
34112	Lionelville Fieldstone House, *03*		17	___
34113	Lionelville Large Suburban House, 2, *03*		17	___
34114	Late Illuminated Station and Terrace "128", *03*		475	___
34117	Early Illuminated Station and Terrace "128", *03*		475	___
34120	TMCC Direct Lockon, *04–07*		CP	___
34121	Lionelville Bungalow, *04*		20	___
34122	Lionelville Bungalow w/ garage, *04*		20	___
34123	Lionelville Bungalow w/ addition, *04*		20	___
34124	Lionelville Anastasia's Bakery, *04*		20	___
34125	Lionelville Cotton's Candy, *04*		20	___
34126	Lionelville Market, *04*		20	___
34127	Lionelville O'Grady's Tavern, *04*		22	___
34128	Lionelville Pharmacy, *04*		15	___
34129	Lionelville Kiddie City Toy Store, *04*		20	___
34130	Lionelville Jim's 5&10, *04*		25	___
34131	Lionelville Al's Hardware, *04*		30	___
34144	Santa Fe Scrap Yard, *05–06*		80	___
34145	New Haven Scrap Yard, *06*		CP	___
34149	Sly Fox and the Hunter Historic Layout, *05–07*		CP	___
34150	Reading Room Historic Layout, *05–06*		CP	___
34158	Ring Toss Midway Game, *05–06*		CP	___
34159	Camel Race Midway Game, *05–06*		CP	___
34162	Operating Oil Pump, *04–07*		CP	___
34163	Speeder Shed, *04–06*		CP	___
34164	Nutcracker Operating Gateman, *05–06*		CP	___
34190	Carousel, *04–06*		165	___
34191	Hobo Depot, *04–05*		CP	___
34192	Operating Lumberjacks, *04–06*		CP	___
34193	UPS Animated Billboard, *04*		30	___
34194	UPS Package Station, *05*		CP	___
34195	UPS Centennial People Pack, *06–07*		CP	___
34500	Rio Grande FT Diesel "5484", traditional, *06*		CP	___
34501	Southern FT Diesel "4102", traditional, *06*		400	___
34504	B&O Non-Powered F3 A Unit "2368", *06–07*		CP	___
34505	B&O E7 A-A Diesels "1425/1429", CC, *07*		CP	___
34508	PRR E7 A-A Diesels "5848/5849", CC, *07*		CP	___
34509	PRR Non-Powered E7 B Unit (Std. O), *07*		CP	___

		Exc	New	Cond/$
34510	PRR Powered E7 B Unit, CC, *07*		CP	___
34511	NYC F7 A-B-A Diesels "1684, 2438/1685", CC, *07*		CP	___
34512	NYC Powered F7 B Unit "2439", CC, *07*		CP	___
34513	WP F7 A-B-A Diesels "918/918B/918D", CC, *07*		CP	___
34514	WP Powered F7 B Unit "918C", CC, *07*		CP	___
34515	NYC F7 Diesel Breakdown B Unit "2440" w/ RailSounds, *07*		CP	___
34518	PRR E7 Diesel Breakdown B Unit w/ RailSounds, *07*		CP	___
34519	NYC Sharknose A-A Diesels "3817/3818", CC, *07*		CP	___
34520	NYC Non-Powered Sharknose B Unit "3818" (Std. O), *07*		CP	___
34521	Santa Fe F3 A Unit "17", traditional, *07*		CP	___
34522	Santa Fe Non-Powered F3 B Unit "17" (Std. O), *07*		CP	___
35100	NYC Vista Dome "7012", *07*		CP	___
35101	NYC Baggage Car "5028", *07*		CP	___
35102	Santa Fe El Capitan Streamlined Diner, *07*		CP	___
35751	New York City Transit Authority R27 Subway Train Set, CC, *07*		CP	___
36000	Route 66 Flatcar with 2 red sedans, *98*		44	___
36001	Route 66 Flatcar with 2 wagons, *98*		42	___
36002	Pratt's Hollow Passenger Cars 4-pack, *98*		445	___
36006	Uranium Flatcar "6508", *99*		60	___
36016	Flatcar with propellers, *98*		45	___
36020	Flatcar "TT-6424" w/ auto frames, *99*		32	___
36021	Alaska Flatcar w/ airplane "6424", *99*		44	___
36024	J.B. Hunt Flatcar w/ trailer "64245", *99*		44	___
36025	J.B. Hunt Flatcar w/ trailer "64246", *99*		50	___
36026	Flatcars w/ J.B. Hunt trailers 2-pack, *99*		85	___
36027	Tredegar Iron Works Flatcar w/ cannon, *99*		45	___
36028	Heavy Artillery Flatcar w/ cannon, *99*		45	___
36029	SP Auto Carrier "516712", *99*		44	___
36030	Troublesome Truck #1, *99*		35	___
36031	Troublesome Truck #2, *99*		35	___
36032	Christmas Gondola w/ presents "6462", *99*		35	___
36036	C&O Gondola, *99*		20	___
36038	Construction Zone Gondola, *99 u*		NRS	___
36040	Bethlehem Flatcar w/ block (SSS), *99*		75	___
36041	Bethlehem Ore Car (SSS), *99*		40	___
36043	Custom Consist Flatcar w/ pickup truck, *99*		40	___
36044	Custom Consist Flatcar w/ dragster, *99*		40	___
36045	Flatcar w/ Lionel dragster, *04*		30	___

		Exc	New	Cond/$
36046	Flatcar w/ custom truck, *04*		30	___
36047	Construction Zone Gondola, *99 u*		NRS	___
36048	Construction Zone Gondola, *99 u*		NRS	___
36054	Archaeological Expedition Gondola w/ eggs, *00 u*		55	___
36055	Flatcar with dragster, *01 u*		30	___
36056	Flatcar with roadster, *01 u*		30	___
36059	Season's Greetings Gondola, *99 u*		50	___
36062	NYC 6462 Gondola, *99–00*		22	___
36063	Conrail Gondola "604768", *99–00*		20	___
36064	Billboard Flatcar "6424", *00*		41	___
36065	Wabash Flatcar "25536" w/ trailer, *00*		35	___
36066	Christmas Gondola w/ presents, *00*		32	___
36067	King Auto Sales Flatcar w/ pink Caddy "6424", *00*		40	___
36068	Pine Peak Tree Transport Gondola, *00*		NRS	___
36079	Service Station Ltd. Flatcar with trailer, *00*		34	___
36082	Whirlpool Flatcar with trailer, *00 u*		NRS	___
36083	Santa Fe "168998" Gondola, *01*		17	___
36084	Grand Trunk Coil Car, *00*		32	___
36085	FEC Coil Car, *00*		29	___
36086	SP Flatcar w/ trailer, *01*	34	35	___
36087	Flatcar w/ wooden whistle "6424", *01*		25	___
36088	Allis Chalmers Condenser Car "6519", *00*		43	___
36089	Frisco Flatcar w/ airplane, *00*		35	___
36090	TT Flat w/ Pepsi truck "6424", *01*		44	___
36091	Maersk Flat w/ die-cast tractors "250129", *00*		55	___
36092	Maersk Flat w/ die-cast frames "250130", *00*		55	___
36093	Soo TT Auto Carrier "906760", *00*		49	___
36094	PC F-9 Well Car "768122", *01*		41	___
36095	Christmas Chase Gondola, *01*		37	___
36098	PRR Gondola "385186", *01*		20	___
36104	Area 51 3-Dome Tank Car, *07*		CP	___
36200	Quaker Life Cereal Boxcar, *00*	400	420	___
36203	Whirlpool Boxcar, *00 u*		105	___
36205	eBay Boxcar, *00*		205	___
36206	REA Boxcar, *01*		25	___
36207	Vapor Records Christmas Boxcar, *01*		34	___
36208	Father's Day Boxcar, *00*		35	___
36210	Burlington Hi-Cube Boxcar "19825", *01*		40	___
36211	NP "659999" Hi-Cube Boxcar, *01*		33	___
36212	Lionel Employee Christmas Boxcar, *00 u*		390	___

		Exc	New	Cond/$
36213	Vapor Records Christmas Boxcar, *00*		38	___
36215	Train Station 25th Anniversary Boxcar, *00 u*		46	___
36218	Snap-On Boxcar, *00 u*		110	___
36220	Pioneer Seed Boxcar, *00 u*		NRS	___
36221	PRR Boxcar "569356", *01*		20	___
36222	NYC Boxcar "162440", *01*		20	___
36223	Chessie System Boxcar, *01*		20	___
36224	Santa Fe Boxcar "16263", *01*		20	___
36225	C&O Boxcar "250549", *01*		20	___
36226	E-Hobbies Boxcar, *01 u*		155	___
36227	Monopoly Community Chest Boxcar, *00 u*		50	___
36228	Lionel Visitor Center Boxcar, *01 u*		34	___
36229	Island Trains 20th Anniversary Boxcar, *01 u*		29	___
36232	Farmall Boxcar, *01 u*		NRS	___
36236	TM Books & Video "I Love Lionel" Boxcar "7474-1", *01 u*		43	___
36238	Snap-On Tool Team ASE Racing Boxcar, *01 u*		NRS	___
36239	LL Bean Boxcar, *01 u*		110	___
36240	Do It Best Boxcar, *01 u*		100	___
36242	Erie-Lackawanna Boxcar "73113", *02*		24	___
36243	Christmas Boxcar "2002", *02*		31	___
36244	Teddy Bear Centennial Boxcar, *02*		36	___
36245	Lionel 20th Century Boxcar "1900-1925", *00 u*		30	___
36246	Lionel 20th Century Boxcar "1926-1950", *00 u*		30	___
36247	Lionel 20th Century Boxcar "1951-1975", *00 u*		30	___
36248	Lionel 20th Century Boxcar "1976-2000", *00 u*		30	___
36253	2003 Christmas Boxcar (O), *03*		32	___
36254	Goofy Hi-Cube Boxcar, *03*		37	___
36255	Donald Duck Hi-Cube Boxcar, *03*		40	___
36256	GN Boxcar "6341", *03*		23	___
36264	Santa Fe Boxcar "600196, *02*		18	___
36265	Angela Trotta Thomas "Window Wishing" Boxcar, *02*		38	___
36267	Mickey Mouse Hi-Cube Boxcar, *03*		50	___
36270	Angela Trotta Thomas 10th Anniversary Boxcar "Holidays", *02–03*		30	___
36272	New Haven Boxcar "6501", *04*		20	___
36273	Railbox Hi-Cube Boxcar "15000", *04*		21	___
36275	2004 Christmas Boxcar, *04*		35	___
36276	Angela Trotta Thomas "Tis the Season" Boxcar, *04*		30	___
36277	Pluto Hi-Cube Boxcar, *04–05*		CP	___

		Exc	New	Cond/$
36278	Winnie the Pooh Hi-Cube Boxcar, *04–05*		CP	___
36291	Simpsons Boxcar, *04*		36	___
36294	UP Hi-Cube Boxcar, traditional, *05*		CP	___
36295	CN Boxcar, traditional, *05*		CP	___
36296	2005 Holiday Boxcar, *05*		CP	___
36297	Angela Trotta Thomas "Christmas Eve" Boxcar, *05*		CP	___
36305	eBay Boxcar "9700", *00 u*		100	___
36500	Western Pacific Caboose "36500", *04*		23	___
36501	D&RGW Caboose "36501", *04*		22	___
36502	Reading Caboose "36502", *04*		25	___
36515	North Pole Central Lines Caboose "36515", *04*		36	___
36519	Lionel Lines Caboose "36519", *04*		22	___
36520	Santa Fe Caboose "36520", *04*		22	___
36525	CSX Lighted Work Caboose, *05*		CP	___
36526	Pennsylvania Work Caboose, traditional, *05*		CP	___
36527	Santa Fe Work Caboose, traditional, *05*		28	___
36528	Chesapeake & Ohio Work Caboose, traditional, *05*		CP	___
36529	North Pole Central Lines Work Caboose w/ presents, traditional, *05*		38	___
36530	Pennsylvania Caboose, traditional, *05*		33	___
36531	Erie Caboose "C150", traditional, *05*		33	___
36532	SP Caboose "1097", traditional, *05*		CP	___
36533	Reading Caboose "92803", traditional, *05*		33	___
36534	NYC Center Cupola Caboose, traditional, *05*		CP	___
36535	LL Center Cupola Caboose, traditional, *05*		28	___
36536	Southern Center Cupola Caboose, traditional, *05*		CP	___
36547	Bethlehem Steel Transfer Caboose, traditional, *05*		CP	___
36548	Transylvania RR Work Caboose, traditional, *05*		CP	___
36550	Halloween Transfer Caboose, traditional, *06–07*		CP	___
36551	Christmas Caboose, *06*		CP	___
36552	U.S. Steel Work Caboose, traditional, *06–07*		CP	___
36554	SP Work Caboose, traditional, *06*		CP	___
36555	Pennsylvania Transfer Caboose, *06*		CP	___
36556	Lionel Lines Work Caboose, *06–07*		CP	___
36557	Rio Grande Work Caboose, traditional, *06*		29	___
36558	Virginian Center Cupola Caboose "316" traditional, *06*		CP	___
36559	WM Center Cupola Caboose "1863" traditional, *06*		CP	___
36560	C&O Center Cupola Caboose "90876" traditional, *06*		CP	___

		Exc	New	Cond/$
36562	Army Transportation Work Caboose traditional, *06*		CP	___
36563	Reading Work Caboose, traditional, *06*		CP	___
36565	UP SP-Type Caboose, traditional, *06*		CP	___
36566	NYC SP-Type Caboose, traditional, *06*		CP	___
36567	GN SP-Type Caboose, traditional, *06*		CP	___
36580	B&O Center Cupola Caboose "C2047" traditional, *05*		CP	___
36587	SP Caboose "1121", *07*		CP	___
36589	PRR Work Caboose, *07*		CP	___
36590	UP Work Caboose, *07*		CP	___
36592	Santa Fe Caboose "999471", *06*		CP	___
36593	NYC Caboose, *06*		CP	___
36601	UP Caboose, *06*		CP	___
36602	UPS Centennial Caboose, *06*		CP	___
36607	K-Line By Lionel Caboose, *06*		CP	___
36611	Conrail Caboose "19674", *07*		CP	___
36612	Alaska RR Caboose "1080", *07*		CP	___
36613	NYC Caboose, *07*		CP	___
36701	Baldwin Locomotive Works Operating Welding Car "36701", *02*		60	___
36702	Postwar Bosco Milk Car w/ platform "3672", *02*		115	___
36703	Lionel Postwar Circus Horse Car and Corral, *06*		CP	___
36704	Animated Reindeer Stockcar and Corral, *02*		145	___
36718	AEC Security Caboose, *02*		42	___
36720	Aladdin Aquarium Car, *03*		40	___
36721	101 Dalmatians Animated Gondola, *03*		45	___
36722	Peter Pan Bobbing Head Boxcar, *03*		45	___
36726	Santa Fe Searchlight Car "36726", *03*		50	___
36727	Weyerhaeuser Moe & Joe Flatcar, *03*		65	___
36728	SP Walking Brakeman Boxcar 163143", *03*		42	___
36729	Lionel Lines Animated Caboose "36729", *04–05*		CP	___
36730	U.S. Army Missile Launch Sound Car "44", *03*		175	___
36731	Motorized Aquarium Car "3435", *03*		85	___
36732	C&NW Jumping Hobo Car, *03*		41	___
36733	Christmas Music Boxcar, *03*		35	___
36734	Santa Fe Operating Searchlight Car "20611", *02*		25	___
36735	WP Ice Car "7045", *02*		55	___
36736	D&RGW Stockcar w/ RailSounds "39268", *04*		45	___
36738	T&P Poultry Dispatch Car "36738", *02*		50	___
36739	Postwar Lionel Lines Log Dump Car "3461", *03*		50	___

		Exc	New	Cond/$
36740	Postwar Lionel Lines Coal Dump Car "3469", *03*		49	___
36743	Santa Claus Bobbing Head Boxcar, *03*		40	___
36744	Little Mermaid Aquarium Car, *03*		55	___
36745	Toy Story Animated Gondola, *03*		70	___
36753	LFD Firecar with Ladder, *02*		60	___
36757	Southern Searchlight Car, *03–04*		NRS	___
36758	Patriotic Lighted Boxcar, *02*		60	___
36760	Lionel Archives B&O Sentinel Operating Brakeman Boxcar, "3424", *02*		65	___
36761	Wellspring Capital Management Illuminated Boxcar, *02 u*		210	___
36764	West Side Lumber Log Dump Car "36764", *03*		55	___
36765	Alaska Coal Dump Car "401", *03*		50	___
36767	Santa's Radar Tracking Car, *03*		40	___
36769	Fourth of July Lighted Boxcar, *03*		70	___
36770	American Refrigerator Transit Ice Car "23701", *04*		42	___
36771	CN Barrel Car "74208", *04*		48	___
36772	Spokane, Portland & Seattle Log Dump Car "36772", *04*		46	___
36773	Jersey Central Coal Dump Car "92926", *04*		45	___
36774	Pennsylvania "Moe & Joe" Lumber Flatcar "36774", *04*		50	___
36775	Santa Fe Animated Caboose "999010", *05*		CP	___
36776	Santa Fe Walking Brakeman Car "19938", *04*		43	___
36778	C&O Searchlight Car "216614", *04*		30	___
36780	Sea-Monkeys Motorized Aquarium Car, *04*		45	___
36781	Finding Nemo Aquarium Car, *04*		50	___
36782	Goofy and Pete Jumping Boxcar, *05*		CP	___
36783	Disney Operating Boxcar, *04–05*		CP	___
36784	Monsters Inc. Bobbing Head Boxcar, *04*		40	___
36786	Postwar MP Operating Boxcar "3494-150", *03*		40	___
36787	M.O.W. Remote Control Searchlight Car "36787", *04*		45	___
36788	Lionel Lines Steam Tender w/ TrainSounds, *04*		75	___
36789	Railbox Boxcar w/ TrainSounds, *04–05*		CP	___
36790	Christmas Music Boxcar, *04*		70	___
36793	Pennsylvania Derrick Car "36793", *03*		22	___
36794	NYC Log Dump Car "36794", *03*		25	___
36795	Southern Coal Dump Car "36795", *03*		25	___
36796	GN Searchlight Car "36796", *03*		24	___
36797	Operation Iraqi Freedom Minuteman Car		45	___

		Exc	New	Cond/$
	"36797", *03*			
36803	Santa Animated Caboose, *06*		CP	___
36804	Candy Cane Dump Car, *06*		CP	___
36805	Reindeer Jumping Boxcar, *06*		CP	___
36809	NYC Derrick Car, *07*		CP	___
36810	PRR Searchlight Car, *07*		CP	___
36811	UP Dump Coal Dump Car, *07*		CP	___
36812	British Columbia Log Dump Car, *07*		CP	___
36814	D&RGW Animated Caboose "01415", *07*		CP	___
36815	Santa Fe Moe & Joe Flatcar, *07*		CP	___
36818	U.S. Steel Searchlight Car, *07*		CP	___
36823	Halloween Spooky Smoke Boxcar, *07*		CP	___
36824	AlienSmoke Boxcar, *07*		CP	___
36829	Alien Radioactive Car, *07*			
36830	Trick or Treat Aquarium Car, *07*		CP	___
36831	Maintenance-of-Way Welding Car, *07*		CP	___
36834	Santa Fe Transparent Instruction Car, *07*		CP	___
36838	K-Line By Lionel Lionel Power Co. Voltmeter Car, *06*		CP	___
36839	K-Line By Lionel Operating Milk Car w/ unloading platform, *06*		CP	___
36900	Depressed Center Flatcar w/ backshop load, *99*	110	115	___
36913	Allied Chemical 1-D Tank Car, 2-pack, *00*		150	___
36914	Allied Chemical 1-D Tank Car, die-cast, white "ACDX 68075", *00*		90	___
36915	Allied Chemical 1-D Tank Car, die-cast, white "ACDX 68076", *00*		90	___
36916	Allied Chemical 1-D Tank Car, 2-pack, *00*		175	___
36917	Allied Chemical 1-D Tank Car, die-cast, black "ACDX 65124", *00*		95	___
36918	Allied Chemical 1-D Tank Car, die-cast, black "ACDX 65125", *00*		90	___
36921	Simpsons Boxcar, *05*		CP	___
36927	B&O DC Hopper 6-pack "435040/45", *01*		520	___
36935	Maersk Maxi-Stack 2-pack "250131/2", *00*		135	___
36937	SP Maxi-Stack "513957", *02*		65	___
38004	Virginian 4-6-0 10-wheeler "203" Locomotive CC, *01–02*		570	___
38005	Long Island 4-6-0 10-wheeler "138" Locomotive CC, *01–02*		510	___
38007	UP Auxilary Tender, black, CC, *01*		200	___
38008	UP Auxilary Tender gray, CC, *01*		205	___
38009	DRG 4-6-6-4 Challenger "3803", CC, *01*		1550	___

		Exc	New	Cond/$
38010	Clinchfield 4-6-6-4 Challenger "673", CC, *01*		1400	___
38012	Wheeling & Lake Erie 2-6-6-2 "8005", CC, *01*		610	___
38013	D&H 4-6-6-4 Lionmaster Challenger "1527" CC, *01*		720	___
38014	DRG 4-6-6-4 Lionmaster Challenger "3800", CC, *01*		710	___
38016	Southern 0-8-0 Yard Goat "6536" Locomotive, CC, *01–02*		530	___
38017	CN 2-6-0 Mogul "86" Locomotive, CC, *03, 05*		CP	___
38018	Wabash 2-6-0 Mogul "826" Locomotive, CC, *03*		485	___
38019	B&M 2-6-0 Mogul "1455" Locomotive, CC, *03, 05*		CP	___
38020	PRR 4-4-4-4 Lionmaster Duplex T1 "5514" Locomotive, CC, *02–03*		630	___
38021	WP 4-6-6-4 Challenger Locomotive "402", CC, *02*		650	___
38022	WM 4-6-6-4 Challenger Locomotive "1206", CC, *02*		690	___
38023	UP 4-6-6-4 Challenger Locomotive "3976", CC, *02*		620	___
38024	Pennsy S-1 Duplex-TMCC "6100", *03*		1000	___
38025	PRR 4-6-2 K4 Pacific "1361" Locomotive CC, *02*		950	___
38026	N&W 4-8-4 J Class Northern "606" Locomotive CC, *02*		1450	___
38027	Meadow River Lumber Co. Heisler Geared "6" Steam Locomotive, CC, *03*		880	___
38028	PRR 6-8-6 S2 Class "6200" Steam Turbine, *01*		650	___
38029	UP 4-12-2 "9000" Steam Locomotive, CC, *03*		570	___
38030	Santa Fe 2-8-8-2 "1795" Locomotive, CC, *03*		920	___
38031	SP 2-8-8-4 AC-9 "3809", CC, *04*		1100	___
38032	Virginian 2-8-8-2 "741" Locomotive, CC, *03*		860	___
38036	Long Island 2-8-0 Consolidation, *01*		500	___
38037	PRR-Reading Seashore 2-8-0 Consolidation "6072" Steam Locomotive, CC, *01*		495	___
38038	D&RG Auxilary Water Tender, *01*		230	___
38039	Clinchfield Auxilary Water Tender, *01*		220	___
38040	LV 4-6-0 Camelback, *01*		405	___
38042	C&NW 4-6-0 10-wheeler "361" Locomotive, CC, *02*		450	___
38043	Frisco 4-6-0 10-wheeler "719" Locomotive, CC, *02*		525	___
38044	PRR 4-6-2 K4 Pacific "5385" Locomotive, CC, *02*		920	___
38045	NYC 4-6-4 Lionmaster Hudson J-3a "5418" Steam Locomotive, CC, *03*		495	___
38046	GN 0-8-0 Steam Locomotive "815", CC, *02*		530	___
38047	N&W 0-8-0 Steam Locomotive "266", CC, *02*		550	___
38048	NPR 0-8-0 Locomotive "303", CC, *02*		530	___
38049	N&W 2-6-6-4 Articulated Steam Locomotive "1234", CC, *02*		690	___

No.	Description	Exc	New	Cond/$
38050	Nickel Plate 2-8-4 Berkshire "779" Locomotive CC, *03*		925	___
38051	Erie 2-8-4 Berkshire "3315" Locomotive, CC, *03*		810	___
38052	Pere Marquette 2-8-4 Berkshire "1225" Locomotive CC, *03*		1000	___
38053	NYC 4-8-2 Mohawk L-2a "2793" Locomotive CC, *03*		1000	___
38055	Santa Fe 4-8-4 Northern "3751" CC, *04*		1100	___
38056	Pennsylvania 4-8-2 Mountain M 1 a "6759" Steam Locomotive, CC, *03*		850	___
38057	Weyerhaeuser Shay Steam Locomotive, CC, *03*		1000	___
38058	C&O 2-8-8-2 H7 "1580", CC, *04*		1200	___
38060	UP 2-8-8-2 H7 "3590", CC, *04*		1200	___
38061	Cass Scenic RR Heisler Geared "6" Locomotive CC, *03*		940	___
38062	Lionel Lines 4-6-2 Pacific "8062" Locomotive, CC, *02–03*		275	___
38065	UP 2-8-8-2 Mallet Locomotive "3672", CC, *02*		980	___
38066	Elk River Shay Locomotive, CC, *03*		1000	___
38067	Milwaukee Road 4-6-2 Pacific "6316" Locomotive CC, *03*		300	___
38068	WM 4-6-2 Pacific "204" Locomotive, CC, *03*		300	___
38069	Erie Hudson w/ whistle, *05*		150	___
38070	C&O 4-6-2 Pacific "489", CC, *04*		300	___
38071	SP Cab Forward AC 12 "4294" Locomotive, CC, *05*		CP	___
38075	UP 4-8-8-4 Lionmaster Big Boy "4024" Steam Locomotive, CC, *03*		800	___
38076	C&O 2-8-4 Berkshire "2699", CC, *04*		860	___
38077	Virginian 2-8-4 Berkshire "508", CC, *04*		1000	___
38079	SP 4-8-4 Northern GS-2 "4410" CC, *04*		980	___
38080	WP 4-8-4 Northern GS-64 "485" CC, *04*		1000	___
38081	C&O 2-6-6-6 Allegheny "1650", CC, *05–07*		CP	___
38082	Pennsylvania 2-8-8-2 Y3 "374", CC, *04*		1000	___
38083	N&W 2-8-8-2 Y3 "2009", CC, *04*		910	___
38085	NYC 4-6-4 Lionmaster Hudson J-3a "5422" Steam Locomotive, CC, *03*		495	___
38086	B&A 4-6-4 Lionmaster Hudson "607" Steam Locomotive, CC, *03*		495	___
38087	Nickel Plate 2-8-4 Berkshire w/ RailSounds, *05*		190	___
38088	NYC 2-6-0 Mogul "1924" Locomotive, CC, *03, 05*		CP	___
38089	Pennsylvania 4-6-2 Pacific "3678", CC, *04*		300	___
38090	Clinchfield 4-6-6-4 Lionmaster Challenger		640	___

		Exc	New	Cond/$
	"672" CC, *04*			
38091	NP 4-6-6-4 Lionmaster Challenger "5121" CC, *04*		660	___
38092	Pickering Lumber Heisler "5", CC, *04*		1000	___
38093	UP 4-6-6-4 Lionmaster Challenger "3980" CC, *04*		700	___
38094	Milwaukee Road Hiawatha 4-4-2 Atlantic Steam Locomotive, CC, *06*		950	___
38095	N&W 4-8-4 J Class Locomotive "611", CC *05–06*		CP	___
38100	Texas Special F3 AB Set "2245", *99*	860	930	___
38103	Texas Special F3 "2245", *99*	435	510	___
38114	AT&SF FT B Unit, *99–00*		170	___
38115	NYC FT B Unit "2403", non-powered, *99–00*		130	___
38116	B&O FT B Unit, *99–00*		130	___
38144	C&O F3 AA "7019/7021", *00*		700	___
38147	GN Alco FA-2 AA Diesel Set, CC, *02*		405	___
38150	Platinum Ghost "2333", *99*		495	___
38153	Spirit of the Century "2333", *99*		800	___
38160	Pennsylvania Alco FB-2 Unit, *02*		125	___
38161	MKT Alco FB-2 Unit, *02*		125	___
38162	Burlington FT B Unit, *01*		NRS	___
38167	Burlington FT AA, *01*		225	___
38176	Pennsylvania Alco FA-2 AA Diesel Set, CC, *02*		405	___
38182	MKT Alco FA-2 AA Diesel Set, CC, *02*		360	___
38188	Southern F3 ABA "2356", *00*		600	___
38194	GN Alco FB-2 Unit, *02*		125	___
38196	Santa Fe FT A Unit "171", *00*		NRS	___
38197	SP F3 ABA "2387", *00*		640	___
38600	UP 0-6-0 Dockside Steam Switcher "87" traditional, *07*		CP	___
38601	Lionel Lines 0-6-0 Dockside Steam Switcher "1" traditional, *07*		CP	___
38605	PRR 0-4-0 Steam Locomotive "94", traditional, *07*		CP	___
38606	SP 0-4-0 Steam Locomotive "71", traditional, *07*		CP	___
38607	Southern 2-8-4 Berkshire Locomotive "2718" w/ RailSounds, *07*		CP	___
38608	Lionel Lines 2-8-2 Mikado Locomotive "57" w/ RailSounds, *07*		CP	___
38609	NYC 2-8-2 Mikado Locomotive "1843", CC, *07*		CP	___
38610	Nickel Plate Road 2-8-4 Berkshire Locomotive "779", CC, *07*		CP	___
38619	K-Line By Lionel Santa Fe 4-6-2 Pacific Steam Locomotive "2037", traditional, *06*		CP	___

38620	K-Line By Lionel B&O Porter Steam Locomotive "16", traditional, *06*		CP	___
38621	K-Line By Lionel 4-6-2 Pacific Steam Locomotive traditional, *06*		CP	___
39008	PRR Heavyweight Passenger Set, 4-pack, *00*	225	___
39009	PRR Heavyweight Passenger Set Combo "Indian Rock", *00*	50	___
39010	PRR Heavyweight Passenger Set Coach "Andrew Carnegie", *00*	60	___
39011	PRR Heavyweight Passenger Set Coach "Solomon P. Chase", *00*	60	___
39012	PRR Heavyweight Passenger Set Observation "Skyline View", *00*	50	___
39013	B&O Heavyweight Passenger Set, 4-pack, *00*	400	___
39016	B&O Heavyweight Passenger Set, 4-pack, *00*	200	___
39017	B&O Heavyweight Passenger Set Combo "Harper's Ferry", *00*	50	___
39018	B&O Heavyweight Passenger Set Coach "Youngstown", *00*	50	___
39019	B&O Heavyweight Passenger Set Coach "New Castle", *00*	50	___
39020	B&O Heavyweight Passenger Set Observation "Chicago", *00*	50	___
39028	LL Madison Passenger Set, 3-pack, *00*	195	___
39029	LL Madison Passenger Set Coach "Irvington 2625", *00*	60	___
39030	LL Madison Passenger Set Coach "Madison 2627", *00*	60	___
39031	LL Madison Passenger Set Coach "Manhattan 2628", *00*	60	___
39032	UP Madison Passenger Car 4-pack, *00*	275	___
39038	SP Madison Baggage Car "6015", *01*	NRS	___
39039	SP Madison Coach Car "1978", *01*	NRS	___
39040	SP Madison Coach Car "1975", *01*	NRS	___
39041	SP Madison Observation Car "2951", *01*	NRS	___
39042	N&W Heavyweight Passenger Car 4-pack, *00*	325	___
39047	B&O Heavyweight Passenger Car 2-pack, *01*	160	___
39050	PRR Heavyweight Passenger Car 2-pack, *01*	215	___
39053	Alaska Streamliner Passenger Car 2-pack, *01*	90	___
39056	NYC Streamliner Passenger Car 2-pack, *01*	75	___
39059	Santa Fe Streamliner Passenger Car 2-pack, *01*	100	___
39062	B&O Streamliner Passenger Car 2-pack, *01*	75	___
39065	PRR Streamliner Passenger 4-pack, *01*	165	___

		Exc	New	Cond/$
39079	SP Heavyweight Passenger Car 2-pack, *01*		NM	___
39082	Blue Comet Heavyweight Passenger Car 2-pack, *02*		325	___
39085	Freedom Train Heavyweight Passenger Car 3-pack, *03*		260	___
39092	PRR 027 Streamline Passenger Car 2-pack, *01*		70	___
39099	Alton Limited Heavyweight Passenger Car 2-pack, *03*		230	___
39100	Congressional Set "William Penn" Coach, *00*		115	___
39101	Congressional Set "Molly Pitcher" Coach, *00*		100	___
39102	Congressional Set "Betsy Ross" Vista Dome, *00*		100	___
39103	Congressional Set "Alexander Hamilton" Observation, *00*		100	___
39104	Phoebe Snow Car w/ StationSounds, *99*		255	___
39105	Milwaukee Road Hiawatha Car w/ StationSounds, *99*		235	___
39106	CP Aluminum Passenger Car Set, 2-pack, *00*		185	___
39107	CP Aluminum Passenger Coach "Blair Manor 2553", *00*		115	___
39108	CP Aluminum Passenger Coach "Craig Manor 2554", *00*		110	___
39109	Spirit of Century Aluminum Passenger Car 4-pack, *99*		520	___
39110	Spirit of the Century Full Vista Dome Car, *99–00*		100	___
39111	Spirit of the Century Full Vista Dome Car, *99–00*		100	___
39112	Spirit of the Century Full Vista Dome Car, *99–00*		100	___
39113	Spirit of the Century Skytop Observation Car, *99–00*		100	___
39118	Texas Special Aluminum Passenger Car w/ StationSounds, "1203 Garland", *99–00*		220	___
39119	Southern Aluminum Passenger Car Set, 4-pack, *00*		350	___
39120	Southern Aluminum Passenger Baggage "Grand Junction 1701", *00*		280	___
39121	Southern Aluminum Passenger Coach "Charlottsville 812", *00*		90	___
39122	Southern Aluminum Passenger Coach "Roanoke 814", *00*		250	___
39123	Southern Aluminum Passenger Observation "Memphis 1152", *00*		90	___
39124	Amtrak Superliner Aluminum Passenger Car 4-pack, *02*		405	___
39129	Santa Fe Superliner Aluminum Passenger Car 4-pack, *02*		305	___
39141	RI Aluminum Passenger Car 4-pack, *01*		400	___
39146	UP Aluminum Passenger Cars, 4-pack, *01*		285	___

		Exc	New	Cond/$
39151	CP Aluminum Passenger Car 2-pack, *01*		315	___
39154	PRR Congressional Aluminum Passenger Car 2-pack, *02*		195	___
39155	PRR Congressional Baggage Car, *02*		105	___
39156	PRR Congressional Coach "Robert Morris", *02*		100	___
39157	Southern Aluminum Passenger Car 2-pack, *01*		290	___
39160	KCS Aluminum Passenger Car 2-pack, *01*	200	260	___
39163	E-L Aluminum Passenger Car 2-pack, *01*		230	___
39166	Texas Special Aluminum Passenger Car 2-pack, *01*	300	430	___
39169	ACL Aluminum Passenger Car 4-pack, *01*		360	___
39179	NP Aluminum Passenger Car 2-pack, *02*		305	___
39182	WP Aluminum Passenger Car 2-pack, *02*		280	___
39185	Rio Grande Aluminum Passenger Car 2-pack, *02*		290	___
39194	UP Aluminum Passenger Car 2-pack, *02*		220	___
39197	CP Aluminum StationSounds Car, *02*		225	___
39198	PRR Aluminum StationSounds Car, *02*		210	___
39200	Hellgate Bridge Boxcar #2 "1900-2000", *00 u*		55	___
39202	Lionel Centennial Boxcar "1900-2000", *00*		46	___
39203	6464 Boxcar Series X, 3-pack, *01*		115	___
39204	New Haven Boxcar "6464-725", *01*		44	___
39205	Alaska Boxcar "6464-825", *01*		55	___
39206	NYC Boxcar "6464-900", *01*		40	___
39207	UP Boxcar 6565 "508500", red, *00*		50	___
39208	UP Boxcar 6565 "903658" silver, *00*		42	___
39209	UP Boxcar 6565 "500200" yellow, *00*		40	___
39210	6530 Fire Fighting Car, *00*		37	___
39211	6464 Archive 2 Boxcar 3-pack, *00*		85	___
39212	6464 Archive SP&S, *00*		NRS	___
39213	6464 Archive Wabash, *00*		NRS	___
39214	6464 Archive Kansas, OK, & Gulf, *00*		NRS	___
39216	PRR 2-Door Boxcar "47211", *01*		46	___
39220	B&LE Heavyweight Boxcar 6565 "82101", *01*		41	___
39221	L&N Heavyweight Boxcar 6565 "109829", *01*		41	___
39222	Conrail Heavyweight Boxcar 6565 "269198", *01*		44	___
39223	Postwar 6464 Boxcar Series 3-pack, *02*		125	___
39227	Postwar 6468 Automobile Boxcar 3-pack, *01*		95	___
39236	Postwar WP Boxcar "6464-250", *01*		55	___
39238	Elvis Boxcar, *03*		36	___
39239	P&LE Boxcar "22300, *02*		35	___
39240	Pennsylvania Boxcar "118747", *02*		32	___

		Exc	New	Cond/$
39241	PC Boxcar "252455", *02*		28	___
39242	Archive 6464 Boxcar Series 3-pack, *03–04*		80	___
39247	Postwar NYC Double-Door Boxcar "6468", *02–03*		32	___
39250	Campbell's Kids Centennial Boxcar, *03–04*		40	___
39252	Lenny Dean 60th Anniversary Boxcar, *04*		38	___
39253	Archive 6464 Boxcar Series 3-pack #2, *04*		100	___
39257	Boy's WP Boxcar "6464-100", *03*		50	___
39258	Elvis Presley Boxcar, 2, *03–04*		40	___
39259	Buick Centennial Boxcar, *03*		35	___
39262	Elvis Presley Boxcar #3, *04*		38	___
39267	Archive No. 6464 Boxcar 3-pack, *05*		CP	___
39273	Archive No. 6464 Boxcar 3-pack, *06*		CP	___
39281	Florida State University Boxcar, *07*		CP	___
39284	Penn State University Boxcar, *06–07*		CP	___
39286	University of Illinois Boxcar, *06–07*		CP	___
39287	University of Alabama Boxcar, *06–07*		CP	___
39289	University of Oklahoma Boxcar, *06–07*		CP	___
39291	University of Michigan Boxcar, *06–07*		CP	___
39400	Republic Steel Slag Car 3-pack (Std. O), *04*		100	___
39404	Republic Steel Hot Metal Car 3-pack (Std. O), *04*		130	___
39411	Jones & Laughline Hot Metal Car 3-pack (Std. O), *05*		CP	___
39423	Postwar No. 3460 LL Flatcar w/ piggyback trailers, *05*		45	___
39424	#6418 U.S. Steel 16-wheel w/ girders, *05*		CP	___
39425	Hood's Flatcar w/ milk container, traditional, *05*		CP	___
39426	Nestle Nesquik Flatcar w/ milk container traditional, *05*		CP	___
39428	Bethlehem Steel Slag Car "4" Std. O, *05*		CP	___
39429	Bethlehem Steel Hot Metal Car "8" (Std. O), *05*		CP	___
39430	Youngstown Sheet & Tube Slag Car "7" (Std. O), *05*		CP	___
39431	Youngstown Sheet & Tube Hot Metal Car "11" (Std. O), *05*		CP	___
39435	Postwar No. 6477 Miscellaneous Car, *06*		CP	___
39436	Postwar No. 6262 Wheel Car, *06*		CP	___
39437	Supplee-Wills-Jones Flatcar w/ milk container, *06*		CP	___
39443	U.S. Steel Slag Car 3-pack #2 (Std. O), *06*		CP	___
39447	Postwar Archive No. 6561 LL Cable Reel Car, *06–07*		CP	___
39450	Postwar Archive No. 6414 Evans Auto Loader, *06*		CP	___
39452	White Bros. Flatcar w/ milk container, *07*		CP	___
48423	Alaska RR Rotary Snowplow, *06–07*		CP	___

		Exc	New	Cond/$
51008	Burlington "Pioneer Zephyr" Diesel Passenger Set w/ RailSounds, *04*		875	___
51009	Prewar No. 269E Steam Freight Train Set w/ TrainSounds, *06*		CP	___
51010	Prewar No. 246E Steam Passenger Train Set w/ TrainSounds, *07*		CP	___
51201	Lionel Lines Rail Chief Passenger Set, *90*		410	___
51220	NYC "Imperial Castle" Passenger Car, *93 u*		500	___
51221	NYC "Niagara County" Passenger Car, *93 u*		500	___
51222	NYC "Cascade Glory" Passenger Car, *93 u*		500	___
51223	NYC "City of Detroit" Passenger Car, *93 u*		500	___
51224	NYC "Imperial Falls" Passenger Car, *93 u*		500	___
51225	NYC "Westchester County" Passenger Car, *93 u*		500	___
51226	NYC "Cascade Grotto" Passenger Car, *93 u*		500	___
51227	NYC "City of Indianapolis" Passenger Car, *93 u*		500	___
51228	NYC "Manhattan Island" Observation Car, *93 u*		500	___
51229	NYC Dining Car "680", *93 u*		500	___
51230	NYC Baggage Car "5017", *93 u*		500	___
51231	NYC "Century Club" Passenger Car, *93 u*		500	___
51232	NYC "Thousand Islands" Observation Car, *93 u*		500	___
51233	NYC Dining Car "684", *93 u*		500	___
51234	NYC Baggage Car "5020", *93 u*		500	___
51235	NYC "Century Tavern" Passenger Car, *93 u*		500	___
51236	NYC "City of Toledo" Passenger Car, *93 u*		500	___
51237	NYC "Imperial Mansion" Passenger Car, *93 u*		500	___
51238	NYC "Imperial Palace" Passenger Car, *93 u*		500	___
51239	NYC "Cascade Spirit" Passenger Car, *93 u*		500	___
51240	NYC Dining Car "681", *93 u*		500	___
51241	NYC "City of Chicago" Passenger Car, *93 u*		500	___
51242	NYC "Imperial Garden" Passenger Car, *93 u*		500	___
51243	NYC "Imperial Fountain" Passenger Car, *93 u*		500	___
51244	NYC "Cascade Valley" Passenger Car, *93 u*		500	___
51245	NYC Dining Car "685", *93 u*		500	___
51249	UP Overland Sleeper		120	___
51300	Shell Semi-Scale 1-D Tank Car "8124", *91*		200	___
51301	Lackawanna Semi-Scale Reefer "7000", *92*	175	210	___
51401	PRR Semi-Scale Boxcar "100800", *91*	135	155	___
51402	C&O Semi-Scale Stock Car "95250", *92*	150	165	___
51501	B&O Semi-Scale Hopper "532000", *91*	110	115	___
51502	Lionel Lines Steel Die-Cast Ore Car "6486-3" (SSS), *96*		80	___

		Exc	New	Cond/$
51503	Lionel Lines Steel Die-Cast Ore Car "6486-1" (SSS), *96*		80	___
51504	Lionel Lines Steel Die-Cast Ore Car "6486-2" (SSS), *96*		70	___
51600	NYC Depressed Center Flatcar w/ transformer "6418", *96*		105	___
51701	NYC Semi-Scale Caboose "19400", *91*	135	145	___
51702	PRR N-8 Caboose "478039", *91–92*	300	385	___
52054	Carail Boxcar, *94 u*		NRS	___
352065	Penn-Dutch Grain Operating Boxcar "9028", *96 u*		100	___
52066	Trainmaster Tractor and Trailer, *94 u*		100	___
52069	Carail Tractor and Trailer, *94 u*		60	___
52070	Knoebel's Boxcar, *95 u*		60	___
52075	United Auto Workers Boxcar, *95 u*		110	___
52082	Steamtown Lackawanna Boxcar, *95 u*		90	___
52098	National Bureau of Standards Boxcar (Std. O), *96 u*		60	___
52099	MP TOFC Flatcar, *96 u*		60	___
52100	Grand Rapids Station Platform, *96*		NRS	___
52105	Superstition Mountain Operating Gondola "61997", *97 u*		80	___
52110	CSPM&O Boxcar, *97 u*	17	47	___
52113	NDG&W 3-Bay Hopper, *97 u*		46	___
52114	NYC Flatcar w/ trailer, *97 u*		65	___
52116	Milwaukee Road Flatcar w/ tractor and trailer "194797", *97 u*		70	___
52121	Mobilgas 1-Dome Tank Car "238" (Std. O), *97 u*		65	___
52123	LIRR "Ronkonkoma" Full Vista Dome "9783", *97 u*		300	___
52123	LIRR "Hicksville" Dining Car "9883", *98 u*		300	___
52132	Knoebel's #2, *99 u*		85	___
52133	Knoebel's Boxcar, *98 u*		85	___
52134	Knoebel's Phoenix #4 Boxcar, *00 u*		85	___
52135	Santa Fe Refrigerator Car "22739", *98 u*		50	___
52136A	Christmas Special Tractor and Trailer, *97*		NRS	___
52136B	Frisco Special Tractor and Trailer, *98*		NRS	___
52137	Red Wing Shoes Boot Oil Tank Car, *98*		55	___
52141	Zep Manufacturing Co. Boxcar, *96*		85	___
52142	Mass Central Maxi-Stack Flatcar, *98 u*		125	___
52145	LIRR "Jamaica" Coach "99831", *99 u*		345	___
52145	LIRR "Penn Station" Coach "99832", *99 u*		300	___
52146	Ocean Spray Plug Door Refrigerator Car "OSCX 1998", *98 u*		170	___

		Exc	New	Cond/$
52147	Frisco/Campbell 66 TOFC Flatcar, *98 u* "52148-558", *99 u*		75	___
52150	Frisco/Campbell 66 TOFC Flatcar, *98 u*		130	___
52151	Amtrak Express Baggage Boxcar "71998" (Std. O), *98 u*		60	___
52152	Ben Franklin Philadelphia Wood-sided Refrigerator Car, *98 u*		105	___
52153	6414 Auto Set, 4-pack, *98*		75	___
52154	Pacific Fruit Express Refrigerator Car "459403" (Std. O), *98 u*		65	___
52158	Monopoly Mint Car "M-0539", *98*		310	___
52159	Monopoly Depressed Center Flatcar w/ transformer, *98*		95	___
52160	Monopoly Water Works Tank Car, *98*		105	___
52161	Monopoly SP-type Caboose "M-1006", *98*		55	___
52167	AT&SF Flatcar w/ Navajo trailer "83199", *99 u*		80	___
52168	Carail Flatcar with Trailer "17455", *99 u*		95	___
52169	Zep Manufacturing Co. Flatcar w/ trailer "62734", *99 u*		50	___
52172	L&N Boxcar, *99 u*		70	___
52173	Long Island RR F3 AA Shells, *00*		NRS	___
52174	REA Baggage Car "0083", *00 u*		400	___
52176	CB&Q Boxcar "8277", *99 u*		65	___
52180	Milwaukee Road Flatcar w/ trailer "194799", *99 u*		80	___
52181	Monopoly Set #2, 4-pack, *99*		290	___
52182	Monopoly Railroads Boxcar "M0636", *99 u*		85	___
52183	Monopoly Jail Car "M-1131", *99*		75	___
52184	Monopoly Free Parking Flatcar w/ 2 autos, *99*		60	___
52185	Monopoly Chance Gondola "M-0893", *99*		50	___
52186	Grucci Fireworks Boxcar "2000", *00 u*		85	___
52187	Madison Hardware Flatcar w/ 2 trailers "1909-1999", *99*		80	___
52188	Carail Aquarium w/ 2 autos, 25th Anniversary, *99*		95	___
52189	Monopoly 4-6-4 Hudson Locomotive "1999", *99*		530	___
52198	Frisco Boxcar "5477000", *00 u*		46	___
52205	SP Overnight Merchandise Service Boxcar 5-pack "6464-2000", *00 u*		170	___
52207	Lionel Lines SD40, traditional, *00*		600	___
52208	Lionel Lines E/V Caboose, *00 u*		200	___
52209	World's Fair Sleeper/Roomette Car "0183", *01 u*		170	___
52210	Rico Station, *00*		34	___
52218	Monopoly 4-4-2 Steam Freight Set, *00 u*		370	___

GET STARTED TODAY!

- Get track planning ideas and tips in every issue
- Keep up-to-date on the newest trains and accessories
- Learn more about layout wiring and train repairs
- Packed with valuable information on operating and collecting toy trains

The top-selling toy train magazine

CLASSIC TOY TRAINS

Operating • Collecting • Fun

Engine reviews & more

Build this layout!
Benchwork • track • wiring • scenery

• Repair
• Wiri
• Ins

Save 25%

Yes! Send me a 1-year subscription to *Classic Toy Trains* (9 **BIG** issues) for only $39.95. I'll save 25% off the newsstand price.

Name

Address

City   State   Zip

Canadian price $50.00 (GST included, payable in U.S. funds). Foreign price $50.00 (payable in U.S. funds, checks must be drawn on a U.S. bank). Make checks payable to Kalmbach Publishing Co.

Savings based on annual newsstand price of $53.55

4616RH   **SEND NO MONEY NOW!**   L87AC1

Visit www.ClassicTrains.com

BUSINESS REPLY MAIL

FIRST-CLASS MAIL   PERMIT NO. 16   WAUKESHA, WI

POSTAGE WILL BE PAID BY ADDRESSEE

CLASSIC TOY TRAINS
MAGAZINE

PO BOX 1612
WAUKESHA WI 53187-9950

NO POSTAGE
NECESSARY
IF MAILED
IN THE
UNITED STATES

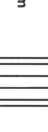

		Exc	New	Cond/$
52219	Monopoly 4-6-4 Bronze Hudson "2000", *00 u*		530	___
52221	Norfolk Southern Boxcar "2001", *01 u*		50	___
52222	SP Daylight Flatcar with trailer, *01 u*		50	___
52224B	SP Flatcar w/ Trailer Flatcar Service tractor and trailer, *01*		25	___
52224A	SP Flatcar w/ Navajo tractor and trailer, *01*		25	___
52225	Monopoly 4-6-4 Pewter Hudson "2001", *01 u*		495	___
52226	Angela Trotta Thomas Boxcar "2000", *01 u*		100	___
52228	Milwaukee Road 1-D Tank Car, *00 u*		50	___
52229	Milwaukee Road 1-D Tank Car, *00 u*		50	___
52230	Milwaukee Road 1-D Tank Car 2-pack, *00 u*		115	___
52231	British Columbia RR 1-D Tank Car, *00 u*		65	___
52232	Central RR of Long Island Boxcar, *01 u*		70	___
52235	World's Fair Vista-Dome Car "0283", *02 u*		NRS	___
52243	National Toy Train Museum 1-Dome Tank Car "1954" (Std. O), *01 u*		50	___
52244	Louisville & Nashville Horse Car, *01*		50	___
52246	Milwaukee Road 2-Door Boxcar "194701", *01 u*		75	___
52248	Tombstone & Western RR Ore Car, *01 u*		40	___
52249	Knoebel's Amusement Park 75th Anniversary Boxcar "9700", *01 u*		85	___
52251	PRR Customized Mail/Cargo Car, *01 u*		55	___
52253	San Pedro Boxcar, *02*		NRS	___
52257	Season's Greetings Gondola "4002", *01*		60	___
52258	UP Flatcar with UP tractor and trailer, *02*		NRS	___
52262	Plasticville Boxcar, *01 u*		120	___
52263	World's Fair Combine Car "0383", *02*		NRS	___
52264	Durango & Silverton Operating Hopper "9325", *02 u*		55	___
52266	PRR "Coal Goes to War" Hopper "707025", *02*		100	___
52267	PRR "Coal Goes to War" Hopper "707026", *02*		100	___
52271	National Toy Train Museum Wheel Car "1957", *02 u*		NRS	___
52272	Lionel Gondola "2002" Gold, *02*		80	___
52276	California Gold Mint Car "2003", *03*		80	___
52290	UP Flatcar w/ tractor trailer, *03 u*		NRS	___
52295	National Toy Train Museum Gondola w/ pipes, *03*		NRS	___
52297	Milwaukee Road 40-foot Boxcar, *03 u*		75	___
52315/52320	PRR FM and Caboose, *04 u*		440	___
52336	U.S. Army Flatcar w/ tractor trailer, *04 u*		115	___
52371	NYC Flatcar w/ tanker trailer, *05 u*		150	___
52422	North Georgia Tinplate Trackers Boxcar, *06 u*		CP	___

No.	Description	New	Cond/S
62162	Automatic Crossing Gate and Signal "262", *99–07*	27	___
62180	Railroad Signs, set of 14, *99–04*	4	___
62181	Telephone Pole Set "150", *99–04*	5	___
62283	Die-Cast Illuminated Bumpers "260", *99–07*	CP	___
62709	Rico Station Kit, *99–00*	46	___
62716	Short Extension Bridge, *99–03*	7	___
62900	Lockon, *99–07*	CP	___
62901	Ives Track Clips, 12 pieces (O-27) , *99–07*	5	___
62905	Lockon with wires, *99–07*	CP	___
62909	Smoke Fluid, *99–07*	CP	___
62927	Lubrication/Maintenance Set, *99–07*	CP	___
62985	The Lionel Train Book, *99–03*	12	___
65014	Half-Curved Track 27" (O27), *99–07*	CP	___
65019	Half-Straight Track (O27), *99–06*	0.75	___
65020	90° Crossover (O27), *99–07*	CP	___
65021	Left Manual Switch 27" (O27), *99–07*	17	___
65021	Left Manual Switch 27" (O27), *99–07*	17	___
65022	Right Manual Switch 27" (O27), *99–06*	18	___
65023	45° Crossover (O27), *99–07*	CP	___
65024	Straight Track 35" (O27), *99–07*	CP	___
65033	Curved Track 27" (O27), *99–07*	CP	___
65038	Straight Track 9" (O27), *99–07*	CP	___
65041	Insulator Pins, 12 pieces (O27), *99–04, 06–07*	CP	___
65042	Steel Pins, 12 pieces (O27), *99–04, 06–07*	CP	___
65049	Curved Track 42" (O27), *99–07*	CP	___
65113	Curved Track 54" (O27), *99–07*	CP	___
65121	Left Remote Switch 27" (O27), *99–07*	CP	___
65122	Right Remote Switch 27" (O27), *99–07*	CP	___
65149	Remote Uncoupling Section (O27), *99–07*	CP	___
65165	Right Remote Switch 72" (O), *99–07*	CP	___
65166	Left Remote Switch 72" (O), *99–07*	CP	___
65167	Right Remote Switch 72" (O27), *99–07*	25	___
65168	Left Remote Switch 42" (O27), *99–07*	25	___
65500	Straight Track 10" (O), *99–07*	CP	___
65501	Curved Track 31" (O), *99–07*	CP	___
65504	Half Curved Track 31" (O), *99–07*	CP	___
65505	Half Straight Track (O), *99–07*	CP	___
65514	Half Curved Track (O-27), *99–03*	3	___
65523	Straight Track 40" (O), *99–06*	CP	___
65530	Remote Uncoupling Section (O), *99–07*	CP	___

		Exc	New	Cond/$
65540	90° Crossover (O), *99–07*		CP	___
65543	Insulator Pins, 12 pieces (O), *99–07*		CP	___
65545	45° Crossover (O), *99–07*		CP	___
65551	Steel Pins, 12 pieces (O), *99–06*		CP	___
65554	Curved Track 54" (O), *99–07*		CP	___
65572	Curved Track 72" (O), *99–07*		CP	___
81024	Christmas Train Set, *02–04*		150	___
81027	Thomas the Tank Engine Set, *01–04*		120	___
99000	Keebler Elf in Express Steam Freight, *99 u*		930	___
99001	Mickey's Holiday Express Freight Set, *99 u*		230	___
99002	Looney Tunes Square Window Caboose, *99 u*		NRS	___
99006	Keebler Flatcar with bulkheads, *99 u*		NRS	___
99007	Smuckers Fudge 1-D Tank Car, *99 u*		75	___
99008	Mickey's Merry Christmas Boxcar "9700", *99 u*		NRS	___
99009	Mickey's Holiday Express S/W Caboose, *99 u*		NRS	___
99013	Case Cutlery Tank Car "1889", *00 u*		NRS	___
99014	Case Cutlery Gondola "1889", *00 u*		NRS	___
99015	Case Cutlery Boxcar "1889", *00 u*		NRS	___
99018	Case Cutlery Rolling Stock 3-pack, *00 u*		200	___
UCS	Remote Control Track (O), *70*	4	7	___

Unnumbered Items

	Exc	New	Cond/$
Amtrak Passenger Set, *89, 89 u*	640	770	___
B&A Hudson and Standard O Car Set, *86 u*	1500	1700	___
Baltimore & Ohio Set, *94, 96*		NRS	___
Black Cave Flyer Playmat, *82*		8	___
Blue Comet Set, *78–80, 87 u*	560	620	___
Burlington "Texas Zephyr" Set, *80, 80 u*	980	1150	___
C&NW Passenger Set, *93*	385	460	___
Cannonball Freight Playmat, *81–82*		8	___
Chesapeake & Ohio Set, *95–96*		NRS	___
Chessie System Special Set, *80, 86 u*	560	620	___
Chicago & Alton Limited Set, *81, 86 u*	560	620	___
Commando Assault Train Playmat, *83–84*		8	___
D&RGW "California Zephyr" Set, *92, 93*		900	___
Erie-Lackawanna Passenger Set, *93, 94*	940	980	___
Erie Set (FF #7), *93*	385	460	___
Favorite Food Freight Set, *81–82*	245	325	___
Frisco Set (FF #5), *91*	405	425	___

	Exc	New	Cond/$
"The General" Set, *77–80*	240	285	___
GN "Empire Builder" Set, *92, 93*	620	730	___
Great Northern Set (FARR #3), *81, 81 u*	620	690	___
IC "City of New Orleans" Set, *85*, 87, *93*	885	1045	___
Illinois Central Set, *91–92, 95*	255	285	___
Jersey Central Set, *86*	345	370	___
Joshua Lionel Cowen Set, *80, 80 u, 82*	540	580	___
L.A.S.E.R. Playmat, *81–82*		8	___
Lionel Lines Madison Car Set, *91, 93*	560	620	___
LL Set, *82–84* u, *86, 86–87* u, *94–95*	530	620	___
Mickey Mouse Express Set, *77–78, 78 u*	980	1600	___
Milwaukee Road Set (FF #2), *87, 90 u*	380	405	___
The Mint Set, *79 u, 80–83, 84 u, 86 u 87, 91 u, 93*	940	1050	___
Missouri Pacific Set, *95*		390	___
N&W "Powhatan Arrow" Set, *81, 81 u 82 u, 91 u*	1450	1700	___
New Haven Set, *94–95*		400	___
New York Central Set, *89, 91*	240	270	___
Nickel Plate Road Set (FF #6), *92*	385	460	___
Norfolk & Western "Powhatan Arrow" Passenger Set, *95*	370	445	___
Northern Pacific Set, *90–92*	190	250	___
NYC "20th Century Limited" Set *83, 83 u, 95*	980	1150	___
Pennsylvania Set, *87–90, 95*	240	270	___
Pere Marquette Set, *93*	720	770	___
PRR Set, *79–80, 79–80* u, *81 u, 83 u*	1200	1350	___
PRR Set (FARR #5), *84–85, 89 u*	600	660	___
Rock Island & Peoria Set, *80–82*	240	315	___
Rocky Mountain Platform, *83–84*		8	___
Santa Fe Set (FARR #1), *79, 79 u*	460	580	___
Santa Fe "Super Chief" Set *91, 91 u, 92 u, 93, 95*	1400	1700	___
Southern Crescent Limited Set *77–78, 87 u*	540	650	___
Southern Pacific Daylight Diesel Set *82–83, 82–83 u, 90 u*	2150	2300	___
Southern Set (FARR #4), *83, 83 u*	620	690	___
SP Daylight Steam Set, *90, 92, 93*	790	940	___
Spirit of '76 Set, *74–76*	570	690	___
Station Platform, *83–84*		8	___

	Exc	New	Cond/$
Toys "R" Us Thunderball Freight Set, *75 u*		NRS	___
Union Pacific Set, *94*	430	500	___
Union Pacific Set (FARR #2), *80*, *80 u*	540	580	___
UP "Overland Route" Set, *84*, *92 u*	770	840	___
Wabash Set (FF #1), *86*, *87*	755	905	___
Western Maryland Set (FF #4), *89*	345	405	___

Section 4
MODERN TINPLATE

O Gauge Classics

		Exc	New	Cond/$
1-263E	Lionel Lines "Blue Comet" 2-4-2		NRS	___
350E	Lionel Lines "Hiawatha" 4-4-2		NRS	___
882	Lionel Lines Combination Car		NRS	___
883	Lionel Lines Passenger Car		NRS	___
884	Lionel Lines Observation Car		NRS	___
1612	Lionel Lines Passenger Car		NRS	___
1613	Lionel Lines Passenger Car		NRS	___
1614	Lionel Lines Baggage Car		NRS	___
1615	Lionel Lines Observation Car		NRS	___
51000	Milwaukee Road "Hiawatha" Set, *88 u*		900	___
51001	Lionel #44 Freight Special Set, *89*		600	___
51004	Blue Comet Set, *91*		1600	___
51100	Lionel Lines Electric "44E", *89*		NRS	___
51201	Rail Chief Passenger Cars, Set of 4, *90*		500	___
51202	Lionel Lines Combination Car "892"		NRS	___
51203	Lionel Lines Passenger Car "893"		NRS	___
51204	Lionel Lines Passenger Car "894"		NRS	___
51205	Lionel Lines Observation Car "895"		NRS	___
51400	Lionel Lines Boxcar "8814", *89*		NRS	___
51500	Lionel Lines Hopper "8816", *89*		NRS	___
51700	Lionel Lines Caboose "8817", *89*		NRS	___
51800	Lionel Lines Searchlight Car "8820", *89*		NRS	___

Standard Gauge Classics

		Exc	New	Cond/$
1-318E	Lionel Lines Electric		NRS	___
1-4390	American Flyer "West Point" Baggage Car		NRS	___
1-4391	American Flyer "Academy" Passenger Car		NRS	___
1-4392	American Flyer "Army/Navy" Observation Car		NRS	___
5130	Lionel Lines Flatcar w/ lumber		NRS	___
5140	Lionel Lines Reefer		NRS	___
5150	Lionel Lines "Shell" Tank Car		NRS	___
5160	Lionel Lines Caboose		NRS	___
13001	1-318E Freight Express Train Set, *90–91*		960	___
13002	Fireball Express Set, *90 u*		1600	___
13003	American Flyer Mayflower Passenger Car Set, *92*		2000	___
13004	Milwaukee Road Hiawatha Passenger Set, *01–02*		2000	___
13008	NYC Commodore Vanderbilt Passenger Set, *02*		1600	___
13100	Lionel Lines 2-4-2 "1-390E", *88 u*		610	___

		Exc	New	Cond/$
13101	Lionel Lines 2-4-0 "1-384E", *89 u*		650	___
13102	Lionel Lines Electric "1-381E", *89 u*		880	___
13103	Lionel Lines "Blue Comet" 4-4-4 "1-400E", *90*		1350	___
13104	Lionel Lines "Old #7" 4-4-0 "7E", *90*		900	___
13106	Lionel Lines "Fireball Express" 2-4-2 "2-390E"		NRS	___
13107	Lionel Lines Electric "1-408E", *91*		880	___
13108	Lionel Lines 4-4-4 "2-400E," Gray, *91*		1100	___
13109	American Flyer Mayflower Electric "1-4689", *92*		2500	___
13200	Lionel Lines Searchlight Car "1520", *89 u*		110	___
13300	Lionel Lines Gondola "1512", *89 u*		75	___
13303	Lionel Lines Sunoco Tank Car "1-215", *92*		135	___
13400	Lionel Lines Baggage Car "323", *88 u*		155	___
13401	Lionel Lines Passenger Car "324", *88 u*		135	___
13402	Lionel Lines Observation Car "325", *88 u*		135	___
13403	Lionel Lines State Passenger Car Set, *89 u*		1100	___
13404	Lionel Lines "California" Passenger Car "1412"		NRS	___
13405	Lionel Lines "Colorado" Passenger Car "1413"		NRS	___
13406	Lionel Lines "New York" Observation Car "1416"		NRS	___
13407	Lionel Lines "Illinois" Passenger Car "1414", *90*		450	___
13408	Lionel Lines "Blue Comet" Passenger Car Set, *90*		1500	___
13409	Lionel Lines "Faye" Passenger Car "1420"		NRS	___
13410	Lionel Lines "Westphal" Passenger Car "1421"		NRS	___
13411	Lionel Lines "Tempel" Observation Car "1422"		NRS	___
13412	Lionel Lines "Old #7" Passenger Car Set, *90*		800	___
13413	Lionel Lines Combination Car "183"		NRS	___
13414	Lionel Lines Passenger Car "184"		NRS	___
13415	Lionel Lines Observation Car "185"		NRS	___
13416	Lionel Lines "New Jersey" Baggage Car "326"		NRS	___
13417	Lionel Lines "Connecticut" Passenger Car "327"		NRS	___
13418	Lionel Lines "New York" Observation Car "328"		NRS	___
13420	Lionel Lines State Passenger Car Set, *91*		1300	___
13421	Lionel Lines "California" Passenger Car "2412"		NRS	___
13422	Lionel Lines "Colorado" Passenger Car "2413"		NRS	___
13423	Lionel Lines "Illinois" Passenger Car "2414", *92 u*		450	___
13424	Lionel Lines "New York" Observation Car "2416"		NRS	___
13425	Lionel Lines "Benard" Passenger Car "1423", *91 u*		1350	___
13600	Lionel Lines Cattle Car "1513", *89 u*		90	___
13601	Season's Greetings Boxcar, *89 u*		105	___
13602	Season's Greetings Boxcar, *90 u*		100	___
13604	Season's Greetings Boxcar, *91 u*		110	___
13605	Lionel Lines Boxcar "1-214", *92*		155	___
13700	Lionel Lines Caboose "1517", *89 u*		105	___
13702	Lionel Lines Caboose "1217", *91*		115	___
13800	Lionelville Passenger Station "1115", *88 u*		390	___

		Exc	New	Cond/$
13801	Lionelville Station "126", *89 u*		290	___
13802	Lionel Runabout Boat, *90*		400	___
13803	Lionel Racing Automobiles "8" and "9", *91*		770	___
13804	Lionelville Switch Tower "437", *91*		400	___
13805	Lionel Racing Boat "1-44", *91*		410	___
13807	Racing Automobiles Straight Track, *91 u*		NRS	___
13808	Racing Automobiles Inner Radius Curve Track, *91 u*		NRS	___
13809	Racing Automobiles Outer Radius Curve Track, *91 u*		NRS	___
13900	Electric Rapid Transit Trolley "200", *89 u*		290	___
13901	Electric Rapid Transit Trolley Trailer "201", *89 u*		150	___
51900	Signal Bridge and Control Panel "4400C", *89 u*		399	___

Section 5
CLUB CARS AND SPECIAL PRODUCTION

Artrain

___	**9486**	GTW "I Love Michigan" Boxcar, *87*
___	**17885**	1-D Tank Car, *90*
___	**17891**	Grand Trunk Boxcar, *91*
___	**19425**	Artrain 25th Anniversary CSX Flatcar w/ trailer, *97*
___	**52013**	Norfolk Southern Flatcar w/ trailer (Std. O), *92*
___	**52024**	Conrail Auto Carrier, *93*
___	**52049**	Burlington Northern Gondola w/ coil covers, *94*
___	**52097**	Chessie System Reefer, *95*
___	**52140**	Union Pacific Bunk Car, *97*
___	**52165**	SP Caboose "6256", *97*
___	**52197**	Santa Fe GP38 Diesel Locomotive, *00*
___	**52227**	Space Boxcar, *01*
___	**52255**	30th Anniversary Flatcar w/ billboard, *01*

Carnegie Science Center

___	**26750**	Great Miniature Railroad and Village Boxcar "9700", *99*
___	**36202**	Great Miniature Railroad 80th Anniversary Boxcar "9700", *00*
___	**36234**	Great Miniature Railroad and Village Boxcar "9700", *01*
___	**52277**	Carnegie Science Center 10th Anniversary Boxcar "9700", *02*
___	**52332**	Carnegie Science Center Boxcar, *03*
___	**52362**	Carnegie Science Center Boxcar, *04*
___	**52399**	Carnegie Science Center Boxcar, *05*

Chicagoland Railroad Club

___	**52081**	C&NW Boxcar "6464555", *96*
___	**52101**	BN Maxi-Stack Flatcar w/ containers "64287", *97*
___	**52102**	Santa Fe E/V Caboose "999556" w/ black roof, *96*
___	**52103**	Santa Fe E/V Caboose "999758" w/ red roof, *96*
___	**52120**	Shedd Aquarium Car "3435-557", *98*
___	**52148**	REA/Santa Fe Boxcar "52148-558", *99*
___	**52170**	SP Operating Boxcar "52170-561", *99*
___	**52171**	UP Operating Boxcar "52171-561", *99*
___	**52178**	Burlington Operating Boxcar "52178-559", *00*
___	**52179**	ACL Operating Boxcar "52179-500", *00*
___	**52215**	CNW 3-Bay Cylindrical Hopper, *01*
___	**52216**	C&NW Cylindrical Hopper (Std. O), *02*
___	**52223**	Santa Fe REA Operating Boxcar, 00
___	**52251**	PRR Customized Mail/Cargo Car, *01*
___	**52259**	MP GP20 "28500," traditional, *01*
___	**52279**	Dragoon & Northern Ore Car, *02*

___ **52282** Western Pacific Feather Boxcar, red "2003", *03*
___ **52287** Minute Man Operating Boxcar, *03*

Classic Toy Trains

___ **52126** MILW Boxcar w/ CTT Logo "21027", 97

Dept. 56

___ **16270** Heritage Village Boxcar, *98*
___ **52096** Snow Village Boxcar "9756", *95*
___ **52139** Square Window Caboose "6256", *97*
___ **52157** Holly Brothers 3-D Tank Car, *98*
___ **52175** 4-6-4 Hudson "NO. 56" Steam Locomotive, CC, *99*
___ **52199** Real Plastic Snow 4-Bay Hopper "6756", *00*
___ **52254** "Happy Holidays" Gondola, *01*

Eastwood Automobilia

___ **16275** Radio Flyer Boxcar "16275", *96*
___ **16757** Johnny Lightning Auto Carrier "3435", *96*
___ **16985** Flatcar w/ 2 Ford vans, *97*
___ **26049** Disney Speed Boat Willie with boat, *05*
___ **36219** UP Boxcar "183518", *2002*
___ **52044** Vat Car, *95*
___ **52083** PRR Flat w/ tanker, "21697", *95*
___ **52130** Hot Wheels TOFC w/ tank trailer, *97*

Houston Tinplate Operators Society (HTOS)

___ **8901** Miracle Petroleum 1-Dome Tank Car, *01*
___ **8999** Lone Star Aquarium Car, *99*
___   Sam Houston Mint Car "8901", *00*

Inland Empire Train Collectors Association (IETCA)

___ **1979** Boxcar, *79*
___ **1980** SP-type Caboose, *80*
___ **1981** Quad Hopper, *81*
___ **1982** 3-D Tank Car, *82*
___ **1983** Reefer, *83*
___ **1986** Bunk Car, *86*
___ **7518** Carson City Mint Car, *84*

Lionel Central Operating Lines (LCOL)

___	**1981**	Boxcar, *81*
___	**1986**	Work Caboose, shell only, *86*
___	**5724**	Pennsylvania Bunk Car, *84*
___	**6508**	Canadian Pacific Crane Car, *83*
___	**9184**	Erie B/W Caboose, *82*
___	**9475**	D&H "I Love NY" Boxcar, *85*

Lionel Collectors Association of Canada (LCAC)

___	**5710**	Canadian Pacific Reefer, *83*
___	**5714**	Michigan Central Reefer, *85*
___	**6100**	Ontario Northland Covered Quad Hopper, *82*
___	**8103**	Toronto, Hamilton & Buffalo Boxcar, *81*
___	**8204**	Algoma Central Boxcar, *82*
___	**8507/8508**	Canadian National F3 AA, shells only, *85*
___	**8912**	Canada Southern Operating Hopper, *89*
___	**9413**	Napierville Junction Boxcar, *80*
___	**9718**	Canadian National Boxcar, *79*
___	**17893**	BAOC 1-D Tank Car "914", *91*
___	**52004**	Algoma Central Gondola w/ coil covers "9215", *92*
___	**52005**	Canadian National F3 B Unit "9517", *93*
___	**52006**	Canadian Pacific Boxcar "930016" (Std. O), *93*
___	**52115**	Wabash Lake Railway 2-Tier Auto Carrier "WL 9519", *98*
___	**52125**	Toronto, Hamilton & Buffalo Gondola 2-pack "2346-2354", *99*
___	**86009**	Canadian National Bunk Car, *86*
___	**87010**	Canadian National Express Reefer, *87*
___	**88011**	Canadian National Woodside Caboose (Std. O), *88*
___	**830005**	Canadian National Boxcar, *83*
___	**840006**	Canadian Wheat Board Covered Quad Hopper, *84*
___	**900013**	Canadian National Flatcar w/ trailers, *90*

Lionel Collectors Club of America (LCCA)

LCCA National Convention Cars

___	**6112**	Commonwealth Edison Quad Hopper w/ coal load, *83*
___	**6323**	Virginia Chemicals 1-D Tank Car, *86*
___	**6567**	Illinois Central Gulf Crane Car "100408", *85*
___	**7403**	LNAC Boxcar, *84*
___	**8068**	Rock Island GP20 "1980", *80*
___	**9118**	Corning Covered Quad Hopper, *74*
___	**9155**	Monsanto 1-D Tank Car, *75*
___	**9212**	Seaboard Coast Line Flatcar w/ trailers, *76*

CLUB CARS AND SPECIAL PRODUCTION

___	**X9259**	Southern B/W Caboose, *77*
___	**9358**	Sands of Iowa Covered Quad Hopper, *80*
___	**9435**	Central of Georgia Boxcar, *81*
___	**9460**	D&TS Double-Door Boxcar, *82*
___	**9701**	Baltimore & Ohio Double Door Boxcar, *72*
___	**9727**	TA&G Boxcar, *73*
___	**9728**	Union Pacific Stock Car, *78*
___	**9733**	Airco Boxcar w/ tank, *79*
___	**17870**	East Camden & Highland Boxcar (Std. O), *87*
___	**17873**	Ashland Oil 3-D Tank Car, *88*
___	**17876**	Columbia, Newberry & Laurens Boxcar (Std. O), *89*
___	**17880**	D&RGW Wood-sided Caboose (Std. O), *90*
___	**17887**	Conrail Flatcar w/ Armstrong Tile trailer (Std. O), *91*
___	**17888**	Conrail Flatcar w/ Ford New Holland trailer (Std. O), *91*
___	**17899**	NASA Uni-body Tank Car "190" (Std. O), *92*
___	**18090**	D&RGW 4-6-2 "1990", *90*
___	**52023**	D&TS 2-bay ACF Hopper "2601" (Std. O), *93*
___	**52038**	Southern Hopper w/ coal load "360794" (Std. O), *94*
___	**52074**	Iowa Beef Packers Reefer "197095" (Std. O), *95*
___	**52090**	Pere Marquette DD Boxcar "71996" (Std. O), *96*
___	**52107**	On-Track Pickup, orange, *96*
___	**52108**	On-Track Van, blue, *96*
___	**52110**	CStPM&O Boxcar "71997" (Std. O), *97*
___	**52151**	Amtrak Express Baggage Boxcar "71998" (Std. O), *98*
___	**52176**	Fort Worth & Denver Boxcar "8277" (Std. O), *99*
___	**52195**	CP Maxi-stack Flatcar "200030", *00*
___	**52206**	SD40 w/ E/V Caboose "2000", *00*
___	**52244**	Louisville & Nashville Horse Car "2001", *01*
___	**52266**	PRR "Coal Goes To War" Hopper "707025", *02*
___	**52267**	PRR "Coal Goes To War" Hopper "707026", *02*
___	**52273**	Flatcar w/ submarine, *02*
___	**52299**	UP Las Vegas Jackpot Security Transport "2003", *03*

LCCA Meet Specials

___	**6014-900**	Frisco Boxcar (O27), *75-76*
___	**6483**	Jersey Central SP-type Caboose, *82*
___	**9016**	Chessie System Hopper (O27), *79-80*
___	**9036**	Mobilgas 1-D Tank Car (O27), *78-79*
___	**9142**	Republic Steel Gondola w/ canisters, *77-78*
___		Lionel Lines Tender only, *76-77*

Other LCCA Production

___	**9739**	D&RGW Boxcar, *78*
___	**9771**	Norfolk & Western Boxcar, *77*
___	**17895**	LCCA Tractor, *91*
___	**17896**	Lancaster Lines Tractor, *91*

CLUB CARS AND SPECIAL PRODUCTION

___ **29232** Lenny the Lion Hi-Cube, signed by Lenny Dean, *99*
___ **52025** Madison Hardware Tractor and Trailer, *93*
___ **52039** "Track 29" Bumper, *94*
___ **52055** SOVEX Tractor and Trailer, *94*
___ **52056** Southern Tractor and Trailer "206502", *94*
___ **52091** Lenox Tractor and Trailer, *95*
___ **52092** Iowa Interstate Tractor and Trailer, *95*
___ **52100** Station Platform, *98*
___ **52100** Grand Rapids Station Platform, *96*
___ **52152** Philadelphia Reefer, *98*
___ **52153** 6414 Auto Set (4-pack), *98*
___ **52207** Lionel Lines SD40 and Caboose, Traditional, *00*
___ **52257** Season's Greetings Gondola, *01*
___ **52343** Milwaukee Reefer, *04*
___ **6464-2002** Maddox Retirement Boxcar "02", *02*
___ RJ Corman RR Boxcar "4002", *01*

Lionel Opoerating Train Society (LOTS)

LOTS National Convention Cars

___ **303** Stauffer Chemical 1-D Tank Car, *85*
___ **3764** Kahn Boxcar, *81*
___ **6111** L&N Covered Quad Hopper, *83*
___ **6211** C&O Gondola w/ canisters, *86*
___ **9414** Cotton Belt Boxcar, *80*
___ **16812** Grand Trunk 2-bay ACF Hopper "16812" (Std. O), *96*
___ **16813** Pennsylvania Power & Light Co. Hopper
w/ coal load (Std. O), *97*
___ **17874** Milwaukee Road Log Dump Car "59629", *88*
___ **17875** PHD Boxcar "1289", *89*
___ **17882** B&O DD Boxcar w/ ETD "298011", *90*
___ **17890** CSX Auto Carrier "151161", *91*
___ **18890** Union Pacific RS-3 "8805", *90*
___ **19960** Western Pacific Boxcar "1952" (Std. O), *92*
___ **20061** OSBC Refrigerator Car, *06*
___ **38356** Dow Chemical 3-D Tank Car, *87*
___ **52014** BN TTUX Flatcar set w/ N&W trailers "637500A/B", *93*
___ **52041** BN TTUX Flatcar set w/ Conrail trailers "637500D/E", *94*
___ **52067** Burlington Ice Car "50240", *95*
___ **52135** AT&SF Reefer "22739", *98*
___ **52162** GM&O DD Boxcar "24580", *99*
___ **52196** CP Maxi-stack Flatcar w/ 2 containers "524115", *00*
___ **52234** WM F9 Well Car with transformer, *01*
___ **52261** Schlitz Beer/URT Refrigerator Car "92132", *02*
___ **52280** Product Mint Car, *02*
___ **52281** PRR Operating Boxcar, *03*

CLUB CARS AND SPECIAL PRODUCTION

___ **52309**   Patriotic Tank Car, *03*
___ **52342**   Stockcar w/ Sound, *04*
___ **52346**   D&H PS-2 Hopper, *06*
___ **52347**   SF SD-80 TMCC, *04*
___ **52381**   Virginian Hopper, *05*
___ **52382**   SF Caboose, *05*
___ **52413**   Steel-sided Reefer, *06*
___ **52419**   Layout Mint Car, *04*
___ **52425**   SP&S Boxcar (Std. O), *07*
___ **52456**   Alpenrose Dairy Milk Car, *07*
___ **80948**   Michigan Central Boxcar, *82*
___ **121315**   Pennsylvania Hi-cube Boxcar, *84*

Other LOTS Production

___ **1223**   Seattle & North Coast Hi-cube Boxcar, *86*
___ **12958**   LCCA/LOTS Banquet Water Tower, *00*
___ **52042**   BN TTUX Flatcar w/ Canadian National trailer "637500C", *94*
___ **52048**   Canadian National Tractor and Trailer "197993", *94*
___ **52129**   Lighted Billboard (Scranton), *97*
___ **52217**   LCCA/LOTS 2000 Convention Billboard, *00*
___ **52260**   National Aquarium in Baltimore Car "2001", *01*

Lionel Century Club (LCC)

___ **14532**   PRR Sharknose AA Set, LCC II, *00*
___ **18053**   Berkshire Steam Locomotive 2-8-4 "726", *97*
___ **18057**   Steam Locomotive 6-8-6 "671", *98*
___ **18058**   Hudson Steam Locomotive 4-6-4 "773", *97*
___ **18135**   NYC F-3 AA Diesel "2333", *97*
___ **18178**   NYC F-3 B-Unit, *99*
___ **18314**   PRR GG-1 "2332", *97*
___ **18340**   FM Demo Train Master Set, "TM-1," "TM-2", LCC II, *00*
___ **28069**   NYC 4-8-6 Niagara "6024" Steam Locomotive, CC, LCC II, *00*
___ **29204**   Boxcar "1900-2000", *96*
___ **29226**   Berkshire Boxcar, *97*
___ **29227**   GG-1 Boxcar, *98*
___ **29228**   Turbine Boxcar "671", *99*
___ **39201**   Century Club Hudson Boxcar "773", *00*
___ **29248**   F3 Boxcar "2333", *99*
___ **38000**   NYC 4-6-4 Hudson Empire State Steam Locomotive, LCC II, *00*
___ **38195**   Santa Fe FT A Unit "170", *00*
___ **39215**   Niagara Boxcar, LCC II, *01*
___ **39217**   Boxcar, LCC II, *00*
___ **39218**   Gold Boxcar, LCC II, *00*
___ **39249**   Christmas Boxcar, *03*
___ **51007**   UP M-10000 Passenger Set, LCC II, *00*

Lionel Railroader Club (LRRC)

___	**0780**	Boxcar, *82*
___	**0781**	Flatcar w/ trailers, *83*
___	**0782**	1-D Tank Car, *85*
___	**0784**	Covered Quad Hopper, *84*
___	**12875**	Tractor and Trailer, *94*
___	**12921**	Illuminated Station Platform, *95*
___	**16800**	Ore Car, *86*
___	**16801**	Bunk Car, *88*
___	**16802**	Tool Car, *89*
___	**16803**	Searchlight Car, *90*
___	**16804**	B/W Caboose, *91*
___	**18680**	Countdown Hudson 4-6-4 "2000", *00*
___	**18684**	Pacific 4-6-2 "1999", *99*
___	**18818**	GP38-2 "1992", *92*
___	**19437**	Flatcar w/ inside track trailer "1997", *97*
___	**19473**	Operating Log Dump Car "3351", *99*
___	**19685**	Western Union Dining Car, *02*
___	**19695**	Western Union 1-Dome Tank Car, *03*
___	**19774**	Caboose Porthole "1999", *99*
___	**19775**	Stock Car, *99*
___	**19924**	Boxcar, *93*
___	**19930**	Quad Hopper w/ coal load, *94*
___	**19935**	1-D Tank Car "1995", *95*
___	**19940**	Vat Car, *96*
___	**19953**	Lionel Corporation Boxcar "6464-97", *97*
___	**19965**	Aquarium Car "3435", *99*
___	**19966**	Gondola "9820" (Std. O), *98*
___	**19978**	LRRC Membership Kit, *99-00*
___	**19991**	LRRC Gold Member Boxcar, *00*
___	**19992**	Western Union Tool Car "3550", *00*
___	**19994**	Western Union Sleeping Car "1307", *01*
___	**19995**	25th Anniversary Boxcar (Std. O), *01*
___	**26089**	Western Union Gondola w/ handcar, *05*
___	**26165**	Western Union Refrigerator Car, *04*
___	**26521**	Western Union Searchlight Caboose, *04*
___	**28062**	Century 4-6-4 Hudson "2000", *00*
___	**28665**	Western Union Berkshire 2-8-4 Locomotive "665", *05*
___	**29200**	Lionel Corporation Boxcar "9700", *96*
___	**36769**	4th of July Boxcar, *03*
___	**39264**	Holiday Boxcar, *04*

Lionel Railroad Club Milwaukee

___	**52116**	Milwaukee Road Flatcar w/ tractor and trailer "194797", *97*
___	**52163**	Milwaukee Road Double Door Boxcar "194798", *98*
___	**52180**	Milwaukee Road Flatcar w/ trailer "194799", *00*
___	**52228**	CMSt&P 1-Dome Water Tank Car "908309", *00*
___	**52229**	Milwaukee Road 1-Dome Fuel Tank Car "907797", *00*
___	**52230**	Milwaukee Road 1-Dome Tank Car 2-pack, *00*
___	**52246**	Milwaukee Road 2-Door Boxcar "194701", *01*
___	**52265**	Milwaukee Road/Zoological Society Aquarium Car "4701", *02*
___	**52278**	Milwaukee Road/Zoological Society Aquarium Car, *03*
___	**52297**	Milwaukee Road Reefer "194703", *03*
___	**52298**	Milwaukee Road Flatcar w/ trailer "194704", *04*
___	**52337**	Milwaukee Road/Zoo Motorized Aquarium Car "4703", *04*
___	**52368**	Milwaukee Road Flatcar, black "472004", *05*
___	**52370**	CMSt&P Milk Car "364", *05*
___	**52369**	Milwaukee Road/Trailer Train Auto Carrier "194705", *05*
___	**52387**	CMSt&P Flatcar "194706", *06*
___	**52400**	Milwaukee Road PS-2 2-Bay Hopper, orange, "99607", *06*
___	**52401**	Milwaukee Road PS-2 2-Bay Hopper, yellow, "98809", *06*
___	**52402**	CMSt&P URTX Ice Car "4706", *06*
___	**52428**	CMSt&P 0-4-0 Engine and Caboose set, *06*
___	**52429**	CMSt&P 0-4-0 Engine, *06*
___	**52430**	CMSt&P Offset Cupola Caboose, *06*

Nassau Lionel Operating Engineers (NLOE)

___	**8389**	Long Island Boxcar, *89*
___	**8390**	Long Island Covered Quad Hopper, *90*
___	**8391A**	Long Island Bunk Car, *91*
___	**8391B**	Long Island Tool Car, *91*
___	**8392**	Long Island 1-D Tank Car, *92*
___	**52007**	Long Island RS-3 "1552", *93*
___	**52019**	Long Island Boxcar "8393", *93*
___	**52020**	Long Island B/W Caboose "8393", *93*
___	**52026**	Long Island Flatcar w/ Grumman trailer "8394", *94*
___	**52061**	Long Island Stern's Pickle Products Vat Car "8395", *95*
___	**52072**	Grumman Tractor, *94*
___	**52076**	Long Island Observation Car "8396", *96*
___	**52112**	Long Island Full Vista Dome Passenger Car "9783", *97*
___	**52122**	Meenan Oil 1-D Tank Car "8397" (Std. O.), *97*
___	**52123**	Long Island Aluminum Diner Car, "9883", *98*
___	**52144**	Long Island Flatcar w/ Grumman van (TT), *99*
___	**52145**	Long Island Passenger Coaches, "9983-1", "9983-2", *99*
___	**52166**	Long Island Flatcar w/ Grumman trailer "8398", *98*
___	**52173**	Long Island RR F3 AA Shells, *00*

CLUB CARS AND SPECIAL PRODUCTION

___	**52174**	REA Baggage Car "0083", *00*
___	**52186**	Grucci Fireworks Boxcar, *00*
___	**52209**	World's Fair Sleeper/Roomette Car "0183", *01*
___	**52232**	Central RR of Long Island Boxcar, *01*
___	**52235**	World's Fair Vista-Dome Car "0283", *02*
___	**52256**	New York & Atlantic Boxcar "8302", *02*
___	**52263**	World's Fair Combine Car "0383", *02*
___	**52296**	Republic TOFC, *03*
___	**52341**	Long Island Flatcar w/ trailer, *05*

Railroad Museum of Long Island

___	**52416**	LIRR 15th Anniversary Boxcar, *06*
___	**52433**	Atlantis Marine World Aquarium Car, *06*
___	**52453**	North Fork Bank Car, *07*

St. Louis Lionel Railroad Club (St. Louis LRRC)

___	**52099**	MP Flatcar w/ St. Louis trailer, *96*
___	**52104**	St. Louis T&T, *96*
___	**52117**	Wabash Flatcar w/ REA tractor and trailer, *97*
___	**52136A**	Christmas Special Tractor and Trailer, *97*
___	**52136B**	Frisco Special Tractor and Trailer, *98*
___	**52147**	Frisco Campbell TOFC Flatcar (TT), *98*
___	**52150**	Frisco Campbell TOFC Flatcar (TT), *98*
___	**52167**	AT&SF Flatcar w/ Navajo trailers "831999", *99*
___	**52190**	IC Flatcar w/ trailers, *00*
___	**52222**	SSW (Cotton Belt) Flatcar w/ SP tractor and trailer, *01*
___	**52224A**	SP Flatcar w/ Navajo tractor and trailer, *01*
___	**52224B**	SP Flatcar w/ Service tractor and trailer, *01*
___	**52258**	UP Flatcar w/ UP tractor and trailer, *02*
___	**52392**	PRR Flatcar w/ Hoods Milk tractor and tank, *06*

Train Collectors Association (TCA)

TCA National Convention Cars

___	**0511**	St. Louis Baggage Car "1981", *81*
___	**5734**	REA Reefer, *85*
___	**6315**	Pittsburgh 1-D Tank Car, *72*
___	**6464-1970**	Chicago Boxcar, *70*
___	**6464-1971**	Disneyland Boxcar, *71*
___	**6926**	New Orleans E/V Caboose, *86*
___	**7205**	Denver Combination Car "1982", *82*

CLUB CARS AND SPECIAL PRODUCTION

__	**7206**	Louisville Passenger Car "1983", *83*
__	**7212**	Pittsburgh Passenger Car "1984", *84*
__	**7812**	Houston Stock Car, *77*
__	**8476**	4-6-4 "5484", *85*
__	**9123**	Dearborn Auto Carrier "1973", 3-tier, *73*
__	**9319**	Silver Jubilee Mint Car, *79*
__	**9544**	Chicago Observation Car "1980", *80*
__	**9611**	Boston Hi-cube Boxcar, *78*
__	**9774**	Orlando Southern Belle Boxcar, *75*
__	**9779**	Philadelphia Boxcar "9700-1976", *76*
__	**9864**	Seattle Reefer, *74*
__	**11737**	TCA 40th Anniversary F3 ABA Set "40", *93*
__	**17879**	Valley Forge Dining Car "1989", *89*
__	**17883**	New Georgia Railroad Passenger Car "1990", *90*
__	**17898**	Wabash Reefer "21596", *92*
__	**52008**	Bucyrus Erie Crane Car "1993X", *93*
__	**52035**	Yorkrail GP9 "1750", shell only, *94*
__	**52036**	TCA 40th Anniversary B/W Caboose, *94*
__	**52037**	Yorkrail GP9 "1754", *94*
__	**52062**	"Skytop" Observation Car "1995", *95*
__	**52085**	Full Vista Dome Car "1996", *96*
__	**52106**	"City of Phoenix" Diner "1997", *97*
__	**52142**	Massachusetts Central Maxi-Stack "5100-01", *98*
__	**52143**	"City of Providence" Passenger Car "1998", *98*
__	**52146**	Ocean Spray Reefer, *98*
__	**52155**	"City of San Francisco" Baggage Car "1999", *99*
__	**52191**	"City of Grand Rapids" Duplex Aluminum Passenger, *00*
__	**52198**	Frisco Boxcar "5477000", *00*
__	**52210**	Rico Station, *00*
__	**52220**	"City of Chattanooga" Vista Dome Car "2001", *01*
__	**52221**	Norfolk Southern Boxcar "2001", *01*
__	**52250**	"City of Chicago" Combo Car "2002", *02*
__	**52310**	Working on the Railroad Boxcar, *04*
__	**52333**	Harmony Dairy Milk Car, *04*
__	**52340**	Train Order Building, *04*
__	**52372**	"Working on the Railroad" Baggage Car, *05*
__	**52376**	GN Refrigerator Car, *05*

TCA Museum-Related Cars

__	**1018-1979**	Mortgage Burning Hi-cube Boxcar, *79*
__	**5731**	L&N Reefer, *90*
__	**7780**	TCA Museum Boxcar, *80*
__	**7781**	Hafner Boxcar, *81*
__	**7782**	Carlisle & Finch Boxcar, *82*
__	**7783**	Ives Boxcar, *83*
__	**7784**	Voltamp Boxcar, *84*

CLUB CARS AND SPECIAL PRODUCTION

___	**7785**	Hoge Boxcar, *85*
___	**9771**	Norfolk & Western Boxcar, *77*
___	**16811**	Rutland Boxcar "5477096", *96*
___	**52045**	Penn Dutch Milk Car "61052", *94*
___	**52051**	Baltimore & Ohio "Sentinel" Boxcar "6464095", *95*
___	**52052**	TCA 40th Anniversary Boxcar, *94*
___	**52063**	NYC "Pacemaker" Boxcar "6464125", *95*
___	**52064**	Missouri Pacific Boxcar "6464150", *95*
___	**52065**	Penn-Dutch Grain Operating Boxcar "9208", *01*
___	**52118**	Rio Grande Boxcar "5477097", *97*
___	**52119**	TCA Museum 20th Anniversary Boxcar, *97*
___	**52128**	Pennsylvania Dutch Pretzels Boxcar, *99*
___	**52172**	L&N Share the Freedom Boxcar "5477099", *99*
___	**52198**	Frisco Boxcar "5477000", *00*
___	**52226**	Angela Trotta Thomas Boxcar "2000", *01*
___	**52242**	Lionel Gondola "2002", blue, *02*
___	**52243**	National Toy Train Museum 1-Dome Tank Car 1954, *01*
___	**52271**	National Toy Train Museum Wheel Car "1957", *02*

TCA Bicentennial Special Set

___	**1973**	Bicentennial Observation Car, *76*
___	**1974**	Bicentennial Passenger Car, *76*
___	**1975**	Bicentennial Passenger Car, *76*
___	**1976**	Bicentennial U36B, *76*

Atlantic Division

___	**1980**	Atlantic Division Flatcar w/ trailers, *80*
___	**6101**	Burlington Northern Covered Quad Hopper, *82*
___	**9186**	Conrail N5C Caboose, *79*
___	**9193**	Budweiser Vat Car, *84*
___	**9466**	Wanamaker Boxcar, *83*
___	**9788**	Lehigh Valley Boxcar, *78*
___		Pennsylvania Reading Seashore Bunk Car, *85*

Desert Division

___	**52088**	Desert Division 25th Anniversary On-Track Step Van, *96*
___	**52105**	Superstition Mountain Operating Gondola "61997", *97*

Dixie Division

___	**52127**	Dixie Division 10th Anniversary Southern 3-Bay Hopper "360997", *98*

Eastern Division

___	**52059**	Clinchfield Quad Hopper w/ coal load "16413", *94*

CLUB CARS AND SPECIAL PRODUCTION

Eastern Division: Washington, Baltimore & Annapolis Chapter

___ **9412**   Richmond, Fredericksburg & Potomac Boxcar, *79*
___ **9740**   Chessie System Boxcar, *76*
___ **9771**   Norfolk & Western Boxcar, *78*
___ **9783**   B&O Time-Saver Boxcar, *77*

Fort Pitt Division

___ **1984-30X**   Heinz Ketchup Boxcar, *84*

Great Lakes Division

___ **9740**   Chessie System Boxcar, *76*
___ **1983**   Churchill Downs Boxcar, *83*
___ **1983**   Churchill Downs Reefer, *83*

Great Lakes Division: Detroit-Toledo Chapter

___ **8957**   Burlington Northern GP20, *80*
___ **8958**   Burlington Northern GP20 Dummy, *80*
___ **9119**   Detroit & Mackinac Covered Quad Hopper, *77*
___ **9272**   New Haven B/W Caboose, *79*
___ **9401**   Great Northern Boxcar, *78*
___ **9730**   CP Rail Boxcar, *76*
___ **52000**   Detroit-Toledo Division Flatcar w/ trailer, *92*

Great Lakes Division: Three Rivers Chapter

___ **9113**   Norfolk & Western Quad Hopper, *76*

Great Lakes Division: Western Michigan Chapter

___ **9730**   CP Rail Boxcar, *74*

Lake & Pines Division

___ **52018**   3-M Boxcar, *93*

Lone Star Division

___ **7522**   New Orleans Mint Car w/ coin, *86*
___ **52093**   Lone Star Division Boxcar "6464696", *96*

Lone Star Division: North Texas Chapter

___ **9739**   D&RGW Boxcar, *76*
___   Texas Special F3 A Unit, shell only, *81*
___   Texas Special F3 B Unit, shell only, *82*

CLUB CARS AND SPECIAL PRODUCTION

METCA

___	**10**	Jersey Central F3 A Unit, shell only, *71*
___	**9272**	New Haven B/W Caboose, *79*
___	**9754**	New York Central "Pacemaker" Boxcar, *76*

Midwest Division

___	**4**	C&NW F3 A Unit, shell only, *77*
___	**00005**	Midwest Division Covered Quad Hopper, *78*
___	**1287**	C&NW Reefer, *84*
___	**1988**	Illinois Central Boxcar, *88*
___	**7600**	Frisco "Spirit of '76" N5C Caboose "00003", *76*
___	**9725**	Midwest Division Stock Car "00002", *75*
___	**9872**	PFE Reefer "00006", *79*
___	**52237**	Lionel Gondola "2002," yellow, *01*
___	**52238**	Lionel Gondola "2002," red, *01*
___	**52239**	Lionel Gondola "2002," silver, *01*
___	**52240**	Lionel Gondola 3-pack "2002", *01*
___	**52241**	Lionel Gondola "2002," black, *02*
___	**52242**	Lionel Gondola "2002," blue, *02*
___	**52272**	Lionel Gondola "2002," gold, *02*

Midwest Division: Museum Express

___	**9264**	Illinois Central Gulf Covered Quad Hopper, *78*
___	**9289**	Chicago & North Western N5C Caboose, *80*
___	**9785**	Conrail Boxcar, *77*
___	**9786**	Chicago & North Western Boxcar, *79*

NETCA

___	**1203**	Boston & Maine NW-2, shell only, *72*
___	**5710**	Canadian Pacific Reefer, *82*
___	**5716**	Vermont Central Reefer, *83*
___	**6124**	Delaware & Hudson Covered Quad Hopper, *84*
___	**8051**	Hood's Milk Boxcar, *86*
___	**9181**	Boston & Maine N5C Caboose, *77*
___	**9400**	Conrail Boxcar, *78*
___	**9415**	Providence & Worcester Boxcar, *79*
___	**9423**	NYNH&H Boxcar, *80*
___	**9445**	Vermont Northern Boxcar, *81*
___	**9753**	Maine Central Boxcar, *75*
___	**9768**	Boston & Maine Boxcar, *76*
___	**9785**	Conrail Boxcar, *78*
___	**52001**	Boston & Maine Quad Hopper w/ coal load, *92*
___	**52016**	Boston & Maine Gondola w/ coil covers, *93*
___	**52043**	L.L. Bean Boxcar "1994", *94*
___	**52080**	B&M Flatcar w/ trailer "91095", *95*
___	**52111**	Ben & Jerry's Flatcar w/ trailer, *96*

CLUB CARS AND SPECIAL PRODUCTION

___ **52146** Ocean Spray Plug Door Reefer "OSCX 1998", *98*
___ **52212** Berkshire Brewing Refrigerator Car, *00*
___ **52236** Moxie Boxcar, *01*
___ **52352** Poland Spring Boxcar, *04*
___ **52270** Jenney Mfg. Co. Tank Car, *02*
___ **52306** NE Trans TOFC, *03*
___ **52418** Indian Motocycle Boxcar, *06*
___ **52434** Cabots TOFC, *07*
___ **52457** Cape Cod Potato Chip Boxcar, *07*

Ozark Division: Gateway Chapter

___ **5700** Oppenheimer Reefer, *81*
___ **9068** Reading Bobber Caboose, *76*
___ **9601** Illinois Central Gulf Hi-cube Boxcar, *77*
___ **9767** Railbox Boxcar, *78*
___ **52003** "Meet Me In St. Louis" Flatcar w/ trailer, *92*

Pacific Northwest Division

___ **52077** Great Northern Hi-cube Boxcar "9695", *95*
___ Pacific Northwest Division F3 AA, shells only, *74*

Rocky Mountain Division

___ **1971-1976** Rocky Mountain Division Reefer, *76*

Sacramento Sierra Chapter

___ **6401** Virginian B/W Caboose, *84*
___ **9301** US Mail Operating Boxcar, *76*
___ **9414** Cotton Belt Boxcar, *80*
___ **9427** Bay Line Boxcar, *81*
___ **9444** Louisiana Midland Boxcar, *82*
___ **9452** Western Pacific Boxcar, *83*
___ **9705** D&RGW Boxcar, *75*
___ **9723** Western Pacific Boxcar, *73*
___ **9726** Erie-Lackawanna Boxcar, *79*
___ **9730** CP Rail Boxcar, *77*
___ **9785** Conrail Boxcar, *78*
___ Lionel Lines Tender, shell only, ***84***

Southern Division

___ **1976** Florida East Coast F-3 ABA, shells only, *76*
___ **1986** Southern Division Bunk Car, *86*
___ **6111** L&N Covered Quad Hopper, *83*
___ **9287** Southern N5C Caboose, *77*
___ **9352** Trailer Train Flatcar w/ circus trailers, *80*
___ **9403** Seaboard Coast Line Boxcar, *78*
___ **9405** Chattahoochie Boxcar, *79*

CLUB CARS AND SPECIAL PRODUCTION

___	9443	Florida East Coast Boxcar, *81*
___	9471	ACL Boxcar, *84*
___	9482	Norfolk & Southern Boxcar, *85*
___	16606	Southern Searchlight Car, *88*

Toy Train Operating Society (TTOS)

TTOS National Convention Cars

___	1984	Sacramento Northern Boxcar, *84*
___	1985	Snowbird Covered Quad Hopper, *85*
___	6076	Santa Fe Hopper (O27), *70*
___	6476-1	LV Hopper, gray, *69*
___	6582	Portland Flatcar w/ wood load, *86*
___	9326	Burlington Northern B/W Caboose, *82*
___	9347	Niagara Falls 3-D Tank Car, *79*
___	9355	Delaware & Hudson B/W Caboose, *82*
___	9361	Chicago & North Western B/W Caboose, *82*
___	9382	Florida East Coast B/W Caboose, *82*
___	9512	Summerdale Junction Passenger Car, *74*
___	9520	Phoenix Combination Car, *75*
___	9526	Snowbird Observation Car, *76*
___	9535	Columbus Baggage Car, *77*
___	9678	Hollywood Hi-Cube Boxcar, *78*
___	9868	Oklahoma City Reefer, *80*
___	9883	Phoenix Reefer, *83*
___	17871	NYC Flatcar w/ Kodak and Xerox trailers "81487", *87*
___	17872	Anaconda Ore Car "81988", *88*
___	17877	MKT 1-D Tank Car "3739469", *89*
___	17884	Columbus & Dayton Terminal Boxcar (Std. O), *90*
___	17889	Southern Pacific Flatcar w/ trailer "15791" (Std. O), *91*
___	19963	Union Equity 3-bay ACF Hopper "86892" (Std. O), *92*
___	52010	Weyerhaeuser DD Boxcar "838593" (Std. O), *93*
___	52029	Ford 1-D Tank Car "12" (O27), *94*
___	52030	Ford Gondola "4023", *94*
___	52031	Ford Hopper "1458" (O27), *94*
___	52057	Western Pacific Boxcar "64641995", *95*
___	52087	New Mexico Central Boxcar "64641996", *96*
___	52114	NYC Flatcar w/ Gleason & SASIB trailers, *97*
___	52149	Conrail Flatcar w/ Blum coal shovel, *98*
___	52192	SP Crane & Gondola 2-pack, *00*
___	52193	SP Gondola "SPMW 6060", *00*
___	52194	SP Crane Car "7111", *00*
___	52231	British Columbia RR 1-D Tank Car, *01*
___	52288	D&RGW Cookie Boxcar, *03*
___	52293	D&RGW 1-Dome Tank Car, *03*
___	52378	Las Vegas & Tonopah Boxcar, *05*

TTOS Division Cars

___ **52009** Sacramento Valley Division Western Pacific Boxcar "64641993", *93*

___ **52040** Wolverine Division GTW Flatcar w/ Lionel Lines tractor and trailer, "52033", *94*

___ **52058** Central California Division Santa Fe Boxcar "64641895", *95*

___ **52086** Canadian Division Pacific Great Eastern Boxcar "64641972", *96*

Southwest Division: Cal-Stewart

___ **19962** Southern Pacific 3-Bay ACF Hopper "496035" (Std. O), *92*

___ **52047** Cotton Belt Wood-sided Caboose w/ smoke "1921" (Std. O), *93-94*

___ **52073** Pacific Fruit Express Reefer "459402" (Std. O), *95*

___ **52098** National Bureau of Standards Boxcar (Std. O), *96*

___ **52121** Mobilgas Tank Car "238" (Std. O), *97*

___ **52154** Pacific Fruit Express Reefer "459403" (Std. O), *98*

___ **52205** SP Overnight Merchandise Service Boxcar 5-pack, *00*

___ **52385** Ward Kimball Boxcar, *05*

TTOS New Mexico Division Cars

___ **52264** Durango & Silverton Operating Hopper "9325", *02*

Other TTOS Production

___ **1983** Phoenix 3-D Tank Car, *83*

___ **17894** Southern Pacific Tractor, *91*

___ **52021** Weyerhaeuser Tractor and Trailer, *93*

___ **52022** Union Pacific Boxcar, *93*

___ **52032** Ford 1-D Tank Car "14" w/ Kughn inscription (O27), *94*

___ **52046** ACL Boxcar "16247", *94*

___ **52053** Carail Boxcar, *94*

___ **52068** Toy Train Parade Contadina Boxcar "16245", *94*

___ **52078** Southern Pacific SD9 "5366", *96*

___ **52079** Southern Pacific B/W Caboose "1996", *96*

___ **52084** Union Pacific I-Beam Flatcar w/ load "16380", *95*

___ **52113** Northeastern Division Genesee & Wyoming RR 3-Bay ACF Hopper "10000" (Std. O), *97*

TTOS Gadsden Pacific Ore Cars

___	**17878**	Magma Ore Car w/ load, *89*
___	**17881**	Phelps-Dodge Ore Car w/ load, *90*
___	**17886**	Cyprus Ore Car w/ load, *91*
___	**19961**	Inspiration Consolidated Copper Co. Ore Car w/ load, *92*
___	**52011**	Tucson, Cornelia & Gila Bend Ore Car w/ load, 93
___	**52027**	Pinto Valley Mine Ore Car w/ load, 94
___	**52071**	Copper Basin Railway Ore Car w/ load, *95*
___	**52089**	SMARRCO Ore Car w/ load, *96*
___	**52124**	EPSW Ore Car w/ load, *97*
___	**52164**	SP Ore Car w/ load, *98*
___	**52177**	Arizona Southern Ore Car w/ load, *99*
___	**52213**	BHP Copper Ore Car, *00*
___	**52248**	Tombstone & Southern Ore Car, *01*

Virginia Train Collectors (VTC)

___	**7679**	Boxcar, *79*
___	**7681**	N5C Caboose, *81*
___	**7682**	Covered Quad Hopper, *82*
___	**7683**	Virginia Fruit Express Reefer, *83*
___	**7684**	Vitraco 3-D Tank Car, *84*
___	**7685**	Boxcar, *85*
___	**7686**	GP7, *86*
___	**7692-1**	Baggage Car (O27), *92*
___	**7692-2**	Combination Car (O27), *92*
___	**7692-3**	Dining Car (O27), *92*
___	**7692-4**	Passenger Car (O27), *92*
___	**7692-5**	Vista Dome Car (O27), *92*
___	**7692-6**	Passenger Car (O27), *92*
___	**7692-7**	Observation Car (O27), *92*
___	**52060**	Tender w/ whistle "7694", *94*

Section 6
CATALOGS

Year	Type	Size	Pages	Exc	New
1945	Consumer	8½" x 11"	4		NRS
1946	Consumer	8⅜" x 11¼"	20	50	85
1947	Consumer	11¼" x 7⅝"	32	30	45
1948	Consumer	11¼" x 8"	36	30	50
1949	Consumer	11¼" x 8"	40	75	100
1950	Consumer	11¼" x 8"	44	45	75
1951	Consumer	11¼" x 7¾"	36	25	45
1952	Consumer	11¼" x 7¾"	36	20	35
1953	Consumer	11¼" x 7⅝"	40	20	30
1954	Consumer	11¼" x 7⅝"	44	20	30
1955	Consumer	11¼" x 7⅝"	44	20	30
1956	Consumer	11¼" x 7⅝"	40	12	24
1957	Consumer	11¼" x 7½"	52	11	22
1958	Consumer	11¼" x 7⅝"	56	10	17
1959	Consumer	11" x 8½"	56	11	17
1960	Consumer	11" x 8⅜"	56	6	10
1961	Consumer	8½" x 11"	72	6	10
1962	Consumer	8½" x 11"	100	8	12
1963	Consumer	8⅜" x 10⅞"	56	4	6
1964	Consumer	8⅜" x 10⅞"	24	4	6
1965	Consumer	8½" x 10⅞"	40	4	6
1966	Consumer	10⅞" x 8⅜"	40	4	7
1967	Same as 1966			4	6
1968	Consumer	8½" x 11"	8	4	6
1969	Consumer	11" x 8½"	8	3	5
1970	Consumer w/ foldout poster	8½" x 11"	8	3	5
1971	Consumer	8½" x 11"	12	3	5
1972	Consumer	8½" x 11"	16	3	5
1973	Consumer	8½" x 11"	16	2	4
1974	Consumer	8½" x 11"	20	2	4
1975	Consumer	8½" x 11"	24	2	4
1976	Consumer	8½" x 11"	24	2	4
1977	Consumer	8½" x 11"	24	2	4
1978	Consumer	8½" x 11"	24	2	4
1979	Consumer	8½" x 11"	24	2	4
1980	Consumer	8½" x 11"	28	2	4
1981	Consumer	5½" x 7"	32	1	2
1982	Traditional Series	8½" x 11"	20	2	4
1982	Collector Series	8½" x 11"	12	2	4
1983	Traditional Series	8½" x 11"	20	2	3

CATALOGS

Year	Type	Size	Pages	Exc	New
___ 1983	Collector Series	8½" x 11"	16	2	3
___ 1984	Traditional Series	8½" x 11"	20	2	3
___ 1984	Collector Series	8½" x 11"	16	2	3
___ 1985	Traditional Series	8½" x 11"	20	2	3
___ 1985	Collector Series	8½" x 11"	12	2	3
___ 1986	Traditional Series	8½" x 11"	16	2	3
___ 1986	Collector Series	8½" x 11"	16	2	3
___ 1986	Stocking Stuffers Brochure	8½" x 11"	4	2	3
___ 1987	Consumer	8½" x 11"	40	3	4
___ 1987	Large Scale Brochure	11" x 8½"	6	1	2
___ 1987	Stocking Stuffers Brochure	8½" x 11"	4	2	3
___ 1988	Consumer	8½" x 11"	40	2	3
___ 1988	Large Scale	8½" x 11"	16	1	2
___ 1988	Classics Brochure	8½" x 11"	4	1	2
___ 1988	Hiawatha Brochure	8½" x 11"	4	2	3
___ 1988	Stocking Stuffers Flyer	8½" x 11"	1	2	3
___ 1989	Pre-Toy Fair Consumer	8½" x 11"	20	2	3
___ 1989	Toy Fair Consumer	8½" x 11"	28	2	3
___ 1989	Pre-Toy Fair Classics Brochure	8½" x 11"	4	1	2
___ 1989	Toy Fair Classics Brochure	8½" x 11"	4	1	2
___ 1989	Large Scale	8½" x 11"	20	1	2
___ 1989	Stocking Stuffers Brochure	8½" x 11"	4	2	3
___ 1990	Book 1 Consumer	8½" x 11"	20	2	4
___ 1990	Book 2 Consumer	8½" x 11"	36	2	3
___ 1990	Large Scale	8½" x 11"	16	1	2
___ 1990	Stocking Stuffers Brochure	8½" x 11"	6	2	3
___ 1991	Book 1 Consumer	8½" x 11"	24	2	4
___ 1991	Book 2 Consumer	8½" x 11"	60	2	3
___ 1991	Stocking Stuffers Brochure	8½" x 11"	6	2	3
___ 1992	Book 1 Consumer	8½" x 11"	32	2	4
___ 1992	Book 2 Consumer	8½" x 11"	48	2	3
___ 1992	Stocking Stuffers Brochure	8½" x 11"	8	2	3
___ 1993	Book 1 Consumer	8½" x 11"	32	2	4
___ 1993	Book 2 Consumer	8½" x 11"	52	2	3
___ 1993	Stocking Stuffers/ 1994 Spring Releases	8½" x 11"	28	2	3
___ 1994	Consumer	8½" x 11"	64	3	4
___ 1994	Thomas the Tank Engine	8½" x 11"	8	1	2
___ 1994	Trainmaster Transformer	8½" x 11"	8	1	2

CATALOGS

Year	Type	Size	Pages	Exc	New
___ 1994	Stocking Stuffers/ 1995 Spring Releases	8½" x 11"	32	2	3
___ 1994	Preschool Brochure	8½" x 11"	4	1	2
___ 1994	Crayola Brochure	8½" x 11"	4	1	2
___ 1994	Gift Collection	8½" x 11"	12	1	2
___ 1995	Consumer	8½" x 11"	88	3	4
___ 1995	Stocking Stuffers/ 1996 Spring Releases	8½" x 11"	32	2	3
___ 1996	Consumer	8½" x 11"	24	2	3
___ 1996	Consumer, illustrated	10" x 8"	24	2	3
___ 1996	Accessories	10" x 8"	32	2	3
___ 1997	Heritage	10" x 8"	12	2	3
___ 1997	Century Club	10" x 8"	16	2	3
___ 1997	Classic I	10" x 8"	24	2	3
___ 1997	Classic II	10" x 8"	36	2	3
___ 1997	Lionel Brochure	10" x 8"	4	2	3
___ 1997	Fall '97 Heritage II	10" x 8"	12	2	3
___ 1998	Classic	8½" x 9"	76	2	3
___ 1998	Heritage	11" x 8½"	24	2	3
___ 1998	Legendary Trains	10⅞" x 8½"	64	2	3
___ 1998	Gilbert American Flyer Brochure	8½" x 11"	4	1	2
___ 1999	Classic Trains, Vol. 1	8¼" x 10½"	63	2	3
___ 1999	Classic Trains, Vol. 2	8¼" x 10½"	45	2	3
___ 1999	Classic Trains, Vol. 3	8¼" x 10¾"	58	2	3
___ 1999	Heritage	11" x 8½"	26	2	3
___ 2000	Classic Trains, Vol. 1	8" x 10¾"	110	2	3
___ 2000	Classic Trains, Vol. 2	8" x 10¾"	85	2	3
___ 2001	Classic Trains, Vol. 1	8" x 10¾"	122	2	3
___ 2001	Classic Trains, Vol. 2	8" x 10¾"	122	2	3
___ 2001	Challenger Brochure	8½" x 11"	4	1	2
___ 2001	Hiawatha Brochure	11" x 8½"	4	1	2
___ 2002	Classic Trains, Vol. 1	8" x 10¾"	122	2	3
___ 2002	Classic Trains, Vol. 2	8" x 10¾"	110	2	3
___ 2003	Classic Trains, Vol. 1	8" x 10¾"	132	2	3
___ 2003	Classic Trains, Vol. 2	8" x 10¾"	152	2	3
___ 2004	Train, Vol. 1 "The Polar Express"	8" x 10¾"	164	4	5
___ 2004	Train, Vol. 2	8" x 10¾"	188	4	5
___ 2005	Train, Vol. 1	8" x 10¾"	144		CP
___ 2005	Train, Vol. 2	8" x 10¾"	164		CP
___ 2006	Train, Vol. 1	8" x 10¾"	184		CP
___ 2006	Christmas, Vol. 2	8" x 10¾"	16		CP
___ 2007	Train, Vol. 1	8" x 10¾"	216		CP

ABBREVIATIONS
Descriptions

AAR	Association of American Railroads (truck type)
Blvd.	boulevard
B/W	bay window
CC	command control
CP	current production
DD	double-door
dz.	dozen
EMD	Electro-Motive Division
ETD	end-of-train device
E/V	extended vision
FARR	Famous American Railroad Series
FF	Fallen Flag Series
FM	Fairbanks-Morse
GE	General Electric
LL	Lionel Lines
M.O.W.	maintenance-of-way
MU	multiple unit (commuter cars)
mv	many variations
NM	never manufactured
NRS	no recorded sales
O	Lionel gauge (1¼" between outside rails)
OO	Lionel gauge (¾" between outside rails)
PFE	Pacific Fruit Express
pr.	pair
RC	remote control
REA	Railway Express Agency
SSS	Service Station Special
Std.	Standard gauge (2⅛" between outside rails)
Std. O	Standard O (scale length and dimension)
S/W	square window
TMCC	TrainMaster Command Control
u	uncataloged
USMC	United States Marine Corps
w/	with
w/o	without
1-D	one dome
2-D	two dome
3-D	three dome

Railroad Names

ACL	Atlantic Coast Line
AT&SF	Atchison, Topeka & Santa Fe
B&A	Boston & Albany
BAR	Bangor & Aroostook
B&LE	Bessemer & Lake Erie
B&M	Boston & Maine
BN	Burlington Northern
B&O	Baltimore & Ohio
C&IM	Chicago & Illinois Midland
CB&Q	Chicago, Burlington & Quincy
CN	Canadian National
CNJ	Central of New Jersey
C&NW	Chicago & North Western
C&O	Chesapeake & Ohio
CP	Canadian Pacific
D&H	Delaware & Hudson
DL&W	Delaware, Lackawanna & Western
DM&IR	Duluth, Missabe & Iron Range
D&RG	Denver & Rio Grande
D&RGW	Denver & Rio Grande Western
D&TS	Detroit & Toledo Shore Line
EJ&E	Elgin, Joliet & Eastern
Erie-Lack.	Erie-Lackawanna
FEC	Florida East Coast
GM&O	Gulf, Mobile & Ohio
GN	Great Northern
GTW	Grand Trunk Western
IC	Illinois Central
ICG	Illinois Central Gulf
L&N	Louisville & Nashville
LIRR	Long Island Railroad
LNAC	Louisville, New Albany & Corydon
LV	Lehigh Valley
MD&W	Minnesota, Dakota & Western
MKT	Missouri, Kansas, Texas
MNS	Minneapolis, Northfield & Southern
MP	Missouri Pacific
MPA	Maryland & Pennsylvania
MILW	Milwaukee Road
M&StL	Minneapolis & St. Louis
NC&StL	Nashville, Chattanooga & St. Louis
NdeM	Nacionales de Mexico Railway

NH	New Haven
NKP	Nickel Plate Road
NP	Northern Pacific
N&W	Norfolk & Western
NYC	New York Central
NYNH&H	New York, New Haven & Hartford
PC	Penn Central
P&E	Peoria & Eastern
PHD	Port Huron & Detroit
P&LE	Pittsburgh & Lake Erie
PRR	Pennsylvania Railroad
RI	Rock Island
SCL	Seaboard Coast Line
SMARRCO	San Manuel Arizona Railroad Company
SP	Southern Pacific
SP&S	Spokane, Portland & Seattle
SR	Southern Railway
TA&G	Tennessee, Alabama & Georgia
T&P	Texas & Pacific
UP	Union Pacific
V&TRR	Virginia & Truckee Railroad
W&ARR	Western & Atlantic Railroad
WM	Western Maryland
WP	Western Pacific

Build your toy train library

Classic Toy Trains magazine

Captures your imagination and sparks your enthusiasm for toy trains! Issues include reviews of the latest locomotives and accessories, track planning ideas, great photos of the best layouts, and information on collecting.
9 issues/year

Greenberg's *Repair and Operating Manual for Lionel Trains, 1945–1969, 7th Edition*

Offers more than a thousand repair and maintenance tips for Lionel locomotives, operating cars, accessories, transformers, light bulbs, and switches. Provides Lionel technical advice as well as handy techniques submitted by toy train collectors and operators. 6 x 8½; 752 pgs.; softcover.
10-8160 • $24.95

Lionel Accessories at Work on Toy Train Layouts

Add classic accessories to your toy train layout! Lionel's electronic accessory items from the 1940s and 1950s through the present day have been very popular with toy train enthusiasts. Former *Classic Toy Trains* editor Neil Besougloff helps you incorporate these accessories, both originals and modern reproductions, into your layout.
8¼ x 10¾; 80 pgs.; 180 color photos; softcover.
10-8355 • $17.95

Available at your favorite hobby shop!
Or at www.cttbooks.com
And 1-800-533-6644

Shipping and handling charges apply. Call for details or view online.